P9-BYU-989

LINCOLN DREAMT HE DIED

ALSO BY ANDREW BURSTEIN

Madison and Jefferson (with Nancy Isenberg)

The Original Knickerbocker: The Life of Washington Irving

Jefferson's Secrets: Death and Desire at Monticello

The Passions of Andrew Jackson

Letters from the Head and Heart: Writings of Thomas Jefferson

*America's Jubilee: How in 1826 a
Generation Remembered Fifty Years of Independence*

Sentimental Democracy: The Evolution of America's Romantic Self-Image

The Inner Jefferson: Portrait of a Grieving Optimist

EDITED BY ANDREW BURSTEIN

Mortal Remains: Death in Early America (with Nancy Isenberg)

LINCOLN DREAMT HE DIED

The Midnight Visions of Remarkable Americans from Colonial Times to Freud

ANDREW BURSTEIN

palgrave
macmillan

LINCOLN DREAMT HE DIED
Copyright © Andrew Burstein, 2013.
All rights reserved.

First published in 2013 by PALGRAVE MACMILLAN® in the U.S.—a division
of St. Martin's Press LLC, 175 Fifth Avenue, New York, NY 10010.

Where this book is distributed in the UK, Europe, and the rest of the world, this
is by Palgrave Macmillan, a division of Macmillan Publishers Limited, registered
in England, company number 785998, of Houndmills, Basingstoke, Hampshire
RG21 6XS.

Palgrave Macmillan is the global academic imprint of the above companies and
has companies and representatives throughout the world.

Palgrave® and Macmillan® are registered trademarks in the United States, the
United Kingdom, Europe, and other countries.

ISBN: 978-1-137-27827-2

The Library of Congress Cataloging-in-Publication Data:

Burstein, Andrew.
  Lincoln dreamt he died : the midnight visions of remarkable Americans from
colonial times to Freud / by Andrew Burstein.
     p.   cm.
  1. Dreams. 2. Celebrities. 3. United States—History—19th century. I. Title.
BF1091.B98   2013
154.6'30973—dc23

2012038454

A catalogue record of the book is available from the British Library.

Design by: Letra Libre, Inc.

First edition: June 2013

10 9 8 7 6 5 4 3 2 1

Printed in the United States of America.

Our life is two-fold: Sleep hath its own world,
A boundary between the things misnamed
Death and existence: Sleep hath its own world,
And a wide realm of wild reality.
And dreams in their development have breath,
And tears, and torture, and the touch of joy;
They leave a weight upon our waking thoughts.

—Lord Byron (1816)

CONTENTS

ILLUSTRATIONS

PREFACE
THE LANGUAGE WE SPEAK TO OURSELVES

Dreams. They are like most of the people we have brushed past in life, remaining in the forefront of our minds for only a short while and then fading into the background. Some are gone forever, others called to mind when we are given the right stimulation. The saying "Life goes on" applies to mind-stories as much as to our memory of old acquaintances. For without a written or visual reminder, memory displaces what is past in order for us to focus on the immediacy of our strenuous, need-driven personal lives.

Dreams. Like the dead, they linger inside us by the strength of imagination. Think of all the personal history that has vanished from your mind, matters you once cared about but have long since ceased to reflect on. There is just too much to remember. New events create new kinds of longing. The dream is one means by which half-forgotten emotions—sometimes in the form of half-forgotten people—return to our active thoughts.

The American dream. It is our timeworn metaphor for a life of opportunity that builds self-confidence and affords security. Yet the popular phrase was not coined until 1931—in the depths of the Great Depression, oddly enough. In the first decades of the republic's history, the word "dream" was more often applied to illusory and easily dismissed ideas than to the collective hopes of a people.

The literal dreams of Americans past cannot be easily summed up. They are, in a word, astonishing. Also, conflicted. A surprisingly superstitious Abraham

Lincoln memorized the dream-infused poems of Lord Byron and firmly believed in the most ominous of his own involuntary visions. According to the president's intimate friend Ward Lamon, who served as a personal bodyguard, Lincoln manifestly prophesied his own violent death when, in a dream, he saw two versions of himself: one appeared hale and hearty, the other deathly pale. This unbanishable dual-image dream said to Lincoln that he would stay safe for a time, but not live out his life beyond the presidency. Photographs show that he aged considerably in office while prosecuting the bloodiest of America's wars. As to how much he dwelled on the contrivances of his unconscious mind, we have some good and provocative testimony.

The sixteenth president was not alone among American notables in contemplating dream life. Like Lincoln, Mark Twain was quite credulous when it came to prophetic possibilities within certain of his dreams. Far from home, Louisa May Alcott, the celebrated author of *Little Women,* surrendered to her sister an exquisite example of one night's time-bending encounter with absent family members. Founding-era dreamers John and Abigail Adams communicated their tortured feelings by telling each other what they saw in their sleep. What did Thomas Jefferson think of dreams? How about the idealistic essayist and lecturer Ralph Waldo Emerson, or his younger neighbor, the beloved dissident Henry David Thoreau?

Answers are forthcoming. But the most pressing, pathos-driven dreams of earlier generations are those of ordinary people whose private letters and diaries tell precious stories. The sweethearts of Civil War soldiers visited them on the battlefront in the only way it could be done safely—by entering each other's nocturnal visions. For many, the literal and metaphorical dream converged, hope of a happy reunion fixing in the conscious mind the morning after a night's fantasy played itself out.

Nor is it anachronistic to speak of an "American subconscious" in historical relief. The word *subconscious* was first tried in the time of Lord Byron. The dream-spinning author Thomas De Quincey, whose *Confessions of an English Opium Eater* was tremendously popular in America, used "subconscious" in the 1830s and 1840s in the same sense we employ it today—a somewhat mysterious hidden self. The feeling that "something was there" predated our modern prodding of the subconscious mind.[1]

Some changes in perception were more dramatic. Toward the end of the nineteenth century, bizarre content in dreams came to be interpreted in less arbitrary ways than it had in previous decades. Many dream narratives exited the realm of fright and intimidation to become downright playful; exultant dreams gradually took on shades of complexity. Then Sigmund Freud ventured across the ocean. It was as if Americans had been waiting for his assurances that their dreams contained something worth knowing; in the early twentieth century, they embraced Freud's theory of dream interpretation and readily succumbed to the psychiatrist's couch.

—⁊∂—

Dreams are a formative element in the construction of individuality. They are unusual, but nonetheless real, delineators of culture, exposing the fragile nature of belief while sketching the boundaries of popular imagination. As a historian and biographer, I found the prospect of doing an investigative history of eighteenth- and nineteenth-century Americans' dreams completely irresistible.

Pleasing nostalgia comes as easily to the sleeper as horrifying images do, as most of us have experienced for ourselves. Early American literature contains a strong sampling of both kinds of emotion. It is only natural to wonder about errant nighttime thoughts, and to ask what, if anything, they explain over the course of a human life. But a cultural history of American dreams? Until now, no one has meticulously studied these widely archived but poorly indexed scraps of a broad demographic, isolating recorded dreams and charting change over time. Weaving their absurd sensations into a crazy quilt of a no-longer-existing consciousness promises, in the end, to tell us new things about the life of the mind, then and now.[2]

So how, in terms of cultural knowledge, should we define the phenomenon of a dream? It is a combination of impulse and art, more than a text and less than an oracle. We are attempting here to tell history from the inside out. We are explaining how individual identities merged into a recognizably American personality, one so invested in categorizing selfhood (and, not inconsequentially, Americans' special place in the world) that citizens in the twentieth century jumped at the opportunity, almost en masse, to transform themselves into psychological subjects.

I hope to satisfy the curiosity of all who are seduced by mysteries, and any who have wondered what their ancestors were dreaming about when they closed their eyes at night. We see past lives through an unusual window when we recover the strange, portentous, quirky night visions people found striking enough to write down. You don't have to be a historian to imagine the huddled masses who once trod in our footsteps, and to raise the obvious question: When it comes to inner states, to their personal issues, were they like us?

"Were they like us?" tags along on nearly every page of what follows. Presumably, our descendants will wonder about us, too, as they extract DNA from our tombs for some as yet unknown knowledge-producing purpose. Every self-appointed family genealogist and every antiquarian who is quick to connect a newly discovered artifact to a once-beating heart knows the lure of the lost past. The naturally curious mind is attracted to the message in a bottle that has floated on the ocean and lands at someone's feet—which is, incidentally, just the sort of thing that happens in a dream!

If they have lain fallow, the dreams of historical actors are more than mere curiosities. From dreams we take notice of the manner in which people characterized their lives when they felt powerful, and how they coped when they felt powerless; how they approached conscience and consciousness; how and what they were prepared to let escape the privacy of their thought.

History is comprised of many elements. Political history, the best known, is of least import in this study. Cultural, intellectual, and emotional history all explore the life of the mind and combine to monitor the beating heart of the past. Ranging across these subdisciplines, I am chiefly interested in literal dreams as a distortion of lived reality. The challenge is obvious, insofar as the mind is a cryptic place and in many ways unfathomable. Dreams disappear from memory quickly, and few diarists (judging by their own statements) committed thoughts to paper until late in the day, often by candlelight. Also, for much of the period under our observation, the educated tended to regard dream interpretation as unproductive.

So, the trick is to avoid speculating unduly. At the same time, who would deny that manipulation of memory is the very definition of history? Writers invent, narratives are ego driven, and books labeled as nonfiction are on some level dreamt up by their authors; otherwise, they would lack personality. Not enough readers—or even critics—sufficiently take into account this simple fact of human nature.

I presume no further justification is required, then, for writing a book about an underused resource of historical consciousness that is a tangible component of culture. Dreams exist at the crossroads of imaginative memory and individual identity. They escort us into lost emotional worlds. Dreams are evocative texts, kernels of authenticity.[3]

~ɔ·

I n giving shape to daily life that is creatively disfigured by the unbound consciousness, I am guided not just by the historian's rule book but also by the
latest in dream research. An emerging consensus among researchers differenti-
ates the wakeful from the sleeping/dreaming brain in ways not previously recognized. The wakeful brain leads an individual to temper emotion with reason,
whereas the sleeping/dreaming brain engages emotional memories haphazardly.
When people dream, reason is literally (in biochemical terms, that is) muted,
if not turned off entirely.

Past social interactions and our loving relationships exist and shape us for as
long as our minds hang together. They can be plucked from "memory banks"—
those disorderly, permeable storage spaces somewhere in the midst of our complex, electrified neural pathways—when something triggers their retrieval. If
we define memory as testimony about the past that joins thought to language,
dreams are, to employ an active metaphorical image, thoughts that bounce off
memory. We wake, remembering what we have "seen" in our thoughts, and
wonder if these imaginative exercises within sleep have something to teach. In
"Demonology" (1839), Ralph Waldo Emerson wrote: "Dreams have a poetic
integrity and truth." He could not be dissuaded that "this limbo and dust-hole
of thought is presided over by a certain reason, too." Otherwise, we would have
to conclude that nature endowed us with throwaway faculties along with essential sensations. "They pique us by independence of us," Emerson added, "yet
we know ourselves in this mad crowd, and owe to dreams a kind of divination
and wisdom."[4]

The proof that we treat our dreams as potentially meaningful thought-
objects—marks of personality—is the fact that we rely on memory to convey
them back to us when we reawaken and our rational faculties are reengaged. It
takes work to make our dreams rationally significant. Once we start doing that,
though, they lose something of their pure energy. Dreams are most real and alluring to us when raw and relatively unprocessed, before reason recasts them.[5]

Like memory, dreams describe the mystery of association that takes place
inside us. And while both dreams and memory spontaneously produce energy,
dreams do so without the same strong relationship to established conceptions
and connections. As an excitation experienced emotionally, a dream is not a

concrete whole but a combination of images comprehended in coherent segments, images that may seem plausible and well integrated on some nights,
bizarre and digressive on others. We accept that the narrative forms we enjoy—
history, literature, film—tend to produce endings. But dreams (both raw and
reasoned through) are less invested in endings. They become visible without
always being purposeful, and they are easily forgotten in the light of day. To call
them narratives is not quite right, then. They have narrative characteristics, but
no obvious rules.

We can appreciate dreams in a new way by acknowledging what civilized
society has generally resisted: the close relationship between "normal" behavior
and the delusions under which the clinically insane struggle. It is only when
the delusions that feed our dreams overtake everyday reality that psychosis is
presented. Feelings of suspicion, of being chased and spied on and persecuted,
of being manipulated by the voices in one's head, are all common features of
dreams. Put another way, the dream is an obsessive pulling on the unresisting
mind, a healthy form of psychosis. As it turns out, late eighteenth-century British and American physicians drew upon the same analogy, though their theories
about health and disease were in many other respects completely ludicrous.[6]

For literally millennia, people have communicated dreams and visions.
Over the past three centuries, our language has added "daydreams," "musings,"
"reveries," and "hallucinations" to the mix. All have in some way been associated with supernatural possibilities of extraordinary understandings. Visions, in
particular, are linked to a sudden religious awareness. It is a phenomenon I do
consider in these pages, without giving special emphasis to the tenets of sectarian movements, as this is not a history of American religion.[7]

Science informs us that older memories are more stable in the brain, which
explains, for instance, how experiences from decades past often find their way
into what Thomas Jefferson, in private correspondence, once called "our nightly
incoherencies." Jefferson himself did not see much potential in the fractured
stories within sleep, though, as we shall discover, the last dream of his life took
him back a half century to a dramatic moment in his wartime governorship.
An obsessive recorder of all kinds of minutiae and intellectually interested in
the dream state, he did not grant posterity access to his own raw dreams. But
some of his peers did. As we will soon find out, his good friend Dr. Benjamin
Rush made dream-telling a mark of intimacy in communicating with others.[8]

Although we "see" in our dreams, seeing and dreaming are two completely
different functions. The eyes provide information about light and dark but

nothing of sensory perception. The brain converts information, stores memory, and gives an emotional charge to all that lies within. As one dream researcher recently put it: "We do not have emotions about our dreams so much as dreams about our emotions." This seems to me a particularly meaningful observation, and one that guides this study as much as its pursuit of the fundamental question, "Were they like us?"[9]

Let me underscore that this book, while an emotional history, is not an "interpretation of dreams" sort of book. Dream-interpretation guides have been disseminated across centuries and across cultures. Their chief value is as cultural artifacts. Modern neuroscience has determined that the symbolic character of dreaming, so central to past analysis, has been overdrawn. This includes the work of Freud, whose sexualization of dream symbols is now widely discredited. Yet dream researchers around the world are asking more questions than ever before about the meaning of our dreams. Influenced by their writings, I engage repeatedly with the imagery, labyrinthine stagecraft, and identifiable feelings exposed in dreams. We may not understand them fully, but to any historian, impulses matter.

History is an art, and it changes even faster than science. Understanding that memory's tendency is to marginalize what does not serve the immediate present, we never quite know what the historian is capable of discovering that will reframe a popular argument about an entire era. In *History as an Art of Memory,* Patrick Hutton shows that there is an overwhelming human desire for the recovery of lost memories, something primal and identity-consolidating in the grand pursuit of a magical, almost godlike historical memory. I argue along similar lines that images of emotional time, as collected in our dreams, say something about the larger attachment to history: *we are nothing if we do not belong somewhere.* The historically anchored mind wants to explain the relationship between individual and collective identity.[10]

─◆─

This book is about Americans who lived from the late colonial era to the opening of the twentieth century. Its cutoff date is the arrival of modern psychoanalysis with the publication of Freud's *Interpretation of Dreams* in 1900. I say with confidence that you cannot understand the twentieth century's fascination with psychology unless you first understand prior generations and their fascination with dreams. We know how our American ancestors communicated across distance. We have a pretty good sense of how the modern world became modern. We tend to be less sensitive to the subtler changes taking place across time and space in the moral imagination and in face-to-face communication. As a product of culture, dreams offer new clues to the boundaries within which emotions were allowed to be revealed and recorded.[11]

Medical thinkers of the eighteenth and nineteenth centuries assessed the human condition in unconditional terms. Their materialist explanation was that dreams indicated some organic pain not consciously understood. If not meaningless noise, then they reported what the physical body was telling the brain. For religious practitioners, dreams spoke in symbols, were connected to divine spirit, and bore properties of prophecy. Yet many in the past also thought, as we, their descendants, do, that dreams belong first and foremost to the search for insight into the self. Modern dream specialist Stephen LaBerge puts it this way: "Dreams may not be messages, but they are our own most intimately personal creations." And that is what this book is chiefly interested in: the intimate creations of a people whose world is not ours but whose belief systems help us track how modern conceptions evolved.[12]

Freud remains a marginal figure in all this. Although dreams may indeed reflect a certain amount of repressed thought, the latest research suggests that nature does the job of "flushing out" negative emotion at least as well as psychotherapy. This is not to say Freud is irrelevant: it is useful to regard sleep as narcissistic, a moment of withdrawal into the self.

We know the dream as a window to the interior, where personal memories dredge up half-forgotten personal histories. But even if dreams mean less than what dream enthusiasts going back centuries, even millennia, have imagined, they are still the stories human beings tell themselves. And that means they belong to history, the discipline that records and assesses stories to forestall collective memory loss.

The meditation on bygone lives that follows recaptures American—and, to a certain extent, transatlantic—culture at key moments. It treats the rise of individualism as a political value from a perspective one does not see in any standard history. Most dwell on a public vocabulary of national self-definition. Here, we look at a more spontaneous language, the language we speak to ourselves.

ACKNOWLEDGMENTS

Friends and colleagues brightened immediately when I told them I had embarked on so unusual a book. At the same time, they almost all automatically asked, "How do you go about doing something like that?" By obliging me to frame new questions at various stages in the process, they kept me busy thinking. So I will be greatly pleased if this study opens a conversation about untried alternatives in squeezing new material from history.

Of the many who weighed in with ideas, I owe special thanks to Lizzie Reis and Matt Dennis, T. J. Stiles, J. Christoph Hanckel, Maurizio Valsania, Bill and Joan Witkin, and Jennifer Blakebrough-Raeburn. More good ideas flowed from LSU colleagues Alecia Long, Bill Cooper, Gibril Cole, Reza Pirbhai, MaryKatherine Callaway, Janet McDonald, and Jerry Kennedy; and elsewhere in academia, Amy Greenberg, Jim Broussard, Richard Bell, Doug Egerton, Carolyn Eastman, Jack Larkin, Sari Altschuler, and John Ferling.

For all kinds of kindnesses, I am indebted to Barbara Oberg, at Princeton; and to Jim McClure, also at Princeton, who is keeper of the faith for Salmon Chase studies. Warm thank-yous go to Lucia McMahon, for sending the poignant dreams of Elizabeth Bayard Kirkpatrick; to Rachel Hope Cleves, for sharing her exciting work on Charity Bryant and Sylvia Drake; and to Douglas L. Wilson, for his particular insights into Lincoln's superstitious nature. I am also grateful to the capable and generous people who make the American Antiquarian Society a temple of knowledge: Ellen Dunlap, Tom Knoles, Caroline Sloat, Elizabeth Pope, Tracey Kry, Laura Wasowicz, Maury Bouchard, Andrew Bourque, Paul Erickson, and John Keenum. I received gracious assistance from Jim Green, John Van Horne, Nicole Joniec, and Connie King at the Library Company of Philadelphia; and nearby, at the American Philosophical Society,

Marty Levitt contributed smart suggestions of places to look and detours worth pursuing.

I had valuable encouragement from off the beaten path as well, where Alicia Allain, Jean David, Mike Thibodeaux, Moss Harbeck, and Lucy Moore have separately resided. I would be remiss not to give a shout-out to energetic LSU graduate students Andrew Wegmann, Spencer McBride, Terry Wagner, and Geoff Cunningham—living proof that my generation will not be the last to explore and improve upon the discipline of history.

To my agent, Geri Thoma, who believed in the dreams project despite its refusal to fit neatly into a single discipline, I am once again deeply thankful for all the good guidance. In more than one critical respect, Luba Ostashevsky, my editor at Palgrave, knew what this book needed to say before I did. She gave me a slew and a half of excellent advice and greatly improved the book's focus. Assistant Editor Laura Lancaster patiently helped navigate the unruly seas of permissions and illustrations. She and Production Editor Carla Benton treated my book with great tenderness.

My son Josh took an early interest in the project and helped with the title and chapter headings, declaring that I'd finally written a book he could read painlessly. It goes without saying that my partner, Nancy Isenberg, has helped shepherd this book along from start to finish—we have been sharing dreams for some time now.

PART ONE
TO 1800

ONE

GEORGE WASHINGTON APPEARS BEFORE BRYAN FAIRFAX

Though there are not many natural appearances more familiar to us than DREAMING, there are few which we less understand.

—James Beattie, *Dissertations Moral and Critical* (1783)

Dreams and foreboding have been mystifyingly linked throughout history. We sense, amid a dream disturbance, that we are inadequate for the task of the moment. Without mobility we feel vulnerable. We know then that the mind is dangerous to the body, that in its accidental impulses it incites us to believe what purely rational thought wants us to deny. In short, life in the dark adds a strange new wrinkle to everyday uncertainties.

Before the modern age, as the last embers burned before total darkness took over, people performed rituals. Not our rituals of brushing the teeth or applying lotion to the skin. They combed the lice out of their hair, checked to see that no heat source would set their home on fire, and hunted down bedbugs. If they could afford it, they slept on mattresses stuffed with horse-tail hair, in beds framed on all sides with decorative curtains. If they prayed, and most did, they appealed for divine protection from mortal threats that loomed as they let down their guard by shutting off their attentive minds for untold hours:

Now I lay me down to sleep;
I pray the Lord my soul to keep.

If I shall die before I wake
I pray the Lord my soul to take.

This eighteenth-century American children's prayer bespoke a very real possibility. The phrase "dead of night" did not enter the English vocabulary idly.[1]

~⌇⌇~

Philadelphia, June 15, 1738. Benjamin Franklin's *Pennsylvania Gazette* reports "a most melancholy account" of a five-year-old boy who hanged himself. He was discovered when a younger sibling was heard crying out, "Brother won't speak to me." It was thought that the boy had been privy to a conversation about the executions of slaves for poisoning their master, and it got into his head that he should see what it was like, having little concept of death. "It is said, that he dreamt much of that Execution the Night before, and telling his Dream in the Morning, added, *And I shall die to Day,*" which was not then regarded. The unspoken moral here could be that dreams, when shared, were not to be left unheeded. They testified to something—but what?[2]

~⌇⌇~

Before attending Harvard in the mid-1760s, twenty-one-year-old Silas Bigelow of Shrewsbury, Massachusetts, taught Latin. He had broken his ankle, and it was poorly set. For months Silas walked everywhere with a cane. He was acutely conscious of his debility when he wrote in his diary about going swimming with "ye scholars"; and when his unconscious was in command of his thoughts, he knew precisely where he had laid his "staff" so that he could get back to his horse:

> This night I dreamed I was riding along, presently came to Doct. Porters house.
> I got off and went in (setting aside my staff by ye side of ye door) and none
> were at home but Mrs Porter. She said ye Doct. was gone half a hundred miles.
> I walked about ye house considerable. She seemed very glad to see me.

At this point, he is walking without needing assistance. Does he really require a doctor? He is feeling welcome, cared for, and free to move about. Then, "just as I was going away she gave me some bread and cheese to put in my pocket." Mrs. Porter's generosity adds to the level of comfort the dreamer is feeling.

All at once, something changes. "I went out and my horse was broke loose and was feeding in the street." (Chaos, temporary loss of control.) Regaining the horse, young Silas rides to the home of "Revd. Mr Lockwood," who is "glad to see me and talked considerable." Silas makes small talk with the preacher. All seems to be going well, until another sudden, uninvited event occurs, presenting challenges and requiring action:

> There came up a shower of rain. I ran to take off my saddle, and as I run I tried to jump over ye gate (which was about four or five feet high) but could not quite, so I opened it, fetched in my saddle, and a little afterward as I was sitting, Miss Lockwood brought me a letter directed to me but had never been sent to me.

We all know this kind of dream sequence: we feel we are being tested. Silas has to gauge the height of the gate; he has to deal with a surprise letter. Wait. Is the letter what he thinks it is? Neither can he figure out the contours of his immediate environment or the size and volume of the letter in his hand: "I opened it, then it seemed like a book. I opened it, found some copper, one piece of silver, then one of the new-fashioned things to wear about ye neck." What's going on? Nothing is making sense, because this is that species of dream that presents one puzzle after the next.

While he copes with the absurd, the diarist tries to put everything in orderly language as his dreaming self unpacks the mysterious letter/book: "There was many other things to wear and I thought some more money down at ye bottom, while I knew not who sent it, but it was some of my good friends."

Is he anxious about money? Perhaps.

And then, the dream's inconclusive final scene: "Mr Lockwood's two puellas [Latin for young daughters] I thought looked very smiling on me, so I began to fix up to go to Deacon May's, intending to lodge there, but I waked before I set out."[3]

The language may sound as foreign as the life he leads, but Silas Bigelow's dream, like those of us moderns, resists narrative (or at least a thorough and logical one). The plot is a series of loosely connected fragments that all seem to involve, on some level, the desire for acceptance and stability of place. The physical pain of a badly broken ankle adds intensity to the young man's quest for emotional steadiness. We can read his satisfaction when people talk to him easily and engage with him in earnest, but we are hard-pressed to glean more from his diary.

All history knows about Silas is that he subsequently graduated from Harvard, was ordained as a minister in the town of Paxton, outside Worcester, and died at the age of thirty. His dream is of a piece with others of his time, and ours today, in the way it mixes positive and negative sensations, selfhood and a loss of power, and describes movement without settled purpose—he never quite knows where he is going or why. Cataloguing the components of a dream such as this, noting the dreamer's awkwardness, if not embarrassment, we can start to gauge how the exhibition of a dream plays a role in personality development.

To Silas, the dream simply interrupts more useful thought. Because he is young and single, and has no plan to publicize his dream, he contributes plenty of raw data without fear of appearing psychologically unfit, but in no way does he indicate that dream content is reckoned meaningful in his world.

∼∾∂

To Dr. Benjamin Rush (1746–1813), dream content did matter. Some of it directly prodded him to monitor his behavior toward fellow human beings.

Rush was a signer of the Declaration of Independence and a celebrated healer. He established himself in Philadelphia as a young man and for decades trained doctors at the University of Pennsylvania. As a clinician, he treated many of the famous and many unknown, in what was for a time America's most populous, politically central, and culturally significant city.

In 1780, amid some of the most uncertain days of the Revolutionary struggle, Rush fell ill with "break bone" (dengue) fever. During his convalescence, he dreamt that a poor woman had come to see him, begging him to attend to her husband. But Rush was feeling so exhausted that he sent her to another doctor. She protested: "O! Sir (said she lifting up her hands) you don't know how much you owe to your poor patients. It was decreed that you should die by the fever which lately attacked you, but the prayers of your poor patients ascended to heaven." The dreamer awoke in tears.

As a scientist, he had been taught to reject superstitious belief and wrote that dreams were rooted in "obvious physical principles." The dengue fever— and nothing of supernatural character—had brought on the memorable dream that Rush worked into his late-in-life autobiography. The experience "left a deep and lasting impression on my mind," he said. "It increased my disposition

Dr. Benjamin Rush (1746–1813).

to attend to the poor, and never, when I could not serve them, to treat them in an uncivil manner." A mid-twentieth-century Harvard psychiatrist who weighed in on the dream interpreted it to mean that Rush was anxious to return to his clinical practice. For our purposes, it is more interesting as an example of disease and mortality as spectacle in early America. As he sat with his patients, grateful that he was valued by them, Rush persuaded himself that he made a tangible difference in their lives.[4]

Of the dreams he wrote down (more of which we will see in chapter 2), there were those that played on, and others that allayed, a sense of guilt in bearing witness to human suffering. The characters Rush's brain produced were often dead persons resurrected, and their reanimation was a transparent means of reshaping his personal history so that it communicated hope.

He taught, among other subjects, nervous physiology. For him and for most of his medical colleagues, the science of sleep commanded individuals to eat the right kinds of foods at appropriate intervals in order to refresh their spirits. The widely owned popular guide *Domestic Medicine* (first published in 1769) urged moderation. It recommended taking "sufficient exercise in the open air; to avoid strong tea or coffee; next, to eat a light supper; and lastly, to lie down with a mind as cheerful and serene as possible." Rush affirmed in his *Commonplace Book* that the "moral powers" were restored after a night's sleep: "They recover . . . in solitude." He firmly believed that nothing gave more advantage than "consulting our morning pillow in cases where there is a doubt or what is right, or duty." Still, he resisted granting dreams more authority than the science of his time allowed.[5]

Owing as much to his central location and amiability as to his medical knowledge, Rush was often the "go-to guy" for philosophic acquaintances. In the autumn of 1799, one year before his election as president, Thomas Jefferson wrote from Monticello to his Philadelphia friend concerning the nature of dreaming. "Do we dream more in age than in infancy?" the Virginian posed. Rush believed so, at least according to the lecture notes he left behind. But Jefferson had other ideas on this small point. "I suspect not," he answered his own question. "Dreams seem to be the consequence of some embarrassment in the animal system. A supper, or the undigested dregs of a dinner interrupt our sleep with dreams, but when all the functions of life are perfectly performed, sound sleep seems to be the consequence in every age." At least in believing that there was an inextricable connection between diet and quality of sleep, Jefferson and Dr. Rush were on the same page.[6]

Rush reviewed his own medical cases as well as those of physicians over the ages when he gleaned theories of human nature in the context of nervous physiology and biological functions. On this basis, he understood sleep to be chiefly a loss of motion in all the muscles (which were otherwise under the influence of the will), a suspension of sensation (hearing, smelling, tasting, and feeling), and a slowing of "involuntary motions" (respiration). In pathological terms, he judged the life of the mind during sleep as a form of manic incoherency akin to hallucination: "Dreaming may be considered a low grade of delirium," he wrote, "and delirium as a high grade of dreaming."

Delirium was not all. Physicians of the Revolutionary era drew analogies between the dream state and mental distractedness or insanity. The passivity of the mind during sleep, and disruption of communication between the brain's sensorium (nerve terminus) and the rest of the body, left the mind susceptible. Some believed that a dreamer, like a madman, acted out the role of another, who was not himself (a strange new self having awakened in sleep). Others emphasized nightmares, wherein the new (altered or invented) persona embodied secret fears or hidden panic. No one was quite sure what was going on.

Thomas Arnold, author of *Observations on the Nature, Kinds, Causes, and Prevention of Insanity, Lunacy, or Madness,* wrote of a species of mental disease that he called "ideal Madness." A person was so diagnosed who could not distinguish the real from the ideal, who lacked a clear sense of his physical environment. "The mind is nearly in the same state as that of a person in a dream," Dr. Arnold asserted. "He has a world of images within itself." For normal people, self-restraint in the waking hours was the prescribed means of resisting the stuff of dreams and achieving mental order; moderation in all phases of one's daily routine (especially diet and resting on one's side) could help recover the kind of sleep that was most desired—dreamless sleep. The madman had it much worse: if his senses were not proactively restored, he was doomed to exist in that imagination-rich otherworld all the time.[7]

A close cousin to insanity in this uncertain time of medical reasoning was the unusual, embarrassing, or simply unacceptable sexual practices doctors read about or came across in their communications with patients. Special attention was paid to masturbation. In *A Guide to Old Age, or a Cure for the Indiscretions of Youth* (1795), Dr. William Brodum felt compelled to address the "abuse of amorous pleasures" among recent college graduates. Citing the venerable ancient Greek physician Hippocrates, he discussed a disorder that arose from "some defect in the spinal marrow" and revealed itself in unhygienic moments: "Every time they go to stool or have occasion to urine, they shed a great quantity of seminal liquor." These young masturbators, Brodum said, "are incapable of procreation, though they frequently dream of the act of coition." He added that those with active sex dreams tended to appear old for their age, "frail, effeminate, benumbed, lazy, stupid." Didactic medicine, lost in its own self-righteousness, was bent on changing behavior through shaming. With other avenues of understanding behavior closed off, dreaming was seen as a sign of abnormal impulses.[8]

Rush did not shy from discussing sex or anything else. He inferred that it was impossible to dream of anything that did not preexist in the mind. As memory (what at some point in the past existed in the waking state) became excited, old ideas revived. Excitation explained sexual stimulation during sleep,

"Sexual appetite acquires strength in dreams." A page from Dr. Rush's lecture notes. Courtesy of the Library Company of Philadelphia.

which he described to his students in terms of the male-specific "wet" dream: "*The sexual appetite* acquires strength in a Dream. This is proved by the Seminal emissions which take place in Sleep—and which never takes place from the base influence of the will in the waking State." He meant that a man of morals could not mentally see his way to orgasm while asleep unless reduced to the dream state.[9]

∽ე∾

I n 1786, John F. Mifflin, a Philadelphia lawyer in his late twenties, wrote down an intense, active dream. It concerned a student at Princeton, James Gibson, of whom he was excessively fond. Either for reasons of privacy or literary convention, Mifflin and Gibson had agreed to refer to each other as "Leander" (Mifflin) and "Lorenzo" (Gibson) when they kept their respective diaries. At any rate, Mifflin fully intended to show Gibson his diary when they reunited

Philadelphia attorney John F. Mifflin dreams of his "stark naked" friend and a harrowing experience navigating home in a strong river current. Courtesy of the Historical Society of Pennsylvania.

"Dreamt a very odd dream last night," Mifflin began. "I thought Lorenzo & I (& I know not whether there was another person present) were in a very small boat inside of a long kind of pier-wharf which was a great way into the river."

This is a dream about a physical struggle that undoubtedly reflects an emotional one. "I thought we had neither oar paddle or anything else to guide our course & we were driving fast into the current which was very strong." He tried to find his way back to the pier, came close to succeeding, but was then pushed away again, "the people on the shore all the time hallowing to us & very anxious for our safety." Finding the pier, he took charge, climbing back up—it was "very high," like the gate in Silas's dream—and pulled his friend "Lorenzo" up after him. But then he suddenly noticed something about Lorenzo: "He seemed to be stark naked & as we were running along hand in hand to the place where his cloaths were—I awaked—greatly agitated by the danger from which we seemed to have escaped."

Freud must wait, because the world of Lorenzo and Leander is not his. And we, as well, must temper any inclination to read blatant lust into Mifflin's thoughts. When it comes to sexual expression, our rules, typologies, and suspicions are not interchangeable with theirs. A bachelor who set up housekeeping with another man was thought to be learning behaviors that prepared him for married life; bachelor roommates were jokingly referred to as each other's "wife" without the imputation that he and/or his partner was exclusively attracted to men. In the late eighteenth century, a fifteen-year-old girl was considered marriageable, and her husband might be anywhere from eighteen to fifty or older.

So, if it is generally difficult to equate male sexual identity in early America with modern perspectives on gay, straight, or bisexual behavior, Mifflin makes it abundantly clear in his diary that his attraction to the sixteen-year-old Gibson is deep. A month or so following his naked hand-holding dream, he found himself sick to his stomach one day, for no evident reason. At that moment, he panicked. The feeling eventually passed, but it elicited a diary entry in which he reflected on "the slender thread of life by which mortality hangs"; from here, his thoughts went immediately to his younger friend. "Oh my Lorenzo!" he recorded, "at that moment did I think of thee & how did I wish for thee that I might unbosom my thoughts & my fears."

Mifflin celebrated every March 14, at 6:00 p.m., the anniversary (right down to the hour) of his "acquaintance & friendship" with Gibson. He gushed: "I felt the *dawnings* of a friendship for him as soon as I saw him—a presentiment of that native worth which a close intimacy hath since confirmed, & taught me to esteem & love." It was at a lecture on electricity that their connection was sparked. The "electricity" of the moment presents a common metaphor to our minds, a metaphor that did not exist for them.

It is hard to know what to make of John Mifflin. He had a delicate frame and, like Silas Bigelow, walked with the help of a cane. He took a series of young men under his wing, and in at least one other case, the mother knew and approved. He and Gibson had traveled together before this and no doubt shared a bed when they did—for this was standard procedure in roadside inns. He visited Gibson at Princeton, and when he called on Gibson's mother, he spent the night in her son's bed whether or not James was at home. In short, Mifflin's fantasies and outward tendencies did not seem to bother those in his wide social circle. In fact, before he turned thirty, John Mifflin tied the knot with an eighteen-year-old, eventually giving her six children. James Gibson, in contrast, did not marry until he was in his late forties.

Mifflin's self-defined "odd dream," with its strong river current, his friend's nakedness, and the two men's hand-holding, struck the dreamer as evidence of an enduring commitment. If the physicality of the dream narrative is unmistakable, so is the dreamer's competitive instinct: he pays attention to his surroundings and acts decisively; he is tested; he overcomes adversity. Yes, there is nakedness, but it is not attached to feelings of extreme anxiety or embarrassment. No naked truth emerges from the lawyer's dream, only naked ambiguity.[10]

If Leander had his Lorenzo, John Adams had his Diana. When he and Abigail Smith were courting, Adams knew his future wife by her chosen pen name: Diana, Roman goddess of the moon, of the hunt, and, not insignificantly, of virgins. It was to "Diana," then, that he wrote of a dream in the summer of 1763: "I saw a Lady, tripping it over the Hills, on Weymouth shore, and Spreading Light and Beauty and Glory, all around her. At first I thought it was Aurora [goddess of the dawn], with her fair Complexion, her Crimson Blushes and her million Charms and Graces. But I soon found it was Diana, a Lady infinitely dearer to me and more charming."

A classical scholar from an early age, he dressed his literal dream in Roman garb, because it was a pleasant vision, and as such reminded the excitable Adams of his future wife. He next told her: "Should Diana make her Appearance every morning instead of Aurora, I should not sleep as I do, but should be all awake and admiring by four, at latest." To sum it all up: "You may be sure I was mortifyed when I found, I had only been dreaming." He got right out of bed, inspired by "Diana" to admire "Miss Aurora."[11]

Another summer, when John was off doing the people's business in the early stages of the War for Independence, Abigail felt the heat of the moment in more ways than one. In Boston, the thermometer registered over ninety degrees. "I have slept many Nights this Summer with all my windows open which I do not remember ever to have done before," she told him. Although Mrs. Adams was an extraordinarily skillful manager of the family's farm and finances, she did not enjoy her husband's long absences at all. "Yesterday compleated Eight months since you left me," she complained. "I often dream of you, but the other Night I was very unhappy. Methought you was return[e]d but met me so Coldly that my Heart ackd [ached] half an hour after I waked." This, she said, was the regrettable cost of caring for someone. He replied nobly: "Your Dream will never come to pass. You never can be cooly received by me, while my Heart beats and my senses remain." We would call hers an abandonment dream.[12]

If John Adams subscribed to the maxim that absence makes the heart grow fonder, it appears that his often lonely wife depended on her nocturnal imagination to fill in some of the gaps. "Tis only in my Night visions," she wrote, "that I know any thing about you." With John gone so much—and as the war went on, sons John Quincy and Charles went to Europe with him—Abigail had only letters and dreams to alleviate the feelings of dejection that routinely crept up on her: "O that I could realize the agre[e]able reverie of the last Night," she wrote in 1781, "when my dear Friend [i.e., her husband] presented himself and two Sons safely returnd to the Arms of an affectionate wife and Mother. Cruel that I should wake only to experience a renewal of my daily solicitude."[13]

Sixteen years later, during her husband's tempest-tossed presidency, the oft-besieged Mrs. Adams, who on the surface bore up so well, expressed feelings of being under attack. This one must have been a particularly vivid dream:

> I seldom think twice of a Dream but last night I had one of so singular a nature
> that it has amused my mind today with various conjectures. I was riding in my
> Coach, where I know not. but all at once I perceived flying in the Air a number
> of large black [cannon] Balls of the size of a 24 pounder. they appeard to be all
> directed at me. All of them however burst and fell before they reach'd me. tho I
> continued going immediately toward them, I saw them crumble all to Attoms.
> but during this scene, two Guns were dischargd at my left Ear the flash of which

I saw[,] and heard the report. I still remained unhurt, but proceeded undaunted
upon my course. how would the soothsayers interpret this Dream?[14]

Any soothsayer worth his sooth would tell her that the cannonballs were political attacks on her husband, the president, which she felt as keenly if not more
than he.

Senator William Maclay of Pennsylvania, a hypersensitive friend of Dr.
Rush's and a principled opponent of Mr. Adams, saw himself as a duty-bound
public servant and righteous republican critic. While holding office in 1790,
he dreamt of deadly events: "I had one strange dream of seeing a man fall from
a place like a saw-mill," he wrote in his diary. "I thought the mill was mine, yet
it differed from my mill at Sudbury. What a heap of idleness! My head ached,
hence I suppose my dreams. A dead child plagued me at another time." Attributing his "ugly" dreams to bad food and physical aches, he did not try to
interpret the bizarre imagery, preferring instead to dismiss it all as nonsense:
"Dreams are but fallacious things. . . . What a heap of idleness!"

Another curmudgeonly politico, onetime president of the Continental
Congress Henry Laurens, of South Carolina, stormed: "I don't Know any thing
more troublesome than the conversation of those people who are eternally pestering one with recitals of their dreams." But he quickly qualified: "This does
not however aim a blow against all dreams." He had his own printed in a
newspaper two days after writing this letter. It was unsigned, at the dreamer's
insistence.[15]

In a good many of the privately recorded dreams of this era, the dreamers,
especially the males, were likely to dismiss their visions, even as they found
them somehow worthy of being preserved. They spoke and wrote of their physical ailments with total unreserve, but when it came to the life of the mind,
their grip on reason had to be firm and steady if they were to retain the full
respect of their peers (and retain their self-respect). Thus, they stood aloof from
dreams, theirs and those they heard recited secondhand.

George Washington was not a believer in dreams as portents, though he
understood the genre and in a good many letters used "appears to me as a
dream" as a catchphrase to indicate some idea of questionable substance or
implausibility. According to a British diarist with access to an intercepted communication in 1776, Washington referred disparagingly to some of his own
officers as "dreaming, sleepy-headed men." But in the middle of his presidency,
he received a letter from one of his oldest friends, Virginia neighbor Bryan

Fairfax, which alters the picture slightly. "I lay myself open to You more than to any man," wrote Fairfax refreshingly. "Such is my Regard that I have some times been uneasy lest you should be displeased with me." The letter sounds confessional, all the more intriguing in that Washington was an emotionally guarded individual.

Boyhood companions, Fairfax and Washington had an unusual history. They stood side by side at the start of the French and Indian War. They traded in land. But when the Revolution was just under way, Fairfax admitted to Washington that he did not want any part of violence and was not sure which side he was on. It is clear that the personal respect each felt for the other did not waver; yet it is as easy to understand why, despite the passage of time, Fairfax doubted how his views would be received. Though he had made amends for his earlier defection, he felt lingering concern over how much liberty to take in a letter to the supreme symbol of the Revolution he had shunned.

Fortunately, something occurred to his mind that convinced him not to worry that his actions or gestures might be misconstrued. As he told the president, "I believe the Lord does sometimes make things known by a Dream." He was, he went on, "relieved from the Uneasiness I was then under by a Dream, in which You appeared to me in no ways displeased." Whatever it was that Washington might have regarded as a slight, Fairfax now could take heart: a dream had informed him to set aside his fears.[16]

Being Washington could not have been easy. In and out of office, the demands on his time were considerable. Like others of a high station, he was barraged by requests for favors of one kind or another. Beyond the good wishes, prayers, and abject flattery, needy people wrote to him begging for loans or gifts of money. One of these, toward the end of Washington's life, found a creative way to get the point across: "I find it impossible to Borrow Money of any Person of my Acquaintance in Consequence of my Reduest [i.e., reduced] Sircumstances being destitute since my Fathers Death," the writer began. "Thus I have given you to understand my unhappy Situation all my Happiness is now depending on your Goodness." He would not have thought to appeal in this manner, he said, "had it not been in consequence of a Vision by Night since my Fathers Death who appeared to me in a Dream since my Misfortunes three times in one Night telling me to make application to you for Money, and that you would relieve me from my distresses. . . . He appeared the other Night again and asked me if I had obay'd his commands."

One can only imagine the expression on the ex-president's face (after all, he chose to save the letter) as he read: "I toald him I thought it Vain presumtion in me to trouble your Excellency again on the Subject he then in a Rage drew his Smal Sword and toald me if I did not he would run me through." This threat from the cruelest of dead parents startled the dreamer awake, leaving him feeling intimidated and at the same time stimulated.[17]

It was not the first time that George Washington held a man's fate in his hands. Nor will this be the last time we encounter the psychological inalienability of dreams and the grave. In Greek mythology, Sleep and Death were brothers.

~ひ~

The most literate of the era placed paramount value on an incisive mind impervious to the seductive pull of superstition. Acknowledging the stakes, the renowned Samuel Johnson (1709–1784), innovative writer and lexicographer, readied himself for death by declaring that he feared only the prospect of a slow mental deterioration. He aimed, he said, to "render up my soul to God unclouded."

For Dr. Johnson, dreaming was the opposite of history. When one retrieved a memory, it was either ordered (as organized history), or it was unorganized thought—much as it would be for a member of a primitive culture or the nonliterate generally. For this latter type of individual, Johnson wrote, memory could only be "perplexed with distant Transactions resembling one another, and his Reflections be like a Dream in a Fever, busy and turbulent, but confused and indistinct." Johnson stuck to his principles. In pain near the end, he refused opiates so that he could die with his mind clear.[18]

The transitory dream could feel like a reprieve from loneliness, a simple, liberating wish fulfillment, as it occasionally was for Abigail Adams. Or it could feel like imprisonment. That was certainly the case for William Widger, whose imprisonment was anything but imagined. Thirty years old in 1781, and already confined by the British in Mill Prison for nearly two years as a captured privateer, he had a dream in which he saw a former shipmate named Silvester who had since been freed from captivity. In the dream, they were back in Marblehead, Massachusetts, where they had originally sailed from, and Widger was saying that he felt frustrated in being so close to home but unable to navigate the last leg of the journey. Soldiers stood sentry where he needed to go.

The frustration reached fever pitch as the dreamer left his friend and "went a little further & met Georg Tucker down by the end of Bowden's Lain where he Stouped and shook hands with me and Said he was Glad to See me[;] he Said my Wife was Just Deliver'd a Boy." Now the emotions came on full force: "I Started at that and Said it was a dam'd Lye it was imposable for I had been Gone tow [two] years. . . . I Left him in a Great pashan [passion] and I was going Down toward Nickes cove I met my Mother and Stopt and talked with hur She asked me wheir [whether] I was not Going home to see my Wife." His response to this was to exclaim that he never wanted to see his wife again.

His mother had other ideas. She sought to reassure her son that the child was "honest begotten." He did the math (in his dream!) and repeated that it was impossible, and that he'd be a "dam'd foule" to return to his wife. His mother would not let up, even as he said that he would prefer to take to the sea again. And then he awoke, still behind bars in England, as the American Revolution moved toward its conclusion and his wife went on living without him.[19]

~∿∂~

In the era of the Revolution, there were many like William Maclay, who rejected dreams as meaningless noise. In "Of Prognostications," sixteenth-century French essayist Michel de Montaigne wrote that dreams, like divination by the stars, represented "the frenzied curiosity of our nature, which wastes its time anticipating future things, as if it did not have enough to do digesting the present." Learned men of the Revolutionary age, who had all read Montaigne, remained as skeptical. But culture does not exclusively flow from the top, and this was also a time when sensational books and pamphlets highlighted incidents of dream-induced prophecy. So-called dream books, vernacular guides, combed ancient history to deliver the message that one not only found meaning in the symbols contained in a dream but could also use them to good advantage.[20]

At one end of the spectrum, then, were the popularly conceived dream books. On the other end stood the young republic's medical experts, such as Benjamin Rush, who decried superstition while devising their own set of empirically weak conjectures. Rush passed on his views to a rising generation, no better example of which exists than Samuel Forman Conover of New Jersey, whose dissertation was addressed, "with all due respect and gratitude," to teachers Rush, Caspar Wistar (professor of chemistry), and Benjamin Smith Barton (professor of natural history).

Conover's "Inaugural Dissertation on Sleep and Dreams" (1791) broke no new ground. For us, it neatly encapsulates the consensus view of the late eighteenth century. Venturing immediately into mysteries of the human soul, the doctor-in-training concurred with the thinking of John Locke, the esteemed English philosopher first trained as a physician; and he backed up his academic advisor wherever possible, too. Locke, Rush, and Conover all accepted that "the soul does not think [or dream] during profound sleep," when, for all intents and purposes, time stands still. Conover espoused Rush's theory that dreams could be a premonitory sign of serious illness, and that the music-loving ears awaken each morning before the eyes do.

As he endeavored to get to the heart of the science of sleep, Conover made associations we would never consider. He had a particular interest in the sleeping habits of vegetables, arguing, along with the Swiss philosopher Charles Bonnet (1720–1793), that "the leaves of vegetables possess the power of voluntary motion." It was axiomatic, Conover held, that "the *sleep of vegetables,* is more or less profound in proportion to their vigour or debility." After satisfying himself that he had said all there was to say on this subject, he moved to animal hibernation, encompassing bear and badger as well as the lowly dormouse (whose very name may be derived from the French *dormir,* to sleep). All this was meant to relate to human sleep patterns.[21]

This invocation of Bonnet, whose work is little known anymore, adds useful context to the beliefs of Conover and others coming of age in American medical circles at the end of the eighteenth century. Bonnet was a central figure in a deepening conversation about science and religion. We can take as a prime example of his reach a pamphlet published in Charleston, South Carolina, in 1800, titled *Conjectures concerning the Nature of Future Happiness.* In it, the Swiss thinker was quoted theorizing about natural senses known and unknown to man: "The germ of the spiritual body may contain at present the organic element of new senses which will not be unfolded till the resurrection." There were powers, he supposed, "at the seat of the soul," that lie dormant until we reawaken in "that future world, our true country."[22]

Despite the way it sounds, Bonnet's first allegiance was to the rational and empirical. His discovery of parthogenesis in aphids—that an insect could reproduce without fertilization from the male—lent itself to the idea that God was unnecessary to the creation of life. But in his public writings, Bonnet insisted that his discoveries did not contradict revealed religion. He just would not agree to the notion of preformation—a static world in which all nature was prearranged by God and all organisms were created at the same time. Before Charles Darwin's theory of evolution, this was where the contest stood between science and faith, and where thinking about the properties of sleep and the physiology (and metaphysics) of dreaming all belonged.[23]

On the subject of our foremost concern, Conover adopted the consensus view, convinced that the character of dreams was fundamentally pathologic. Recurring again to Locke on the soul, Rush's student drew the seemingly self-evident conclusion that dreaming occurred "in times of morbid sleep," when external causes excited internal processes. In a delightful aside, though, he credited the otherwise depraved minds of professional thieves for making their entry during "the dead hour of the night," the time of profound sleep, rather than in the period just before dawn when the external world could creep into an impressionable mind and expose them. And while on the subject of evil impulses, Conover expressed his conviction that the moral faculty was easily compromised in dreams: fantasies of "perpetuating crimes without scruple or remorse" flowed from the nocturnal "desertion" of judgment. Dreams, he said, affected those most who were "of a debilitated and delicate habit." While the eighteenth century liked to tie up all the loose ends, the medical student could not but admit here that the human machine resisted a complete cataloguing.

Continuing to negotiate that nebulous boundary between science and faith, Conover quoted the Scottish thinker Dr. James Beattie (1735–1803): "Superstition is one of the worst diseases of the soul." The superstitious, in this case, were the "weak and ignorant" who still believed dreams to be "prophetical" and "ominous" as of old. There was reason-inspired history, one was to understand, and then there was "sacred" history. Separate truths. No overlap.[24]

The last section of volume one of Beattie's 1783 *Dissertations Moral and Critical* featured an examination of dreams, and he opened volume two with a discourse on memory. Dreams were not always "extravagant," he said. They were as often "not unlike real life." Because they belonged to nature, dreams were not to be dismissed as nonsense. Beattie was more conventional in associating pleasant dreams with a mind at ease and a temperate diet. An early seventeenth-century poet wrote colorfully of dreams: "Some bred by dayes-discourse, or dayes-delight, / Some from the stomacke fuming to the braine." Beattie translated the notion this way: "When therefore we have an uncommon dream, we ought to look not forward with apprehension, as if it were to be the forerunner of calamity; but rather backward, to see if we can trace out its cause." Some of Beattie has a proto-Freudian ring to it.

The Scottish thinker had a significant following in America. And like most of his contemporaries, he was drawn to classical models. He took at face value the observations of Greek philosophy when he discussed the physiological basis of dreams. "In sleep," he wrote, "a weak impression made on an organ of sense may make us dream of a strong impression." This was an Aristotelian premise, purporting to explain the mystery of dreaming. Here is another from the same source, in Beattie's re-airing: "A slight warmth in the feet . . . will sometimes cause us to dream of walking on burning coals." No one was saying no to Aristotle.

The logic underlying eighteenth-century scientific discourse led Beattie to further infer that dreams were influenced by "the state of the air. . . . If the external air can affect the motions of so heavy a substance as mercury, in the tube of a barometer, we need not wonder, that it should affect those finer fluids, that circulate through the human body." We see once again that among students of the dream state, every explanation begins assertively and ends ambiguously.

Like Dr. Rush, Beattie reckoned that while dreams were generally traceable to food or environmental factors, and lacked prophetic properties, there were exceptions in the dreams that could be useful "in the way of physical admonition . . . [and] serviceable, as a means of moral improvement." Beattie upheld the spirit of Enlightenment optimism, which assumed that the active memory prescribed right conduct. The memory that arose during sleep was defined as impaired memory, proven so by the fact that "a person shall dream of conversing with his deceased friends, without remembering any thing of their death."

According to Beattie, speech was one vessel of personality development, reading literature another. Both gave the mind a "lively sensation," which, after migrating from conscious remembrance to the place of pure imagination, became reactivated by a further stimulus. Thus, Beattie concluded, we have the common phrase "I either saw such a thing, or I dreamed it." Dreams conveyed the imagination stored in memory; sometimes that imagination contained useful knowledge. The problem lay in determining whether a dream brought back fact or fiction.[25]

As to Dr. Rush's student who invoked Beattie, Samuel Conover brought his dissertation to a close by counting out the numerous physiological causes of dreams: bodily fatigue. Exposure to heat (sometimes simply a matter of heavy bedclothes). Worms in the alimentary passage. Urine in the bladder. Too much drinking. Too little drinking or eating. "An accumulation of the venereal stimulus." "Air rendered very impure, from its being impregnated with any noxious particles." "A penury of blood." Too much study. Too much business. Too much love or joy or anger. It was, all in all, a work meant to dot the i's and cross the t's in synthesizing what he had been taught.

Yet by Mr. Conover's reasoning, to exchange "morbid sleep" for a good night's sleep, one would presumably have to banish from thought all but sober matters. With his wide and sundry list of symptoms, he had effectively equated morbidity with the very act of breathing. By this measure, nature would have to have done something wrong, contradicting one of Aristotle's dictums: "Nature does nothing in vain." It was a contradiction the Enlightenment mind could not accept, and it meant that the eager medical student had merely added to existing confusion.[26]

～๑～

The archive contains an unending supply of unique Americana. One of the stranger finds comes from the diary of a Revolutionary War surgeon from Connecticut with the unique name of Albigence Waldo, who endured the infamous Valley Forge winter. While in the town of Mount Holly, New Jersey, he happened upon a German-born hermit who had been living in a tiny bark hut in the nearby woods for twenty-seven years. The man's bed was a hole in the ground ("which he calls his grave"); he had a routine of crawling twice a day, on hands and knees, to a particular tree where he prayed. "He says he was warned of God in a remarkable Dream when he first came to America to take this course of life," recorded the army surgeon. "He has many Latin and other Books in his lonely Cell and is said to write considerably. He kisses every man's hand that visits him."

It wasn't some kind of Freudian rehash of experience that commanded the hermit, but a simple dictate. Dreams and foreboding had driven the eccentric to take up an ascetic existence, and, somehow, the choice granted him peace.[27]

TWO

FROM A LOFTY SCAFFOLD, JOHN ADAMS SPIES AN ELEPHANT

We live and feel just as much in dreams as in our waking moments.
—Georg Christoph Lichtenberg (1742–1799), physicist

I n the humanely ambitious Dr. Benjamin Rush we have an unusually forth-coming witness to early American history who was uniquely positioned to testify about the contested inner territory that concerns us. What makes Rush especially interesting is that he not only recorded his dreams but also lectured and published on the phenomenon. And he shared his dreams with the best-known thinkers and statesmen of his day, including the ornery John Adams.

From 1775 until the end of his life, Dr. Rush was a trusted friend and avid correspondent of both Adams and Jefferson, strong-minded men of vastly different temperaments. Their lives intersected on two continents, they battled each other in two national elections, and they finally gave up on their party-crossing friendship on March 4, 1801, the day Jefferson succeeded Adams as president. Eight years after that uneasy parting in the unpretentious new capital city of Washington, the good Dr. Rush picked up his pen one day and told Adams of a prophetic dream he had had a few nights earlier. He thought he had spied his son reading a book with a grand title: *The History of the United States*. On the page before him was a retrospective on the year 1809, when, the book stated, ex-Presidents Adams and Jefferson renewed their broken friendship, magnanimously carried on a fruitful correspondence, and eventually, as very old men, "sunk into the grave nearly at the same time."

It is historical fact that Adams and Jefferson did die on the same day, and not just any day either: it was July 4, 1826, the fiftieth anniversary of the nation's founding. Dr. Rush's dream incontestably came true, though he did not live to see it and call it prophecy. Newspapers around the country reported on the perfectly timed departure of the second and third presidents as—what else could it be?—a providential event, auguring well for the future of America. Historians have, from time to time, used Rush's prediction as a literary device, never suggesting that the dream was other than a ploy, a gentle push that resulted in the restoration of a rich epistolary exchange and recovery of a historic friendship.

It is easy to dismiss Rush's dream as no dream at all, as purely wishful thinking or a lucky guess. But to do so is to give short shrift to a lively corpus of dream writings. Rush was a kind of bellwether, for reasons that will become apparent. Among the many productions of his that have been archived, his published *Travels through Life* and *Commonplace Book* are solid examples of a restless, humane mind. One of his biographers aptly named Rush the "Revolutionary Gadfly," which speaks to his perked-up ear and voluble tongue, as he registered his expectations from Revolutionary character. He credited his good grooming for civil society to Reverend Dr. Samuel Finley (great-grandfather of the inventor Samuel F. B. Morse), whose academy he attended in Rising Sun, Maryland. "I owe my present ideas of the misery connected with great wealth to a dream which the Revd. Mr. Richd. Treat related at [Dr. Finley's] table when I was about 12 years old," Rush wrote in *Travels through Life*. He did not detail the dream, only its moral that happiness could not be bought.[1]

With a commitment to candor and an unusual range of interests, Rush constantly interrogated memory, gamely speculating on all that gave rise to sensations and visions in the ancient world as well as his own. In his zealous engagement with patients and his equally avid concern with the fragility of mind, he informs us how people of his generation lived and acted, imagined and obsessed. And how they strained to make out a nocturnal horizon.

~∿~

There are certain species of dreams that modern researchers consider universal across cultures. Prominent among these are two related phenomena: dreaming of someone who is every bit alive appearing to have died, and dreaming of someone who has died returning in some form or fashion. It is by no means unexpected, then, that as America's story began to unfold, dreaming of the dead should have been the most common nocturnal narrative recorded. The graveyard was as fraught with possibility as it continues to be in a Hollywood that specializes in ghost-assisted horror, haunted houses, and the like.

Dr. Rush, as a restless soul and persistent note-taker, wrote down a protracted dream that had him navigating between the worlds of the living and the departed, a dream he considered momentous. Unlike most, this one has a clear beginning, middle, and end.

> I imagined I was walking in a grave yard in this city when suddenly I heard a noise in the air which I supposed to be the last trumpet. Soon afterward I saw the dead arise from their graves clad in shrouds in which they had been interred. Contrary to my expectations, I saw neither confusion nor distress among them.[2]

We can see right away that this promises to be an interesting excursion. Rush's dream greets us with auditory illusions as well as visual ones, so let us first consider his choice of words. Suddenly hearing a trumpet *in the air* (we'll get to the trumpet momentarily) tells us he is trying to place sound in a dimension where communication—the movement of air—naturally occurs. Is there "air" in a person's dream? Is the need to construct a credible narrative, even if he is writing for himself, leading him to imagine, after the fact, that his mind senses the weight and feel of air? But let us accept the premise that neither his dreaming mind nor the grave itself is airless or inert, because the dreamer owns his dream, and this one belongs to Dr. Rush.

In reconstituting past societies, all sensations matter. Yet as automatically as we privilege visual description, few would think to register the historical environment in terms of the human ear. Fortunately, in the past decade a pair of historians, Richard Rath and Leigh Eric Schmidt, have independently done absorbing work on this very subject. The prominence of noncorporeal voices in a land where religious singing was part of life is but the first piece in a chain of evidence, as "noise in the air" becomes integral to our study of historical dreamscapes.

At the outset of his book *How Early America Sounded,* Rath declares: "Sound was more important to early America than it is to you." From church bells to natural phenomena, to sobs and sighs and wails and cries, acoustic space fed the colonial imagination. In Schmidt's book *Hearing Things,* we learn that mid-eighteenth-century studies of the physics and physiology of sound supported the kind of republican government Rush fought for in the 1770s, when reason became the oracle of the sovereign mind. In the age of Enlightenment, Schmidt writes, "submissive listening sounded ever more tyrannical." History was only now beginning to herald what might be called "the autonomous ear."[3]

There was, and still exists today, a culture of the senses. People of other times and places interpreted the power of sensations in distinct ways. In sensory terms, Rush's was a time of transition, when vision-oriented mass print culture was in the process of supplanting the force of sound. Obviously, this does not mean he and his contemporaries interpreted whispers, murmur, hubbub, inner voices, or the sound of an instrument the same as we would. But if reading resonated differently in his culture, and the range of a bell described a known territory and a feeling of security, what else is there to reckon with? To reiterate, then, it matters what our ancestors heard, as well as saw, in their own minds.

They confronted a less busy soundscape than the one we know, and, if Professor Rath is correct, one they were more attuned to than we are to ours. Their homes were poorly insulated, and their sleep habits differed markedly from those of modern times. They retired earlier and woke after what they termed "first sleep," which meant rising after midnight and sitting alone with one's thoughts for up to an hour before returning to an even deeper sleep. In that quiet, ruminative interval after "first sleep" (which a modern researcher has found to exhibit unique hormonal characteristics), early Americans experienced an altered state of consciousness. When they listened to the dark world, relying on no light other than that which the moon gave off, they probably perceived the contours of their immediate surroundings, and any irregularities at night, not just differently but also better than we do.[4]

"The day has eyes, the night has ears," went a Scottish saying. In fact, all the senses were differently engaged in the preindustrial world. Night, sometimes called "shutting-in," was part of an emotional inheritance we have all but forgotten. The time of day when dreams descended felt understandably suspect. Their road map was dark. Journeys had to stop because paths were unlit and therefore dangerous. Inside towns, watchmen made their rounds. Inside homes, the residual smells of candle wax, lamp oil, and fireplace embers remained full. Fire was everywhere essential and everywhere feared; the slightest spark could, and often did, bring down a house or even a city.

Family members learned every inch of their dwellings. In his work on education, Jean-Jacques Rousseau recommended clapping one's hands on entering a strange room: "You will perceive by the resonance of the place whether the area is large or small, whether you are in the middle or in a corner." No, they were not "like us" when it came to expectations of comfort.[5]

It does not take long to come up with ways in which the physical environment affects us. On a daily basis we hear car engines, phone calls, and an electronically enhanced soundscape. More problematically, though, we need to consider how this kind of experience alters collective psychology. It seems reasonable to assume that the interplay of silence and sound—sensations that affect memory—varies over time. The built-up Philadelphia of Dr. Rush's adult years would have been more alive in the dark than the less congested farming town of his younger years, but both would have had a place in his subconscious.

Sound could mean a clock striking, wind whistling, angry and ungovernable thunder and lightning, or some other no-longer-familiar bridge between music and providence. An eighteenth-century man of science could certainly enjoy fantastic sounds in his dreaming mind without surrendering outright to the imagined power of magic. One way or another, he engaged with a world that bustled unlike ours; its "air," returning to Dr. Rush's dream, was not our air.

So, what did he hear in his mind? "The last trumpet." This was the dreamer's description of the Day of Judgment. It was also something of a trope, and would probably carry little weight if Rush did not repeatedly come back to the subject in his writings. Indeed, when he alighted on musical metaphors, he engaged with the human condition in a particular way: "We are all necessarily Religious as we are reasoning and musical animals," he wrote significantly near the time he recorded this dream. As a philosophic Christian, he pronounced: "It is true we are disposed to false Religions; so we are to false reasoning and false music."[6]

If we know what false reasoning is, it is not absolutely clear what "false music" meant to him. But there are other such resonances in his library of thought that help fill in more of what is missing: Rush's *Medical Inquiries and Observations upon the Diseases of the Mind* (1805) used "chords" and "strings" to suggest the fragility of mind, and how loss of mind, or derangement, was to be understood. Medical theorists and sensational fiction writers of this generation found a similar resonance in "chords" of sympathy and harmonious music-making. "Chords" and "harmony" helped them imagine the body's internal processes, just as the metaphor of the telegraph—the sympathetic nervous system as a system that could be explained through electrical communication—would be found useful in a later generation. The *Oxford English Dictionary* informs us that eight hundred to a thousand years ago, the word alternately written as *dream, dræm,* and *dreme* could mean "joy, pleasure, mirth, gladness" and also "the sound of a musical instrument," "melody," and "sound."

Muses, musing, music. This kind of word association actually describes Rush's mind well. He interpreted the noise in his dream as the sound of not just any trumpet, but the final trumpet: Judgment Day. In reporting his grave-yard dream, he whose mind was constantly immersed in the study of mortality and prolongation of life is telling us that he aimed to find a logical (and musical) correlation between his two belief systems: science and religious worship. Pointedly, in his *Medical Inquiries and Observations,* he wrote: "Music suspends the fear of death." Making the sound in his head mean what he wanted it to mean was a rush to judgment—the Day of Judgment—so that the judgmental Rush might dream meaningfully.[7]

～∂

One whom he knew and admired was Joseph Priestley (1733–1804), a man who spent his career attempting an enlightened marriage of science and theology. The English scientist embraced liberal-minded religious views and controversial political stances that eventually forced him to flee to America in 1794, and Rush was prompt to make his acquaintance. In the 1770s, Priestley had become world famous for experiments leading to the discovery of oxygen; in the same decade, he helped found English Unitarianism, upholding reason and conscience in asserting the singular nature of God. In 1782, he extended his theological critique by publishing a *History of the Corruptions of Christianity.*

After they had dined together, Dr. Rush recorded his thought. Dr. Priestley's conversation was highly instructive, but his opinions were prone to what were, for Rush, strange and uncomfortable transmutations. Rush was combative in defending what he believed in, going so far as to insist that the new American republic was part of a divine plan. Priestley, long established as a critic of fabulous beliefs, never stopped questioning.

It was as a Pennsylvanian that Priestley wrote "Some Thoughts concerning Dreams," conveying his belief that "few or no impressions ever made on the mind are wholly lost." To help explain the sensory power that reigns in the midst of sleep, he recounted one of his own dreams, in which he echoed Rush's awareness of music and voice.

> I thought I was attending a public speaker, whose vociferation was very loud, and his tones very peculiar. Before the harangue concluded, I awoke. But still, though no articulation could be perceived, I had a distinct hearing of the peculiar tones of the speaker, resembling notes in music; and, lying perfectly still, I attended to the sound a sensible space of time. To satisfy myself that I was really awake, I opened my eyes, and saw distinctly every thing in the room in which I lay. How long I may have retained the sound, remaining from my dream, I cannot tell; but on a very slight motion of my head it instantly disappeared.

Further expressing dream experience compatible with Rush's, the scientist-theologian stated anecdotally that most of his acquaintances "seldom dream of anything recent"; that the dead, in dreams, "speak and act in their proper characters." Why is this important? Priestley was encountering his dreams as natural curiosities, owning them without regarding them as dispiriting objects or embarrassing signs of a compromised mind. His openness, like Rush's, was fairly remarkable.[8]

Rush was raised Presbyterian, but by middle age, he was a Universalist Unitarian. If he did not accept the Trinity, he believed nonetheless in the divine attributes of Jesus. Having urged Priestley to assume the chair in chemistry at the University of Pennsylvania, Rush considered the English émigré a "genius," though he continued to find some of his religious doctrines, in his word, "peculiar." There were differences among Unitarians, and for Priestley, not even the resurrection of Jesus (which he was not quite prepared to deny) indicated divine character.[9]

Most important to Rush's view of life and love was an unshakable faith in God. "There is no man," he wrote, "so wicked that does not under a sudden sense of good say 'Thank God' or feel gratitude to Him." And elsewhere: "To the Deity, the whole human race probably appears as much a unit as a single human body appears to be a unit to the eye of man." For the practicing physician who saw suffering on a constant basis, hell did not exist and salvation was universal; the only agony men knew was earthly.

~∿∂~

N ow that we understand something of his convictions and predilections, the opening of Rush's dream says more to us—in short, that the grave-yard did not frighten him. He was not having a nightmare in the conventional sense, because the risen dead whom he encounters are in no distress.

As the dream proceeds, he recognizes many of his old friends and acquain-tances. One of them asks the way to a tavern. Another asks the whereabouts of a woman Rush had never heard of. A third asks the price of national bank stock. Well-dressed men walk "hastily" to the churchyard gate; he asks where they are going. "The Coffee house," he is told. Others move toward a second gate. "Make haste," says one, "or we shall lose our chairman." The dreaming one, deprived of control, infers from what he is hearing that those who populate his dream are to participate in a town meeting.

His attention is now drawn to others among the dead. Tom, a schoolmate of long ago, his face "bloated and full of pimples," takes Rush's hand. Someone else stands behind them, gesticulating loudly, and it turns out to be a former neighbor. "Damn you, Tom, is that you?" he says. "Damn your blood, Sir how are you? A damn fine day, Tom." Dreamer Rush is disturbed by the profane greeting and tries to ignore it.

In another area of the graveyard, he happens upon two who, in life, had begun as friends but spent their final two decades refusing to talk to each other. Rush watches anxiously as one offers the other his hand, only to be rebuffed with "a look of malignity such as I had never before seen in a human creature." From here, "I heard a woman vociferating to a man I supposed to be her hus-band in an angry and petulant tone, 'But I want more, I want—' to which he meekly bowed and made no reply. At a little distance I saw the reverse of this scene. It was a man kicking his wife and dragging her by the hair of her head along the ground, and then leaving her by saying, 'There, take that, you bitch.'"[10]

It is unusual to find such uncensored language in the recorded dreams of this generation of Americans—or such sensitivity to gender politics. Though misguided in his medical theories, relying heavily on the practice of therapeutic bloodletting, Rush was ahead of his time in the treatment of women and would never have engaged in the bawdy humor that was common among eighteenth-century misogynists. Few educated men were willing to challenge prevailing notions of biological determinism: a woman was made to breed and to love God and children. She was ill suited for the rough-and-tumble of a man's public world; her intellect was not meant to be overstimulated. For her, imagination was a concept fraught with danger, and she was warned against reading the kinds of novels that made the heart beat fast. As her body was the site of dangerous impulses, she was especially prone to "hysteria," "nymphomania," "melancholy," and other emotional torments. Her pursuit of happiness consisted of monitoring a delicate sensibility. More to the point, she had to be protected from herself. By men.[11]

Since the time of John Locke, physician-philosophers maintained that women and men exhibited markedly different states of mind. Men were outwardly active and robust, women more naturally dreamy, given to hypochondria, and therefore less logically driven. Literature portrayed them as frail, amiable creatures, unable to arrest their own dark thoughts. The menstrual cycle was held up as a partial explanation for these distresses: it was called an "eruption" and an "oppressive Disease" and, of import to our study, thought to be productive of nightmares. After menopause, still assailed by their bodies, women grew "fat, heavy, and sickly" and even more susceptible to night terrors. In some ways to be pitied, woman was formed for a pampered life. She was often referred to as an "ornament," the tenderness of her nerves making her adept at conversation and, in general, a desirable companion.[12]

Benjamin Rush respected women and reckoned their intellectual ability the equal of men's. In 1775, courting Julia Stockton, the teenager who would shortly become his wife, he wrote determined, expressive letters: "O! my love—my hope—my joy—my life—my Julia—my Julia!" Recurring to the musicality of his thoughts, he told her of the gift of a mockingbird from a grateful patient: "There was a time when his singing would have delighted me, but I can now relish no music but yours." The sentimental doctor completed their premarital correspondence in January 1776 with a further conjuring of living music: "Your mocking bird sympathizes in the joy of the whole family. He has prepared a song to welcome you home."[13]

Julia eventually gave him thirteen children, four of whom died in infancy. Over the long span of his demanding career, Rush proposed a course of education for young women that went beyond basics: English grammar, poetry, history, mathematics, and "vocal music" to augment their contribution to public worship as well as (more traditionally) to "soothe the cares of domestic life." In Charles Willson Peale's 1776 portrait of newlywed Julia Stockton Rush, the serene subject is—to conform to the musical metaphor that pervades his life—strumming a mandolin. Most notably, Dr. Rush embraced the uncommon belief that young women, and not only young men, should be taught an appreciation for political liberty. If they lacked the citizen's right to vote, they should still be politically literate.[14]

So it would appear that Rush's conscious argument carried over into dream life with his representation of the pain women endured. Conscious argument emerged, as well, in the detail orientation of the man of science. In conversing with the deceased, he set down dialogue that was specific and numbers that were precise: "it cost 5/ a yard," he notes from within the dream. Another unusual aspect of his graveyard dream is the fact that his questions all had answers: "'What is your hurry?' 'I am looking, said he, to know what has become of my father and mother.'" The characters in his dream valued freedom of thought and movement. They were all people in need, dead people with unresolved issues—just what one might expect from the mind of an anxious healer.

As the dream approaches its conclusion, the dreamer witnesses a young boy reading to a man at the churchyard gate. He peers over the boy's shoulder and sees that it is the Bible. At last, Rush exits the gate: "I was undertaken by a plain-looking little man whom I had seen in the church yard. I asked him if I might accompany him." Whether there is significance in this choice of words, "undertaker" already had multiple meanings, including that of the profession of burying the dead. On the surface, anyway, by "undertaken," Rush meant simply that the man had taken an interest in him.

The pair proceed to Pennsylvania Hospital, where the plain-looking man is instantly surrounded and one of the patients calls him "father." Another, his brother, "thanked him for the fruit he had sent." Someone else "kissed his hand and thanked him" for a further good deed. Yet another "stroked his back, and said, 'Ah! the pot of sweetmeats you brought me saved my life.'" The voices in the dreamer's head become louder and louder until they wake him: "when lo! I discovered that I was lying in my bed, and that all I saw and heard was nothing but a dream."[15]

—

Rush's *Commonplace Book* is filled with dated entries that begin, "This day died . . ." followed by a name or names. Yet Rush refused to allow the nature of his profession to crush his spirit. This from a 1798 entry: "As medicines sometimes lie many days or weeks in the body without being felt . . . , so does moral and religious instruction. Years after being administered it produces good effects."[16]

The combination of his avid opinions and wide sociability made Rush one of the most visible and remarked-about Philadelphians. He was known for his humanity and sense of fairness. As a family man, he took a deep interest in his children's education. He was especially proud of his son Richard, attorney general of Pennsylvania at the time of the graveyard dream, who would soon thereafter serve as attorney general of the United States and a close aide to President James Madison. But Dr. Rush was also laboring under the knowledge that his eldest son, John, a physician like his father, suffered from pronounced mental problems. He had killed a navy lieutenant—his erstwhile friend—in a duel and slashed his own throat with a razor. Of late, John languished at the same Pennsylvania Hospital where Benjamin Rush's dream companion found himself lionized. In his daily life, our dreamer endured the trials of many parents, balancing a commitment to home life against his public occupations.[17]

Rush took the measure of his fellow creatures, because it was a physician's job to do so. He was compassionate yet also judgmental; for a man of the eighteenth century, a time when outward stoicism was especially valued, he had an extraordinary capacity for sharing personal thoughts and experiences. In letters to favorite correspondents, idealism and empathy usually dominated, even in the midst of terrible political and social upheaval. To his friend Thomas Jefferson, he used a poignant medicalized simile in reflecting on the attempt of Napoleon's forces in Haiti to still a revolution: "Does our globe, like a diseased body, stand in need of a perpetual issue of blood?" As people died, the mix of acceptance and impotence that a doctor of the Revolutionary era felt grieved Benjamin Rush more than it did most people, making the setting for his dream—a church graveyard—entirely predictable.[18]

As a humanist, Rush was an early opponent of the death penalty. His enthusiasm for moral reform occasionally led him to make ecstatic predictions. "In the year 1915," he wrote in 1788, with no explanation for why he alighted on that particular year, "a drunkard I hope will be as infamous in society as a liar or a thief, and the use of spirits as uncommon in families as a drink made of a solution of arsenic or a decoction of hemlock." In the same letter, he exhibited compassion for the plight of African Americans: "I love even the name of Africa, and never see a Negro or freeman without emotions which I seldom feel in the same degree towards my unfortunate fellow creatures of a fairer complexion." While this kind of hyperbole was a common feature of eighteenth-century letter writing, as a medical practitioner Rush exceeded in ardor, and sometimes self-delusion, what others expressed. He was blind to the primitive character of eighteenth-century medicine, and he reached conclusions on the basis of insufficient evidence. Most critically, he refused to outwardly acknowledge failure in his treatment of the sick.[19]

If Benjamin Rush were less complicated, he would not be worthy of this amount of scrutiny. As distrustful of human judgment, in general, as he was utterly certain of his own professional judgments, he somehow extrapolated a hopeful theology. Prayer, he said, was as "natural to man" as sin. Nature's mysteries were fully intelligible only to God, and human beings required their rational faculty to discern the mind of their Creator: "God reveals some truths to our senses and to our first perceptions, but many errors are conveyed into the mind through both. . . . Thus the Sun appears to our eyes to revolve around the earth. Astronomy corrects the error." He is both professor of science and student of God's nature.

At this point in his personal exegesis, Rush invoked the substance of Matthew 24: "There have been many disputes about those words of our Saviour in which he says he was ignorant of the 'time' of the Day of Judgement." As we know, the doctor's dream engages with this very question. He could not get that trumpet out of his mind.[20]

~∞~

It is we who seek insights by probing Rush's recorded dreams. In fact, the doctor spent comparatively little time on his fantasy life. Broadly curious, he collected and applied what he learned from the case studies of other medical professionals. He tended to be wrong about nearly everything in life-and-death determinations, but he regularly updated his university lectures and constantly sought clarity.[21]

Rush treated the poor as well as the wealthy. He worked in military hospitals during the dark days of the Revolutionary War and famously risked his life during the yellow fever epidemic of 1793, staying in Philadelphia and treating—ineffectually, we might add—all sufferers who came his way. President George Washington and most others who were mobile enough fled to unaffected areas, but for months Rush heroically challenged a death that he believed was brought on by "putrid exhalation," as it enveloped the temporary national capital.

Society fell apart. People dropped dead in the street, and many bodies were left untouched for days. A woman went into labor as her husband lay lifeless beside her—after her cries went unheeded, she too was found dead, though her infant survived. The beleaguered Dr. Rush saw it all. As thousands expired from the mosquito-borne virus, he retained his awe for the power of the eternal without ceasing in efforts to earn respect for his idiosyncratic manner of practicing medicine. At the height of the epidemic, he wrote of his state of mind in a letter to his wife: "While I depend upon divine protection and feel that at present, I live, move, and have my being in a more especial manner in God alone, I do not neglect to use every precaution that experience has discovered to prevent taking the infection. I even strive to subdue my sympathy for my patients; otherwise I should sink under the accumulated loads of misery I am obliged to contemplate." This straightforward description of a conflicted conscience plainly attests to the strategy of coping that one of early America's best-known medical practitioners deployed.[22]

Conflict is not limited to Rush's conscience. In the graveyard dream, the dead behave much as the living do. They move, they speak. There is no mortal dread for the dreaming Rush, only the desire for communion, and for answers. Death is not annihilation for him. He could not let it be so.

This leaves us with an interesting contradiction. In his graveyard dream, the dead emerge from their tombs, fully human; in the dengue fever dream discussed in chapter 1, he is told that the prayers of his impoverished patients ascended to heaven and had effect. What, then, is heaven to Benjamin Rush? The worshipper of God and careful Bible reader believes in a realm where the dead are no longer weighed down by all that preoccupies the living; yet those who survive as figments of his dreaming imagination remain engaged with life.

Rush contemplated the powers of creation and destruction at once. His religion was not evangelical in character, though he listened to preachers of varying stripes. He was consoled by the strong belief that God presented mysteries—beautiful mysteries that natural scientists were working on understanding better. That was good enough for him.

⁓∂⁓

W HEN young, Rush saw more of the wider world than most of his peers. After attending Princeton in his teens, he went on to the prestigious University of Edinburgh to study medicine. Much later, in his position as a professor of medicine in Philadelphia, he taught students about the causes of dreams and the nature of the dream state in part by drawing on examples from his own life. In one such instance, he wanted to offer proof that memory became "excited" in a dream, so excited, in fact, that ideas that had by all indications "perished" from the mind could be revived.

"I sailed from this city in the month of August 1766 for Edinburgh by the way of Liverpool," he would tell his classes, recalling that his brother had gone to the wharf to see him off. Then the story got interesting, as he skipped ahead to the summer of 1802, when he had a dream in which he was embarking for Edinburgh from the same wharf. Except this time, a Princeton classmate, Jonathan B. Smith, "appeared to me on the same Spot." The professor of medicine explained: "Had I been asked the night before whether any other person accompanied me to the wharf besides my brother, I should have said, no." So, the morning after the dream, he rapped on the door of the same Jonathan Smith and "was assured by him that he perfectly recollected that this was the case." Rush's point was that the excitement of blood vessels—"the most moveable part of the brain"—had worked on his memory while he slept.

In the same lecture, he told of a widow in neighboring New Jersey who had been sued for a debt contracted by her late husband. She believed it had been paid but needed proof. "She dreamed at this time that her husband appeared to her, & directed her to look into a certain drawer & she would there find a receipt for the money. She ascribed this to supernatural influence, but there is little doubt she had been told by her husband in his life time where he had lodged the receipt, and that the remembrance of it was excited by the more than common action of her memory in her Dream." And now Rush would cast his eyes across the classroom. "See! here gentlemen how the Science of the mind as a branch of physiology, corrects superstition."

Yet Rush believed Old Testament dreams to be divine and declared it so to his students. "Let it not be supposed that I deny the existence of revelations in dreams in the ages of the prophets and apostles," he said. "But I believe they all ceased with the lives of the apostles." To admit even one contemporary dream to be prophetic was to admit all, he said; and "in so doing, we reject the Bible." That is how strong his faith was and how strong his need to corporealize dreams was, even when they produced moral effects.[23]

In handwritten notes that he used in his university lectures, Rush elaborated on the mechanism of sleep and its biological features. Once again, he was preoccupied with sound, intrigued when he read that "the inhabitants of the falls of the Nile are unable to sleep when they leave home from the absence of the customary Stimulus of Sound." He was convinced of the phenomenon, because the rhythm of rain on the roof and the humming of bees also tended to induce sleep. He knew a watchmaker in Philadelphia, he said, who made a habit of taking home the ticking watches from his shop, keeping them at his bedside to make sure he was never robbed of his livelihood. When the watchmaker traveled, he found he could not fall asleep unless he borrowed the watches of the people at whose homes he boarded, wound them, and left them by his ear.[24]

The general assumption among physicians was that bad food produced bad dreams. Dr. Rush was one who emphasized this in lecture. He was apparently not apprised of the puzzle presented to the mind of John Mifflin. The young attorney who, as we earlier saw, dreamt of his friend "Lorenzo" naked on a Philadelphia pier noted one autumn night in 1786: "Slept uncommonly sound last night—the way I account for it is, that I made an unusual supper of mush of milk last evening—a supper I have not made (perhaps) for years. Nevertheless I had a very disagreeable dream. . . . I awoke I believe with the agitation of it." So, he had a sound sleep, but it was punctuated by an anxiety dream. The simple dish he consumed explained the restful sleep but not its lamented end. Impossible that Dr. Rush should have had access to Mifflin's health record or state of mind? Not impossible, as Mifflin and he were close acquaintances. Rush had more than once seen him in "Lorenzo's" company. He even served as a courier of their letters when traveling between Princeton and Philadelphia. America was a smaller world then.[25]

Though celebrated, Dr. Rush was not above criticism. One student, the self-important Charles Caldwell (Samuel Conover's contemporary), really wanted to rub it in. This exacting son of Irish immigrants repeatedly confronted his teacher and chief examiner at the time of his thesis defense. The issue at hand was nothing less than the student's spirited claim of a discovery he had made: "the cure of fever by a shower of rain." The South Carolina–born Caldwell insisted that Rush had stolen his imaginative idea and had lectured on the same subject without giving due credit. The discovery was a momentous one for Caldwell, being cured of a fever in this manner. He thought himself a genius on the order of Isaac Newton watching an apple fall to the ground and being able to explain the force of gravity.

Young Caldwell's defiance of Rush did not let up. He quibbled so much at his thesis defense that the established professor refused to sign off on the dissertation. Never doubting that he was smarter than his teacher, the fiery student could not resist questioning whether his examiner was of sound mind. He inserted in his autobiography, several decades later, that in the midst of the yellow fever outbreak, Rush was seen walking the streets alone, gesticulating as if conversing with several people at once. As a professor, Caldwell charged, Rush was "overbearing." But not he himself, apparently.

The disagreements between Caldwell and Rush were as trivial as they were intractable. To round out our portrait of the self-satisfied student, we need only add that Caldwell claimed that the three and a half hours of sleep (1:30–5:00 a.m.) he allotted himself while he was under Rush's direction, because it was "dreamless and profound," earned him "a higher degree of sound and renovating repose, than does the dronish, time-wasting dozer in seven hours." And boasting that the only exercise he required was "manly . . . swordsmanship," he crowed: "When I retired to my couch, moreover, my business was to sleep—not to 'skim the sky' or 'build castles in the air.' Hence no sooner was my head on my pillow, than my eyes were closed, and consciousness was gone." Without encouragement from Dr. Rush, the insufferable Dr. Caldwell earned his degree and went on to found a medical school in Louisville, Kentucky. In the process, however, he alienated his first wife and was eventually forced into an early retirement by his unsurprisingly unappreciative colleagues.[26]

Another young man not known for self-doubt, John Quincy Adams, had the good fortune to get his education abroad. He served as French translator for the U.S. minister to Russia while in his mid-teens before attending Harvard, where, of course, he excelled. Though he never studied medicine, the young Adams read deeply in philosophy. As a twenty-year-old in 1786, and not yet out of college, he committed thoughts to his diary as he was reading the same passages in Locke (on whether the soul is always thinking) that so interested Samuel Conover. Adams detected a problem in the fact that some people walk and talk in their sleep without knowing, upon waking, that they have done so. "The author seems to think," he wrote of Locke, "that dreams, are no proof of the soul's being active, but supposed it may be caused by some faculty like that possessed by Beasts. This Idea is ingenious, but it is not sufficiently proved true, to be admitted as an argument." For Locke there existed an uncertain tension between consciousness and life. In the daily repetition of sleep-wakefulness-sleep, there had to be some way for ideas to regenerate; what that was, he could not say. For Adams, though, the vitality of a dream, the diversity of images presented in sleep, suggested a greater distinction between the faculties of men and instincts of animals.

As John Quincy Adams read, he entertained doubts—for him, this was the way to constantly build and rebuild the inner life. A Renaissance man if

America ever had one, he protested blandness of thought at every turn. Unfortunately, he did not record his own overnight narratives. But at least he gives us evidence that the accomplished son of two avid dreamers took seriously the study of the soul—the essence of individuality—in the context of debating the physiology of a dream.[27]

～✠～

Antithetical to the ideas of the medical Enlightenment were the superstitious tracts of popular hacks and the overreaching grasp of ecstatic religion. Thus the most frequently reprinted dreams in the Revolutionary era were those that concerned prophecy. A dream did not have to be nocturnal, or even literal, to be prophetic. The Puritans had lived in a "world of wonders" and were quick to personalize acts of nature: thunder and lightning could express God's wrath. Their world was gone, but irrational belief was not. People wanted sensory activity explained, one way or another.[28]

While history focuses on the power of Newtonian science, alternative explanations resonated in many minds—and not just among the uneducated lower classes. The Royal Society of London reported the case of Henry Axford, who had been struck dumb "by means of a frightful Dream." Four years after the event, though not normally much of a drinker, he drank heavily one evening and dreamt he had "fallen into a Furnace of boiling Wort." Screaming out in the middle of the night, he instantaneously recovered his lost voice.[29]

In a memoir prepared for her family, Janet Livingston Montgomery (of New York's land-rich Livingstons) seized on something her grandfather had announced two years before his death. She was the older sister of Robert Livingston, a signer of the Declaration of Independence, and wife of the much-lamented General Richard Montgomery, who led the American invasion of Canada in 1775, where he was martyred for the cause of independence. "My husband said, 'I have always told you my happiness is not lasting,'" she related before her own death, subtly revealing to her family that fatalism had long been a part of her worldview. "We had peace and plenty in the land," she recalled of the lead-up to the Revolution. "War was the dream, we thought, of my grandfather. He alone foretold war with England. We laughed at his credulity."

The point of the story was its irony. Her grandfather had turned to her father, who was a judge, and said to him: "You and I will never live to see this country independent." Next, he addressed Janet's new husband: "Montgomery, you *may*." And to a grandson: "You *will*." Janet regarded the "you may" as a less-than-assuring remark, which could be seen in retrospect as the warning of an old man, his consciousness half in this world and half in another, to the ill-fated General Montgomery. Her grandfather, she went on, was "in raptures" at the outbreak of war in the spring of 1775, and he died not long after the Battle of Bunker Hill that June, uttering last words of: "What news from Boston?"[30]

Beginning in 1776, in printed works and popular lore, the cause of independence was routinely associated with reassuring dreams and visions. The distinction between these two phenomena is fairly straightforward: dreams are narratives of a sleeping person; visions, more broadly, occur in whatever state an individual receives instructive pictures or clearly laid-out ideas that seem to come from a supernatural, or otherwise wondrous, source. It is hard to ascertain which—dreams or visions—were designed to cause the greater stir.

The first hint of this trend actually appears a full decade before the Revolution, at the onset of discord between the political parent and her wayward child. In New London, Connecticut, an anonymously authored pamphlet, titled *A Dream or Vision of the Night,* attested: "One Night, not long after King George IIId came to the THRONE, I had the following DREAM, real not feign'd." Not feigned. It was often the case in such a publication that assurances of the writer's reputation for honesty preceded the text, in part because dreams were a known vehicle for disreputable literary inventors.

Asking to be taken at his word, the dreamer of 1766 saw a cosmic shift about to happen. It was so distinct in his mind that he even imagined he understood the direction in which he was pointed when he looked into the future: "And lo I stood on the Western Bounds of a great Sea, which was alive with People, almost as numerous as the Trees of the Forest, all moving their Course to the East."

Who were the people in his dream? Some sailed in ships, others rode on horseback, and still others were swimming: "I stood—I paused—I wondered—How, said I, can this be?" The water was hard, and the color of parchment, as he took his first step onto it. He proceeded until he came to a magnificent house, which appeared to him as a customhouse, or perhaps an accounting firm. He counted four floors, at the top of which a watchtower stood, "wherein were royal and sacred Spies, to see and give timely notice of foreboding Good or Evil." In time (however time is measured in a dream), he moved on, picturing heaven's clear light, "the Air pure and aromatic, the Fruits mature and gustful." In a sacred stream, written in gold, was the word *Liberty,* repeated three times.[31]

Another pamphlet, *The American Wonder,* was first published in 1769 and republished in 1776. Addressed to "All Christian Readers," it was attributed to an unnamed Gloucester, Massachusetts, man, and it described "a strange road . . . attended with many evils." The dreamer had heard a voice saying, "Woe to mortal man," while predicting "great trouble, that is coming upon *New-England.*" The line is asterisked, and at the foot of the page, the editor of 1776 recounts the "ever-memorable" battles of Lexington and Concord as evidence of the prophetic content of a dream that had occurred six years earlier, when a night watchman cried out ominously, "What of the times? What of the times?"[32]

In the autumn of 1776, a contributor to the *Maryland Gazette* reported a politically charged dream. It was probably based on a literal dream the writer experienced; at least, that is what is suggested by the cumbersome parenthetical assertion that takes up a chunk of the opening paragraph. The writer wanted it both ways: for the dream to be accepted as prophetic, and also as the product of a thoroughly rational mind. Here is how his piece began: "A dream or vision (don't rashly pronounce me superstitious, for it was not a dream from any disorder of body or mind, as both were healthy and clear, and the same was presented to me twice in the same night, though I have not had a dream to be before regarded these twenty years) represented to me a very great luminary (call it the Sun) in the west, under a great but not total eclipse."

He went on to describe the cosmic phenomenon in scientific detail. It was not a total eclipse, as luminosity was evident at the top of the celestial orb. But as many as thirteen moons loomed before him, plainly located to the southeast of his position. They were "of different magnitudes" and appeared to be "like a polished white metal, but giving no light." Within each moon he beheld "a very deformed black spot" with corrosive tendencies. He was guessing at the number thirteen, in designating the moons as American colonies, but he had no doubt that the dark spots eating away at the bodies were the Tory populations of each moon. They were obstructing Congress and aiming "to produce darkness and confusion" so as to wipe out the independent republics.[33]

It is interesting that the writer of the above dream parable first expresses uncertainty as to whether what he experienced was a dreamlike vision or a full-blown dream. He rejects a strictly medical explanation, instead interpreting what he sees as something meaningful that the public deserves to know about. The implication is clear: even one inspired, ecstatic encounter could smash the edifice of a strong, rational-conscious self.

In 1775 and early 1776, the *Pennsylvania Magazine* was edited by a new-comer from England, Thomas Paine. Several articles addressed the dream state. "A Curious Conjecture Concerning Time" noted that the passage of a brief moment could seem like "whole seasons" to a dreamer: "I have fallen in love, courted, married, and had a family in one night's time." Another issue offered up the fantastic "Dream of Irus," modeled on classical narratives illustrating the elusive nature of happiness. Like an actual dream, Irus's flits from scene to scene: a "mighty prince" receives his people's adulation but is unfulfilled; an "Asiatic sovereign" is assassinated. Topping them all, an impoverished young couple enjoy "unaffected chearfulness" in their "thatched hovel" of a dream home.

Between contrived pieces and philosophic exercises, contradictions appeared that were never challenged. The very next month, the pages of Paine's magazine contained a history of dream theory, emphatically denying the legitimacy of seers, religious visions, and prophecies meant to influence individual perspectives or government actions. The Enlightenment held that the best explanations were those predicated on scientific methods of analysis and observation. Wandering thoughts could be studied, if not codified. And so a dream of "stenches" related to "putrid matter" in the body of the dreamer. A dream of falling had predictive properties—not in a supernatural way, but only in previewing an episode of vertigo.[34]

This framework accorded with Dr. Rush's well-regarded *Medical Inquiries and Observations,* in which he cautioned that dreams presented as a sudden and temporary onset of mental confusion, often with "the premonitory signs of acute diseases." Despite his own imaginative engagement with dreams, Rush officially dressed them in pathological terms as, for instance, "a transient paroxysm of delirium," and he proposed as a "cure" the only behavior that made sense to an eighteenth-century physician-philosopher: the removal of "disquieting passions," the acquisition of balanced eating habits and balanced work patterns—essentially the "cures" recommended in his student's dissertation.[35]

In patriot Joel Barlow's attempt at national epic poetry, "Vision of Columbus," published in the year of the Constitutional Convention (1787), the Connecticut scholar and future diplomat developed the conceit that America's moral essence could be captured in visionary strains. His America was an empire of the imagination even before it began to resemble a continental empire. It was a vision that had prodded Christopher Columbus to persist in his appeals for sponsorship, despite the illiberal attitude of an "ungrateful and timid" King

Ferdinand of Spain. In Barlow's poem, an angel came to the explorer and described the great diversity that existed within the human race; the heaven-sent creature presented to his mind's eye the future American Revolution in its most glorious aspect. America was a "happy shore" in the poem, "Immortal Washington" the explorer's spiritual son, and the other Revolutionaries "Fruits of his cares and children of his toil." In his supposed vision, Columbus was permitted to see "Stretch'd over Virginia hills . . . beauteous Alleghenies . . . sultry Mobile's rich Floridian shore . . . Hudson's winding bed . . . fair Mississippi," and the remainder of that land whose "liberation" his voyages would make possible.[36]

Such productions were timed to react to awe-inspiring events and to occurrences of frightening proportions as well. A broadside distributed in 1793, year of the massive yellow fever epidemic in Philadelphia, told of a certified dream of 1757, repeated in 1768, which predicted that calamity would descend on the city. The dream was replete with "screeches and lamentations," "great pits dug like the foundation of houses," black plumes of smoke, and a parade of black horses leading a parade of mourners.

A private, unpublished, unsigned "memorandum" of 1799, a time when Federalists and Democratic-Republicans were at each other's throats, illustrates the providential phenomenon in its most undisguised form: "I Thought (in my sleep) I was invited to a Meeting such an one as had never before been held on the Contenant of America. . . . [W]hen I came within the Door I saw the Assembly which was Composed of a Considerable Number of men, who sat in the most solemn pause [i.e., pose]." Most strikingly, it was "a native Indian of this Land" who rose from the middle of the crowd to deliver the warning that a scourge would befall the country as an expression of God's wrath. The Indian finished speaking and took his seat, "the Tears still streaming from his Cheeks." Others in the room felt the power of his words, and they cried, too.[37]

New settlements took shape, and the nation's population doubled from one generation to the next. The number of churches was ever expanding; new sects came into being. In this rapidly changing environment, the inner world was made less dangerous, or at least less incomprehensible, by the interposition of a guiding light. When subsumed in moral texts, the dream was a godsend.

~⁊∂~

Given the traumatic character of the many dreams that found their way into newspaper columns and hand-sewn pamphlets, it should not be surprising that there was an increase in the dissemination of popular dream guides. The first to be published in the colonies was *The New Book of Knowledge* (1767). Three decades later, the genre was alive and well. A typical title, *The Complete Fortune-Teller* (1799), sought to be reassuring: "To dream you see the air clear, blue, calm, and serene, shews that the point you then aim at will be prosperous; if it is streaked with white, you will get over your difficulties." But read on, because for every prediction its opposite was always looming: if the air is filled "with thick and dark clouds, you will meet with disappointments or fall sick."

Angel dreams were common to a good many of these published pamphlets, wherein the dreamer received a glimpse of heaven and hell. A self-styled guide to "the hidden decrees of fate" stated confidently: "If you dream of angels, this is proof that there is one near you, and that the rest of the dream shall prove true; therefore be mindful of it." Not surprisingly, there was never an emotionally neutral angel dream in this period.

Why did so many early Americans dream of guiding angels and dead relatives, receiving glimpses of heaven from their keen, all-knowing nocturnal visitors? Think of the regular church-bell ringing as funerals took place in every community. This was their world: burying children, burying neighbors. A modern scholar has tracked dreams copied down by Jesuit missionaries in seventeenth-century China, taken in interviews with the local men and women they had converted. Of sixty-four dreams collected, twenty-five concerned the Virgin Mary (four times bearing the infant Jesus); eleven dreamers saw dead relatives; eight saw a heavenly bright light; seven saw angels; seven saw demons or monsters; and five saw heaven itself. Power of suggestion explains a lot.[38]

Another popular volume to appear in the 1790s was *The Oneirocritic.* The editor defined oneirology as "the science of foretelling future events by dreams." Many dream guides were alphabetized by subject: under "A" alone were adultery (never good), adversary (your business will succeed), almonds (trouble awaits), alms, anchors, angels, anger, ants, apes, apparel, apples—and so on.[39]

The *Dreamer's Class-Book* was one of the more ambitious of the genre. "Eagles are harbingers of promotion; ravens indicate a funeral," it declared. "Birds in a cage denote domestic harmony; but to see a wild bird caught and thus confined, admonishes you, if you are in debt, to settle with your creditors as soon as possible." The book not only promised knowledge; it hinted at outright happiness. Problem: "How any person may dream of his or her Sweetheart." Solution: "Write the name and age of the person in full length

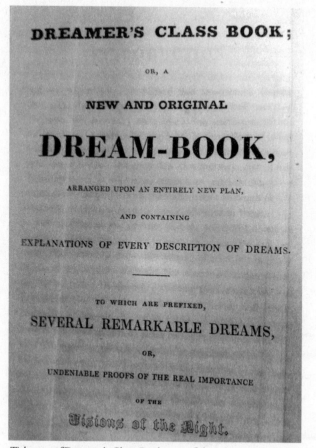

DREAMER'S CLASS BOOK;

OR, A

NEW AND ORIGINAL

DREAM-BOOK,

ARRANGED UPON AN ENTIRELY NEW PLAN,

AND CONTAINING

EXPLANATIONS OF EVERY DESCRIPTION OF DREAMS.

———

TO WHICH ARE PREFIXED,

SEVERAL REMARKABLE DREAMS,

OR,

UNDENIABLE PROOFS OF THE REAL IMPORTANCE

OF THE

Visions of the Night.

Title page of Dreamer's Class-Book, *one of the many popular dream interpretation guides published in the late eighteenth and nineteenth centuries.*

with red ink, on a half-sheet of paper, cut in the form of a heart . . . and place the paper in your left-hand-glove under your pillow. By this means you will most likely dream of the person, and by the circumstances of the dream, may give a shrewd guess, as to the honour and fidelity of the party, and of their sentiments towards you."

The level of absurdity is self-evident, and the genre hardly worth delving into at any length, other than to uncover examples of creative fraud. The *Dreamer's Class-Book:* "To dream you have a glass eye, shows you have misplaced your affections." And, "It is good to dream of white, purple, pink, or green; brown or black, is rather ominous; but the worst colours are red and yellow." Which begs the question: How did the compilers of *The Universal*

Dream-Dictionary, before there were zoos (indeed, before any American had ventured to the interior of Africa), imagine a citizen of the young republic dreaming of apes? Needless to say, the authors of these unoriginal works were neither scientists nor philosophers, but scrappy printers aiming to collect.[40]

The entirely unplayful *Universal Interpreter of Dreams and Visions* supplied over two hundred pages of examples of dream lore from classical antiquity forward, mixing historical with spiritual messages. This compendium avowed that the "ever blessed Creator" did not stop with holy men of old, but had persisted in sending angels, "those glorious ministering spirits, to reveal to the sons of wisdom his divine good pleasure, sometimes to admonish them of things to come."[41]

In "Good Effects of Dreams," *The Astrologer's Magazine; and Philosophical Miscellany* made reference to some lesser known dreams that came to pass in the Roman Empire, adding as a reminder of oneirological force the story of Joan of Arc, "a virgin, who dreamed, that she herself should be the only means to put Charles the seventh in possession of his kingdom." The magazine's lessons were helped along by excerpts from the work of a Swiss entrepreneur, Johann Caspar Lavater (1741–1801). Lavater's books on physiognomy, the "science" of determining character on the basis of facial construction, were exceptionally well received in America. The author and illustrator attributed distinct personality traits to certain shapes of chins, noses, foreheads, and eyes. "Each part of an organized body is an image of the whole," he asserted. For the thin-lipped it was hard to avoid being thought of as naturally deceitful.[42]

A course in physiognomy, like dream interpretation, fed a thriving curiosity about the secret impulses of human beings. Such practices matter as we enfold our discussion of literal dreams in cultural prejudices that existed at the crossroads of medical theory and popular belief. Of note, then, is the early work of Charles Caldwell, Dr. Rush's unpleasant student, who in 1807 published an "Essay on the Truth of Physiognomy." Lavater had written that each country possessed its own indelible "national physiognomy," and he praised English women for their tall, slender tendencies and uniform softness of disposition. When Dr. Caldwell visited the bustling port city of Liverpool, he remained true to character and deliberately irritated his hosts by insisting that English women paled in comparison to their American rivals in terms of "elasticity, vigor, and springiness." On the whole, he said, the British suffered from "a want of cellular tissue." No one had a better head (structurally speaking) than the majestic George Washington.[43]

-ꝏ-

N ary a one of the dream guides of this era failed to highlight Artemidorus, the Roman dream master from the second century A.D., who
lived in what is today western Turkey. The greatest of ancient interpreters
to have had his teachings preserved, Artemidorus saw nocturnal visions as
lighting the way to the future. Greek temples as early as the seventh century
B.C. show dream therapy being practiced, and Artemidorus famously placed
all dreams into one of two categories, as either *oneroi,* the future-directed, or
enhypnia, the mundane and meaningless. Consistent with the eighteenth-
century medicalized association of anxiety dreams with obvious biological
processes, he dismissed dreams that taught nothing or simply went over the
day's events—dreams that did not predict—as deriving "from an irrational
desire, and extraordinary fear, or from a surfeit or lack of food." And he
added: "People who live an upright, moral life do not have *enhypnia* or any
other irrational fantasies . . . , for their minds are not muddled by fears or
expectations." Instead of wasting their time on bad dreams, they allow their
souls to wander into the place of oracles.

As a man of his time, Artemidorus wandered only in directions that legiti-
mized the hierarchical social order he wished to uphold. Thus the same dream
changed meaning according to the public standing of the dreamer. He never
questioned the divine origin of dreams either, insisting that the gods sent specific kinds of dreams to the dreamer's soul according to the nature of the prayer
being conveyed. These observations are borne out in the following excerpt from
his writings:

> Seeing Zeus himself as we have imagined him or seeing his statue wearing his
> proper attire is auspicious for a king or a rich man. For it stabilizes the one's
> good fortune and the other's wealth. It foretells recovery for a sick person and it
> is also good for other people. It is always better to see the god standing still or
> seated upon his throne and not moving.

The basic structure of dream interpretation that Artemidorus set forth,
featuring contingencies for every dream symbol, was reflected in dream guides
of the last years of the eighteenth century. Indeed, the road from Artemidorus
to Freud is not as long as one might suppose.

After Artemidorus, it was Aristotle whom American classicists of the post-Revolutionary period consulted for thoughts on dreams. Though open to the metaphysical, Aristotle adopted medical explanations first: dreams were the result of external factors acting on the sense organs during sleep and were therefore of principal value to medical diagnosticians. He allowed that some dreams foretold future events, but in most cases even these could be chalked up to coincidence.[44]

Dream interpreters in early America were as widespread as forgers, purveyors of instant cures, and other hucksters. This encouraged satirists to capitalize on the dream industry in less serious ways. Philadelphia wit Francis Hopkinson wrote of a dream, circa 1787, that did not seem contrived until he offered his self-serving interpretation of it. "I thought I had lost myself in a thick wood, without any road or path to direct my way," it began. "Whilst I was considering what course I should take, a wild goose and a parrot descended from a large tree, and after several circuitous flights, alighted, the one on my right shoulder, and the other on the left: These birds were certainly figurative of my authorship and genius." The idea was to make light of a genre that appealed most to the modestly educated.[45]

And then there was the one about the New Hampshire farmer who took advantage of the gullibility of his neighbors. He told them he had dreamt that a treasure lay hidden beneath a dunghill on his land, and if they would only assist him in digging it up they could share in the profits. The men brought their carts and relished the otherwise thankless work. When they had dug so far, the sly farmer apprised them, according to the newspapers, "that his dream went no further than the removal of the dunghill, which he was obliged to them for doing, as he could not himself have effected it before the snow came on." And that was as far as the story went, too.[46]

When Benjamin Franklin was in Paris during the American Revolution, he became devoted to the widow Helvétius. In his effort to charm a woman who had declared herself faithful to the memory of her late husband, he told her that Monsieur Helvétius had appeared to him in a dream and gave his blessing to their terrestrial union. To advance his purpose, the mischievous Franklin wrapped the words of the late Helvétius in direct quotes, as the dead man spoke about the virtues of his widow: "Ah!" he said, "you remind me of my former happiness. But we must forget it if we are to be happy here. For several years at first I thought of nothing but her. At last I am consoled. I have taken another wife; the most like her I could find." As their conversation proceeds, "the new Madame Helvétius" enters the picture, and it is none other than the late Deborah Franklin. "I was a good wife to you for forty-nine years and four months," she tells dreaming Ben. "Be content with that. I have formed a new connexion here which will last for eternity." However he might try to enlist messengers from heaven, our conniving dreamer's comical ruse did not succeed with Madame.[47]

Approaching eighty, Franklin wrote an essay titled "The Art of Procuring Pleasant Dreams," which was so well received that it was appended to his celebrated autobiography in published collections of the early nineteenth century. He begins the piece by suggesting that, as dreams are unavoidable, it makes sense to manage them: "for, whether real or imaginary, pain is pain. . . . If, while we sleep, we can have any pleasant dreams, it is, as the French say, *tant gagné*, so much the better." Near the end of his life, Franklin would remark of his nine years in Paris that the time spent was so "sweet" that "now, even in my sleep, I find that the scenes of all my pleasant dreams are laid in that city."

"The Art of Procuring Pleasant Dreams" recommended exercise before meals and eating "sparingly" to render digestion "easy and good" and keep the body "lightsome." A great swimmer before becoming portly, Franklin, two centuries in advance of the invention of junk food, believed that an "improvement in cookery" had exacerbated matters: big eaters, consuming "twice as much as nature requires," did not acknowledge the damage it was doing to their bodies since "it costs them only a frightful dream, and an apoplexy; after which they sleep till doomsday." He warned: "when the body is uneasy, the mind will be disturbed by it, and disagreeable ideas of various kinds will, in sleep, be the natural consequences." One's best recourse, if startled awake in the middle of the night, was to "get out of bed, beat up and turn your pillow," undress, "shake the bed-clothes well, . . . walk about your chamber" (allowing the bed to cool a bit), and then return to bed.[48]

There is yet another source for the popular wisdom of the Revolutionary era: *The Spectator*. Benjamin Franklin and Benjamin Rush, though born four decades apart, were alike reared on *The Spectator* essays. Every gentleman possessed them, in several volumes, and their reputation did not falter even a century and a half after their initial publication in 1711–1712. Written by Oxford scholars Joseph Addison and Richard Steele not long before young Franklin entered the world of printing and publication, *The Spectator* was a model of superior wit, ribbing human nature, and commenting critically on the ways of the world. The young were expected to read these essays to develop character as much as to feed a literary imagination.

"The Artist's Dream" (1840) (print by George H. Comegys; engraved by John Sartain) captures the essence of the dream recounted in Spectator *83. Courtesy of the Library of Congress.*

Franklin, Rush, and many others would have known of Addison's little dream escapade in *Spectator* 83. On wet and miserable days, the author tells us, "when the earth swims in rain," he made it a habit to escape the weather by visiting an art gallery. The diversion so affected him that, after one such occasion, he replayed the experience in a "short morning's dream," in which he entered a gallery that was contained by two walls: one that featured living artists, another that featured the grand masters of times past. "On the side of the living," writes Addison, "I saw several persons busy in drawing, colouring, and designing"; "on the side of the dead painters, I could not discover more than one person at work, who was exceedingly slow in his motions, and wonderfully nice in his touches."

He inspected the living first. (Each was named for an archetypal human quality.) There was "Vanity," whose portrait subjects, whether male or female, displayed "a certain smirking air"; "Fantastique," who "had an excellent hand at chimera, and dealt very much in distortions and grimaces"; and "Industry," a Dutchman who captured every last detail. Having "taken a cursory view" of the one wall, the author of the dream turned toward the masterpieces: "I fancied myself standing before a multitude of spectators, and thousands of eyes looking upon me at once; for all before me appeared so like men and women, that

I almost forgot they were pictures." He was transfixed by these lifelike subjects, until he gave his attention over to the one old man he had seen when first sizing up that side of the gallery, who was now retouching one of the canvases and worked "without rest or intermission." At length, he recognized the "ancient workman . . . by the long lock of hair upon his forehead" to be "*Time*" himself. Upon which discovery Addison concluded his essay: "Whether it were because the thread of my dream was at an end, I can not tell, but upon my taking a survey of this imaginary old man, my sleep left me."[49]

The tract could have been inspired by an actual dream. It possesses that fragmentary, emotionally wrought drama we expect from dreams; and the old man, who does not speak (no one in the dream does, in fact), is industriously, almost compulsively at work. Whether the dream is deliberately plotted or creatively adjusted, the reader can't quite tell. However, in *Spectator* 167, by Steele, the writer identifies himself as a "castle-builder," who admits to chasing "chimerical happiness" in phantom-laden "reveries" and "day-dreams." The daydreamer was already known to history as one with an overactive, and often self-defeating, imagination. The self-anointed genius Charles Caldwell, M.D., said he had no patience for "castle-builders" at all.[50]

~∂

What we see, by and large, is a people living as "Spectators," encouraged to contribute to their communities by observing what lay about, without saying too much about what lay within. They wrote of their public activities and made their inner urges as inconspicuous as possible. But if they allowed adornment to mask essence (and this is what is most interesting), they certainly communicated in a language that stressed self-examination.

Early Americans were not distrustful of emotion so much as they found a moral vocabulary more accessible than an emotionally laden one. The reality of frequent early death predisposed them to prize personal memory. They thrived on their social encounters, sent their thoughts, wrote and shared, and kept careful records. We understand these impulses. As the philosopher Paul Ricoeur (1913–2005) put it: "Forgetting makes us afraid. . . . We welcome as a small happiness the return of a sliver of the past, wrestled away, as we say, from oblivion." This urge was no less existent for the eighteenth century. Yet because dreams let loose something potentially dangerous from the darkest bottom of the well of memory, most people were reluctant to characterize their dreams as a component of emotional identity.[51]

~y~

Having encountered Benjamin Rush as dreamer, physician, husband and father, and man of faith, let us return to the matter of his political connections, and to that moment in 1809 when he conveyed his prophetic dream to John Adams. Even as a signer of the Declaration of Independence, with a close-up view of much of what took place during the war, Rush never sought national office. He commented freely, and often provocatively, on people and events, sharing in Adams's wartime criticism of the "superstitious veneration" shown toward General Washington, while maintaining, he later wrote, only "a slender intercourse with public men" during Washington's presidency. He was a great fan of Benjamin Franklin's, however, and when this most famous citizen of the City of Brotherly Love died in 1790, Rush obtained a souvenir lock of his hair.[52]

If he tried to stay aloof, he continued to take the pulse of the nation. In one searching letter, he reached out to Horatio Gates, hero of the Battle of Saratoga, which turned the tide of the war in America's favor in 1777. General Gates had enjoyed a period of popularity after Saratoga and briefly threatened Washington's preeminence. He was discredited, however, owing to a stupendous failure on the battlefield in South Carolina. In 1795, Rush strongly empathized with the belittled general, who was excluded from the councils of government. "Many of us have been forced to expiate our sacrifices in the cause of liberty," he reminded Gates, "by suffering every species of slander and persecution."

And he would know. According to his critics, Dr. Rush was often seen walking the streets alone during the deadly summer and fall of 1793, as the yellow fever raged, and there was that story about him talking to himself distractedly. He was supposed by some to be going insane. Rush was a proud man, acknowledging to Gates the hurt done to him by "resentful . . . enemies" of his work. But he was quick to add: "A kind and bountiful providence has showered a thousand blessings upon me which more than compensate." William Cobbett, an abusive English-born columnist, published a political gazette in the United States under the pseudonym "Peter Porcupine" and seemed to enjoy making enemies. He claimed that Rush had killed more patients than he saved, and Rush successfully sued his accuser for libel. The good-hearted doctor was a poor epidemiologist, but at least he found in the courts a profitable antidote to the barbed quill of Cobbett.[53]

He extended himself to all who suffered. This was who he was. As he felt compassion for General Gates, so did he feel for two of the most harassed politicians of the age, Adams and Jefferson. Intimates since their time in the Continental Congress, they severed relations as Jefferson assumed the presidency and his predecessor rode home to Massachusetts in defeat. It was Rush, then, who stage-managed the resumption of the Adams–Jefferson correspondence and the restoration of a historic friendship. The question for us is whether his dream truly was the work of the sleeping Rush or whether it was a complete concoction.

He advanced his vision to seventy-four-year-old Adams on October 17, 1809. Jefferson, sixty-six, had retired from the presidency only months earlier. The dream (as Rush related it) began with a question: "'What book is that in your hands?' said I to my son Richard, a few nights ago in a DREAM." If his dream were purely fictitious, one wonders why Rush would have written "a few nights ago," situating the dream on a date he could recollect. Richard answers him: "It is the History of the United States." Rush, as dreamer, is unmoved at first, until his son says that the page before him concerns his friend Adams.

Rush tells Adams what he "read" in this supposed chronicle of the American past: "1809. Among the most extraordinary events of this year was the renewal of the friendship and intercourse between Mr. John Adams and Mr. Jefferson. . . ." According to the publication, Adams's letter reopening the dialogue "did great honor" to his reputation, and Jefferson's response likewise expressed "regard and esteem." For years after, Rush continued to project, the two statesmen "reviewed the scenes of business in which they were engaged" and "candidly acknowledged" the partisan hyperventilation they had acquiesced to. Miraculously, "These gentlemen sunk into the grave nearly at the same time, full of years and rich in the gratitude and praises of their country."

Rush was wrong only about the year 1809. It was not until New Year's Day, 1812, that Adams initiated the correspondence; otherwise, the doctor was dead-on in the essentials. And, as we know, old Adams outlasted Jefferson by a few short hours, both of them paying their debt to nature on July 4, 1826, the day of America's jubilee as a nation.[54]

As we consider whether, unlike his other dreams, Rush had simply manufactured this one as a friendly conspiracy, we should note that, by 1809, he was already much in the habit of telling Adams his dreams. It also explains why, in his response to the reconciliation dream, Adams exclaimed: "A Dream again!

I wish you would dream all day and all Night. . . ." The New Englander was positively entertained by Rush's uninhibited style.

Nor did Rush cease relating dreams with that of 1809. In 1812, a few months after Adams and Jefferson began writing to each other again, he gave Adams a charming account of a visit he had just paid to the farm where he was born and to the graveyard where four generations of his ancestors lay buried. As he came to the end of the story, he described the daydream that overtook him as he stood before his grandfather's tomb. "My thoughts became confused," Rush reported. He imagined his farmer ancestors arising suddenly and speaking among themselves about the stranger in their midst. As soon as he received this letter, Adams wrote back: "Is it a dream? Or is it Biography?"[55]

For a brief time, Adams and Rush took to exchanging dreams. Toward the end of 1812, Adams told of one he had had years before, in which he stood on a "lofty scaffold in the center of a great plain in Versailles," as the prospect of democracy in France was under discussion. Before him were "a multitude" that included elephants, lions, wolves, bears, and lesser beasts. Adams was attempting to persuade them all to unite under a free government based upon principles of "fraternity among all living creatures." The elephant "pouted his proboscis . . . in contempt," the lion roared, the wolf howled. A scene of carnage ensued, and Adams turned and ran. "Frightened out of my wits," he told Rush, "I leaped from the stage and made my escape—not, however, without having all my clothes torn from my back and my skin lacerated from head to foot." He awoke in terror. Rush replied by patently acknowledging that however evocative his own dreams were, Adams remained the master of this genre: "You have so far outdreamed me," he wrote of their frivolous rivalry, "that I shall be afraid hereafter to let my imagination loose in that mode of exposing folly and vice."[56]

The difference between their dreaming experiences is interesting. Rush reports complex dialogue, whereas in Adams's dream fierce animal sounds communicate the emotion he felt. His vision takes place across a wide expanse, as historic issues are under consideration and events spin out of control. Rush tends to focus on singular places: the graveyard, the hospital, a room in his house. The metaphors of Adams are almost literal—"frightened out of my wits," "clothes torn from my back." For him, bad dreams evoke the panic of mental deprivation. Think of what we mean by the expression "losing one's senses"—it is akin to having the covering of one's mind exposed, like clothes being removed, which leaves one feeling vulnerable and unable to perform essential functions at peak level.

The competition for self-revelation between these two emotionally driven men had been building for years, mainly at Rush's instigation. A March 1805 letter to Adams had cited a "singular dream" of 1790 concerning a man who had "discovered a method of regulating the weather." In the dream, this man carries a trident and waves it to change the direction of the wind or bring on rain; but in each such instance he witnesses, Rush the dreamer sees no actual effect. "This man is certainly mad," he says (in his mind) to a friend standing beside him. All of a sudden, "a figure dressed like a flying Mercury" is holding a "streamer" that reads: "De te fabula narratur" ("The tale is told of you yourself"), upon which Rush "instantly" awoke. What makes this one especially interesting is that Rush is a professor who lectures more than he listens and who confesses to his scientific shortcomings only in dreams.[57]

As the election of 1808 approached, Rush related a dream to Adams while it was fresh, and he went on for pages. "I dreamed I had been elected President of the United States," he began. "At first I objected to accepting the high and honorable station, but upon recollecting that it would give me an opportunity of exercising my long-cherished opposition to ardent spirits . . . I consented." One day, "President Rush" received a visitor, "a venerable but plain-looking man," who remonstrated with him over the prohibition policy. People were getting disgusted with their cold water diet, and "the plow and the wagon stood still from the want of that strength in the men which they formerly derived from their morning dram." (Strength derived from a dram? Strength derived from a dream?) Clergy could not preach and lawyers were unable to plead, "from the want of a little grog to moisten and oil their organs of speech."

Again, we find in Rush's dream a remarkable vocality. Yes, the length of the dream exposition suggests embellishment. But his failure as a president does smack of the common anxiety formula; he is told, point-blank: "Mr. President, I am sorry to tell you, you are no more of a philosopher than you are of a politician. . . . [G]o back to your professor's chair and amuse your boys with your idle and impracticable speculation, or go among your patients and dose them with calomel and jalap——" (medicinal plants used for purging). The climax of the insult awakens the dreamer, the effect of which made Rush, as he told Adams, "happy in discovering that the whole of the scene I have described was nothing but a dream."[58]

A dream the following year dealt with current political events brought to Rush's mind by something Adams had written to him. This time, Rush encountered a pair of men preparing elixirs. One is "a stout man with a flushed face," the other a "little old man" who accosts him. The dream doesn't make a great deal of sense, but the detail Rush provides—a man "shaking a bottle in which were infused a number of rare gums and roots"—surely suggests that his dream is other than a fiction.

Based, then, on the compilation of evidence over the course of many years, it seems unlikely that the dream of an Adams–Jefferson reconciliation would have been completely and deliberately calculated. In addition to the signs of raw imagery in it, why would Rush invoke by name his son Richard in introducing the substance of the dream? We should not be surprised, given his presence at the center of Revolutionary activity, that the map of emotions that crisscrossed Rush's mind illuminated national personalities who framed his historical recollection. We should recall, too, that the first graveyard dream contained a reconciliation drama.

Rush copied down dreams other than his own. On the general subject of extrasensory communications, he recorded in his *Commonplace Book* several examples within the scope of his hearing or reading. A "pious merchant" of England in the seventeenth century had dreamt of the death of his wife when she was at a distance of fifty miles, only to learn later that she expired precisely at the time he was dreaming her death. Closer to home, two Philadelphians gave similar reports; one heard a voice call to him, "Da! Da!" as his child was dying some seventy miles away.

Also remarkable is the case of Judith Sargent Murray, a prominent poet and essayist from Boston. Around the time she published "On the Equality of the Sexes," a groundbreaking essay arguing that women were no less rational, no more emotion driven, than men, she testified to a strange occurrence that she believed was no coincidence. Confiding in Dr. Rush, she explained that her first husband (who had died in the Caribbean three years earlier) came to her in a dream just as his soul was taking flight. According to Rush, "she saw him easy and happy at the very moment on which the accounts of his death said that he died, on March 8th, 11 o'clock at night." Despite his tendency to reflect on observations made by others, Rush opted not to elaborate on any of the above events.[59]

It is hard to know what to say about the enlightened Judith Sargent Murray. We might note that more scientists of the twenty-first century are asking how, not whether, thoughts travel. They have discovered that the brain has other ways of picking up signals from the eye than through the optic nerve. How does a person sense from behind that someone is staring at him or her? Consciousness generates something beyond itself. We are not always aware of what we know.

~∂~

N orth American Indians certainly took their dreaming seriously. The Sac chief Black Hawk, born in 1767, in what is now Illinois, grew up with the story of his great-grandfather's encounter with early French settlers in Canada. Na-nà-ma-kee was a prolific dreamer and learned four years before the event that he would come to meet a white man "who would be to him a father." When the dreamt-of day arrived, the Great Spirit pointed him to the French encampment, where Na-nà-ma-kee discovered that the white man, "the son of the King of France," had similarly dreamt of meeting, on that very day, "a nation of people who had never yet seen a white man."[60]

Numerous early publications by missionaries and explorers in regular contact with eastern and Midwestern tribes remarked on the ways in which dreams were stimulated and then put to use. The Algonquian word "manitou" was known to white students of Indian practices in the late eighteenth century. It bespoke a supernatural power or good spirit to which humans had access through dreams. "God, they say, does not require men to pay offerings or adoration immediately to him," the Moravian George Henry Loskiel wrote of the Indian worldview, using "God" for lack of a better term in the early 1790s. "He has therefore made known his will in dreams, notifying to them what beings they have to consider as *manittos,* and what offerings to make of them." One Indian might find his personal manitou to be the sun, another the moon, and another an owl. The dream-inspired manitou was represented in wood and either worn as a necklace or carried in a small bag. "An Indian is dispirited, and considers himself as forsaken by God, till he has received a tutelar spirit in a dream." Just as a Christian might wear a cross, or medallion, as a metaphor for belief in God and as a bid for his protection, an Indian felt a connection to the manitou symbol.[61]

Indians fasted in order to excite dreams. In the missionary's words, the more intense the fasting, the more "extravagant" the dream. Young boys were "made to fast" and their dreams analyzed by the elders who assigned them positions in the tribe accordingly. One's dream might suggest a future as a healer, a hunter, or a warrior. Some fasted and dreamt before the seasonal hunt: "They say that fasting peculiarly helps them to dream, and in dreams they pretend to be informed of the haunts of the game." This missionary writer respected the culture he studied, insisting that while in superficial ways uncultivated, Indians were virtuous and kind, their behavior "solid and prudent," deliberative, and never impulsive. They chose, he said, not to waste time on "empty compliments" among themselves or in greeting strangers.[62]

Modern studies confirm the traditional practice, or vision quest, as a form of encounter with sources of personal empowerment. Seeking out images in their visionary realm was "a medium of knowing" that shaped Indians' communal experience, no less than Christians' recitation of passages from the Bible within the walls of a church secured a much-sought cohesion in their communities. Both cultures used commonly understood tools to reshape their realities.[63]

West African–born Olaudah Equiano traveled widely during and after his years of enslavement in colonial America and the Caribbean. Living in England as a free man, he managed to straddle dual identities, African and European. In the narrative of his life published in 1789, he wrote of his experience in the "elegant" town of Philadelphia. At about the age of twenty, he was directed to a "wise woman" who possessed the power to prophesy. "I put little faith in this story at first," he wrote, "as I could not conceive that any mortal could foresee the future disposals of Providence." But that very night he saw the woman in a dream, and because he had yet to meet her, he grew especially eager to do so, to confirm or dispense with his vision. On locating the "wise woman," he found that she was wearing the same dress as the woman of his dream. She told him (correctly, it turned out) that he would not long be a slave.

In a later instance, on board a vessel in the West Indies, he dreamt of an encounter with another ship, and it came to pass only hours later. A third instance of a dream making a difference concerned a morally indifferent gunner on Equiano's ship, who awoke one night in abject fear. The nightmare was so dispiriting that he had to leave his cabin and climb onto the deck. He told his shipmates of the wake-up call that had shown him the error of his ways, but they laughed at him. A short time later, in the darkness, a forty-gun ship rammed theirs, and the gunner's cabin was torn apart. The dream had proven lifesaving.

What are we to make of all this? While there is doubt about Olaudeh Equiano's stated place of birth—he has little to say about life in Africa—his narrative otherwise appears to be a fairly credible account of an eighteenth-century man who came to stand for abolition of the slave trade. We know that every life admits a certain number of unexplainable coincidences. In the case of the "wise woman" who prophesied, this was an event Equiano remembered years later when he was inspired to tell of his success in overcoming adversity. Memory plays tricks, and his mind could have redressed the woman of his dream, either at the moment of their real-life meeting or in his later memory, to satisfy a need to make her a reliable authority. Nor can we dismiss the possibility that he embellished in order to sell books. After all, dreams made for good parables.[64]

Benjamin Rush emphatically used the dream formula in putting forward his views in opposition to slavery. In 1789, he heard from a preacher that South Carolinian Charles Cotesworth Pinckney, one of the best known of Revolutionary figures, had left his dying wife to attend a backcountry court. Alarmed by this report, Rush felt his sense of racial justice engaged, no less than his protofeminism. "Does the small share that women take in the management of their families in S. Carolina render them less necessary to their husbands?" he posed. If so, he deduced, "it furnishes a new & strong argument against negro Slavery." To Rush's thinking, if a plantation wife sat back while the family's slaves made sure she never had to lift a finger, she was a superfluous adornment in her husband's world, and slavery diminished the value of her life as well as the African American's. It was with his social activism as it was with Rush's dreams: he craved instant answers and easy explanations.[65]

An early and vehement opponent of slavery, Rush possessed an ardent sense of commitment to the dispossessed. Given his coupling of dreams with social justice, it should mean more now that he titled an 1806 essay in opposition to slavery "Paradise of Negro Slaves—A Dream." The tract contains monologues far too lengthy to constitute a literal dream. A number of different individuals paraded before him, in a country of superior "cultivation and scenery," all of them happy former slaves. The land does not appear to be America, though Rush neglects to say whether those who spoke to him in the dream—young and old, men and women—were in fact repatriated Africans. Even so, as one of the emancipated told him, this was the earthly "paradise" where they were "destined" to remain "'till the general judgement.'"[66]

"Color coding" was more than skin-deep in dream dictionaries, as the historian Mechal Sobel has shown in her book *Teach Me Dreams*. *The Universal Dream Dictionary* counterintuitively held that to dream of white or pale skin was "a sign of trouble, poverty, and death," whereas to dream of a black face meant "long life." More ominously, a white woman who dreamt that her flesh had become "spotted" or "black, like a moor" would be "taken in adultery, and . . . repudiated by her husband." White clothing portended "joy," black clothing "temptation to sin."[67]

Though "Paradise of Negro Slaves" was completely contrived, we can see how Rush found in literary escapism a useful supplement to his everyday concerns. He attended to symptoms; he dispensed words; he attempted to treat.

⁓ɷ

B enjamin Rush died in April 1813 at the age of sixty-seven. Many years before, he had composed his own epitaph and inserted it into a bound volume of "Letters & Thoughts." The epitaph read: "Here *first* found rest, the *body* of Benjamin Rush MD." It was meant to indicate that he knew himself as one who did not allow his body any rest. The very next entry in his "Letters & Thoughts," beginning on the same page, is no less intriguing: "a *Dream,* containing a Dialogue between Dr. James Finley, Mr. James Davis & Dr. Wm Cullen, & Dr. B. Rush." These were his "beloved masters"—teachers—and his dialogue with them involved the dreamer asking each in turn to forgive his pupil for having diverged from the recommended course in religion, politics, and medicine. At the end, Rush bade his teachers en masse: "Do me the justice to believe that I *have aimed well.*"[68]

The historical record is clear. He did aim well. Rush's world was haunted by death. It was terrifying, and how could it not be? Awake, he rendered professional judgments, some of them based on his own dreaming history. He was sufficiently convinced by his dream studies to employ absolute terms when addressing America's rising generation of physicians: "It is certain that labouring people dream but seldom," he lectured them. Additionally, he presented empirical evidence (obviously misguided) in contending that vegetarians were incapable of dreaming. Restating the faith he held on to most aggressively, he wrote that biblical dreams carried a "mark of authenticity" and consisted of "visible ideas" emanating from a divine light. "Lovers," he said with equal conviction, "dream of each other only in the beginning, or in the declining State of their love for each other." This was because in everyday married life, the imagination and memory were so absorbed in seeing the partner happy that the active mind became "worn down" and the nocturnal imagination "exhausted of . . . excitability." On this basis, he put out a friendly warning to woman in general: she should seriously doubt the veracity of any suitor who claimed to dream of her every night.[69]

As the example of Dr. Rush broadly reveals, eighteenth-century science was as assertive as twenty-first-century science, with far less cause. But science periodically requires correction, in any century, and the meaning of our dreams is nowhere near being settled. Today's dream scientists speculate that the evolutionary function of dreams may be to restore body and mind, assist with learning, and prepare the brain for managing threats and disturbances. Dreams, it seems, help resolve conflicts that occur in the waking state, recalibrating identity.

It could be some or all of these things. Unless everyone is wrong, and dreams are a fluke, an accident of nature serving no evolutionary purpose at all. The point is, we do not know for certain what dreams do, though there is every indication that they feed a collective compulsion to reconcile past and present.

THREE

DEPLETED OF ENERGY, HEMAN HARRIS LEAVES HIS BODY

The world's all face; the man who shews his heart,
Is whooted for his nudities, and scorn'd.
—Edward Young, *Night Thoughts*

A Norwegian-born sailor based in Manhattan remained haunted by a dream he had at the age of six, in 1790, when he and his parents lived in the seaside town of Larvik, southwest of Oslo. On the windy night that his father, a fisherman, crashed his boat into a rock and was heard crying out, young Nicholas Peter Isaacs awoke from a dream. It was a happy dream at first; he was on a freshwater lake with his father, rowing out to an island. It was a place where they had gone together before. In the dream, his father was able to cast his net across the entire island: "He took a long pole with a heavy knob at the end, and pushed it into the water, and through the holes in the island, to drive the fish into his net. . . . While thus engaged he fell overboard and was drowned. This sad termination of the dream frightened me, and I awoke, and told it to my mother."

The clock in their home had just chimed eleven. The mother of Nicholas Peter expressed concern about the great gale and her husband's late return. It was not until morning, though, that news arrived of the fisherman's fate. He had been swallowed up by the North Sea, and his body was never found. A witness who had heard the dying man's cries the night before reported that it was eleven o'clock when the tragedy struck. "Though varying from the facts in many circumstances," wrote the son in his memoir of later years, "it was certainly a remarkable dream, especially for a child."[1]

Nathaniel Newlin tells an equally poignant tale. "It is now upwards of 40 years since I had a dream so remarkable, and which made so great an impression on my mind, that now in my 84th year [I recall] every circumstance attending it." He dreamt of a human form, "of a clear transparent substance, without the appearance of materiality, and yet plainly visible." When it came closer, he recognized it to be his sister, who had died young. "She spoke to me in a pleasant manner and after some conversation solemnly said 'I have come to tell thee that thou shalt die and not live.'" The dreamer felt a sense of alarm, and so conveyed to his sister, should she not know the details of his life, that he had a wife and several small children to care for. But, he added, if this was how it had to be, "I could submit."

"At this crisis," Nathaniel continues his retrospective, "a niece of mine, then a young woman, and who is still living, walked between us, and addressing herself to my sister, pleasantly said that I could not yet be spared—To which my sister seemed to assent, and walked away from us. As she was going my eyes followed her to a great distance and I distinctly remember the appearance of the path which she took over a bridge." With this, his dream came to an end—but his narrative proceeded, so as to explain why the dream had remained with him through old age:

> During the next three days I felt much alarm and anxiety and at the end of that time I was taken ill—the only dangerous illness that ever came upon me. I gradually grew worse until almost every hope was given up of my recovery. I however, still told my wife, that I believed I would not die at that time; and my brother, coming to see me, and finding my wife in want of assistance in nursing me, offered to send his daughter, my niece, who, in my dream, had so opportunely interfered. She accordingly came, I recovered, and here I remain to this day. I have never ceased to feel the closest attachment and warmest gratitude to my niece, and never see her without thinking of my dream.[2]

There is a certain similarity between Newlin's dream and Benjamin Rush's dengue fever dream. Recall that an impoverished woman had forced Rush to look into his soul after he had refused to treat her: "It was decreed that you should die by the fever which lately attacked you," she said, "but the prayers of your poor patients ascended to heaven." In both instances, the dreamer was saved by a merciful, all-knowing female.

In 1789, the *Freeman's Oracle,* a New Hampshire newspaper, reported the spooky story of a young woman whose father was wealthy—but from smuggling rather than a noble profession. She married a midshipman whose father, the captain of a frigate, had left him penniless. Theirs was a love match by all accounts, and she willingly (as the law demanded) ceded control of her inheritance to him. One day, he received an invitation to dine on board at the captain's table. The young wife bade him to decline, because she had dreamt the night before that she saw her husband's dead body floating along the coast. He, however, thought too little of the premonition and more of the respect owed to the captain and went off. When her dream came to pass and she saw his corpse, she was so distraught that she herself died of heartbreak only days later.[3]

What these stories of warning and woe have in common is a problem with plausibility. To take them one at a time, the sailor was very young when he had his dream, so it is reasonable to assume that his mother was enough moved by the tragic coincidence that she reminded him of it as he was growing up. The imagery makes sense: a child could easily dream of an island that his larger-than-life fisherman-father reached across with a net that seemed impossibly large to young eyes. As to Nathaniel Newlin, despite a forty-year gap between his dream and its retelling, his style is simple and earnest, and it is hard to see what he would gain from lying.

If these two accounts appear convincing, let us remain at least a little skeptical. Sailors (and others from the lower classes) were known for their attachment to popular dream books. In the decade of the American Revolution, one fisherman along the Massachusetts coast said he saw his future wife in a dream, recognizing her instantly when they met because of the moles on her cheek, which he had pictured while dreaming. Herman Melville, who plied the Pacific before he became a writer, included sailors' dream books and would-be prophets in his stories.[4]

The New Hampshire wife's premonition is the least credible of the preceding vignettes. It does not give the protagonists' names, nor does it move much beyond the literary trope of the unlucky, hardworking husband and his devoted helpmeet. This does not make all newspaper reports fictional—though it underscores the need to carefully evaluate sources.

Pennsylvanian Elizabeth Drinker is a diarist well known to historians of early America. For decades, through the Revolution and beyond, she kept a credible personal record that came to reflect the trials of life in her native Phila-delphia. Her diary records the funerals she attended, and the list is long. Hav-ing lived through the yellow fever epidemic of 1793, she had already witnessed a lot of death by the time of the following dream, which has an indisputable ring of truth to it.

It was a sleeting autumn night in 1798. Her mind fed her stark images of the choking death of a man named Thomas, who had dined with her on the day preceding. Drinker had served him roast pork, and in her dream it was once again pork on the menu. The only difference was that the dream scene took place at her son's home, and she and Thomas were the guests. As the meat lodged in Thomas's throat, "Dr. Jardine was sent for, who rubb'd and shook him 'till he said in a horse [sic] voice, I have choaked myself with a rine of pork. I thought the Doctor with an instrument got it out, but Thomas died directly afterward."

What happened next explains why it was that she remembered her dream at all, given that she penned her diary entries late in the day, well after the prior night's dream narrative had been shunted aside. In this case, though, another son's housemate had chanced to stop by before noon, hours before she would, by habit, be sitting with her diary. He told her that the remains of a man had been found in the woods behind Dr. Jardine's place. The corpse was propped up against a tree, his legs gone, and one of his arms "knaw'd almost off" by an animal. "A hat was on his head, but no resemblance that he could be known by." Dr. Jardine believed the unrecognizable man was someone who had done work for him in the past, and so he "collected a [coroner's] Jury, and afterwards had the body bury'd."

"I dont call every thing that is accidental, remarkable, or am I much of a dreamer," Drinker wrote, "but last night. . . ." And now it was clear to her that she was recalling the dream because her visitor had triggered a memory by speak-ing of the same Dr. Jardine calling a jury to authorize burial of the mutilated corpse. Quite by coincidence, in her dream about the choking guest, "it was concluded to call a Jury, which I was helping them to name, all the near neigh-bours was named, but they were not enough . . . how it finish'd I cannot tell."

She did not bother to interpret the dream: serious illness and horrible death were real enough for her that a clinical assessment captured the moment. Our interest in the disquieting dream resides in the fact that the diarist was intent on visualizing time and dispassionately exploring the nature of memory, but was loath to describe her own feelings.[5]

-ᴠᴧᴃ-

We have already encountered enough such examples to understand how large death loomed for early Americans. Their letters and diaries reveal plenty. The literature they read only intensified what they already felt. The Philadelphia mystery writer Charles Brockden Brown wrote in *Edgar Huntly; or, Memoirs of a Sleep-Walker* (1799): "I never sleep but with a candle burning at my pillow. If, by any chance, I should awake and find myself immersed in darkness, I know not what act of desperation I might be suddenly impelled to commit." In a candlelit world, disorder lurked nearby.

Inner doubt was fed by a quiet passion for poetry. Add to this early Americans' familiarity from an early age with the axioms of devotional literature. Metaphors of light (revelation) and darkness (concealment) resonated in all they read and kept death close.

The ever-present mystery of the dream was suited to poetic conversation:

> *By passionately loving life, we make*
> *Lov'd life unlovely; hugging her to death.*
> *We give to time eternity's regard;*
> *And dreaming, take our passage for our port.*

The above are lines from the once greatly popular and widely quoted *Night Thoughts* by Edward Young. He was an active dreamer who took dreams to be evidence of the immortality of the soul. *Night Thoughts,* first published in 1742, was compared by Young's contemporaries to John Milton's classic *Paradise Lost.* Young presented in cryptic verse an intense picture of the vain hopes mortals shared, combining nocturnal imagery with such pregnant phrases as "death's admonitions" and "suffocating sorrows." The opening pages of a popular dream guide likewise asserted: "There is scarce any thing that yields so true and great a figure and similitude of the condition of the soul after death, or in the state of separation, as dreams."[6]

We are reminded again that Native American cultures coexisting in time and space with the young American republic maintained cultural forms (chants, dances, stories) in which the living remained in contact with their ancestors. In the Southwest, Zunis and Navajos were using a psychoactive cactus, peyote, to induce dreams for this purpose. In the Northeast, the symbolic spiderweb opened the minds of the Abenaki, yielding an "awakening" to a lucid, or controllable, dream, accented by streams of light, inviting an ancestral "spirit guide" into the dreamer's world.

The Senecas of western New York State are of particular interest. In 1799 and again in 1800, in visions that had an enduring and transformative effect on the tribe, the prophet Handsome Lake was warned by a spirit to beware of alcohol and witchcraft. Historian Matthew Dennis emphasizes the syncretistic character of Handsome Lake's program in bringing together Christian and traditional Indian values. Commenting on the Seneca's dream encounter with the late President Washington, Dennis writes: "The prophet's divine conversations and communion with the dead—departed family members as well as more famous and remote figures—sanctified his mission." In many Indian nations, seeing the dead in dreams was a social convention with broad repercussions.[7]

Mainstream white America, meanwhile, remained fixed on melodramatic, if not lurid, dream depictions. Though visions of night were less significant to citizens of the new republic than they were, in ritualized form, to Indians, they remained symbols of something. As a literary talisman to counteract the more sensational gothic depictions, some paper would publish a squib on the order of "An Essay in Praise of Morning," in which an unidentified writer delighted in the curative sounds of daybreak outside his window. Recovery from darkness was as simple as replacing the memory of a sleep vision with the instantly cheerful reception of a bird's song: all it took was "to start out of a most troublesome dream, and immediately to find my tortured senses regaled with such innocent harmony." Innocence, indeed. Each generation attempts to circumscribe its reality; each subsequent generation taps a new universe of sensations and redraws the cultural map of the past. It does so purposefully and judgmentally.

This says something important. All forms of awareness are but a blip in time, as fleeting as dreams are. Before we strut our tools of analysis and deny past actors competence or sophistication in the ability to interpret their own inner lives, it is worth noting that a majority of dream specialists (and dream therapists) in our century insist that the dreamer ultimately gets to decide the meaning of his or her dream. There are no fixed certainties in this exercise we are conducting.[8]

On the subject of early Americans' coping mechanisms, nothing is so striking to the cultural historian looking backward as the frightening regularity of sudden, unexpected death. Approximately one in four women was destined to die in or after childbirth. There was high infant mortality and seasonal epidemics; pneumonia and tuberculosis (which they knew as "consumption") were slow killers.

In every relationship, life's fragility was implicitly understood. Partings were intense, and the tactile pleasure of a letter set hearts beating. Early Americans folded keepsakes into stored correspondence and preserved locks of hair for generations as a soft reminder of one whose physical presence could be reclaimed in no better way. Thomas Jefferson, not known as squeamish or maudlin, lost his wife when he was thirty-nine, after her seventh pregnancy wore her down and she failed to recover strength. For the next forty-four years, he kept a lock of her hair, along with that of one of their daughters who died in infancy, in a private drawer at his bedside; it was found by surviving family as they were doing an inventory of his things after his death.[9]

In their interconnected moral and mortal environments, soulful dreams could easily express a level of pathos, even desperation, that most of us today, living lives of relative comfort, do not feel as viscerally. In their familiar letters, people wrote about Sunday sermons and argued the question of the materiality of the soul—whether it survives physical death—the way we argue politics. "Men in dreams are nearer the condition of departed souls, than when awake," went the dream guide. It is not the sort of connection we would instantly make when contemplating the meaning of our dreams. But it was for them when they were willing to admit it.[10]

~w~

When Charlotte Hutton, sixteen, died in 1795, her character was hailed and her promise tragically buried with her. "She knew several languages, and almost all sciences, in a tolerable degree," the eulogy went, and then listed her numerous intellectual attainments. "She extracted the square roots of most of the second 1000 numbers to twelve places of decimals." And then the most poignant element in Charlotte's sad story: "A very few days before her death, when the family joined her one morning in the parlour . . . she told them a dream she had in the night, which seemed so curious, that they desired to write it down." This is how it went:

> I dreamed that I was dead, and that my soul had ascended into one of the stars. There I found several persons whom I had formerly known, and among them some of the nuns I was attached to when in France. They told me, when they received me, that they were glad to see me, but hoped I should not stay with

them long, the place being a kind of purgatory; and that all the stars were for the reception of different people's souls.

The upshot of the nuns' explanation was that you went to whichever star best suited your particular temperament. And with that, the tribute picked up again, leaving readers to meditate on the meaning of the dream. Had she lived, the piece concluded, Charlotte would have been "a second Hypatia," referring to the great female mathematician of fifth-century Alexandria, Egypt. With her death, a paragon of female virtue had disappeared.[11]

Charlotte had gone to the stars. Or something metaphorically like it. Heaven is spatially imagined in the sky without obtruding on the science of astronomy; it was therefore possible that the post-corporeal "beyond" that all were desirous of knowing more about was combinable with dream studies. One could learn something about death's nonphysical expanse by describing the climate within a sleeping mind and locating its religious properties. All that was required was an all-seeing guide. And faith.

As noted before, angel-accented dreams were among the most regularly reported of dream variations. In personal diaries never intended for publication, one finds narratives in which a dreamer is led into heaven by an "angel" or "guide" and, in numerous cases, given a glimpse of hell—a sneak peek at the world to come, with an inescapable moral attached. (This formula is not greatly different from Indians who welcomed their "spirit guide" character.) According to *The Oneirocritic,* when an angel appeared, one was to "be mindful of the rest of your dream, for it will come to pass, pretty accurately. . . . If a woman with child dreams of them, she will have a good time [i.e., smooth labor], and perhaps twins." *The Universal Dream-Dictionary* noted: "To dream you see an angel or angels is very good; and to dream that you yourself are one, is much better. But to speak with, or call upon them, is of evil signification." Angels, usually associated with the visions of the gravely ill, had been starring in private diaries and public pamphlets from at least as far back as the seventeenth-century divine Cotton Mather. His Puritan elders held that angel visitations were the province of men only. (As historian Elizabeth Reis explains, female angel sightings were automatically discounted in Puritan times and even suspected of being Satan-supplied delusions.) By the late eighteenth century, though, women had risen enough in stature that their angels were as good as men's.[12]

Tucked into the collected correspondence of a Quaker woman who died in 1814 is an account from an unknown dreamer that was written down in 1782, in order to be studied and heeded by future family members:

> I thought I was dead, and beheld my body lay like a corpse. there seemed to be a person in the appearance of a man, his raiment somewhat of a sheep skin or bright fawn colour, who said follow me. he ascended a hill, on the top of which was a large building, the outside appeared built of large rough stone. I followed my guide into the house, but at first did not see the beauty of it to the full. it seemed white and bright, and a large company setting, such a number as I never beheld.

The dreamer goes on to describe, with enlarged metaphors, how stunningly bright the picture in her mind was and how sweet and composed the faces were. It was not clear to her whether these people, though seated, were physically attached to chairs or pews of any kind. She asked her (male) guide if they were in heaven. He did not answer in words but gestured toward the left—note that the dreamer retains a sense of direction.

She felt herself leaving the scene and descending. "I did not perceive the road we went," though she recalled picturing a "lofty" arch, before moving through a large room that seemed to have no end and was painted in a variety of colors (none specifically mentioned). "A number of persons richly dressed passed us, who smelled so strongly of Brimstone that I seemed almost suffocated." That the sense of smell is activated, or imagined, adds a unique dimension to the dream, for the great majority of extant dreams from this period engage exclusively with the senses of sight and hearing.

Eventually, the dreamer escapes the hints of a hellish end and arrives in "a large enclosed Feild," where she espies "many Persons, some of whom are since dead[.] out of it I could see no road." Next comes the first spoken words of the extended dream: "My guide . . . earnestly said thou art now going into the world again. Remember what thou hast now seen, tis not enough to be honest to man, but must be honest and faithful to thy God also."[13]

Mary Grew, another woman with strong religious convictions who emigrated from England to New England, recorded a dream that she could not let go of and finally wrote down a week later. "I thought I was dying & surrounded by my friends whom I addressed not only with composure but joy—telling them I did not find Death so terrible as it once appeard." In her "happy serene" frame of mind, still dreaming, she heard herself reciting lines from Isaac Watts, the composer of many well-known hymns: "Jesus can make a dying Bed / Feel soft as downy Pillows are. . . ." And then she awoke. Elsewhere in her diary, Mary periodically wished that death might come to her peacefully. As things turned out, she lived another four decades.[14]

Then there was Heman Harris, who, feeling depleted of energy, believed he was within an hour of his death. "My increasing weakness, by degrees, locked up my senses, and seemed to extinguish every faculty of my soul." He felt himself leaving his body. "O the change!" He was "independent of matter," he said, "my sight, my hearing, all the perceptive faculties of body and mind were reduced to . . . thought." In this state, he found himself in the company of other spirits. Heaven and hell were blended together, "good and evil spirits promiscuously inhabiting every part of the universe." While in this netherworld, there was no active conversation, because he and all those who surrounded him could read the others' thoughts. Finally opening his eyes, he said he retained the sense of gloom that had been the last sensation he experienced before returning to his body. But rather than assert that anything special had occurred, he concluded: "I am so far from considering it any thing more than a dream, that I have committed it to paper rather as a curiosity than incontestable truth." All well, except that Heman Harris was dead soon after recording the above. According to whoever it was who brought his story to press, there was something sublime, neither exclusively good nor explicitly evil, in "the offspring of darkness and sleep" that was the crossing Heman Harris allegedly experienced.[15]

Aaron Warner's dream of May 20, 1799, is told in even more detail. The premise, once again, is that the experience is so transformative that the dreamer writes it down—and the editor embellishes the circumstances for the undisguised purpose of appealing to readers' religious instincts. Warner had gone to bed with chest pains and proceeded, either in sleep or out-of-body experience, to discover a lightness in his soul that he had not known before. Everything "disagreeable and loathsome" faded away, and he began feeling "the security of a traveller bound to an unknown country, a place not made with hands, eternal in the heavens, and whence I expected to receive judgment."

These sensations yielded to the vision of a staircase, "the sides of which were adorned with flowers of a beautiful green, interspersed with a lively blue." There he perceived people of "all ages and countries" and came to feel a new hopefulness and love of God. But as he gazed forward, he saw the outlines of a

A
DREAM,
OF
MR. *HEMAN HARRIS*,
IN HIS LAST SICKNESS,
A LITTLE BEFORE HIS DEATH.

PRINTED AT *WORCESTER*,
1798.

A Dream of Mr. Heman Harris. *In the Old Testament, Heman, a musician, also served as King David's seer. Courtesy of the American Antiquarian Society.*

dark cloud. His fellow "passengers" on the journey seemed at this moment to fall into shadow, yet he felt no fear. From among the crowd there emerged one "venerable man," aged and shriveled and with silver hair. He appeared to the dreamer to be ridden with guilt. Warner spoke the first words since having been separated from his body: "Says I, good daddy, why in such misery?" The man believed he was bound to pay for his earthly actions: "I have doted upon unlawful gains injuriously taken from the innocent." As the old man wailed, the dreamer saw that he himself was about to be judged. He fell to his knees, and a gentle voice instructed him to "arise, and feast upon the riches of divine grace."

The dream was not quite over. Warner looked in all directions for the guilty old man. He could hear him lament "with redoubled anguish" when the deceiver appeared, "his countenance the most alluring and inviting; his voice flattering and pleasant." As the old man was unceremoniously dragged from the place of clouds and shadows, Warner awoke. It was 7:00 A.M. "To the best of my judgment," he noted, "this dream, or vision, continued about eleven hours." The editor of the posthumous work then steps in to attest: "This narrative is true, and him who relates it, writes it as it was presented to him."[16]

Perhaps he did. Or perhaps the whole story was invented. What matters is that Aaron Warner's encounter with people of "all ages and countries" is meant to underscore the universality of the theme. His dream takes place within cosmic time (the only dimension in which a free soul is to be found), and when he wakes, he is brought back to earth unfinished. The plot is his journey. Because it is almost Homeric, it requires a sure ending. Thus, a fixed number of hours (eleven) are said to have elapsed in preternatural wandering.

Lest it be thought that the genre of the heavenly journey was confined to New England and the northern states, in 1803, Jesse Richardson of Rutherford, North Carolina, dreamt: "I was walking on a public road, and had a call to leave this world (not to die, but after the form of taking a journey in this world) and immediately I found my feet leaving the earth." The act of levitation revealed the light of another world, where he, a Methodist, met John Wesley, the recently deceased founder of the movement. "His garments of a silver white, his countenance serene and pleasing." Wesley was Richardson's "guide" and showed him heaven and hell. Richardson did not know where his dream had come from, but he was confident that it had derived from something other than bodily stress or the sort of pathology a trained physician would ordinarily assign as the cause.[17]

Such dream narratives as these all bespeak a gospel of feeling, yet they are notably unsentimental. Violent prospects may interfere with foreknowledge of post-corporeal bliss and enhance dramatic power, yet there is something left unfelt in the post-Revolutionary autobiography. The unfeeling vocabulary delays the appearance of more positive and palpable expressions of selfhood.

↗∂

Some of the most intellectually engaged Americans evaluated the messages in dreams with all the objectivity they could muster. Ezra Stiles (1727–1795), longtime president of Yale College and a Congregationalist minister, kept a diary in which he occasionally noted the dreams others told to him that he found especially curious. In 1794, twenty-three-year-old Jonathan Osborn, Jr., sick for over two years with a "chronical putrid Disorder," had taken a turn for the worse. A few months prior, he dreamt that he had died and attended his own funeral. "He turned about & went up to the Coffin & viewed his own Corps," wrote Stiles, "& casting his eyes on the Lid of the Coffin, saw it inscribed with the Initials of his name & aetat. 58 from whence upon waking up he was impressed with the Idea that he might recover & live to the age of 58."

Osborn smiled his way through his illness, refusing to accept the dire prognosis of his doctors. Reverend Stiles visited with the patient, telling him about a man he knew who had felt similarly able to predict his time of death—he had given himself fifteen years, and when the date approached, he made his peace with the world. The day of his demise came and went, and he was still alive after some twenty years had elapsed. Jonathan Osborn was not quite as fortunate. While his dream seems to have carried him through one crisis, its full message was not realized, and he died two years later, at twenty-five.[18]

Stiles is a particularly fit example, because he successfully bridged the divide between Enlightenment skepticism and religious ardor. He was a peerless patriot, as literal in his acceptance of the words "God bless America" as anyone who has ever lived and died on these shores. On the occasion of the 1783 Treaty of Paris, which affirmed American independence, he delivered an ecstatic sermon, subsequently published as a pamphlet titled "The United States Elevated to Glory and Honour," which celebrated "GOD'S American Israel."

By the time of his visit to the inspired Mr. Osborn, Reverend Stiles had already interviewed a good number of others who described their experiences with supernatural communications. One of these was an Irish-born Pennsylvania merchant, told in a dream that he would lose one of his four children after eight years. A child of his died after six. Not quibbling about dates, he reckoned this an accurate prediction and went on to tell Stiles that he often found his soul separated from his body and saw angels: "the air was full of them." Inexplicably (as Stiles put it), "His Guardian Angel is of a green color." This man, too, had a pretty good idea of when he was meant to die.

Reverend Stiles never suggested that he thought any of his neighbors deluded who shared their dreams—angel-bearing or otherwise. But his own dreams were, he believed, fairly prosaic. They situated him in places out of his past and at other times in the present, with dream characters who were well known to him. He always wished he could wander farther afield while he slept. "Tho' of a volatile make," he wrote preciously, "yet I am perhaps the least subject to dreams of any Man in Life." Stiles's statement is of special interest given Dr. Rush's assumption (which, the reader may recall, Jefferson disputed) about the elderly, nearer to death, dreaming more—and more meaningfully—than the young. Stiles was unknowingly near death as he penned these lines.[19]

If life were urgent and pain-filled, it was not often explained. Ann Warder woke in the middle of the night when her dreaming husband came out with sighing words: "To Day we are here & Tomorrow seen no more." She noted in her journal the "singularity" of his outburst, "as I never remembered hearing him speak asleep before." She wished she would remember her own dreams more often, because this way—as when she sailed to England without him—she would be with her "best beloved" each and every night.

To judge by the moods we have already isolated, it is hardly surprising that Ann Warder expressed no alarm at the utterance of her husband with regard to the brevity of life. Like Mary Grew, who dreamt she was dying; or Ezra Stiles, who dealt with dreamers who thought they could, with supernatural assistance, establish the date of their own end; or Judith Sargent Murray, convinced that she saw her husband happy, as he was dying in the West Indies; or Benjamin Rush, who designed his epitaph decades before his death, Ann Warder saw nothing unusual in the nature of her husband's dream-sent exclamation, because thoughts of death were an integral part of life. As Edward Young put it in his lugubrious, irresistible *Night Thoughts,* to have faith was, in fact, to reason, because nature would be too impossibly cruel if life on earth was everything, and not simply a station stop on the path to "eternal day":

> *Man's misery declares him born for bliss;*
> *His anxious heart asserts the truth I sing,*
> *And gives the sceptic in his head the lie.*
> *Our heads, our hearts, our passions, and our powers,*
> *Speak the same language; call us to the skies.*[20]

～ֆ～

As we move ahead through the nineteenth century, we will encounter more instances of revelatory dreams expressing the imminence of death, many of these powerfully affecting. Dreams that are preoccupied with death, physical injury, and rejection appear so much more frequently than any other species of dream in personal writings in the period before 1800 that they tend to eclipse such subjects as filial and companionate love, which fill out the American dreamscape in the nineteenth century.

It is worth pausing briefly to meditate on the book's opening query: Were they like us? Are we like them? Conducting research at hospices, two modern experts on the pre-death dream, Kelly Bulkeley and Patricia Bulkley, write: "All dreams, in more or less subtle ways, are searching meditations on the finitude of human life." The coauthors report that even those dreams that engage with people, places, and events from the past still serve to focus us ahead and focus on the end. We are unconsciously preparing ourselves for death over a long stretch of time, not merely at the end of life's journey.

The ultimate metaphor of the human condition is that life is a journey. Death is either a final destination or the beginning of a new journey. Early Americans who traveled great distances on the water, aware of the dangers, repeatedly wrote of themselves metaphorically as "mariners" on a "boisterous" sea. Edward Young's lines resonate: "We give to time eternity's regard; / And dreaming, take our passage for our port."[21]

The boisterous sea has become, in our automobile-reliant time, the bumpy road. As we waste energy, we expect to reach the "crossroads of life" on our metaphoric highways; we "get the green light," recognize when it is "time to move on," fault someone who "has no direction," and hope for a "smooth ride." But, like our seafaring ancestors, we recognize that the road ahead is uncertain at best. Or to adapt the same metaphor to plane travel, our future is "up in the air."

While we may remain conflicted in our waking lives as to whether we are more likely to be "living our dreams" or indulging "pipe dreams," we know bedtime as a hotbed of emotion. In that sense, dreams, Freud's "royal road to the unconscious," dramatize each "crossroad" in our lives. So, no matter how we reckon our ultimate destinies, we are constantly drawing metaphors from our experience with the nature of things to communicate, to augment meaning. A modern dreamer will say of an occurrence within a dream something like "I felt glued to my seat" or "I stormed out of the room," because of how we rely on metaphors to express ourselves.[22]

Early Americans were creative in the pictures and sounds they set forth in recording their dreams, even if the scenarios they describe in words are not as metaphorically endowed as the stories we tend to tell. The emotional woman in Benjamin Rush's dengue fever dream lifted her arms toward the sky as she appealed to heaven; the plain-looking man in the graveyard dream was thanked by two who "kissed the hand" and "stroked his back," figures of expression that conjure softness and fond regard. In his wild dream about Versailles, John Adams told Rush that he felt "frightened out of my wits" in his dreaming persona, after an the elephant "pouted his proboscis . . . in contempt." Losing touch with one's wits is a rich enough metaphor. But if most early dream reports were unadorned narrations, we should not jump to conclusions and say that they were limited in meaning or emotion.

Our metaphors, their metaphors, our dreams, their dreams, all speak to the fragility of the human spirit. We denote ourselves as active forces of nature while recognizing at the same time our utter subordination to nature. So it is not surprising that dreams engage as much as they do in mortal fears and death-defying fantasies. In dreams, we are haunted by memories, sometimes happily, other times unhappily, as we reconnect to nature emotionally. Our mental and linguistic pictures help manage and prolong life, to constantly create anew. But as memory machines, we break down, just as our bodies do, because our nature is imperfect and time is a-wasting.

Dreams, like the religious systems we have invented, are a form of resistance to death and, perhaps more importantly, a form of compensation for death. In dreams, we battle the evidence mortal nature presents to our reason. As for the pre-death dream phenomenon that Bulkeley and Bulkley study, they say we are able to devise fantastic self-regulating imagery in grappling with the force that opposes life in what we anticipate are our last moments. Why do we refer to this time as our "last moments on earth"? This, too, is a convenient, yet unexplored, metaphor. It assumes that the substance of earth cannot contain our souls.

With metaphor, we aim to help ourselves believe in post-death scenarios that are worth dying for, which makes us kin to those of our past who faced mortality without recourse to modern medicine.[23]

∽∂

The early novels of sensibility discovered a "gloomy herald" in every "inward voice." In François D'Arnaud's *Fanny: or, the Happy Repentance*, "melancholy reflections of the day were followed by hideous dreams in the night." An American seduction drama of 1789 forestalled the heroine's fate by conjuring up the power of sympathy in a sleep vision. Fragility of the mind was a clear preoccupation of the age.[24]

. We do not have to travel very far from here to the gothic imagery in the prose of Charles Brockden Brown (1771–1810). Brown, a Philadelphian, was influenced by the French Revolution, writing amid the political upheavals of the late 1790s. The most marked trait his characters share is their inner confusion. In *Arthur Mervyn,* a novel set amid the yellow fever epidemic of 1793, dreams reveal impatience, irregular behavior, and threats of violence. In *Wieland,* as the senses are undercut and privacy intruded upon, the title character is driven by a voice to murder. The mindful narrator Clara, Theodore Wieland's sister, first dreams, and then perceives in waking life, that her brother is out to destroy. Discovering that he murdered his wife and children, Clara cries out: "Wieland! My brother! The husband and the father! That man of gentle virtues and invincible benignity! . . . Surely, said I, it is a dream." But it was not. Making the case that the mind is often incapable of discerning between reality and a nightmarish subversion of reality, Brown employed a vocabulary of emotional extremes: "shadows," "illusions," "frenzy," and "torments" were some of his favorite words in moments of crisis.

He is routinely compared to the British author William Godwin (1756–1836), whose psychologically intense *Caleb Williams* (1794) is a story of obsession and dreams of vengeance. For Brown, deception did not merely lie in the lurid thoughts of seducers; it existed as much in the average mind, where reason could at any time slip away and a phantom consciousness take its place. The age of Godwin and Brown was the age of the disordered imagination. Not insignificantly, Godwin's daughter, Mary Shelley, went on to author the horror fantasy *Frankenstein.*[25]

~w~

Brown was a Quaker. As the historian Carla Gerona lays out in her book *Night Journeys,* American Quakers were different from other religious sects in that they made dreaming mainstream and respectable. Evangelicals found in dreams and visions a secret knowledge of the world beyond, but the credibility of their claims was contaminated by the dire prophecies delivered by the fanatics among their number. The medical Enlightenment, as we know, dismissed all but the pathological element in dreaming and saw dream interpretation as, at best, a diagnostic tool for physicians. For Quakers, dreams were part of a larger ethos, used to intensify appreciation of God. They brought comfort along with a commitment to righteous behavior.

An inquisitive, reform-minded sect, the Quakers circulated their dreams. Though pacifists, many of their visions featured thunderstorms, setting suns, apocalyptic earthquakes, and other kinds of violent imagery that served to exhort their community to heed the Lord's wishes for them. But as Gerona explains, Quakers kept their interpretations deliberately vague. Dream interpreters did not worry about whether dreams proved false; their very ambiguity meant that they could be recycled.

For some, the Quaker tradition had its downside. Grace Galloway, the wife of a prominent Loyalist during the Revolution, stayed behind in Philadelphia after the rest of the family had fled. By and large friendless, she dreamt of her daughter Elizabeth drowning while en route to England; another time, she and Elizabeth were attempting to return, on foot, to their confiscated property, and Elizabeth took ill. In a subsequent dream, a cousin died, and in still another dream, she thought she herself "was going to be hang'd." Not long after this, Grace Galloway died. Daughter Elizabeth, at least, survived the war.[26]

Professor Gerona goes on to highlight the dreams of two well-known African American Quakers, Paul Cuffe and Benjamin Banneker. Cuffe (1759–1817) was the son of a West African father and a Wampanoag Indian mother. Raised in Massachusetts and a Quaker from childhood, he made his fortune in shipping and was instrumental in developing Sierra Leone as a colony for freed slaves. At a Philadelphia Quaker meeting, he reported that he was in low spirits one night when a "form of a man" appeared to him in a dream and told him he had a disease in his heart. With the dreamer's permission, the man used a sharp instrument to remove the heart, which was seen to contain "abominable things." The cleansed heart was returned to Cuffe's body, and he woke a changed man.

Banneker (1731–1806) was a Maryland mathematician, astronomer, and surveyor who in the early 1790s assisted in laying out what was shortly to become the federal city of Washington, D.C. He ruminated on whether a soul could separate from a body and float free, and in one of his recorded dreams, he asked to understand how this could be. He tried, in his dream, to solve the problem scientifically. In another dream, he fought a "hairy" creature whom he threw into a fire, but who would not burn. In a third, which took place at Christmas in 1799, he held a white-haired fawn that he wished to set free, but would first clip on the ear, as an identifying mark so that he would know the fawn if he saw it again.[27]

Whether these dreams were directly related to the abolitionist activities of Cuffe and Banneker is uncertain, but it is worth noting that white America was acutely aware of the dream interpretation tradition among Indian tribes and in African American communities, and did not disparage it. In spite of the pervasiveness of racial prejudice (even, as Gerona points out, among antislavery Quakers), there are signs that the legitimacy of African American dreams was not challenged any more than white dreamers' experiences were.

The tradition of collecting, assessing, and repeating dreams only grew in popularity. The unique situation of African Americans, a people in constant political limbo, no doubt contributed to the perpetuation of this cross-cultural mystery. Fifty years after the American Revolution, with dream interpretation guides being run off presses in greater numbers than ever before, *The Complete Fortune Teller and Dream Book* appeared. The author of the 1824 book, "Chloe Russel, a Woman of Colour," was a West African–born former slave who claimed to have predicted the Revolution in all its twists and turns, without error. The text is packed with life advice on the order of: "Directions to young ladies how to obtain husbands they most desire" (it involved wearing sweet-smelling flowers that touched up against one's naked body). Her nuanced interpretation of angel dreams is taken verbatim from one we have already encountered, *The Complete Fortune-Teller* (1799), which itself was probably derivative. So, while there was, in fact, an African American woman named Chloe Russel living in Boston at the time, the extent of her involvement with the Exeter, New Hampshire, publisher of her guide cannot be known any more than the reputation she may or may not have earned locally for any one-on-one dream interpretation she offered to members of the public.[28]

~∞~

A s a new century was about to get under way, twenty-seven-year-old Louisa Park, a pastor's daughter, married Dr. John Park, a surgeon, who served on board the USS *Warren*. It was named after Dr. Joseph Warren, Harvard-trained physician, Son of Liberty, and the man who dispatched post rider Paul Revere on his historic mission before losing his life at the Battle of Bunker Hill in June 1775. A quarter century later, the ship *Warren* patrolled the southeastern coast of the United States in the wake of a rumor-enhanced "Quasi-War" with Revolutionary France. When her diary begins, in the late fall of 1800, Louisa Park was a new mother of a baby boy, also named after the Revolutionary martyr.

"Today I shall hear from my husband for the last time these sixty days," she writes glumly, knowing that Dr. Park is preparing to embark from a port outside Boston. "These solitary hours pass heavily." Without any precise fear in mind, she is anxious. "There are so many things left unsaid. . . . What an impatient, inconsistent being I am."

A few days later, she marks the third anniversary of the passing of a favorite aunt, demonstrating the powerful hold of death and remembrance in her society. "My beloved Uncle was the most distressed, wretched being I ever saw," Louisa is reminded. A friend comes to dinner that night. The day's entry concludes: "Drink to my husband's return."

In the middle of a New England snowstorm, her worried mind shifts from husband to sick child. "Must my boy die because he has no father here!" Baby Warren, and the *Warren* her husband sailed south on, are both facing rough seas. As the days of December pass, the boy cries incessantly. Louisa tries to cut the fabric for a shirt she is making for her husband. Warren is teething. She endures a weeklong headache. At least, she writes, "it did not prevent some pleasant dreams of my beloved, last night. When shall I again realize those dreams." This is where her pen lingers: "Life is a dream;—all the sweets of our dearest friends are but dreams when past;—and when gone, are no better than our flights of imagination when we sleep."

At Christmas, she is still home alone. "This is the most stupid place I have ever lived in," she cries out. Someone in town is involved in a frivolous dispute with someone else in town. She has no interest in finding out about it.

Then, on December 27, 1800, her husband comes home in the only way possible:

> Last night, I dreamt of sitting at tea, with Mrs. Perkins in the evening as I have often done; some one rapped. Madame Perkins called out—Dr. Park! I trembled; the door opened, and we all sat waiting, while he continued scraping his feet, for it rained violently. I could sit no longer, but flew to the entry, and stole a sweet <u>kiss</u> from my <u>husband</u>. What a moment, for my heart beat.

Because this is a dream, and either a total abstraction of her emotions or a function of some obscure life-affirming force within, she must wait out the drama passively.

> He had grown very poor, and was in very low spirits. He said they had taken a prize from the Havana for France, loaded with dollars, which was the occasion of their returning so soon.

In a dream, Louisa Park "stole a sweet kiss" from her absent husband. *Park Family Papers, courtesy of the American Antiquarian Society.*

A "prize" was a captured enemy vessel, and so his shabby state should not have made sense. The narrative does not carry forward the way it would if she had willed it to unfold logically. He approaches her, but they are unable to enjoy a single private moment.

> Much company kept us up 'till late. I watch him the while as I would my life. At last, we retired. Instead of undressing, he threw himself on the bed and groaned; I begged to know what was the matter. Said he, Louisa, come to my arms; when I have you in my bosom I shall be happy. I flew, and in that close embrace, I lived an age, and drank such draughts as burst my soul, and called me to my solitary chamber. Behold, it was a dream!

She had waited through the contortions of her bizarre dream, and in the end, for one brief instant, husband and wife were able to share unencumbered intimacy. She was able to make him happy and make herself happy, which was the real function of her dream.

"I would that my life were such a dream," she confessed, as she finished recording what she had experienced in sleep, in which, interestingly, baby Warren had no role to play. "O my beloved husband, thou best of men; from whom I derive all my happiness in this world, and with whom I wish and hope to enjoy Eternity. With thee, I would fly to some remote, some solitary home; there would we, with our books and our pens, with our minds at ease and free—far from the wickedness and follies of the world—there would we enjoy the luxuries of life."

In the next dream she had of John Park, there was less to be hopeful about. "January 8, 1801. Go to bed and see my husband very much dejected, and would not tell me the reason—talks to himself, but I could not hear what he said." When at last he communicates with her, he says he wants to draw her and baby Warren. But then, as he attempts to capture their images, he gives up, weeping. He tosses aside the pencil. She is confused. Then he reassures her that no one could ever persuade him to leave his wife and child. "I awoke in tears," she writes, "happy to find it a dream—for when asleep, I thought he intended to leave me for some other."

Louisa Park lived in a constant state of anticipation. Her feelings of abandonment make perfect sense to us. There is nothing not-like-us in the emotional content of these dream narratives.

In all respects, her diary dwells on the elusiveness of happiness, one of the most often repeated themes in magazine essays and the male- and female-authored poetry of her generation. She writes of attending a funeral sermon delivered by her Congregationalist father. "I perceive," she says, "that my father believes that the soul goes immediately after death into a state of happiness or misery. There is no knowing." But then, she protests, "neither is it of much importance."

Louisa was not a simple person. Her vitality and very fortune were inextricably bound to thoughts of her absent husband; she seems, at the same time, to be disengaged from her community. The wife and new mother wondered what her purpose on earth was. In dreams, she exhibits devotion to an ideal of marriage and a life she has yet to enjoy. During the first half of 1801, more dreams dot her diary, with her husband still at sea. "Last night," she wrote one day in February, "I dreamed of reading a charming letter from my husband—and after that, of being with him and kissing him heartily."

By May, long months of watching and waiting ended when the child Warren died, having just passed his first birthday. He was laid to rest, she recorded, in "white robes of innocence and death." A letter from her husband was the only "balm" for her "wounded, aching heart" during this difficult time. "I know not what to do with myself, now I have no Warren to care for, attend to, caress and love."

Later that month, she copied out another dream. "After the usual consequence of reading letters from my husband, weeping until I am exhausted, I go to bed, and dream all night of nursing Warren of meeting my husband, and of scenes too interesting for rest." The "too interesting" scenes, we may presume, are of more of those that involve her yearning for John Park's actual embrace.

A prisoner of time, longing is all she has. She does no moralizing. She has no marked desire to invite drama—it's just there, present in the sensual mind-body experience she won't deny herself and in the agitated directions she receives from the invisible force that brings memory to a boil.

Louisa Park's dreams contain mixed messages. They are a prime source of inspiration, and they repeatedly lie to her. Of course, her dreams also made it possible for her to stave off the forgetting process for as long as it took. In early June 1801, the ship's surgeon returned home at last, and life began again.[29]

PART TWO
1801–1860

FOUR

ELIZA CHAMPLAIN SEES ANGELS OVER CONNECTICUT

A sympathy seemed to arise between the waking and the dreaming states of the brain at one point—that whatsoever I happened to call up and to trace by a voluntary act upon the darkness was very apt to transfer itself to my dreams.
—Thomas De Quincey, *Confessions of an English Opium-Eater*

After leaving the presidency in 1809, Thomas Jefferson retired to Monticello, his mountaintop estate in central Virginia. He stayed as far as he possibly could from the corridors of government. But he still received inquisitive letters from people he knew and just as many from citizens he had never met before. One in particular—among the longest ever addressed to him—came from the hand of one Miles King, who lived on the Chesapeake Bay.

"Dear Sir," it began. "It is not without a considerable struggle in my mind arising from the conflict between a conceived duty, and many weighty and powerful objections, that I have ventured at some length to address you on the all-important subject of vital religion." They had been introduced once, in 1806. The writer, an obscure former navy lieutenant and ship owner, had been won over, he said, by the president's "politeness" and "urbanity." This seemed to qualify him to take extra-special care of his fellow Virginian's soul.

When he finally got around to explaining the impetus for his long letter, King stated that he had awakened at midnight after a dream—"something about you" was all he said about it—and it prompted him to concentrate his thoughts on the great man's "spiritual estate." A good many pages later, as he attempted to wind down his letter, he assured Jefferson that there was "no neuter ground" in religion and urged him to "give Christianity your firm support." In praying for Thomas Jefferson's soul, Miles King took solace in something he had supposedly heard spoken in the light of day, to the effect that Jefferson was immersed in studying the Book of Isaiah, with its multiple dramatic prophecies.[1]

Embracing freedom of conscience, his only certain gospel, Jefferson strenuously sought to keep his ideas about truth and religion to himself. He tended to his farms and to his family, and for a dozen years after King's sprawling letter, he read voraciously. As a young man, he had jotted down bold words of Cicero: "The man who is afraid of the inevitable cannot live with a soul at peace"; as an old man, he wrote conventionally to his peers in the expectation of an end to life that led to an "ecstatic meeting with the friends we have loved and lost." Then, in the first days of summer, 1826, worn down by debts and intestinal troubles, the eighty-three-year-old former president lay on his deathbed. Something was about to happen that the late Dr. Rush had eerily foreseen and that his fellow Americans, always eager for sensational news items, were to find irresistible.[2]

Whenever early newspapers announced the deaths of famous citizens, they enclosed their columns within black borders. But this singular (or dual) event went beyond what Americans had ever encountered in their first half century as an independent republic. The perfectly timed departures of John Adams and Thomas Jefferson on July 4, the day they helped make famous, left the nation dumbstruck. It prompted eulogists far and wide to wonder—quoting one representative newspaper—at "a coincidence marvelous and enviable. . . . It cannot be all chance."

Skilled orators knew how to exploit the founders' deaths. In Fayetteville, North Carolina, Henry Potter, whom Jefferson, as president, had appointed to the federal bench, spoke to a crowd in words that remind us of Dr. Rush's dream of the Last Judgment: "And on the memorable 4th of July, the Jubilee of American Freedom, while the cannon's peal was roaring, the trump of jubilee sounding, the acclamations of joy floating in the heavens. . . ." It was repeated by a eulogist in Newark, New Jersey: "The sound of the Trumpet of Jubilee is reverberated in strange and mysterious echoes." Invariably insisting, in prefatory remarks, that they were immune to all superstition, editorialists in various cities and towns nonetheless evoked the collective belief, generated by a seemingly impossible conjunction, that "the Ruler of Events has chosen to manifest by a signal act of his Providence" the principles laid down by America's founders.[3]

Though Jefferson wrote nothing about the substance of his dreams, he did dwell on the nature of memory and the mind. He was often captive to those "fugitive" moments when sentimental "reveries" took over. Away from his daughter, he wrote her that nothing was so "soothing to my mind" as these indulgences, which involved their past travels together and served to "alleviate the toils and inquietudes" of political life. In 1819, long past active politicking, he wrote of the confidence that he lodged in his two immediate successors as president, James Madison and James Monroe: "I willingly put both soul & body into their pockets. . . . I slumber without fear, and review in my dreams the visions of antiquity." He was being literal, though perhaps less in the content of his dreams than in his reference to the reading matter that he most favored in retirement: ancient Greek and Roman thinkers. Their "visions," as classicists who have studied Jefferson show, put him in loving touch with lyric poets and keen philosophers. His imagination flew to "the heroes of Troy" and to Epicurus, wherein he found, in the words of Karl Lehmann, "that there was no dualistic contrast between ideas and reality, spirit and flesh." This also meant that, despite the "ecstatic meeting" with friends of whom he sometimes fantasized, he had serious doubts about the likelihood of a soul existing separate from the body after death.[4]

His own political history was never far from Jefferson's thoughts, and on the day before his death, given the opiate laudanum to ease bodily pain, he dreamt of the Revolution. It was war again in his still fertile mind. As his grandson looked on, Jefferson went through the motions of writing out urgent letters. He spoke deliriously about the Committee of Safety, which in 1775–1776 had stood guard against the British invaders. "Warn the Committee to be on the alert!" the dying man called to the people his imagination were producing at that moment.[5]

One year before, Jefferson's favorite granddaughter, Ellen, had married Joseph Coolidge, an international trader from New England. Consequently, she did not arrive back in Virginia in time for a last audience with the dying patriarch. Two years later, however, she wrote from Boston to one of her sisters that her memories of life at Monticello kept returning to her when she went to sleep. Though the walls of the historic home were now bare, and the family

obliged to sell everything to pay off Jefferson's debts, Ellen was comforted in
her dreams, where the best in nature crept into her mind. Of the senses activated, it was hearing that most affected her:

> In my dreams I sometime revisit my home, but it is strange that I never find my-
> self within the house. I am always wandering through the grounds or walking
> on the terrace, & the weather is always delightful. I hear the gentle breathing
> of the wind through the long branches of the willows, & see them wave slowly,
> whilst on the other side the aspen leaves quiver & tremble with a justling as
> distinct as ever delighted my waking ear.

Quivering, trembling, breathing—she heard as much as she saw in her dream.

Ellen Coolidge was thirty-one, a mother; but in her dreams of Monticello,
she told her sister, she felt sixteen again. Her young children were absent from
her thoughts, as she regressed and regained a life she once knew. It was invariably the same paradisal vista, and it existed under a sunny sky. And so she
concluded:

> Nothing is a surer proof to me that climate enters very much into our pleasures
> of association & recollection & exercises a decided influence over our imagina-
> tion, than the effects produced on my feelings by a bright southern day, whether
> it comes to me in a dream, or, more rarely still, when a few of the most adven-
> turous of these birds of passage straggles so far north as Boston.[6]

Her grandfather, who had described dreams as mere "incoherencies" and
had shunned the Christian concept of miracles in any form, famously devoted
his nights to quiet reading and denoted the sun as "my almighty physician."
The granddaughter who most took after him—whose style of writing most
resembled his—belonged to a generation that partook more of mystery and
spirit in religious life, and for whom moonlight mended the mind as well as
sunshine did.

Ellen's was the generation we classify as American Romantics. It has been
said that classical and romantic are the systolic and diastolic of time—not
mutually exclusive, but complementary. The chambers of the heart need each
other, of course; and if we recur to the designation of the classicist's sun and the
romantic's moon, one rarely eclipses the other completely, and when an eclipse
occurs, it does not last.

Let us be clear: the generations were not at odds. Though denied any official connection to the political world her grandfather helped create, Ellen was valued by senior statesmen for her poise and judgment. In that way, she was similar to one of her elder acquaintances, former First Lady Dolley Madison, a Virginia-born Philadelphian who for many years captivated Washingtonians. One of Dolley's oldest male friends recalled her debut in society: "I well remember it, in all its freshness & beauty, just as we do the delightful dreams which sometimes visit our slumbers, as if to remind us, that there is some thing, in some region better & brighter than any of the scenes in this world of mix'd pleasure and pain." Dolley had that effect on people, but what a curious comparison he had drawn: the verifiable memory of a teenaged Dolley and the charmed memory that adhered to pleasant dreams.

In 1793, Dolley lost her first husband to the yellow fever epidemic. The following spring she met "the Great Little Madison," and they married that fall. During their courtship, the wife of a Virginia congressman (who ostensibly heard Madison through boardinghouse walls) girlishly informed Dolley: "At night he Dreams of you and Starts in his Sleep a Calling on you to relieve his Flame."

Even if the congressman's wife was toying with Dolley, the Madisons' forty-two-year marriage was marked by as much passion as fortitude. In October 1805, when her husband was serving as secretary of state under Jefferson and they were temporarily separated, she fretted for him. Trusted messengers carried their letters, and it was by this means that she wrote confidentially: "In my dreams of last night, I saw you in your chamber, unable to move, from riding so far and so fast—I pray that an early letter from you may chase away the painful impression of this vision." She closed the letter with: "Think of thy wife! who thinks and dreams of thee!" Years later, when, at eighty-five, the fourth president collapsed and died at breakfast, his ever-affectionate widow would respond to a letter of condolence: "I have been as one in a troubled dream since my irreparable loss of him."[7]

~~⌒ᴎ∂~~

In 1807, one member of the Jeffersonian circle, the keen-witted troublemaker Thomas Paine, wrote "An Essay on Dream." It was the last original work that the Revolutionary published in his lifetime, a prefatory piece in advance of a scathing critique of religious dogma. In early 1776, urged on by none other than Dr. Benjamin Rush, he had authored the momentous pamphlet

Common Sense, which turned up the heat on an already percolating spirit of rebelliousness. Capitalizing on his fame, Paine went public in the 1790s with his freethinking ideology. *The Age of Reason* shocked a sizable number of Paine's former supporters. From then until his death in 1809, he fought off attacks from all who detested his unexpurgated irreligion—which, in reality, fell short of atheism.

His thesis was a recapitulation of the Enlightenment's optimistic, deistic belief in a godly nature. For many intellectuals, the prophetic books of the Bible belonged to ancient poetry, and natural causes and natural laws made far more sense than inherited understandings of Christian revelations. Reasoning men elevated Isaac Newton above the New Testament. Yet even Unitarians like Rush, whose liberal humanism was much closer to Paine than to conservative Christianity, rejected Paine's authority to speak on the subject. Once tarred as an atheist, a person was unlikely to lose that label.

Paine's 1807 essay separated dream narratives from Christian allegory. "In order to understand the nature of dream," he said, "it is first necessary to understand the composition and decomposition of the human mind." Relying on an Enlightenment vocabulary, he proposed that in the waking state, the three main faculties of mind—imagination, judgment, and memory—were equally active. But in sleep, he explained, regularity and rationality could not be relied upon.

What he found most curious about the dreaming mind was its ventriloquizing power "to become the agent of every person, character, and thing of which it dreams. It carries on a conversation with several, asks questions, hears answers, gives and receives information, and it acts all these parts itself." As an unstoppable force in sleep, the faculty of the imagination indulged its wild side, "counterfeiting memory" to the point of confusion: "It dreams of persons it never knew, and talks with them as if it remembered them as old acquaintances. It relates circumstances that never happened, and tells them as if they had happened. It goes to places that never existed, and knows where all the streets and houses are as if it had been there before." For Paine, the matter was one he could cast in the vocabulary of political systems: sovereignty. In the light of day, dreams obligingly yielded their sovereignty over the mind back to memory.

The oft-spoken comparison to insanity impressed him as it did other thinkers: "It may rationally be said that every person is mad once in twenty-four hours, for were he to act in the day as he dreams in the night he would be confined for a lunatic." It was, Paine concluded, "absurd" to ponder too closely the meaning of a dream and just as illogical to center one's religious faith on this odd species of thought.[8]

Ezra Stiles Ely was pastor of the Third Presbyterian Church in Philadelphia and namesake of the Yale College president and dreamer whom we met a bit earlier. Prominent in his own right, Ely authored *Conversations on the Science of the Human Mind* a few years after Paine's death. It was a book on human appetites, organized as a dialogue between a professor and student, and included the following:

PUPIL: What is insanity?

PROF: It is a state of mind in which the mental faculties do not operate in a
    natural manner.

PUPIL: What are the most common mental causes of insanity?

PROF: An excessive indulgence of some affection or passion is the most com-
    mon cause of permanent madness.

This exchange led almost immediately to a teaching moment about dreaming. Not only is the correlation, which we have already seen, worth noting, but the logic is equally fascinating, insofar as it is the one area in which modern science and early American medico-religious thinking are pretty much aligned:

PUPIL: Well, Sir, is not dreaming a species of insanity?

PROF: Any mental operation performed while one is asleep is called dreaming.
    There is some resemblance between the state of an insane person and that
    of a sleeping person who dreams: still, dreaming is not raving. When one
    dreams, he does not generally think himself asleep; and when one is in-
    sane, he is very prone to think all other men are more mad than himself. In
    a state of insanity, some of the faculties seem to be dormant, while others
    perform strange operations: and in sleep the faculties of the dreamer are
    not all equally active, nor equally consistent in their activity.

PUPIL: Do we always dream, when asleep?

PROF: We not always remember what our minds have been doing, when we
    were asleep; nor can we recollect any considerable portion of our mental
    actions done while we are awake. That we do not remember to have been
    at all times conscious of thinking, feeling, willing, and mentally exerting
    ourselves, when asleep, is therefore no proof that we have not been. . . .[9]

Reverend Ely would not have wished to align himself with the radical Tom Paine, but in this one respect—the analogous features of dreaming and raving—they are close.

The difference, of course, is that in segueing from dreams into his larger project, Paine insisted that "the belief that Jesus Christ is the son of God, begotten by the holy ghost, a being never heard of before, stands as the story of an old man's dream." In making the assertion, he repeated the passage from Matthew in which an angel appeared to Joseph in a dream, instructing him with regard to his wife Mary, "for that which is conceived in her is of the holy ghost."

Delineating several dreams from holy scripture, Paine lumped all together and lamented that such a system of belief had undone civilization: "This story of dreams has thrown Europe into a dream for more than one thousand years," he charged. "All the efforts nature, reason, and conscience have made to awaken man from it have been ascribed by priestcraft and superstition to the workings of the devil." Living through an era of massive change, he admitted having hoped for more; that in unleashing a new spirit of inquiry, the American Revolution would have done away with "this religion of dreams" and moved ahead. But he recognized that more time was needed, because preachers, though educated to know better, "still believed the delusion necessary." Paine challenged America's religious leaders, whose hypocrisy was a two-sided coin: "not bold enough to be honest, nor honest enough to be bold."[10]

Paine's posthumous fame remains secure, but his refusal to mince words on the subject of faith marred his reputation in the immediate period after his death. Though a logical extension of Enlightenment thought, his interpretation made many uncomfortable. Indeed, as the century took wing, the thinkers who spoke on behalf of "rational religion," having been so long in the spotlight, were gradually overtaken by a cohort for whom wonderment over the god in nature led to mysticism and new bursts of evangelical enthusiasm. Paine, like Jefferson, saw in unquestioning religion an enslavement of the mind. That was their issue. In the nineteenth century, it became less of one.

~⁊⁊~

As the generation born after Revolutionary times began to make its mark, it revitalized organized religion. The average person was not prepared to jettison physicians' thinking that food consumption and physiology explained what was happening in nightly visions. But prophetic possibilities became increasingly attractive.

Reports of extraordinary dreams circulated widely. Ann Lee, British born and with little education, founded the Shaker sect after an angel apprised her of Christ's second coming. Shakers, like Quakers, were a pacifist sect. Believing sex the root of all evil, their charismatic leader commanded celibacy from her followers in upstate New York and New England. Though Mother Ann Lee died in 1780, by the early decades of the nineteenth century, the group had expanded into the Midwest. An 1816 account of her life and visions emphasized her ability to commune with the dead, identifying them as they swirled around the living.[11]

Around this time, a thirteen-year-old farmhand in western Massachusetts, the "mulatto boy" Frederick Swan, was studying the Bible when he took sick. He experienced a series of dreams over a period of months—seventeen dreams judged remarkable enough that someone wrote them all down. In one of these, Frederick was led to understand "that if he read the Bible three months, he should be well." Well with God, that is.

The "mulatto boy" dreams contain raw elements unrelated to their visionary content: "I dreamt I set out to travel with something to sell, and on the road I saw a large white building"; "I set out to go to my mother in a thunderstorm"; "I dreamt I went to the brook, and saw a boat coming towards me with white sails hoisted—I called to my mother to come see it"; "I dreamt of standing at the foot of my bed on crutches"; "I dreamed of being on the road south of our house."

"South of our house" offers a clear sense of direction, which would not be necessary if the dreams were wholly contrived. The color white, repeated in six of the dreams, was a widely known symbol of purity and part and parcel of religious narrative. (According to the *Columbian Magazine,* the national colors of red, white, and blue denoted "hardiness and valor," "purity and innocence," and "vigilance, perseverance, and justice," respectively.) The devil, "a man all covered with bells," made more than one appearance in the "mulatto boy" collection. And in six of the dreams, Frederick mentioned seeing angels. Consider the likelihood that the mass culture Frederick responded to had designated dreams as supernatural phenomena, whose purpose was to bring people to religion. Thus, the young dreamer lumped all unknown sleep figures into the two extreme categories of devils and angels.[12]

In the more freewheeling environment coming into existence in early nineteenth-century America, the religious and the medical combined in new ways. Samuel L. Mitchill, M.D., was both a professor of medicine at Columbia and a member of Congress from New York. He served in the House of Representatives from 1801 to 1804 and in the U.S. Senate from 1805 to 1809. This overachiever had a well-deserved reputation for pedantry, but his authority was rarely called into question.[13]

In 1814–1815, retired from politics, Dr. Mitchill took extensive notes on the startling case of one Rachel Baker, a devout Presbyterian until age sixteen, and now, at twenty, a Baptist. Though "little prone to talk," she had been praying and preaching in her sleep for years. According to Mitchill, she made a habit of turning in around 9:00 P.M. Not long after falling asleep, she experienced a "fit" and spoke audibly (sometimes in a "forcible" tone). Occasionally, she recited verses from the hymns of Isaac Watts.

Clergymen were the first to sit with her in the dark. They posed questions, and she responded from her stupefied state:

QUESTION: "Are you thirsty?"

ANSWER: "Yes, but not for the water than man drinketh. . . . I long to draw
water out of the well of salvation."

QUESTION: "What is your greatest grief?"

ANSWER: "That the hand of the Lord is lying heavy upon me, and that he
has made me to differ from my brethren and sisters in a strange and unac-
countable manner."

And so forth.

"Her words are poured forth in a fluent, rapid stream," wrote Mitchill, after observing the patient. "At times she is remarkably animated, and gives point to her sentences by the most expressive emphasis." As a physician, he studied her pulse and found it "full, equable, and flowing, without tremor, flutter, or intermission." Nothing that was tried put an end to her unconscious nightly performances. Even bloodletting, "though practised to a degree considerably debilitating, did not break the paroxysm."

Dr. Mitchill was right about one thing. Rachel Baker was a fit subject for medical study, but not as an example of supernatural communication. People were known to talk in their sleep; the difference with Rachel was that she did so regularly and for several minutes at a spell. "In some of its forms," the doctor wrote of her condition, "it manifests its nearness to hysteria and catalepsy. It resembles reverie." He also saw a relationship to somnambulism, or sleepwalking: Dancing around known neurological states, he settled on a mixture of "reverie,

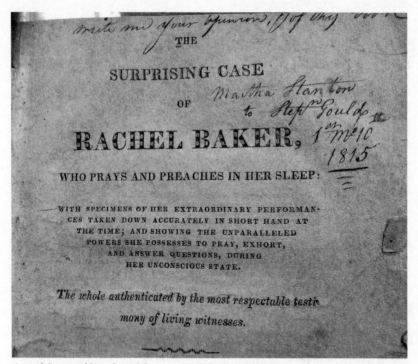

One of the pamphlets of 1814 featuring Rachel Baker, "who prays and preaches in her sleep."

somnambulism and dreaming" for his definition for the Rachel Baker phenomenon: "Strictly its name is Somniloquism; at least as far as speaking goes." His logic was supported by the general belief that memorization of religious teachings came most easily at puberty, "when the female frame acquires additional sensibilities, and undergoes a peculiar revolution."[14]

A second treatment of the Rachel Baker case, which again drew upon Dr. Mitchill, included a feature the earlier edition did not: the doctor's categorization of sleep pathology, or "somnium."[15] Each subcategory within "somnium" had a corresponding Latin classification, amounting to the most developed taxonomy of dreams and sleep disorders known to the early American republic. Under the broad category of "Symptomatic Somnium," Mitchill listed indigestion, with troublesome dreams; classic nightmares; and "debility" (somnium cum debilitate), in which "desultory traces of memory and imagination" were "presented in a confused and irregular manner" and attended by a "muttering delirium."

He designated as the "common dream" a "somnium from fresh and vivid occurrences . . . traced to some conversation or occurrence of the day or evening, or to some actual condition of the body." Calling it a "somnium," though, classified any dream as a pathological event. The only difference between "common dream" and the rest on his list was that the former could be explained away as a reaction to recent experience, whereas each of the latter exhibited an obvious disordered character.

There was "Somnium from old and forgotten occurrences" (somnium ab obsoletis), which arose "when long lost images are renewed to the memory, and dead friends are brought before us." (This would be Rush's notable graveyard dream.) Next, "Somnium of a prospective character," which occurred "when the dreamer is engaged in seeing funeral processions, and foretelling lugubrious events by a sort of SECOND SIGHT, as it is called." This was, by another name, the precognitive, or prophetic, dream, which Mitchill latinized as "somnium a prophetia." He was especially bold in assigning it a hereditary nature: "This disease is symptomatic of a peculiar state of body, running in families, like gout, consumption, and insanity."

His "somnium a toxico" was the dream produced by opium administered for pain, known for "disturbing the will and exciting strange fancies." (This would be the dream that a medicated Thomas Jefferson experienced just before he died.) With similar fearlessness, the doctor explained what it meant to be an oracle or seer. "They see so much," he said with a certain redundancy, that "their sights are termed VISIONS, inasmuch as the eyes are so peculiarly concerned." The pathology of clairvoyance was in eliciting impressions so strong and vivid as to appear (though they were emphatically not) supernaturally derived.

Finally, Dr. Mitchill provided a timely interpretation of the ill-defined word "reverie." At the opening of the era of Romantic poetry, it only seems right that someone should have laid claim to a definition. But unlike his delimitation of the above dream types, Mitchill found reverie to be "idiopathic," of no obvious cause: "the internal senses are so engaged that there is no knowledge, or but an imperfect one, of the passing external events, constituting what is termed REVERIE; where fanciful traces of thought are indulged at considerable length." The word means pretty much the same thing to us: a self-directed indulgence.[16]

We perceive reverie today as a brief respite from our customary focus on ever-present reality, momentary suspension of the will to notice our immediate surroundings. It is an act of summoning memory for no greater end than to find a fleeting harmony. Not every thought has to be concentrated. In the shadows of awareness lies unknown pleasure, even insight.

The modern understanding of "reverie" was about to take hold, and it marked a subtle but important difference between Mitchill's and the rising generation. Where intellectual powers were suspended, the early American medical professor saw a lapse, a decline in condition. He could never luxuriate in reverie. For budding Romantics, though, it was effectively a new human endowment being discovered. Over the next several decades, Americans would open themselves to internal experiences their parents had shied from. They did not abandon the duty to uphold self-control; they transformed the emotional environment by privileging the role of imagination. A literary revolution was under way. In terms of the culture of the dream, it meant enriching the meaning of everyday life, embracing as positive certain of the phenomena Dr. Mitchill labeled "somnia," or disorders.

Every generation has its eccentrics. In the post-Revolutionary period, one of these was named Jonathan Plummer. He was an itinerant peddler and a man of little consequence except in his own mind. Before he died, he claimed in an autobiographical publication that God spoke to him in his dreams. He wrote to inform others that it was possible to train oneself to access the divine in this manner. The night preceding his acquisition of a copyright certificate, Plummer said, he had "a very remarkable dream" and heard the words, "Your noble fame, shall reach the sky!!!" Another dream instructed him to drink chamomile tea; yet another directed him to consume a red liquid (he naturally determined that the Lord meant it to be wine). Poet as well as prophet, Plummer could not understand his inability to find love and, just to set the record straight, pronounced himself "no hermaphrodite"—meaning that he was not incapable of pleasing a woman. After unsuccessfully warning others of the approaching Final Judgment, the unrequited, self-described "old bachelor" officially ended his literary career by starving himself to death in the fall of 1819.[17]

~∂

N ow meet Eliza Way Champlain of New London, Connecticut, and New York City, a watercolor painter and the daughter and niece of accomplished painters. She was born in 1797 and lived to the ripe age of eighty-nine. When Eliza arrived, her mother, Betsy, was twenty-three and already caring for one baby. Eliza was the second of four children, then, the rest boys. But because the eldest, George, turned out to be reckless, Eliza was the family's model citizen as she embarked upon adulthood. Her mother's older sister, the never-married Mary Way, moved to the big city when Eliza was fourteen, establishing herself as a drawing instructor as well as portraitist. In 1820, the year Eliza's father, a shipping merchant, died, Mary went blind and was forced to return to New London to live with the family. Two years later, at twenty-five and still single, Eliza followed in Aunt Mary's footsteps and found herself a place to rent in lower Manhattan.

Eliza's watercolors are inspired and delicate and her familiar letters clearly the product of a high-spirited imagination. One that preceded her move to New York so delighted friends of the family that it prompted the following commentary: "Letters from Eliza, full of fun and nonsense, . . . are in high demand and much approved if laughing is a mark of approbation." Not long after Aunt Mary returned to the family and exchanged places with Eliza, she and her niece were writing self-revealingly and arguing affectionately. On the subject of Eliza's ostensibly plain features, preference for simplicity of dress, and stubborn individuality, Mary charged: "Indeed it appears pretty evident, there is no Doublet and Hose [i.e., opulent Shakespearean garb] in your disposition and more is the pity. You say Fortune has kindly spread a strengthening plaster for your Pericranium to supply the deficiencies of Nature. I say success to the application, but. . . ." The two women, one an old maid, the other, apparently, an old maid in waiting, did not always agree, but they were alike in spirit.

In the same letter, Aunt Mary shared a dream. "I have past many a sleepless night in anticipated pleasure, and when I slept, my dreams were all about it. The other night I heard the voice of Mrs. Fitch [her absent, not deceased, friend] as plain as I ever heard it in my life, I heard her say, 'If I was a Widow, and had no Family, I would go too.' I thought much of her and of my dream, if it was a dream, but to me it appeared reality."

It is not so much the substance of the dream, which made complete sense only to the correspondents, but the dreamer's attitude that tells us something important. The blind Aunt Mary placed emotional value on the words of Mrs. Fitch as they came through her sleeping mind. The mere appearance of Mrs. Fitch was not something worth her comment, because known individuals appear to us in dreams, and we accept this as a common feature, if not function, of the dream. Anna Fitch lived in lower Manhattan—she was formerly Mary's neighbor and now Eliza's. What Mary needed to do, for her own comfort, was to rationalize what her dream said to her about the death(s) she had conjured.

"Now you must know," she went on, "we are great dreamers, here in Yankee town, and we have great faith in dreams also, and in the interpretation thereof. So I determined to interpret my dream in the manner most agreeable to myself, which is in the words of Brutus 'Not that I loved Caesar less, but that I loved Rome more.'"

It sounds like in dreaming Mary wasn't fantasizing the death of Mrs. Fitch's attorney husband, or projecting a fateful decision onto Mrs. Fitch herself, but only expressing the desire to have the flesh-and-blood Mrs. Fitch come and keep her company in New London. Eliza's aunt goes on to say, in fact, that, in interpreting her dreams, "I prefer a more plain and simple exposition. . . . I would then enjoy the company of those I most love and value."[18]

The salutation Eliza used most often in her letters to the painter sisters was "Dear Mother & Co." On at least one occasion, though, it was the especially charming "Dear Sisters of the brush." In October 1822, still building her career in the city and concerned in not having heard from home in two months, she wrote nervously:

> Although I am not at all superstitious, a dream that I had last night may perhaps be the cause of my writing to day. I fancied myself in a house opposite to the one in which you live, and that I saw a coffin brought out from your house and placed in a hearse that stood waiting at the door. It moved slowly round the corner and proceeded to the grave yard followed by more people than I thought New London contained. As the last of the train disappeared from my view I beheld the air filled with angels each having a golden trumpet in their hand and their perfectly "symmetrical" forms enveloped in a robe of the most transparent texture. I can give you no idea of the grandure and sublimity of the scene, or of my sensations while gazing on it.

This was one of those dreams Dr. Mitchill classified as "Somnium of a prospective character," complete with the funeral procession he had outlined; it was not one of those didactic angel dreams that found their way into religious publications, because this dream bore no meaning for the larger world. Indeed, Eliza said about her vision that she felt "loath" to return with the trumpet-bearing beings to the "celestial regions" where they resided. The troubled dreamer just wanted to be reassured, as she awaited a letter, that no loved one in New London was then being mourned.[19]

Her mother wrote back confirming that everyone was fine. A commentary on Eliza's dreaming habit followed, showing that, like her sister Mary, Betsy Way Champlain took an interest in the active life of the nocturnal mind:

"Your dream was truely sublime," writes Betsy Way Champlain to her daughter Eliza in 1822. Way-Champlain Papers, courtesy of the American Antiquarian Society.

Your dream was truely sublime, and though Death is call'd the king of terrors, there was something so soothing in the <u>symphony</u> (excuse me for giving it this term, as I know not what else to call it) that it seemed to ballance those terrors which perhaps are altogeather immaginary. I can only say with some degree of faith that we shall have no more laid upon us than we can bear.

"Some degree of faith" gives us a fair idea of the muted religiosity Eliza had likely experienced growing up—this was not a strictly pious family. Betsy's choice of the word "symphony" in the context of discussing her daughter's troubled dream is also faintly suggestive, even though the trumpets were not sounding for Eliza, and her dream, as laid out, was visual and not auditory in character. From the same source, after a few months had passed, came this maternal piece of advice:

I am of the opinion that your Dreams proceed only from your Dissipation as you term it. Late sitting up has a tendency to weaken the system [and] often causes unpleasant dreams, this I know from experience, and perhaps there is nothing will make a person grow old faster. Mary bid me say to you that there is no meaning in any dream . . . and you may throw all your Devil ones to the wind.[20]

The combined resolve of Betsy and Mary seems hardly different from what Dr. Rush might have prescribed: a peaceful evening without undue exertion so as to yield pleasant dreams. We do not know what "dissipation" Eliza had referred to, because her letter is missing. But it is clear from the tenor of her earlier ones that "dissipation" was a relative term, an exaggeration for effect. She read a good bit of fiction and had a healthy fantasy life. She invested considerable

A watercolor by Eliza Way Champlain captures the creative innocence that enveloped the early nineteenth-century, New York–bound dreamer. Way-Champlain Papers, courtesy of the American Antiquarian Society.

energy in her painting. She wrote with fervor. But that appears to be the extent of her dissipation. At worst, she may have participated in social activities that kept her out late. Whatever it was, it was bringing on the occasional nightmare.

At a dinner party in the city, Miss Champlain, the young, sociable painting teacher, had occasion to meet the former governor of Ohio, Ethan Allen Brown. A New York–educated lawyer who had migrated west, Brown was an attractive man, an eligible bachelor. Blessed with both looks and intellect, he had, in addition, the distinct honor of being born on the same day as the nation he served: July 4, 1776. In May 1825, when he and twenty-eight-year-old Eliza met in Manhattan, Brown was fourteen months shy of fifty.

"Since my residence in New York," she wrote "Mother & Company," "I have not been so charmed with the conversation of any gentleman as his. . . . His person is tall and commanding, his face tho' not strikingly beautiful is nevertheless of the first order of fine faces and there is a fire in the quick fascinating rays of his fine eyes." After continuing on at length about the governor's attributes, she dissected his conversation, which came to encompass the subject of males and females and their respective places in the social order: "He insinuated that woman, lovely woman was an enigma after all."

This was treated as a taunt by one female of their party, none other than the irrepressible Anna Fitch of Aunt Mary's dream, who advocated with intensity for the political rights of women. Interpreting the moment for Betsy and Mary, Eliza noted of Ethan Brown "an ill suppressed smile on his expressive countenance at the soreness she exhibited on the subject on which she feels most sore." Betraying her own comfort with the norms of the day, Eliza wrote critically of her neighbor: "I assure you she fought like an Amazon—she fought with a zeal worthy of a greater cause at least."

Eliza did not understand why some women became "almost wretched because Dame Nature chose to call them the weaker vessel." For her part, "Nature in making me woman has offended me less than in anything else she did when mixing up my composition, for in truth tis a queer medley—she intended me to get along through life by my own exertions." Personable and at no loss for friends in the big city, she was able to support herself as a single woman and did not feel oppressed. Governor Brown, meanwhile, fulfilled Eliza's expectations of masculine self-confidence. Unprovoked by the feminist Fitch, he was "all humility and submission while the storm was venting its rage." It is important to note, however, that even as she bowed to woman's designated social role, Eliza rejected the medicalized assumption about a female imagination naturally inclined to emotional extremes.

In her late twenties, she was already an unusual statistic among eligible women. She was considered too old not to have found a proper husband. Perhaps it was that her favorite aunt, self-sufficient until she lost her sight, had led a fulfilling life without a husband, which altered the timetable for Eliza. It was more than all right for Ethan Allen Brown to remain unmarried—it certainly did no harm to his public image. A friend and fellow governor joked with him: "Have you not violated the great command increase and multiply? Have you not bedewed the pillows of love-sick damsels with tears. . . !" And he joked back that he would rather "scatter" than "concentrate" his manly seed.[21]

It becomes clear in her letters that Eliza Champlain was hoping to find a mate. On some level, the elusive bachelor Brown charmed her. But instead of an older man, she ended up with someone two years her junior. It was right around this time, in fact, that she met Edward Riley, a musical instrument craftsman. In dreaming of an easy camaraderie, though, she was about to find life complicated. Her mother suddenly died, and Eliza was obliged to return to New London to help care for Mary. This made for a prolonged courtship.

The first extant letter from Eliza, in New London, to her fiancé in Manhattan was penned in February 1826 and bore the salutation "my dear Edward." He had thought, on the basis of something she had said, that this woman of poise and maturity might have been belittling him for his "timidity," or unmanly bearing. So she wrote back to reassure him that her uncensored thoughts did not indicate disappointment in him, let alone a desire on her part to take charge: "I could no more love an effeminate man than you could love a masculine girl. They are both out of Character—and of course disgusting."

Eliza painted a miniature of Edward, to have and gaze at while they were apart. Despite the loss of her mother, much of the courtship correspondence reveals her to be as winsome as she had been in years past, resorting to light banter and exhibiting good humor. He wanted her to learn a musical instrument, convinced that one species of art promised good results in every other. But she demurred: "You know I told you I certainly never could learn any thing by rule—I was not born by rule and I know I never should have Painted decently if the rules of Painting had been stuffed into my skull." And then she bade him bring his "pretty face" to New London. Threatening to box his ears—a thinly disguised sexual come-on—she admitted: "I dream of you often—sometimes my dreams are very laughable—at others more grave—tho' never at all gloomy." And then she concluded her mostly playful letter with an earnest "Adieu love I am yours Eliza."[22]

That spring, the couple wrote constantly on subjects far and wide. Eliza said she objected to the British tendency to "mask strong feelings under appearance of coldness." She understood what was expected of a woman of her generation: a delicate blend of liveliness and reserve. "I know if I should attempt to conceal any feelings on some occasions I could not succeed," she wrote. "I am not English and have not yet learnt [i.e., taught] my looks to contradict my feelings." Honest and unafraid, she prized openness in a way we would not have seen in the preceding generation. To take the exceptionally forthcoming Benjamin's Rush's courtship letters as a counterpoint, we find the following: "I am now standing on an eminence. The married life stands before, and the single life behind me. My dearest Julia is the principal figure in the groupe of objects which surround me."

The remainder of his courtship letters adopt a similarly restrained tone. In the Revolutionary of 1775, we encounter hardly any self-reflection. "I admire you for your accomplishments—but I love you chiefly for your virtues" is an axiom, not a revelation. He mentions "the flame of love in my breast," but he does not describe it emotionally. Even a warm sign-off of "Adieu my dearest girl. My whole soul consents when I add that I am your wholly" does not escape convention. We find a good deal more of the inner man in Rush's dreams than in his love letters.[23]

In the writings of young couples in 1826, the imagination is readily engaged. We find Eliza continuing to indulge in dream lore. After Aunt Mary and her brother—Eliza's uncle—attend a New London wedding in April of that year, she writes again to Edward:

> Uncle sent me up some of the cake (as I had <u>retired</u>) with a charge to put it under my pillow in order to dream of you___ Accordingly I placed it there–and instead of your pretty face presenting itself in my dreams I was annoy'd all night by no less a personage than our beautiful Cat Malt. The next morning when I went down I was obliged to give an account of my dreams—Uncle Way laughed hartily at my beau—but I did not care–and determined to dream on the cake again—and again—as the rule is three nights—the next night (which was last night) I made a second attempt to get sight of you—and was prevented exactly as the first by that rascally Cat presenting herself, and no one else—to night is the last and if I dream of her again I will shoot her tomorrow.[24]

Nothing so perfectly captures Eliza's irrepressible humor as her offhanded engagement with rank superstition. She knows better than to indulge the fantasy, but a penchant for clowning around makes her go through with the exercise. It provides her with a great visual punch line, too: her comic resolution to shoot the cat.

~∂~

We have already seen how dreaming of a coffin, mourners, and an angel once caused Eliza a slight twinge, if not quite credible alarm. Shortly after this lighter engagement with dreams, Eliza and Aunt Mary found themselves ruminating about the subject once again—this time while under the same roof. We can read about it because they brought Edward Riley into the conversation.

The dreams, in this instance, were not their own. They were the drug-induced dreams of Thomas De Quincey (1785–1859), who, in 1822, shocked and titillated readers in England and America with his *Confessions of an English Opium-Eater*. Eliza read the book aloud to Mary, and Edward read it independently. "The Opium Eater is certainly very interesting," Eliza wrote to her betrothed, "but I think I never felt more melancholy than when I had finished it—and as I do not fancy melancholy—the book is not altogether to my taste. Aunt Mary was delighted with it." As was Mrs. Fitch, for that matter.[25]

De Quincey's *Confessions,* a testament to the enticements and torments of addiction, stands as the most dream-intensive piece of literature in this era.

Thomas De Quincey (1785–1859), author of Confessions of an English Opium-Eater.

At a very young age, the author lost his father to consumption (tuberculosis) and eventually came to believe that regular use of laudanum—taking a liquid concoction of opium and alcohol—staved off an inherited tendency to the generally fatal disease. Barely five feet tall and sickly, De Quincey was haunted, too, by the early death of a favorite sister. He was defiant toward his devout, emotionally unavailable mother and the guardians appointed to oversee his inheritance.

The books that appealed to his budding imagination were Samuel Johnson's *Rasselas* (1759) and Mungo Park's *Travels in the Interior of Africa* (1799), both of which involved elusive quests and mysteries of the mind. Despite having been tapped as a promising scholar of Greek and Latin, De Quincey quit school to test his mettle, and with little to support his chosen lifestyle, he formed a particular attachment to a teenage prostitute named Ann with whom he lived for a time in an unfurnished house in London. His impulsiveness, despondency, passion for poetry and literature, and the tumultuous dreams that he experienced even before his addiction began made De Quincey an ideal carrier of the Romantic word.[26]

In the *Confessions*, writing as a rehabilitated addict (in fact, though, De Quincey never completely kicked the habit), he dates his earliest acquaintance with the drug to the year 1804 and an incapacitating toothache. During his initial courtship with the medicinal extract, he found that it composed him while encouraging "the great light of the majestic intellect." He would go to the opera house and revel in all that his ears took in: "Opium, by greatly increasing the activity of the mind generally, increases, of necessity, that particular mode of its activity by which we are able to construct out of the raw material of organic sound an elaborate intellectual pleasure."[27]

When, in 1813, he began using opium daily, his nights became increasingly anguished; his happiness yielded to "an Iliad of woes." A turbaned Malay with "small, fierce, restless eyes" who had come to his door one day became, in his dreams, a symbol of all he feared in the Asiatic psyche. For whatever reason, the Malay had caught hold of his passive mind, taking him to a part of the world where humanity was "a weed." Again and again made captive in this cruel, foreign place, De Quincey was forced to live among snakes and crocodiles. He hated the Asiatic with all the patrician intolerance and Tory xenophobia he could muster. By now married and the father of two, he often found that he could be liberated from the "hideous reptile" living in his mind only when his young children woke him at noon with their happy, innocent voices. His frightened wife implored him to stop taking the drug, and he tried to temper his dreams by conversing with her and the little ones just before bed, "hoping thus to derive an influence from what affected me externally into my internal world of shadows."

In 1819, still unable to resist opium but apparently able to sleep securely again, he had a powerful dream in which he reencountered the prostitute Ann, whom he had long since despaired of ever finding alive. In the dream, he believed it was Easter Sunday, and he was standing before the cottage where he now lived with his family, but in the distance loomed a mountain range of Alpine heights. Then, turning back to his garden gate, he beheld the domes of a Jerusalem-like city, and there sat Ann. "So then I have found you at last," he said. She would not answer. She looked the same age as before and even more beautiful. The scene dissolved, and they were back on the lamp-lit streets in Oxford where they had walked side by side. He was young again.

To demonstrate the immoderate power of the dream, De Quincey relates one more, which took place in 1820, a short time before he penned his *Confessions*. It is a dream filled with sound, and louder than all the trumpets we have encountered before. Here is what De Quincey says of it: "The dream commenced with a music which now I often heard in dreams—a music of preparation and of awakening suspense; a music like the opening of the Coronation Anthem [composed by George Friedrich Handel for King George II, in 1727], and which, like that, gave the feeling of a vast march—of infinite cavalcades filing off—and the tread of innumerable armies." This was not a martial moment, but "a day of crisis and of final hope for human nature, then suffering some mysterious eclipse, and labouring in some dread extremity." Great drama was under way, another Last Judgment fantasy, and it came with an overpowering sound track.

De Quincey had no firm idea what was at stake. "I, as is usual in dreams (where, of necessity, we make ourselves central to every movement), had the power, and yet had not the power, to decide it." In the theater where our dreams are staged, whether or not an orchestra plays, the director—who is also the main actor—never knows how the scene will play out.

After this dream, De Quincey cannot carry on as before: "And I awoke in struggles, and cried aloud—'I will sleep no more!'" Now, as he finally begins to wean himself off his opium habit, the reader is given the moral of the story: do not do as I have done. As obvious as the moral is, the author confides that such scenes, once ingrained, never disappear entirely: "One memorial of my former condition still remains: my dreams are not yet perfectly calm: the dread swell and agitation of the storm have not wholly subsided."[28]

When Eliza Champlain wrote to her fiancé Edward about De Quincy's book, though its melancholy strains failed to impress her, she called the author "a true philosopher." Aware that Edward was predisposed to like the book, she lightly praised De Quincey for his originality of style—"this I don't dislike"—while insisting that she could not bear to read it a second time. Separately to Mrs. Fitch, she tried humor: "Aunt Mary is quite delighted with the Opium Eater (what a horrid title the book has). You would fancy her under the influence of Opium while she was listening."[29]

Two Romantic poets directed De Quincey's writing career: William Wordsworth and Samuel Taylor Coleridge. As an Oxford student, De Quincey wrote a letter to the former, begging for his attention, and was rewarded, at twenty-two, by becoming a virtual member of the Wordsworth family. By then, he had successfully conspired to meet his other hero, Coleridge. According to De Quincey's most recent biographer, knowing how much Coleridge needed opium ("and that he had written and spoken great things while on it"), De Quincey may have upped his own dosage, dragging him into worse nightmares. However, even without an opium habit, he was accustomed to brooding trances, in no small measure due to the intensity of his other habit—reading. The same might be said for dreamers at large before the electronic age, dramatically so in this age of expansive poets. Evening reading fed potent sleep visions.[30]

Educated Americans read Wordsworth, Coleridge, and Lord Byron with a passionate engagement most moderns can no longer appreciate. The Romantic poets spoke to the human condition as few could. Coleridge is especially pertinent to the discussion, because of his own admitted obsession with opiated dreams. Most famously (and questionably), he revealed publicly in 1816 that his masterpiece, "Kubla Khan," had come to him in a dream. The poet was convinced of the prophetic potential of "visions of the night," in which powers emerge that do not exist in any "day-dream of philosophy"; this was what Hamlet meant when he said to his closest comrade, "There are more things in heaven and earth, Horatio, / Than are dreamt of in your philosophy."

Artists, poets, and inventors have long insisted that some of their best productions came to them either in dreams or in some other form of "effortless thinking"; they take the imaginative segments and complete their plots. In

Coleridge's case, the poet was unable to let go of the subject of dreams at any time in his life. It continually perplexed him that the sleeping mind accepted every absurd distortion of waking life, such as the transformation of a known person into someone with impossible features or altered shape.

Depending on whose work one read, dreams were either a diagnostic tool or a disease; they meant something, or they meant nothing. Coleridge's notebooks show that he read the history, the medical literature. He did not deny physiological explanations of the sort to which Drs. Rush and Mitchill and their British counterparts subscribed. He believed many if not most dreams to be connected to "motions of the blood and nerves" or "oppressive air" in the stomach and bowels—manifestations of pain somewhere within the physical body. The "fevered imagination" the physicians kept bringing up connected his dark creativity to organic morbidity.

He took an interest in the Rachel Baker case, unwilling to reject the possibility that the young woman did, in fact, communicate with a divine entity when she sermonized from an unconscious state. And like Eliza Champlain, whose coffin dream prompted an urgent letter home, Coleridge wrote about his concerns for the health of a Mrs. Barlow after repeatedly dreaming about her—it all seemed ominous to him.[31]

Poets were the movie stars of the nineteenth century. As with celebrities today, the lives of the Romantic poets were intertwined. Coleridge published "Kubla Khan," with his prefatory explanation of its dream origin, at Lord Byron's instigation. In July 1816, the same year "Kubla Khan" was published, Byron wrote his deeply expressive poem "The Dream," from which this book's epigraph is drawn. It begins, "Our life is two-fold: Sleep hath its own world," and goes on at length to narrate a night's tale of two whose promise of enduring love is diverted and finally crushed.

Byron's dream may be an invention, but its structure resembles that of a raw dream. He chooses to begin six consecutive sections with the line "A change came over the spirit of my dream." (As we shall learn, Abraham Lincoln, a believer in the power of dreams, counted this poem as one of his favorites.) Summering in Switzerland with his poet friend Percy Bysshe Shelley, Byron composed the gloomy "Darkness." It opens with the line, "I had a dream, which was not all a dream," and proceeds to envision the extinction of suns, with desperate men on an icy earth setting forests on fire in a last hope to save the light. It is a beautifully wrought poem for a people who lived with death and could not govern their dreams.[32]

After Shelley's drowning death in July 1822, at the age of thirty, his disconsolate young widow told two female friends that she saw him in her dreams on a regular basis. A diary entry in February 1823 attests to her misery: "I was reading—I heard a voice say 'Mary'—'It is Shelley' I thought—the revulsion was of agony—Never more shall I hear his beloved voice." And a week later, this diary entry: "Visit me in my dreams tonight, my loved Shelley." The next year, it was Byron who died, at thirty-six, succumbing to a fever in Greece, where he had offered his services to a band of revolutionaries.[33]

The rakish poet-adventurer Byron was not always treated kindly in the American press. Eliza Champlain would have read in the *New-London Gazette* a defense of candidate John Quincy Adams's suitability for the presidency that distinguished his "restrained" nature from the "exceedingly alarming and dangerous" passions of "Byron and Buonaparte"—certainly an unflattering pairing. In 1825, advertising an ethereal Byron, the *New-York Mirror* printed a fantasy piece, "Literary Thermometer: A Dream." In it, an angel guided a dreaming "son of the earth" through scenes that eventually led him to a funeral procession: "It was the remains of Lord Byron, attended only by the nine muses." Americans found in Byron a larger-than-life dreamer, a veritable philosopher of dreaming. His open excesses—a profligate life made public—imitated the unrestrained, uncensored character of a dream world.[34]

As for the artist Eliza and the musical instrument manufacturer Edward, the couple married in 1826 and settled in Orange, New Jersey. She accepted painting commissions up to her wedding day, and he continued the family business. As a dream aficionado, she rendered her final decision on De Quincey's opium dreams: chilling, indeed, but not as powerful as what Shakespeare was able to dramatize. "I think Clarence's dream is ten thousand times more dreadful than any of his," she said of *Richard III*. "That dream is too well painted—for I died in reading it."[35]

She was referring to the suspenseful moment in Act I, Scene 4, as Clarence, brother to the murderous king, tells his jailer his dream of drowning:

> *O Lord! methought what pain it was to drown!*
> *What dreadful noise of waters in mine ears!*
> *What sights of ugly death within mine eyes!*

At the bottom of the sea, jewels sat in skulls where eyes once were, "And mock'd the dead bones that lay scatt'red by." Entering the "kingdom of perpetual night," Shakespeare's dreamer remains captive of his dark imagination:

. . . Then came wand'ring by
A shadow like an angel, with bright hair
Dabbled in blood, and he shrieked aloud. . . .

With the Furies of his dream still howling in his ears, Clarence tells of the awful, clamorous vision foreshadowing his fate. Eliza was right: no matter the depth of De Quincey's fear of Asiatics and crocodiles, it would be next to impossible for the opium-eater to shock the bard.

With his keen psychology and close attention to character, Shakespeare was a school unto himself. For his part, Byron dazzled in print. De Quincey constructed a long and successful writing career on the elevated reputation of his confessional book. Dreamers found support, and adopted the vitality they discovered, in the ardent imaginations of their literary models.

~⁊~

Charity Bryant loved women. At thirty, she met Sylvia Drake, eight years younger, and for the next forty-four years, they lived together—married in all but a legal sense. Until Charity's death at mid-century, they were accepted as a couple by the Vermont community in which they lived, leading active lives in the church and co-owning a tailoring business. Charity's affectionate nephew, the poet and newspaper editor William Cullen Bryant, went on to publish a story about their remarkable life together.

Before she met Sylvia, though, Charity was involved with a woman named Lydia Richards. After their physical relationship ended, they remained close friends. On two occasions, years apart, Lydia told Charity that she had appeared to her in a dream. In the first, she wrote: "I was seated in the west room at my Father's, near the bed, when you approach'd me with a radiance and sweet expression in your eyes which made too deep an impression on my mind to be dispell'd or erased by the beams of the morning." The second dream was more mysterious: "I was parting with you and after I had turn'd to leave you, thot of something further I wish'd to say and turn'd back, but seeing your face hid I again turn'd to leave you—but feeling unwilling to go without saying what I wished. . . ." The double take and indecision repeated, until at last Charity let her face be seen. Opening her eyes, she displayed tears, and then, in Lydia's words, she "look'd upon me with a smile which I return'd."[36]

A far less noble dream with sexual implications came to the attention of John Wurts, a prominent attorney in Philadelphia. He had served in the state legislature and was shortly to win election to Congress. In the early months of

1823, he received a confidential letter from an acquaintance, Roberts Vaux, a philanthropist who carried weight in the City of Brotherly Love. One of Vaux's chief interests was providing support to schools that accepted students from poor families. He served as president of the Board of Controllers for Public Schools and was personally involved in shaping school curricula.

It is understandable, then, that he would take a personal interest in the case of a teacher named Seixas, charged with molesting the young teenage girls who sat in his classroom. Somehow, the allegations against him had been kept out of the newspapers. Vaux did not want to see the matter swept under the rug and figured if Wurts knew what was going on in private meetings he might be able to do something. Seixas had a capable attorney working for him, and though the client looked guilty based on the testimony of several individuals, it was the unusual means by which Seixas was first fingered that gave the defense confidence it would win at trial.

According to Vaux, "it appears that the suspicion of improper conduct first originated from the circumstance of the mother of Letitia Ford having been disturbed by a dream, which she interpreted to augur something unfortunate to her daughter who was at that time under the care of Mr. Seixas." Based simply on her dream, Mrs. Ford presented her suspicions to a member of the school board, and "unknown to Mr. Seixas a private and strict examination into his conduct was instituted." Without taking the teacher's side, Vaux was incredulous: Who would believe that "any society of tolerably respectable individuals could play such a disgraceful farce before the community as that of instituting a solemn investigation on the ground of an old woman's dream"?

Pubescent middle-class girls were meant to be protected from masculine vulgarity in whatever form it took. Yet misogyny was also alive and well in nineteenth-century America, evidenced in tavern culture and in the kind of humor newspapers regularly published. A Philadelphia magazine of this era featured an essay on dreams, with a moral directed at women: "Females are most apt to put faith in dreams," it read. "Whether this be owing to a peculiar conformation of the brain [producing visionary thoughts]; or whether from the more secluded and domestic habits of women, they have more leisure to remember and reflect on the thoughts that intrude upon the sleeping hours, we shall not attempt to decide." Deemed easily susceptible to outside forces, weaker in critical apprehension, and, as a rule, more easily impressed than men, females were reckoned "naturally" prone to superstitious suggestion: "The belief in dreams is often strengthened and confirmed by those catch-penny publications, entitled dream books. . . . The most absurd explanations are set down as undeniable truth." This, apparently, is the tradition Roberts Vaux had in mind when he expressed incredulity that Mrs. Ford was actually being taken seriously.

The committee that evaluated the board's report voted that "the Dream of Letitia Ford's mother was utterly ridiculous," and that the investigation would proceed without paying any mind to the alleged victim's mother. By now, however, her claim of special sight was common knowledge, and the case could hardly be separated from the accusatory dream that fed it. Two key witnesses to the teacher's behavior, Letitia Ford and her classmate Catharine Hartman, stated that Seixas had been in their bedroom at night, yet they did not charge him with having "hugged or kissed" either of them. Someone else said he was seen "taking hold of the legs" of both, and for Vaux that was serious enough. When the "Matron" of the dormitory was apprised of this, she put bolts and bars on the girls' door to prevent further intrusion.

The statements of the girls were at this point "uncorroborated," according to the report Vaux cited in his letter to Wurts. Yet Seixas had refocused the attention of those like Vaux when he put his foot in his mouth—or, rather, his hands where they did not belong. "Uncorroborated!" Vaux expostulated. "He said he felt the girls heads." More students were coming forward, all commenting on the man's active hands: "Some of the girls say he put his hands under the clothes & felt their bodies." A teenage boy who did odd jobs around the school said he saw Seixas "taking gross liberties . . . , that when the girls were setting at their writing desks would put his arms over their shoulders and feels their bosoms & thighs."

Letitia Ford's mother had had a dream. Her sixth sense, or whatever it was, was right. But a dream only delegitimized what was otherwise a valid cause. Vaux made clear that he did not wish to get involved. Wurts may have felt the same, insofar as Seixas was known to have vocal supporters. In the end, given that no publicity ensued, the libidinous teacher appears to have escaped punishment.[37]

~∂

From the birth of the republic through the mid-1820s, the majority of recorded dreams were relatively uncomplicated and tended to focus on real-life concerns. Elizabeth Drinker, who saw a great deal of death and described it in her diaries, watched the houseguest in her dream choke on pork. Dolley Madison, who doted on her frail husband, saw him in an enclosed space, unable to move from "riding so far and so fast." From modern science, we learn that whatever emotional issue the person is addressing, the dreaming brain searches for contextualizing metaphors.

Even when early Americans were not dreaming of death directly, mortality was never far from the surface of their communications. They dreamt of distant loved ones, imagining them present. Fear of death bridged the days and weeks between letters received. Of this species of dream, Louisa Park's are probably the most pained and intimate, constituting a detailed record of the odd behavior and uncharacteristic conversation of her long-absent husband each time he visited her in the night.

Here is another of that ilk. Jane Bayard Kirkpatrick of New Brunswick, New Jersey, was fifty-three in 1825 when she had "a sweet vision" of her son Bayard, though he was in South America on business. "I saw him just as he looked in his picture," she recorded. "I thought I was sitting on the sopha—and he came behind—and leaned his head on my shoulder—and with an expression of tenderness & sensibility uncommon in him said to me 'dear mother, how happy I am in the persuasion of your love'—I laid my cheek by his—and waked."

The dream, which she herself described as "vivid," impelled her to reflect—but not on the science of dreaming. Instead, it was on the wonderful mystery dreams conveyed. She noted that she rarely dreamt of her son, and that the Bayard of her dream was a good deal more expressive of emotion than he was in life. This was especially satisfying to her. She had had less pleasant dreams about him a year and a half earlier, and in one of these pictured him in the middle of a war, "wounded—but not mortally." So she knew to suspect dream-borne prophecies.

In insisting (or, at least, confiding to her journal) that it was not "weakness or folly" for a person to pay attention to her dreams, Kirkpatrick defied the medical consensus. "We know so little of the spiritual world," she breathed. "But every one has observed striking coincidences in their feelings with those of absent friends—which could not be accounted for—which seemed some thing more than chance." She is saying: do not discount spiritual communion, though it be little understood.[38]

As the nineteenth century advanced, a new pattern began to emerge. Bizarre content was finding its way into dream records that are more varied and unpredictable. The one element that does not disappear, however, is the presence of morbid imagery.

Benjamin Rush was anomalous among those of the Revolutionary generation in his willingness to confront the bizarre in dreams. Perhaps this was because, as a heralded medical expert, he was freer to experiment with his thoughts. Everyone else was convinced by the likes of Dr. Rush that dreams were only to be associated with dangerous thoughts and delusions, excessive sensibility, hypochondria, hysteria, and mental weakness. The many and varied classifications of insanity and the aggressiveness of doctors who thought they understood more than they really did about the human psyche must have weighed on dreamers' minds and restrained their pens—after all, no one wanted to sound mad.

The bizarreness of dream content (skipping from place to place, people appearing and disappearing, an irrational conflation of images) is something science can explain fairly well now. Bert O. States, a literary theorist who has studied the science of dreams for decades, describes the phenomenon as a "warring process" taking place within the brain when "chaotic 'bottom-up' brain-stem activation" comes into contact with "'top-down' cortical attempts to make sense of the resulting disorder." Bizarreness is "the natural consequence of dreams exercising the power of association while the body is 'off-line.'" Associations collide.[39]

Citizens in the early years of the republic, rather than stigmatize themselves, limited themselves to acceptable scenarios in dreams that they narrated. They wrote down dreams that they could nearly understand. As the nineteenth century proceeded, the necessity of doing that diminished. Workaday people marveled as the poets captured the wild beauty of dreams and artfully imagined the outer limits of what a dream can say. If regular folks could not express themselves in the language of Byron, Shelley, and Coleridge, they still conveyed in dreams, whether plain or adorned, how they confronted their fears, tried to remain psychologically intact, or simply bore up. The dreamy poet, with his broad appeal, stole the show from the straitlaced medical theorist. Byron was more than a showman performing for a voyeuristic public; he could say what others were loath to say or incapable of reproducing.

It is not easy for us, who generally think of poetry as a less infectious, even obscure, form of literature, to appreciate just how deep an impression Lord Byron made on Americans. History commands us to recognize that selfhood has a history. For earlier generations, poetry was a key part of personal development. It stimulated an assertiveness of belief and a quality of mind that sustained faith in the forces of nature—a faith similar in impact to what words of ancient scripture do for the conventionally religious.

FIVE

HENRY DAVID THOREAU GAINS EVIDENCE OF REINCARNATION

The witchcraft of sleep divides with truth the empire of our lives.
—Ralph Waldo Emerson

Caroline Lee Hentz, age thirty-six in 1836, operated a girls' school with her French-born artist-zoologist husband in Florence, Alabama. "I awoke in the night oppressed by a horrible dream," she penned in her diary, not eager to write down the particulars. Clearly feeling anxious, she wondered on the page: "What are dreams? Do they not sometimes assume the form of avenging spirits? Mysterious operations of the imagination, unguided by the will, shadows of the past & images of the future—fearful in their obscurity & intensity, whence do they come & wherefore are they sent?" The French poet Charles Baudelaire, a contemporary of hers known for his haunting language as well as for the use of hashish and laudanum, was more willing to accept what comes: "In sleep, that adventure-filled journey we make every night, there is something positively miraculous; it is a miracle whose mystery has been blunted by its regular occurrence."

Good dreams, bad dreams. Dream researchers nowadays tell us that something like three-quarters of our dreams are of the latter variety. Three nights before Caroline Hentz recorded the above musings, she noted "piercing shrieks" coming from the home of a neighbor who was abusing his wife and family at bedtime; three days after the "horrible" dream, it was: "Oh! how the visions of the past dim & awful floated around me, as I sat by the fading embers, in the loneliness of the midnight hour."

Her own marriage was less than ideal. Caroline's obsessively jealous husband had orchestrated their move to Alabama from Cincinnati two years earlier, owing to her apparently innocent friendship with another man. Oppressed by her neighbor's exhibition of rude passion, Mrs. Hentz remained fixated on evil as darkness fell.[1]

—⁂—

To dream is to create a story, but to do so in a way that resembles writing on a fogged-up mirror. As the air dries, the writing on the mirror disappears; we see ourselves again as we always see ourselves when the mist is not present to divert our attention.

Washington Irving (1783–1859) did more than anyone else in early America to normalize, as well as sentimentalize, the dream. In "Rip Van Winkle," and a number of stories that are less well known today, he blended literal dreams with travel through history. The village good-for-nothing Rip goes into the Catskill mountains with his dog and his hunting rifle and dreams away twenty years, missing the American Revolution while visiting and drinking with gnomish Dutch bowlers who had sailed with Henrik Hudson a century and a half before.

Irving wanted his reader left in awe of the supernatural, but not defeated by it. Going to places where the mind questioned its authority was his specialty. The short epigraph that precedes "The Legend of Sleepy Hollow," drawn from eighteenth-century Scottish poet James Thompson, describes the atmospherics inside the sleeping mind's eye: "A pleasing land of drowsy head it was, / Of dreams that wave before the half-shut eye." In many of his stories over the years, Irving bent and displaced time—just what a dream does—as he toyed with the fragility, with the very insubstantiality, of human memory.

One of the tales in his transatlantic bestseller, the *Sketch Book* (1819–1920), is "The Mutability of Literature," which involves a twisted encounter in Westminster Abbey. It opens with the sentence: "There are certain half-dreaming moods of mind in which we naturally steal away from noise and glare, and seek some quiet haunt where we may indulge our reveries and build our air castles undisturbed." The "solemn monastic air" of the Abbey library creates a half-dreaming mood for Irving's first-person narrator, the lone occupant of the stacks, who literally hears long-unconsulted books speak to him. The story ends with the narrator wondering "whether all this . . . actually took place, or whether it was another of those odd day-dreams to which I am subject." In *Bracebridge Hall* (1822), the second in Irving's *Sketch Book* series, the niece of the estate's housekeeper "has always had her head full of love and matrimony. She knows the dream book by heart, and is quite an oracle among the little girls of the family, who always come to her to interpret their dreams in the mornings."[2]

He is popularly recalled as the author of elegant tall tales, but the real Washington Irving was not so starry-eyed as that. He indulged in as much gothic horror as friendly folklore, and he mocked superstition more than he promoted dreaming. Usually in his stories, mysteries turn out to have logical, rational explanations: the headless horseman is a monster that does not exist beyond Ichabod Crane's oversized imagination. Though a master storyteller and later in his career the hero-worshipping biographer of both Christopher Columbus and George Washington, Irving appreciated the fundamental irony of history—so overwhelming that it obliges us to simplify and forget. His writings, taken together, demonstrate that every individual, in greater or lesser ways, relies on imagination to paint acceptable pictures for the ego.

One would expect that the first American to succeed at making authorship his full-time profession—he whose tale of the twenty-year sleep became a long-running play that toured the country, he who made the metaphor of the dream a staple of his literature—would have written down some raw dreams of his own. But in the several decades worth of notebook-keeping and original sketching he did, Irving provides little insight into his dream world. Among the thousands of pages, fragments of thought, and unfinished stories that have been preserved, there is but a narrow window of time, while he lived in France in the mid-1820s, when Irving revealed the difficulty he often had sleeping. In that one notebook, jarred by the inward experience of one alarm-filled night, he left a trademark anxiety dream.

We begin with his daily notebook in the final month of 1823, when we have the following:

December 7: "Night of troubled dreams." December 8: "Uncomfortable dreams again." December 13: "Woke early—restless and anxious—full of doubts as to literary prospects—After breakfast tried to summon up ideas to write but in vain." December 16: "Night of broken sleep." December 20: "After a night of broken rest and scanty sleep, rise at 8." December 21: "Again a watchful night—rendered more irksome by the intolerable howling of a dog in a neighboring yard." December 22: "Night of broken sleep."

The same pattern continued through 1824, with such notations as: "Out of spirits—distrustful of my work"; "a rainy day—felt good for nothing." He briefly mentions "vivid dreams" about the Fosters, a mother and two daughters who had virtually adopted Irving in Dresden in 1822. Calling on them daily, he studied German and put on plays with the girls, until the lifelong bachelor confessed to the mother that he fantasized about marrying her elder daughter.[3]

In the autumn of 1825, the author was staying in mild, low-lying Bordeaux. He was waiting for an opportunity to cross the Pyrenees and see firsthand the supernaturally eerie landscape of the Man of La Mancha. It was in Bordeaux, then, that he recorded the one noteworthy dream from his time abroad. It happened as he was fretting over a loss of appetite and repeatedly complaining of sleepless nights.

November 15: "A night of frequent waking—broken dreams—about failures of [banking] houses." (As the day proceeds, he receives letters about the financial woes of friends who have invested as he has.) "Seems as if my dreams & forebodings were realized. . . . Went to bed but did not get to sleep until twelve."

November 18: "Awoke at 4. Laid awake with my mind full of anxious thoughts."

November 23: "Awake early. . . . Wrote but very little today."

November 24: "In bed this morning thought of a plan of a miscellany."

And now we arrive at the only dream Irving ever detailed:

November 25: "Last night dreamt of being in a large old house—found it giving way above, escaped and saw it falling to ruins—It took fire—tho[ugh]t all my property & especially my Mss: [i.e., manuscripts] were in it—rushed towards the house exclaiming I am now not worth a six pence—Found one room in the house uninjured—my brother E.I. in it. Arranging papers, wiping books &c, told me that he had just managed to save every thing that belonged to us, by putting them in this one room that remains uninjured—the dream was doubtless occasioned by my letter to E.I. written yesterday requesting him in case of difficulty to place my literary property, &c in the hands of Brevoort or J.T.I."[4]

E.I. was Ebenezer Irving, an older sibling with a more astute business mind, who regularly monitored his complicated brother's U.S. publishing interests. Brevoort was Henry Brevoort, whose financial resources were endless;

he and Washington Irving were former roommates and lifelong intimates. J.T.I. was John Treat Irving, the brother who had risen in legal circles and would cap his career as a prominent New York City judge. Washington, the youngest (and least pragmatic) of the Irving clan, was long accustomed to his elders' guidance and regularly sought their financial backing.

Unlike the dreamy tales for which Irving was famous on both sides of the Atlantic, his own dream did not require imagination to invent. He lived on the edge when he invested a large chunk of his book royalties in much-hyped projects, such as a French canal that lost money. He had also watched his family's Liverpool export business go bust.

Fortunes came and went in the volatile decade of the 1820s. In failing to marry, Irving used the rationale that his writings did not bring in enough for him to support a wife. In his most recent anthology, *Tales of a Traveller,* he had centered a number of stories on robbery, squandered inheritance, a money-lender who preys on his neighbors, and buried treasure found and abandoned. So an anxiety dream about a devastating property loss is hard to read as anything but a reflection of the author's own pressing financial concerns.

But the existence of a secret room in the dream—a room discovered by Ebenezer, a room immune from fire—is indeed curious. Part of Irving's literary stock-in-trade was the unlucky room, the mysterious portrait that gazed out suspiciously, the haunted house, a palpitating heart, characters unable to extricate themselves from unnerving situations. It is entirely likely that a good bit of the literature that emerged from the shadowy recesses of his mind was adapted from his literal dreams. If only this dream-obsessed storyteller had consented to give history more of the inner man.

In surveying the literature of 1820–1850, I find a host of adjectives before the word "dream." Listed here on a scale from neutral to fear inspiring is a fair sampling of such dream modifiers: curious, singular, golden, enchanted, winged, fantastic, frozen, indistinct, misty, idle, unquiet, fearful, troubled, confused, bewildering, disagreeable, wild and weary, wild and baseless, dismal and fading, feverish, ominous, ghastly, treacherous.

Dreams served as a tool for pulp novelists, an easy excuse to add embellishment to their stories. In the literature of the prior century, options were fewer. To draw upon a single, but accurate, example, there was Samuel Johnson's 1759 *Rasselas,* an adventure in search of knowledge, undertaken along the banks of the Nile by a prince of Abyssinia. The word "dream" appears a number of times, but is never once modified. It is: "They dream away their time"; lovers "exchange glances, reciprocate civilities, go home and dream of one another"; men of folly "dreamest" of riches and power; "Life passes in dreams of rapture or of anguish." Surface description seems to suffice—yet it was Johnson who only four years earlier had completed his renowned dictionary of the English language and had every recognized word at his disposal.[5]

Now, dreams in literature could shift from inviting suggestions to grotesque imagery before the reader even noticed. In an 1835 magazine story by Willis Gaylord Clark, the narrator speaks almost euphorically at first about the oddity of dreams. Soon he is coming apart at the seams: "Reader, did you never have queer dreams? Had you ever a vision of being at a fashionable party, and all at once discover that you had no coat on? That one of your feet was a broom, wherewith, in obedience to some superior mandate, you were engaged in both dancing and sweeping?" Then, exploiting the current passion for frontier stories, the author seizes the nearest trope: "It is hard work to run in a dream. I have been chased by Indians thus, and could never get on. Some horrid weight hangs to one's feet; he feels the breath of his enemy on his shoulders and neck—but it seems an age ere he is overtaken. It is folly to say that it is not unpleasant to be killed in a dream."

To convince his reader that everyone speaks the language of dreams, Clark repeats the classic nightmare of being trapped in a primal void. "Methought I was crossing an immense abyss, on a single grape-vine, with Apollyon [the Devil] for a pilot. I forget his appearance exactly, but it was hideous in the extreme. He led me over the dark and dismal void, until I had reached the midway part of the vine, when he attempted the gymnastic feat of throwing me off. I caught him by the hair, which me-seemed was composed of red hot wires. . . ." As the fiend falls away, the narrator claims he can still hear the "thunder" that roared through his dream.[6]

William Dunlap, known mostly for his plays, published a novel in 1836 titled *Thirty Years Ago; or the Memoir of a Water Drinker.* A character named Cooke, "his face buried in the bed-clothes," insists that the terrifying thoughts he has been experiencing were "caused by an imagination distempered from the previous day's excess"—long the standard, medically informed explanation for a dream. He says he does not know whether what he saw was dream or reality, and he tries to rationalize: "I saw her—heard her—in a miserable hovel—sick—stretched on her death-bed—poor—starving—dying! I have had such visions before in my sleep, after my waking thoughts have been employed on the past; but never like this. I heard her voice! It rings in my ears still!" Cooke is consumed by the emotion he has dredged up from old memory and is put off balance by the corrupted state of his present consciousness. He wants "to drown the thought of the past." Seeing a youthful version of himself in his sleep confuses him, and the confusion is his undoing: "I lose time—time! I have lost time, indeed!" In the space of fifteen years, we have moved from Irving's lovable rogue Rip Van Winkle, traveling through time in his sleep, to the sorrows and regrets of a host of haunted minds.[7]

Imagination had become the source of preoccupation for more people—that is what the textual evidence all points to. It was no time for complacency. When Lord Byron wrote of pain and beauty, an alternately tender and intense juxtaposition of words established his power in the reader's mind. But as "wild" as his reality was, he did not completely detach dream from that reality, nor did the dream overpower waking thoughts.

To be sure, the sensations of night were never a matter of indifference. The American literati saw savagery in dream nature. In the democratizing 1830s, their dreams seemed, by some irony, capable of chipping away at the quintessential American value of individual freedom. To describe the shift a bit differently, the term "imagination" had been closely related to "reverie" before this moment arrived. Now imagination loomed somewhere between reverie and monomania, which rendered it suspect. This displacement would not last, however, because early Americans could not stomach cynicism for any length of time.

~ぬ~

William Wirt (1772–1834), the longest-serving attorney general in the history of the United States, held this position throughout the back-to-back administrations of James Monroe and John Quincy Adams. An emotional writer and accomplished orator, he was chosen, in 1826, to deliver the official joint eulogy on the careers of Adams and Jefferson in the U.S. Capitol. Being the chief executive's top legal authority was not a full-time job in the mid-1820s, so Wirt, Maryland born, spent much of his time in Baltimore in private practice. This meant that his wife, Elizabeth, remained at home in Washington, D.C., caring for their large family. Being apart more than they were together for a good many years, husband and wife wrote each other constantly.

In 1825, Wirt's work caused him to miss Christmas. "I am surrounded by the documents in several cases that are pressing for trial," he wrote home.

Elizabeth interpreted his absence differently. "Do you love me?" she wrote back. "Or are you angry with me. I dreamt you had taken to yourself another wife."

Because it was a dream, the irrational could be presented with deadpan credulity. If she saw her husband leaving her for "old Mrs. Turner," the jilted wife did not have to languish, for "she did not live long to tease me." Elizabeth explained: "This was after hearing one of the children read a story of some Indian that had done the like—and the first wife killed herself by rowing to the falls of the Niagara."

The attorney general's reply was blithe spirited. "Do I love you? dearest— Ay, do I love you—and when I love you not, chaos is come again. . . . What a dream was that? another wife!—I promise you that when I take another wife it shall be old Mrs. Turner." Should old Mrs. Turner be dream code for a young bride, Wirt wanted to reassure the mother of his children that he was no more likely to abandon her for a woman in her prime than he was to wed an ancient one. "And now I think your heart may be at ease—another wife, another! Pray does your coach need a fifth wheel?"[8]

Salmon P. Chase (1808–1873) was another cabinet member whose personal papers contain dream records. Best known to history as Abraham Lincoln's secretary of the Treasury, he was born in New Hampshire but came to live with an uncle in Cincinnati after his father, a state senator, went bankrupt and died. Upon graduation from Dartmouth College, Chase traveled to Washington, where he taught school and fell in with none other than William and Elizabeth Wirt, becoming a surrogate member of their active family in 1829. Despite evidence of a flirtation between Chase and two of the Wirt daughters, he concentrated on getting a top-notch legal education and returned to Cincinnati as a practicing attorney. There he met and married Catharine Garniss in March 1834.

Happiness was short-lived. Catherine ("Kitty," he called her) died at the beginning of December 1835, after giving birth to a daughter. Chase had reluctantly left for Philadelphia ten days earlier and hurried back to Ohio by steamboat after receiving a letter informing him that she had taken a turn for the worse. "She passed away almost insensibly—without a struggle—without even a sigh," he recorded, repeating what his father-in-law, at her bedside till the end, communicated to him. The young widower chided himself: "I was far away."

He devised a narrative to feed his memory, but it offered little comfort. "At the moment of her death I was thinking of her, I believe, but little dreaming of her situation." He did not really mean he was dreaming—not yet. He arrived home to find Kitty lying in her coffin. "I kneeled before her, and implored

God to restore her to me. My prayer was not heard. I kissed her cold lips. They returned no pressure as they were wont. I pressed her cold, but still noble, forehead. She was dead."[9]

The aggrieved husband felt powerless. As the bitter month of December slowly passed, he noted in his private journal: "I rose this morning with a heavy heart. I had been dreaming of accompanying my dear wife to church & I awoke to the mournful conviction that never more should we walk to the house of God in company or take sweet counsel together." Kitty had been more religious than he, and he found himself entertaining the errant thought of "meeting my dear-dear wife as an accusing spirit at the bar of God" and being reproached for lacking any real spiritual routine. He took to reading a book on midwifery and wrote: "I feel extremely sorry that I did not study this subject before the sickness of my wife."[10]

As the new year, 1836, arrived, he gave himself over to caring for their child. "My little babe continues to improve," he wrote hopefully. "She enjoys the most perfect health & now takes considerable notice of many things. She smiles & laughs now & then, awake & in dreams." He called upon his own dreams, unsuccessfully, to soften the blow; and he tried convincing himself that the infant's dreams had the potential to communicate across the void. But all hope was tentative: "Dear—dear Kitty—life of my life is it possible that thou art gone?"

In late January, Chase gave a further indication of the release he sought but had not obtained: "I dreamed last night—as I do almost every night—of my dear departed wife: but I cannot now recollect my dream. It has passed from me like the visions of Nebuchadnizzar [*sic*]." In the intense cold of a winter morning, after a dream that he was not allowed to remember, he turned to the Almighty. "Oh how my heart aches," he confessed, "when I think that my dear wife is not permitted to join in these delightful exercises but I do hope that she is worshipping the same God in a better Society."[11]

What should an educated man of the nineteenth century do to offset feelings of impotence? Salmon Chase, suddenly a single parent, was reading about midwifery. As though he might learn enough to save another new mother and establish an emotional equilibrium, he hoped for knowledge and power at a disabling moment in his life.

There was little to hope for in the advance of medicine during this period. In fact, a return to superstition was helping some people find consolation. Phrenology, the pseudoscientific notion that character could be read according to the shape of the skull, was meant to supply the same sorts of answers that dream interpretation provided. While J. L. Comstock, M.D., author of a physiology text, remained skeptical of the practice, he was not completely dismissive. At least one medical thinker he respected associated superior intellect with "a capacious and prominent forehead."

In his male-directed book, Comstock recommended regular physical activity and eight hours of sleep. He warned against the feminization of men: "When we see a person of feeble muscular powers easily thrown into agitation, turning pale, or fainting by slight causes, and morbidly sensitive to every nervous impression, we may conclude that in such persons the sentient-nervous system predominates. . . . In such persons, the flesh is commonly soft to the touch, and has a pallid hue."

The language of medicine had scarcely moved from where it stood in the late eighteenth century: excessive study, the sedentary life, luxurious living, and habitual melancholy were conditions that allowed a dangerous nervous temperament to develop. When the men who read and absorbed such literature had their lives uprooted, as Salmon Chase did, and found in their dreaming an inner world of confusion, they were left to grieve and warned against submitting too long to melancholia. If uncontained emotions unmanned the lovelorn, the unscientific dream book and other kinds of pseudoscience promised to restore at least some measure of control.[12]

Take the curious case of Nahum Capen, a bookseller, whom we know of through the diary of Christopher Columbus Baldwin in the mid-1830s. The self-educated Capen, "a confirmed phrenologist," held the belief that "the fetus in the womb may be disfigured by the imagination of the mother." Baldwin called it nonsense, convinced that God would never be "so cruel as to subject the fetus to the hazard of becoming a monster through the visionary and silly dreams of the mother." But Capen insisted on the correctness of his doctrine, going a step further to state that he had "brought his mind to an elevated state, and permitted nothing to disturb his cogitations" when setting about to conceive a child. What power did the spirit possess? Capen's wacky philosophy was not something he invented, but a holdover from olden times. The question he raised—"What power did the spirit possess?"—mattered to Americans who came of age in the middle decades of the century.[13]

～∞～

The Boston birthplace of Ralph Waldo Emerson (1803–1882) was near that of another of America's famous men of letters, Benjamin Franklin.

Ralph Waldo Emerson (1803–1882), who arguably gave more thought to the nature of dreaming than any other literary figure in early America.

Like Franklin, Emerson influenced conduct and culture in what he wrote. But because the nineteenth-century reading public was so much larger than that of the eighteenth, his celebrity was extended through touring and lecturing. In England, he met Coleridge shortly before the poet's death ("What a living soul, what a universal knowledge!"), and he was entirely charmed by the effervescent

Thomas De Quincey. "The Opium Eater is the ruler of the Night," young Emerson gushed.[14]

He stands out as one who in tangible ways incorporated his personal dream experience into a philosophy of life. Son and grandson of New England ministers, educated at Harvard, he was a moralist, poet, and spiritual teacher, an idealist who believed that divinity attached to all things, that the mind's free expression was glorious. Over his long life, Emerson never retreated from his early sense of transport. Life was not to be divorced from adventure, nor laughter from genius.

His 1839 lecture "Demonology" dramatized the benefit of maintaining a healthy astonishment toward all things. He began the address by defending its title and establishing his purpose of evaluating the mystical bent to human nature: "Demonology covers dreams, omens, coincidences, luck, sortilege, magic and other experiences which shun rather than court inquiry, and deserve notice chiefly because every man has usually in his lifetime two or three hints of this kind which are specially impressive to him." It was an invitation to wander within the mind.

The Emerson of "Demonology" marvels at the mind's defiance of reason. Dreams are marked, he says, by the "painful imperfection" of that which lodges in memory. "Jealous of being remembered," they "dissipate instantly and angrily if you try to hold them." He notes their déjà vu character, too, how they at once toy with waking experience and taunt the sleeping mind with suggestions that something we believe has occurred may actually not have. His emotionally resonant word choice ("painful," "angrily," "jealous") underscores the notion that even a pleasing dream is demanding. As the philosopher for a new age, he hoped to make sense of the difference between the body's architecture and an uncontained nature, between the structured and nonstructured.[15]

As time passed, Emerson ruminated more and more on the psychological trauma that comes into a mind asleep. "Hideous" was an adjective he was apt to use before "dreams" in his personal journals. He was not past querying, as medical tradition demanded, whether his nightmares were "any more than exaggerations of the sins of the day." On one occasion, awakening his demons in order to challenge them, he jotted roguishly: "It is extremely disagreeable, nay, a little fiendish to laugh amid dreams. In bed I would keep my countenance, if you please." He chokes back a droplet of defensiveness in this seemingly harmless squib.

Emerson's dreams must have featured animals from time to time, because he liked to invest his dream commentaries with observations about the puzzles that wildlife presented. "The birds fly from us," he wrote in 1835, "and we do not understand their music." Their literal singing was a language both enrapturing and distant, like the untranslatable part of a dream. "Such is now the discord betwixt man and nature," he lamented, judging it "strange that our life is accompanied by Dreams on one side, and by Animals on the other, as monuments of our ignorance." The inner lives of animals, and dreams in general, left human beings in the dark. Emerson will not let go of the phenomenon. He says in "Demonology" that "Animals have been called 'the dreams of Nature.'" And: "Perhaps for a conception of their consciousness we may go to our own dreams." Beyond the possibility of shared sympathies (here Emerson is conflicted), men and beasts both experience a shared sensation of imprisonment: as a dog must obey, so we must obey—in our dreams.[16]

Lest it appear otherwise, Ralph Waldo was not traumatized. "Dreams have a poetic integrity and truth," he assures in "Demonology." (This pithy assertion copies an entry in his journal made four years earlier: "The dreams of an idealist have poetic integrity and truth.") He has decided that the refusal of dreams to be chained down is a good thing—it is how they can have a freeing effect on the mind.

But nothing about them comes easy; that's always his main point. Dreams "have a double consciousness, at once sub- and ob-jective," he says, before hijacking his philosophical argument through impressment of a seafaring metaphor: "We call the phantoms that rise [in dreams], the creation of our fancy, but they act like mutineers, and fire on their commander." He knows that dreams confuse as well as create ideas, and they backfire when they are misunderstood; but he credits them as integral to the knowledge-gathering process, "the maturation of opinions not carried out to statements." In challenging fixed assumptions about what is real and what is not, they are the putative carriers of future reality.[17]

Having joked or jousted with himself that it was "a little fiendish to laugh amid dreams," he admitted that he enjoyed the absurd, whether awake or asleep. "In my dream," he recorded the same year as he gave the "Demonology" lecture, "I saw a man reading in the library at Cambridge, and one who stood by said, 'He readeth advertisements,' meaning that he read for the market only & not for truth. Then I said,—Do I read advertisements?"

Another vision, a year later, took conventional form, but not for long. "I dreamed that I floated at will in the great Ether, and I saw this world floating also not far off, but diminished to the size of an apple. Then an angel took it in his hand & brought it to me and said, 'This must thou eat.' And I ate the world." One Emerson scholar has interpreted this as a reversal of the story of Genesis, in which eating the fruit of the tree of knowledge is good (a repudiation of original sin). To the dreamer himself, however, it does not seem to matter what it means; in its heckling of philosophy it is already satisfying.[18]

Here is one that went completely haywire: "A droll dream last night, whereat I ghastly laughed." In it, he found himself attending a conference on the institution of marriage, when one of the speakers all of a sudden "turned on the audience the spout of an engine which was copiously supplied from within the wall with water." The man shook the hose in all directions and "drove all the company out of the house." The dreaming Emerson relished the scene: "I stood watching astonished & amused at the malice & vigor of the orator, I saw the spout lengthened by a supply of hose behind, & the man suddenly brought it round a corner & drenched me as I gazed. I woke up relieved to find myself quite dry." With such risk-taking admissions as these, we have clearly moved past the humorless standard of interpretation propagated by the medical community. Emerson rejects the notion that some gastronomical reaction caused his beautiful, bizarre dream. His recorded postscript illuminates his lighter side: "the Institution of marriage was safe for tonight."[19]

Though he welcomed his dreams, Emerson constantly struggled with their jigsaw character: "I passed into a room where were ladies & gentlemen, some of whom I knew. I did not wish to be recognized because of some disagreeable task, I cannot remember what." One of the females was beautiful, and he sensed that they were lovers. Yet she failed to recognize him, which he thought "unpardonable," until he figured out that he had never proposed to her. The scene changed. At the center of the dream now was "a common street-boy . . . walking with an air of determination." But nothing more. "'Tis all vain," Emerson concluded. "I cannot restore the dream."[20]

The motive force in any dream plot is often as ambiguous as the choice of characters is. We are apt, after waking, to wonder why, at the most awkward or immobilizing moment in the dream when we are stuck in place, we could not have simply transformed into our willful selves when we needed to do so to exit the dream gracefully. Add to this the moral ambiguity that can accompany human attraction in a dream. The beautiful woman stood before Emerson as a challenge—he had only half an idea of who she was and how he should handle her presence.

He consciously employed metaphors to contrast the tactile, or tangible, with the illusory. For instance, in an 1838 journal entry: "The landscape and scenery of dreams seem not to fit us, but like a cloak or coat from some other person, to overlap and incumber the wearer." Nature "fit" man when awake, but dreams hung loosely, uneasily. Another aspect of Emerson's dream life, familiar to us, is the arbitrary scene-shifting that invites doubt. He rendered emotional judgments about the content of his dreams, while questioning his capacity to discern correctly. Whether it is his feeling small, fearing rejection, or being pressed into a service he would rather not perform, Emerson seems to speak to the universality of certain dream-enhanced emotions.

We perceive a slow but steady transition in dream construction. In 1800, Louisa Park recorded dreams of yearning. Her husband, long absent at sea, returned without warning, bedraggled but presumably much the richer in having looted an enemy vessel. She did not understand the gloom that shed about him, and company kept them from consummating their love until the last scene of the dream. Events and behaviors may not make logical sense, but the scenes the dreamer describes are literal enough that they can be easily staged. Four decades later, Ralph Waldo Emerson recorded dreams with less plot and greater absurdity: a conference on marriage is interrupted by a water engine drenching those in attendance. The trajectory is from structured narratives with clear components to less structured narratives containing more descriptive (and more implied) emotion.[21]

The background to this transition involves literary representation more generally. American letters and the American picturesque were in sync during the third and fourth decades of the nineteenth century. Artists put the viewer in the position of a privileged observer, comparable to the staging of an autobiographical dream. The painted panorama conjured a superior nature, lofty and imposing, a rarified atmosphere with a psychological impact that was deliberate and irresistible.

When the real was decidedly beyond words, it was dreamlike. After completion of the Erie Canal in 1825, tourists flocked to an as yet undeveloped Niagara Falls and struggled to find words for the majesty of what they beheld. Daniel Webster wrote of the spectacle: "Water, vapor, foam & the atmosphere, are all mixed up together in sublime confusion." Niagara was improbable enough to be compared to the sublime confusion of a dream. James Fenimore

Cooper's *Leatherstocking Tales* and Washington Irving's otherworldly histories of Moorish Spain (and, after 1835, his equally exotic celebrations of the western frontier of America) combined with Byronic verse to offer readers the kinds of moving scenery that helped stimulate new fields of inner vision.[22]

Emerson was part of this movement. In his essays and poems, especially those that concern grand nature and the human soul, we find amazing vistas. His poem "Woodnotes II" removes the boundary between exterior and interior nature:

> *The rushing metamorphosis*
> *Dissolving all that fixture is,*
> *Melts things that be to things that seem,*
> *And solid nature to a dream.*

Inward forces tax the mind, but do not use it up. As such, the Emersonian effect in dreaming is to wake feeling agreeably overwhelmed—responsible for the dream, but not exhausted by it.[23]

~∂

In terms of his commitment of pen to paper, Emerson was the most noble, mobile, and energetic American dreamer since Benjamin Rush. In 1842, he reached out to the financially strapped Nathaniel Hawthorne (1804–1864) and rented his Concord, Massachusetts, home to the shy, little-known writer. An early tale of Hawthorne's, "The Haunted Mind," depicts dreams as gloomy signs. "A funeral train comes gliding by your bed," Hawthorne writes. And little changes, in that regard, as his career takes off.

Dour, almost brooding compared to his beaming landlord, Hawthorne published "The Celestial Rail-Road" in 1844, a short work patterned after John Bunyan's *Pilgrim's Progress,* the seventeenth-century Christian allegory of the path to heaven. Both Bunyan and Hawthorne use the literary conceit that his work is the record of a dream.[24] But Hawthorne, unlike Emerson, saw dreams only as symbols of man's failure to live well; in his stories, they tend to be destructive of spirit. He clearly did not believe that the dream could be used to reflect inspiration or artistry.

Hawthorne's wife, Sophia Peabody, had an abiding interest in the occult, according to the memoir of their son Julian. For a time she communed with the family's governess, whose "mediumistic powers" attracted her, and she listened to "messages seemingly from another world"; but when "pious and heavenly" imagery yielded to the "sinister and unpleasant," she gave up on the prospect of obtaining any extrasensory understanding. As to the essential difference between Emerson and Hawthorne, the son says: "Emerson was always on the trail of the Sphinx; Hawthorne and the Sphinx had been playmates from childhood." In other words, Hawthorne was content to leave mysteries alone.[25]

Another of Emerson's Concord circle, Henry David Thoreau (1817–1862), ruminated often on the potential of dreams. Thoreau, described by Julian as a "short, dark, unbeautiful man," lived under the same roof as Emerson and his family in the early 1840s, serving as the children's tutor, and in 1845 he famously moved out to Walden Pond (on land owned by Emerson). From here, he became a tax resister, graduating to the lecture circuit as a proponent of civil disobedience. He became ever more a student of nature, and in 1854 he published his beloved *Walden, or Life in the Woods*.

It was in his self-published *A Week on the Concord and Merrimack Rivers* (1849) that Thoreau first incorporated the dream theme into his work. This short, digressive book describes a trip that he and his by then deceased brother took ten years before. (Thoreau actually composed the text during his year at Walden Pond.) Englishman Edward Young divided his epic poem *Night Thoughts* into nine nights; the Yankee Thoreau divided his philosophical journey into seven days and nights.

In the concluding passages of Wednesday, Thoreau wrote: "I dreamed this night of an event which had occurred long before." The event in question was an argument he had had with a friend, and he was still pained by the memory of it. "But in my dream," he found, "I received that compensation which I had never obtained in my waking hours." The compensation was satisfaction—deliverance—reconciliation. For Thoreau, an awakening took place in the dream state, rooted in resistance to the self-deception that sleep brought about. "In dreams we see ourselves naked and acting out our real characters," he wrote paradigmatically. "Our truest life is when we are in dreams awake."[26]

His private journals tell us still more. "I awoke this morning to infinite regret," he wrote in 1851. "In my dream I had been riding, but the horses bit each other and occasioned endless trouble and anxiety, and it was my employment to hold their heads apart. Next I sailed over the sea in a small vessel such as the Northmen used, as it were to the Bay of Fundy [off the northeast coast of Maine], and thence overland I sailed, still over the shallows about the sources of rivers toward the deeper channel of a stream which emptied into the Gulf beyond."

Thoreau identified the geography in his dream based on what he was reading the night before: a book about Canadian seafaring that he found particularly absorbing. The Bay of Fundy boasts the world's most extreme range between high and low tide, making it a natural phenomenon. As a lover of natural wonders, the critical dreamer was carried off with the tide of his dream to such an extent that his very emotion surprised him.

"Again I was on my small pleasure-boat," he says, "and I raised my sail before my anchor, which I dragged far into the sea. I saw the buttons which had come off the coats of drowned men, and suddenly I saw my dog—when I knew not that I had one—standing in the sea up to his chin." From this familiar absurdity, he suddenly finds himself elsewhere: "And then I was walking in a meadow, where the dry season permitted me to walk further than usual, and there I met Mr. Alcott."

He is referring to Amos Bronson Alcott (1799–1888), another member of the Emerson group. Although born to an illiterate, hardscrabble Connecticut farmer, and with little formal education, Alcott had become a teacher in Concord and a leader of New England Transcendentalism—which took as its premise the divinity of human nature. Emerson, Hawthorne, Thoreau, and Alcott all sunbathed in the ideal for varying lengths of time.

Alcott was a spiritual man, an intuitive explorer, who came to rely on the generosity of Emerson and others to keep him afloat. His ideas on education (and especially female education) got off the ground with an 1830 tract concerning "infant instruction"—tapping the receptive senses from a very early age. In this plan he was materially supported by the philanthropist Roberts Vaux, in Philadelphia, the same man who had taken a close interest in the 1823 Letitia Ford harassment case, predicated on a mother's dream about teacher misconduct.

Inspired by William Wordsworth's depiction of the soul as "our life's star," Alcott famously experimented on his own children. Once she came to outshine her unbusinesslike father, his affectionate daughter and pupil Louisa May Alcott (1832–1888) reminisced about her spiritually freeing early years among the stimulating Concord crowd. As an eleven-year-old, after lighting some pine cones on fire and listening to them crackle and sing, the future author of *Little Women* recorded in her "Imagination Book" thoughts that sprung from being an Alcott: "Life is pleasanter than it used to be, and I don't care about dying any more. . . . Had good dreams, and woke now and then to think, and watch the moon." While Julian Hawthorne found Thoreau "unbeautiful," young Louisa May found him both beautiful and captivating.

To proceed, then, with Thoreau's dream of his encounter with the elder Alcott, the two had just met up in a meadow: "We fell to quoting and referring to grand and pleasing couplets and single lines which we had read in times past; and I quoted one which in my waking hours I have no knowledge of, but in my dream it was familiar enough."

When morning arrived, Thoreau could no longer conjure the lines, but he knew that what they expressed was a sense of regret: "It had the word 'memory' in it!!!" he exclaimed on the page. "And then again the instant that I awoke, methought I was a musical instrument from which I heard a strain die out,—a bugle, a clarionet, or a flute. My body was the organ and channel of melody, as a flute is of the music that is breathed through it . . . , my nerves were the chords of the lyre."[27]

Thoreau, an ecstatic dreamer, strikes the same metaphorical chord we first associated with Benjamin Rush. He goes beyond Rush's end-of-days trumpet to intuit that his dream (or any dream) can convert the dreamer into the channel for a wind instrument. The vocabulary of an earlier generation was not lost on him: in likening the nerves to a system of vibrations, and dreaming to a musical device, Thoreau was taking the language of sense and sensibility to a new, and clearly a more intense, place.

His remarks on musicality were of a piece with observations he made in *A Week on the Concord and Merrimack Rivers*. On the Monday of his fictive week, he had written of falling asleep to the sounds of a novice drummer, who was preparing for an old-fashioned "country muster." Though the sounds that permeated the forest night were simple, they had had the effect of taking the young Thoreau on a kind of flight in time:

> I see, smell, taste, hear, feel that everlasting Something to which we are allied, at once our maker, our abode, our destiny, our very Selves. . . . What are ears? what is Time? that this particular series of sounds called a strain of music . . . wafted down through the centuries from Homer to me.

Music was a universal form of exhortation for him: "What a fine communication from age to age . . . even as were never communicated by speech, is music! It is the flower of language, thought colored and curved, fluent and flexible. . . ." We know that music inspires; for Thoreau it also spoke and painted, which made it the perfect embodiment of dream life.[28]

Also intriguing are the forgotten lines he recited in his dream—lines that contained the word "memory." He and Alcott were quoting to each other what they most enjoyed committing to memory, only to have it forgotten by morning. Was this portion of the dream really about the problematic nature of memory? If so, what beautiful irony!

One year later, another of his dreams prompted Thoreau to speculate about the inherent power of the dream state. He did not detail the dream, but said that its mystical properties were causing him to consider whether the bizarre in dreams could be best explained by reincarnation. The vision had not come from his own direct experience, leading him to believe that it might have been "based on an experience in a previous state of existence, and could not be entertained by my waking self." This is beyond even Emerson. "Both the thought and the language were equally novel to me," Thoreau wrote, "but I at once perceived it to be true and to coincide with my experience in this state." His description of the energy contained in his dream bore a striking resemblance to the perception of indigenous Americans, who appreciate a dream as the fuel that makes transport through psychic space possible.[29]

"There are some things of which I cannot at once tell whether I have dreamed them or they are real," he mused a few years later. Thoreau was now toying with the idea that the transition to waking thoughts takes the dreamer through a kind of tunnel, in which the dreamed and the experienced cannot be told apart: "Dreams are real, as is the light of the stars and moon, and theirs is said to be a dreamy light." His mind had produced a mountain east of the town of Concord, where no hill of any height actually existed; he had climbed that nonexistent mountain enough times in dreams that it appeared to his mind's eye, remembered and forgotten so many times until it hardly mattered anymore.[30]

~∞~

Thirty miles southwest of Concord, in Mendon, a farming town in cranberry country near the Rhode Island border, lived a man named Ichabod Cook. Despite having served a single term in the Massachusetts House of Representatives, he was a farmer and not a politician. Thoroughly undistinguished in his time, he deserves to go down in history as the "Dream Collector," because in his travels he made a habit of inquiring about people's dreams and graciously offering to help interpret them. The journal he kept during the 1840s contains a good many ordinary Americans' dreams, along with his own.

Ichabod was nearly sixty when he began collecting dreams. Born during the Revolution, he married at twenty-three in 1802. His wife became pregnant each year of their marriage, but only one of their five children survived infancy, and Hannah King Cook herself died in 1808. Ichabod remarried the following year and fathered three sons; their mother, Louisa, died in 1839, leaving Ichabod a widower for the second time. It was then that he began to record dreams in earnest.

As engaged as he was in dream spinning, the everyday life of a farmer came first in his regular writings. To entertain himself as he exercised his brain, Ichabod regularly versified the mundane in his life, peppering his daily journal with the likes of:

> *To sell some cheese I've been away this morn,*
> *And bought me boots. Fine weather for the corn.*
> *Fine showers this afternoon, with thunder's noise,*
> *But nothing outward gives celestial joys. (May 29, 1841)*

A week after his cheese-selling, boot-buying expedition, a neighbor named Cushman came to Ichabod with a dream that had caused him to fear for his life. As Cushman related it, a man named Burr, who had been dead several years, "came into a room where he was." Ichabod is copying this all down. As Ebenezer Scrooge was to tell his deceased partner Jacob Marley in Charles Dickens's *A Christmas Carol* (which would not be published for another two years), Cushman told his ghostly visitor that he thought him dead, upon which the late Mr. Burr confirmed that fact, indicating that he would return again in three months and take Cushman back with him to the place of the dead. In the dream, according to Ichabod, "C thought his wife and several others were in the adjoining room, and wanted they should see him, and was about stepping to the door to call them when B got up, and before he could get them in B disappeared."

We know this species of anxiety. Cushman, in his dream, was dreadfully eager to prove to witnesses that his vision was real and verifiable. This would be one means of reasserting control, rather than allow the dream (as dreams usually do) to string him along.

Ichabod explained to his anxious neighbor that "in visions, a day, a week, or a month might mean a year." This meant that Burr might not be back for years, and poor Cushman could stop worrying that he was fated to die anytime soon. And why not offer such an interpretation? The illusory world was not supposed to be read any other way: a loose-talking character cited in a Macon, Georgia, newspaper pronounced that a wedding dream portended a funeral, "as dreams are interpreted backwards."[31]

The incident with Cushman gives us a fair impression of Ichabod's character, too. He wants to feel welcome in his surrounding community; he wants to be thought clever and to be given credit for his insights. In his collected papers, we are made privy to the mild eccentricities of a self-educated man who exhibits a combination of country manners and calm conceit.

And now for a sampling of Ichabod's own dreams:

February 27, 1836: "Dreamed of being in a room, in a distant house, alone, and took up a large book, in which I read a few words, from which I thought it might be some French history; for I thought it was there stated, that Bonaparte said in his last days, 'when I was young I had tender feelings, and strove to harden myself against them; and when I had grown old, I was like a lobster incased in his shell and could not feel when I would.'"

February 28, 1836: "I dreamed of being at a building which was only planked up on the sides, with open spaces. . . . There was a woman in the upper room, which was as large as the house, who I thought was intending to deliver a discourse; but she did not. After I was down, I stood out north of it, and it came apart from one end to the other. . . . Men were at work on the roof and sides. Clumps of them slid off the roof and fell to the ground, and individuals also. . . . Those left on the house paid no attention to them that fell, but kept steadily at their work."

We can say this much. Ichabod's dreams possess energy and activity while introducing mental challenges. He does not try to explain the absurd or reshape his dream (as he did for Cushman) into a proper life lesson. Events dictate to him in his dream; his immediate environment is in disrepair, and he exercises his will, albeit unsystematically. Perhaps falling men signify the omnipresence of death, or the precariousness of life, but what matters is the dreamer's priority: recording facts accurately and keeping things straight in his mind.

Ichabod also experienced a conflagration dream on the order of Washington Irving's:

> After dreaming last night much which is gone too much from me to be written, I thought there came from the north a fire, rushing along violently, spreading from the east to the southwest, the smoke boiling up from the woodland in great clouds and the [illegible] land so dry as to kindle and smoke in innumerable places; the air being full of burning leaves and other things. I was busy in closing the windows to keep these out, thinking that many buildings must be burned.

Irving feared for his precious manuscripts; Ichabod, a farmer, focused instead on getting a precise reading on wind direction as he battened down the hatches. He was a man who craved order and, as all of us do, wished that everything in his life might fit into place. But he knew, too, that if he left his dreams alone, in their raw state, disorder would prevail. And so, at some point, he would have to exert his will and offer up interpretation—envisioning a world of greater order and less unpredictability. The question is whether he entrusted himself with authority as an interpreter of his own dreams, in the way he was able to reassure his neighbor. And here the answer is less clear.[32]

November 26, 1840: "I dreamed that a female in my family was sick. . . . I went up northward [he imagines it to be the part of Canada from which he had recently returned] and stayed longer than I intended. I felt uneasy about mood, as it was cold and stormy. I returned my house was poor, dirty, and without floors; but better afterwards. In the course of doing her work a female led me from the kitchen to the parlour three times, to a girl that sat doing some light work, to have me give her some instructions—it seemed she was about taking the lead in my household affairs. Thus ended my dream."

Reminiscing, four days later, about his northern tour, he returned from the butcher's shop at midday to find a familiar scene at home. His housekeepers were going about their business cleaning. One was sitting down, "to gain her full strength To be more able at ironing to toil." Odd Ichabod is led to conclude: "And thus it seemed to be much as I dreamed."

It would appear, then, that he did try to maneuver his dreams into his waking life, that they should contain just enough prophetic content to support his goal of regularity and order. It was just too easy, otherwise, to succumb to the bizarre in dreams and experience them as a force that prolonged disorder through the days of his life.

The dreams of others that Ichabod took notes on tend to be more colorful than his own. One of his occasional housekeepers, variously called Anna and

Ann Maria, turns out to be a treasure trove of dream imagery. On March 9, 1841, he recorded: "Ann Maria dreamed, while laying down in the evening, that she went to the house of [left blank] whose wife, when a girl, she loved very much. She went in and inquired of him where his wife was, he replied 'that is her'—a tall woman, who appeared pleasant to her, but looked cross with her eyes and which she considered to be a spirit, rather than a living person, though she treated her pleasantly."

The strategy of standing still and waiting silently didn't do much for Ann Maria. Her dreaming self was very afraid. She ran out of the house and into the barn, "and there she got under the feet of an old ox, she got by him, and awoke." Later the same night, she dreamt again. She was in the same house, this time called there to do some sewing. The woman from her past was there again, looking as she did when a girl, and Ann Maria told her about being there before. The girl smiled. Then, "Ann Maria took up her pressing iron, and as she took it she saw a new horse comeing towards her, she ran into the other room, and the horse caught hold of this girl, and she screemed for her help, but [Ann Maria] could not do any thing but soon awoke."

A dream of confusion marked by extreme vulnerability, this one has two emotionally rich parts: the retrieved image of someone long since gone (a memory displaced by time) and intense raw emotion represented by the belligerent horse—an irrational, but not impossible, contingency. If we were to establish dream typologies, Ann Maria is the dreamer as victim. But her testimony does not so much suggest the long-established cultural assumption, very much a part of Ichabod's world, that females are naturally, neurologically, more susceptible than men; instead, what she admits to her employer suggests a broader awareness of the competition taking place within every mind between force of will and independence of sense impressions. A housekeeper, whose last name we do not even know, is telling us that the imagination modifies established ideas about the range of possible thought in a dream. Her dreams are not a plain representation of a corpse, a coffin, a funeral procession, with an objective order and predictive quality. They hold nothing back; they are ungoverned; they simply exist.

Ann Maria's testimony gives plausible evidence that Americans were reaching for individual dignity in a way they had not done quite so directly in previous generations. It was through confrontation with emotional ignorance, through a more overt rebellion against emotional oppression, that they launched their struggle within. There are no blank stares in such dreams—we begin to feel the dreamer's urge to mount a subjective response. We might expect such creative courage coming from Henry David Thoreau; it is more remarkable that such random expressions of contention were being voiced by an unschooled housekeeper as well.

Ichabod caught another of Ann Maria's dreams the very next day, and it once again speaks to the freeing of thought: "Somebody told her the world was coming to an end, and she walked out towards a river, and she saw a man coming in a carriage with two red horses." At the bridge, the man took the horses out—this is when it gets good: "They dove down into the water, and brought up three of the beautifulest flowers that she ever saw." The man still held the reins, and he returned the horses to the carriage and drove off. "Then she saw a man riding on a white horse down towards the bridge, and when he got to the river he let the horse go into the water and he let go of the reins the horse could not dive and he must swim out; she said well she should like to see a horse swim; she saw him swim[m]ing, and awoke."

It is a fable without a moral. The housekeeper's fear of the unnatural gives way to the marvelous, the magical. Horses were ubiquitous in rural New England, of course, and their often mysterious personalities could well have affected the dreamer. Some horses are nervous and unpredictable; we know that they spook easily. So, whatever emotion Ann Maria is portraying in the dream—feeling small before the unpredictable, let's say—her isolation, even as she attempts to understand what the man with the horses is doing, is not a negation of her volition. Note, too, the identification of colors: if we take the dreams recorded in the decades leading up the 1830s, specific mentions of color (and of animals, for that matter) are less frequent than they are from this period forward.

Ann Maria's dreams grow ever more enticing as the days proceed. A man with whom she had a passing acquaintance shows up with a cape that belonged to "a girl that he had been paying some attention to." He tells Ann Maria that it is "the most beautiful cape that was ever seen, that there was no queen had any that would compare with it." She could not resist desiring to see it, but dared not ask. Then temptation strikes: "The man went out and left the cape rolled up in a paper on the table; she thought she might venture to take the cape up and look at it, and just as she had taken it up, the man came in. Not having time to roll it up, she slipped it under her apron and ran out doors with it; he inquired for the cape; she did not dare to let him know she had it, for fear he would think she took it to keep, so she went into the bedroom and laid it on the bed, and left it, and awoke." Here is a crime of opportunity, followed by pangs of guilt. Though Ichabod was known for his solutions to dramatic puzzles, he did not take the bait this time.

The best of Ann Maria's dreams came the next night. Ichabod, his twenty-one-year-old son William, and a second housekeeper named Elizabeth were all part of it, which obviously piqued the dream collector's interest:

"Anna dreamed that some robbers came, they were in the celler first, we were in the kitchen shut up, they would kill us if we went out of it. I said [to Ann Maria] if we could get out we would take the horse and wagon and get away; they hearing this fenced round the hous[e]." The robbers then said they would shoot everyone if even one should leave.

Ichabod is now at the center of his housekeeper's dream, sending William in search of an officer of the law. Stepping outside the house, dream character Ichabod "saw a paper spread on the ground, with pistols under it, it was written on the paper if I touched it it would kill me." Ann Maria, privy to this threat (it was, after all, her dream), asked how touching a gun could kill him, and then realized the note was written, and the pistols left there, to test Ichabod.

Upon her realization, Ann Maria "went out at the wash room door, and a man drove up with a team of four very beautiful white horses." Two of them were taken and "hitched near the barn"; Ann Maria was obliged to hold on to the unsecured pair by herself. "One stood very good, the other started round and got away and stepped off a few steps, and then ran towards her; she stepped round the other side of the horse; she then left them," and came back inside. In this confused segment, it is once again unpredictable horses that absorb the dreamer.

Now Elizabeth wanted Ann Maria to go out and collect firewood. When she agreed, she saw that the two horses were gone; the other two, still hitched outside the barn, "looked earnestly at her; and having got her wood, she looked up and they were running towards her; she ran into the house and as she stepped into house they were at the door stone, and she awoke." Whatever the robbers had planned for her and the others no longer seemed to matter.

Interestingly, the night before this, Elizabeth also saw a pistol in her dream. She had dreamt of being at her father's old house in the seaside village of Wickford, Rhode Island, looking through a window from just outside. This dream, though in Ichabod's hand (as all of them are), is harder to follow than the others: "The house appeared very empty, and there was a man at the next window, with a pistol both on the outside & same side, he trying to shoot her through the house. As the windows looked into different rooms, he had to shoot through one room out at its door into the next room and out at its window."

It stops there, a fragment. The awkward syntax is all the more difficult to fathom because their dreams, like ours, do not abide by reason. It appears that the shooter had two pistols, one of which was aimed at Elizabeth; and with obstacles in the way, the bullet had to thread a needle. Improved odds did not make the moment any less anxious for the dreamer.

One more of Ann Maria's dream narratives that busy week can be told. It involves an animal, but this time not a horse. In the dream, Elizabeth has just gone outside "to dip some water out of a barrel," when "a small dark coloured snake jumped out of the water and twisted round her wrist under her sleeve, and she was very much frightened. She could not see it, nor get it off—at last she got her sleeve up so that William got hold of its head and pulled it off, and threw it; it turned and went over Anna's head, and fell on the floor and she saw it no more."[33]

It is unusual for us to have such variety to work with. We should try to figure out what Ann Maria's dreams say about her. To generalize, rather than play shrink, she appears to be hopeful of finding solace in her human relationships. Her word and her dignity form as much a part of the overall picture as the threats of violence that permeate her dreaming. The imagery she describes underscores an even larger concern with the indefinite relationship between humans and the natural world. Thus, animals are both beautiful and dangerous in her dreams. A horse gives her an "earnest" look, a snake jumps out at her.

What does this mean, if anything? If we draw a composite of her several dreams, the "life is a journey" metaphor does not really enter into the narrative much at all, though we can see that she seeks refuge; whatever recourse she tries, or others try on her behalf, proves inadequate or impermanent protection. We perceive the obvious: that unpredictability is a consequence of life in the real world.

Insights do not lie in our devising a unique interpretation, but in the overall familiarity we sense as we read of her dreaming experience. An evolutionary function of dreams, we are told these days, is to teach avoidance skills. Being chased or under threat from a wild animal is part of that regimen. Indeed, this is one reason that many scientists believe we were not designed to remember our dreams (and don't remember most), that remembering them only adds confusion; in effect, we're getting an unauthorized glimpse of the brain "off-line," the processing plant, as it were, when all we are meant to experience is the product at retail.[34]

As farmer Ichabod took to the road, he recorded dreams amid a series of chance encounters. Traveling between Philadelphia and New York, he met a stranger and reconstructed their conversation verbatim and at length—it bears witness to his outgoing nature and strong convictions: "Paul Upton: Where dost thou reside? I. Cook: In Massachusetts. P.U.: My mother came from Mass." It goes on for several more rounds until they learn that they are cousins. Concludes Ichabod: "Thus a pleasant acquaintance was begun." His earnest routine reminds us that early America was a smaller world than it has since become.[35]

Ichabod's concern with dream worlds overlaps with his interest in religious community. "I met a man by the wayside who was full of questions," he recorded on July 13, 1841. (The man's words indicate that at different times in his life he had been a Calvinist, Universalist, Deist, and Atheist.) "When he came to doubt of the Creator, I told him that the perfection of every thing we behold is sufficient evidence that there was a God. All had their eyes in the right place; nothing less than supreme Wisdom could form an eye; the eye without light would be of no use; and as all parts of the heavens were full of lights, we must suppose that worlds were there full of eyes." Never entirely at home in any sect, Ichabod grumbled almost as much as he ruminated, but he defended God everywhere he went. As he reached for satisfying explanations for the existence of God, he always avowed that dreams had a role to play.

His dream reporting enlarged in the spring and summer of 1842. One night, he lodged at the home of a man named Peleg. "Some years ago his wife dreamed one night that she had something [plantlike, apparently] grew up in one corner of the room, very flourishing, which she highly valued. She thought that something that appeared like a horse rushed up to the window, as though it was coming in; she told Peleg to stop it; P. sprung up to it, but it ran its head in with a sweep, and bit it all off, and was gone in an instant." (This is remarkably close to Ann Maria's emotionally taxing horse dreams.) Peleg's wife interpreted his dream as a bad omen, and the pair found a tragedy to attach to it. "Trouble . . . came fast enough," Ichabod notes. "Soon after this her darling child was taken sick and died suddenly." Ichabod does not say whether he believes in the connection, though he resists the chance to scoff at it.

Heading home from Peleg's place, he encountered Otis Thayer "by the wayside planting" and was invited to spend the night. Ichabod and the Thayers attended a Quaker meeting together, where a number of dreams were told that related to deaths in the community. In one case, a mother testified that she had heard her four-year-old exclaim: "They are going to bury that child alive! do stop them!" The mother then (in her dream) picked up her own child, "and it was light as a feather; she ran after [the funeral party] after walls and fences, with the greatest ease, through pastures, like those they passed in going to the child's grave." A few days later, the community learned that the four-year-old had died from exposure.

A man named Elisha Sherman told Ichabod of his unhappy marital history, which was in part owing to religious differences. Elisha was a Quaker, his wife a Baptist. "He meant to give her her liberty," Ichabod recorded, alluding to what was still quite uncommon: divorce. "He dreamed that they were away from home, and were going to a certain place, and he was for going one way, and she another. He took his way, she told him they could never get there that way; he told her they could. They came to a turnpike gate. When she saw it she says there I told you we could not get along this way, you have no money and cannot get through. He says we can."

At this point, Elisha, at the reins of his carriage, is arguing with the gate-keeper, a woman. She wants to know when he plans to return. He says he has no idea when, if at all. When she disputes him, he tells her "he owned a right in that road" and barrels ahead. But he finds the terrain "hilly and rough," and his wife continues to protest. "At length they came to the top of a hill and looked down into a swampy place where there was old logs and many obstructions, and it looked to him as though they never could get through." Once again, he resolves to press on. "They went by some old houses up a hill and came to a plain, with the most beautiful road he ever saw. He says then, I told you we could go this way." The "life is a journey" metaphor is about as transparent and decisive as it could be in any dream. Elisha told Ichabod that he had never believed in dreams before, but that this one changed his mind, because after he shared it with his wife, she started going to Quaker meetings with him and their marriage was repaired.

A five-year-old girl dreamt that her grandfather, his legs terribly swollen, was lying in a coffin. Ichabod noted down what happened: In the morning, at breakfast, the girl sat nervously and could not be convinced that her dream was not reality. Because her grandfather lived a short distance away, she was permitted to check in on him. She saw him looking fit and cried as she told him of her dream.

A mother who watched a daughter die dreamt that "three men, dressed in white, appeared to her, and asked her what she was troubled about. She told them that she had lost her daughter, that she wanted to see her once more. . . . On the same day another of her daughters, about the same age, died."

While he was visiting Providence, Rhode Island, a woman told Ichabod a dream in which her eldest son, who "went to the south, many years ago, with a caravan, as a musician, and has not been heard of," came "flying up" to a tavern the family formerly kept. Then, just as suddenly, he vanished again. "He appeared in his likeness without wings," the dreamer explained, hoping Ichabod could tell her what it all meant. But he could not say for certain.

The next one evokes the most common of all themes in seafaring times: a young woman said she had a brother at sea. In her dream, she saw a vessel, and on one side the water was crystal clear, but inside a man lay dead. Subsequent to her dream, a letter she received from her brother mentioned that a man on board had died and was buried at sea on the precise day she had had her dream. We are brought back to the Norwegian fisherman's death, as dreamt by his son; and the astounding dream the writer Judith Sargent Murray told to Benjamin Rush, in which she "saw" her husband at the precise time of his death when he was over a thousand miles distant in the West Indies.

As he aged, Ichabod was drawn deeper and deeper into the netherworld of dreams. Another eerily prophetic one from his 1842 notebook: "Eliza Wheelock who died last [March] dreamed about two years before that her mother had a little baby that was sick and, a little before it died, it looked up to her and said, 'prepare for death, and follow me.' About a year after this [Eliza's] mother did have a little baby. It was always unwell and lived about 6 or 8 months. Eliza was sick about a year, and was very unwilling to think she should not get well."

In 1847, the one-time Massachusetts state representative Ichabod Cook produced a long pamphlet cataloguing his religious views. In the course of his exegesis, he drew upon the extensive dream data he had collected over the years, a strong sampling of which we have cited here. He was not the first pamphlet writer to look for divine signs in dreams, of course. What makes Ichabod's work special is that the two texts—dreams from his journals and dreams from his pamphlet—can be placed side by side and compared. They show him providing religious explanations for dreams that his journal leaves uninterpreted, and he excludes from the pamphlet those dreams (the horse dreams, for example) that cannot be manipulated so as to contain a revelatory Christian message.

That said, we can credit Ichabod for resisting the urge to tamper with dreams to the degree that more arbitrary compilers of religious tracts had.

"Angels have often been permitted to cheer the weaker sex," the *Religious Messenger* observed in typical fashion. "Perhaps in pity to the weak and apprehensive minds, they have been sent to comfort . . . and in a dream or vision of the night, be the messenger of peace to the mind." And from the same periodical, this testament to the efficacy of prayer: "A pious father and mother in Philadelphia were distressed by the conduct of a daughter who was devoted to worldly vanities." After they prayed for her, "she dreamed that she was sinking into hell! She awoke much agitated." This repeated three times until "she could sleep no more." That is when she conformed to her parents' wishes and united with them in praising the Lord.[36]

Ichabod Cook's *A Brief Examination of Some of the Most Prevalent False Doctrines and Ceremonials of the Christian Sect* was published, suitably enough, in the town of Providence. In it he pronounced, with unabashed pride, that "the hand of Providence" had reached out to him and to others of his acquaintance: "Dreams having been occasionally used to confirm me in revelations. . . . I began six or seven years ago to note down in my memorandum dreams of other people, as well as some of my own, that appeared most remarkable; so that I have hundreds to turn to, as occasion requires. Almost daily do I see something transpiring, which was pointed to by these dreams." And as nearly every dream book's preface reminded readers, Ichabod, too, highlighted the Book of Daniel, and Nebuchadnezzar's dream projecting the end of imperial power—in modern times it was "the iron toe of Great Britain, with the toes of clay, [that] must be reduced to dust, and carried away as the chaff of the summer threshing-floors!" All great kingdoms pass away, wrote Ichabod. "The dream [of Nebuchadnezzar] is certain, and the interpretation thereof sure."[37]

He retold his own dreams of 1836: that of the house with the falling roof, which he now interpreted as a reflection of discord and division among Quakers; and that of the large book that he presumed was of recent French history: "A very true representation of the hardening our hearts." As for his housekeeper Elizabeth, he was suddenly less interested in her dream of a man with a pistol and more with her suggestion that Ichabod open the Bible on New Year's Day, and that whatever page he opened to would contain a message of prophetic consequence. In this case, it was the fourth chapter of Exodus, and it convinced him that he was meant to "commence a new denomination of Christians."

Beyond such expressions of confidence, Ichabod's pamphlet focused almost exclusively on the dreams he recorded in 1843, the year he lost his commitment to the Quakers. Mrs. Curtis dreamt of "an immense plain covered with sheep, walking eastwardly, crowded together. . . . At a distance motion was lost to the sight, and they looked like a white ocean." She told Ichabod that she did not understand the vision, but felt it had something to do with him. Subsequently, on a night when Ichabod was under her roof, she dreamt of his son William, who was not there; in the dream, she was wading in a pond, and William led her to safety. The gist of it, as Ichabod explained, was that they had found a common place to worship, "wading in the same pond—walking with the same sheep."

Deborah Ballou dreamt of Ichabod's house being red and situated on a prominence. His late wife, Louisa, was there and gave Deborah a tour of the rooms. But Louisa could not stay: "she seemed to be her spirit." Outside the house, Deborah saw "a fish-pond, full of fish" that "shined like stars." Then she went beyond and saw a lush garden, laid out in squares, and "trees full of fruit, not quite ripe." Ichabod was deeply struck by the details: except for the color (his current house, not the former one, was painted red), Deborah had described "more exactly than I could have described it myself" the house outside Boston where he had lived some years earlier. "The garden, and fish-pond, and fish," he insisted, were "Scriptural figures of the church." Moreover, the "color and star-like appearance of the fish were good."

Milla Aldrich came to Ichabod for help in translating her dreams. She was leading a creature she thought was a lamb. Her right arm tightened around its neck as it tried to break free. But it was dark, and she sensed that it was really the head of a year-old colt. To her left were woods, where she thought she spotted "litters of pigs of all sizes," maybe a hundred in all. She came to a village and encountered a blue-eyed woman. There were large insects on a small hill above the town. These were the principal images in a dream of confused geography. Ichabod said of it: "This dream is so full of Scriptural figures that it almost interpreted itself as she told it." Tortured explanations of spirits good and evil followed. He was on a mission, and each of the dreams of 1843 pointed out a path for him. "How dark-minded must he be," Ichabod concluded, "who doubts that the Most High still speaks to us in dreams."[38]

~⁊~

Whimsical reminders of the America Ichabod Cook lived in come in the form of practical lessons that ordinary folks took from their surroundings. More and more, newspapers carried stories that undercut medical orthodoxy, featuring realistic-sounding dreams designed to deliver hope. Notwithstanding the reputation a Dr. Rush might have retained in his time, the average physician in early America was not trusted. He was often the butt of humor and outright mockery. An upstate New York newspaper, the *Plattsburgh Republican,* reported in 1845 that a patient on the operating table was saved from bad doctors by a bad dream. The abscess in his throat, "which nearly stopped respiration and . . . would have caused death," burst when he woke in a panic. While his doctors were performing a useless operation, applying leeches to bleed him, he dreamt that he was being dissected while still alive. The startled patient lurched from the trauma of the dream and felt the abscess suddenly burst. He was restored, "almost instantaneously," to health.[39]

Religion gripped ordinary people, as the average American's life span declined during the first half of the nineteenth century owing to greater mobility that spread infectious disease. This was not Tom Paine's America and had not been for some time. Religious skepticism was muffled by the many new outlets through which citizens discovered their personal faith. Elizabeth Payson was a twenty-two-year-old Presbyterian who would later go on to compose hymns and to author a religious novel. She left her home in Maine to teach at a school in Richmond, Virginia, and in 1841 replied to a cousin who had written asking whether she saw God in her dreams: "No—I never did, neither should I think it desirable," she said. "But a few days ago, when I woke, I had fresh in my remembrance some precious words which, as I had been dreaming, He had spoken to me. It left an indescribable feeling of love and peace in my mind. I seemed in my dream to be very near Him."

By 1847, married to New England pastor George Prentiss, Elizabeth had increasingly grown more devoted to God. That year she meditated on the numerous dreams she had regarding her sister-in-law Abby, who had passed on eight months earlier: "I used always to dream of her as suffering and dying, but now I see her just as she was when well, and hear her advising this and suggesting that, just as I did when she was here last summer." Elizabeth felt that the shift in what she saw in dreams had fundamentally changed her: "It seems to me that my youth has been touched by Abby's death." In feeding her optimism about the soul's immortality, dreams had fortified her faith.[40]

The flip side of the religious dream was the saucy one. "Did I ever tell you the funny dream I had about you?" a girl named Fanny, away at boarding school, wrote to her friend Octavia Wyche in Meridianville, Alabama, in March 1848. "I dreampt that I got a letter from you in which you said that you were engaged to marry your Uncle John . . . and I didnt know whether your Aunt Lucinda was still alive or not." Neither the evident absurdity nor, more importantly, the dangerous sexual imagery stopped her pen.

In her real-life letter, Fanny repeats the words Octavia wrote to her in the dream-delivered letter: "I was sitting in the dining room and Uncle John came in smiling and came to me and took me in his arms and kissed me and said I was the prettiest and the sweetest thing in the world and he then addressed me and I engaged myself to him." Underscoring how convinced she was that the dream was real, Fanny adds: "In the same letter you invited me to be one of your bridesmaids." Then, at the end of her recitation, she prods Octavia girlishly: "Wasnt that funny." Upon which, recognizing the chance she was taking by refusing to censor herself (though she and Octavia had known each other since infancy), she repeats her initial reticence to retell the dream, lest there be some kernel of truth in it: "I felt so badly about it I was afraid to write to you. I wrote to Ma first and asked her if you were well."

There were good reasons that Fanny, at a distance, was still wrapped up in Octavia's life. Accustomed to sharing confidences, she had openly fantasized that her best friend would come and join her at boarding school; she excitedly imagined them rooming together. In the letter before the one in which she recounted her dream, Fanny had urged Octavia to burn the paper after reading so that no one would ever see its contents. Octavia saved it regardless. With the dream letter, Fanny did not make the same appeal, oddly enough, despite its embarrassing details.[41]

—⁊∂—

In this chapter, we have surely seen an increasing preoccupation with dreams. The times allowed for greater openness, wistfulness, longing—forms of individual expression. We have seen how culture contributes to what the dreamer decides to record or what he or she leaves out owing to reticence, shame, or embarrassment. Culture manages change as it stands guard against the onset of personal anarchy. It tugs at the past it is losing, as it tries to anticipate the future.

Something had happened in America, if the nationally prominent essayist and lecturer Ralph Waldo Emerson was getting drenched by a hose; or a farmer's part-time housekeeper was conjuring armed robbers, finding a threat written on a stray piece of paper, and looking into the eyes of horses that communicate design and emotion. Dreamers were capturing the illogical drama of dreaming in more random ways. Whereas the eighteenth century constantly warned against the "diseased imagination," the middle decades of the nineteenth century allowed incoherent omnium-gatherum to settle on the page without it necessarily serving some cautionary tale. And that's precisely the point: the more unsystematic dream records are, the more we recognize them as dreamlike.

America's first successful storyteller, Washington Irving, launched this trend through literary experiments that found their way from his private journals into his published writings. In his bestselling fiction, whether it was the portrait that came to life or the "spectre bridegroom" who refused to sleep quietly in his grave, Irving manipulated time and memory and through sleight of hand made the unlikely seem possible. His stock-in-trade was striking readers where they were the most sensitive and vulnerable. His subjects were the broken heart, the fear-inspiring apparition, treasure hunts, and, in general, the allure of irrational belief—supporting the stagecraft through which he illustrated the difficulty of silencing the imagination at night.

Ichabod Cook, a man of quirks and queer expectations, happened to share a name and a bit more with Irving's fictional schoolmaster from *The Legend of Sleepy Hollow*. Both Ichabods stuck their noses in other people's business as they lived out their overactive imaginations. As a recorder and interpreter of raw dreams, Ichabod (Cook, not Crane) applied the stuff of his journal to justify his removal from one religious community and then adapted the same material to justify his decision to establish a new one. In his 1847 pamphlet, he issued a public appeal to readers to join him in creating a place to seek God. Four years later, in 1851, Ichabod was dead at seventy-two.

He and the dreamers whose stories he collected bequeath to us something real and remarkable. More people were coming to accept that, just as Henry David Thoreau gushed, "in dreams we see ourselves naked and acting out our real characters." The sudden amplification of autobiographical fragments—the desire to catalogue images as they were impulsively produced—says that people were striving to know themselves better and were less afraid that their dreams might reveal flaws in character. Consequently, they shared fantasies with minimal embarrassment. Dreams were more routinely "sold" to the public in good and bad literature, and they made objects of fascination in the ever-expanding press.

By mid-century, Americans had become eager and effusive dreamers. They had discovered that the sleeping mind was both elastic and imperial in reach and could be tapped for small mercies or large explanations. When dreams were picked apart to explain what lay behind emotion, they portrayed night thoughts as part of living memory. They showed that individual growth was possible.

SIX

CLAY DILLARD LEARNS
A STRANGE LANGUAGE

I'm dreaming. O! I'm dreaming.
—Caroline Clay Dillard, 1855

Madaline Edwards loved in vain. Born in 1816 in Sumner County, Tennessee, she came from patriotic stock. Her paternal grandfather, a Virginian, had been an officer in the Revolution. She was educated for a short time at a female academy in Gallatin and had a clear gift for writing. But she never had a chance, having been pressured into marriage by her father when she was only fourteen. The marriage lasted six years and ended unhappily—as did the relationship between her parents. Her father moved to Mobile, Alabama, and remarried. Madaline did not lose contact with him, but neither did he foster emotional stability in her.

By her mid-twenties, she stood five foot seven, with large green eyes. By then she was residing in bustling New Orleans, as the mistress of businessman Charles Bradbury. She lived a few blocks outside the French Quarter, a short walk from the home of her paramour—"Charley," she called him. When not sitting at home waiting for him to visit her, she was employed (like Eliza Champlain) as a painting teacher. Madaline had an admirer, an unmarried man, whose friendship she valued. But there was no substitution for Charley. For sustenance, she listened to the sermons of Theodore Clapp, a native New Englander who preached at the Congregational Church just off Canal Street.

Before her involvement with Charley began, Madaline was mixed up with one "F.G." in Vicksburg, Mississippi, who, she wrote, "brought me to my ruin." Charley would not improve Madaline's social status either, though she refused to believe that he was stringing her along. And that is what makes her dreams in the sweltering months of 1844 so fraught with pathos.

Charley was heading to Ohio, with his wife, Mary Ann, to escape the heat. He would not return until fall, and Madaline would be unable to get him out of her head. From the diary: May 9, 1844: "The natal day of my beloved C. God grant that he may live to see many, very many more." May 15: "Oh I have spent a melancholy day. I cannot shake off this feeling that so haunts me and the nearer the departure of C approaches, the worse it gets. I do not see how I can live under his absence. God knows my feelings and he alone. It is worse than death itself." May 16: "Still unhappy while nature looks so lovely this spring morning. I have just got some work to do for C and will try to shake off my misery in work. Last night I dreamed I saw a lovely infant boy of his and it was his image. I kissed it and loved it, but it was not mine."[1]

Her married lover had left town. She occupied herself by reading the likes of Milton's *Paradise Lost* and by writing original poems and essays, some of which she was able to publish in respectable local papers. Creativity helped lift her spirits. On the Fourth of July, she listened to the booming guns and recorded her patriotic pride. "I glory in our free born republic, and I venerate the immortal Washington. . . . I had rather boast of being one of America's humblest daughters than to be an empress or Queen of a Monarchy."[2]

The longer Charley was gone, the more she saw him in her generally encouraging dreams. July 8: "Last night I dreamed twice of seeing my dear Charley. One time I thought he filled my lap with gold, which did not make me half so glad as the sight of him." July 23: "Last night I dreamed such a singular dream of my dear Charley surely it portends a letter." Justifying a belief that dreams were portents—whatever that "singular dream" was—she noted that the prior night's had already come partly true when a shipment of "peaches, chickens and other things" arrived from her sister. But in the letter accompanying them, the sister condemned Madaline's life style, saying flatly: "That man will throw you and your child both on a cold world."

What child? All signs pointed to it: Madaline was pregnant. More and more dreams followed, reflective of her loneliness and growing desperation. July 24: "Dreamed last night again of dear Charley. Oh that it was reality and not a dream. When will he come." July 25: "I could sit down and weep half the night but it must not be. Oh such nights are too holy to be spent alone. . . . Dear Charley forget me not. I dreamed again last night I saw him." On the twenty-seventh, she dreamt of being together with him in his home: "Oh! What extacy was mine last night as I sat by Charley at his own table and when he spoke low to me and said he would be here at dark. How happy I was. His wife seemed much pleased with me and I did not feel unjust towards her but alas the morning dawn dispelled all this happiness and I awoke to sigh and long for the reality."[3]

Madaline's wish-fulfillment dream not only delivered Charley to her, but it also allowed her to replace Mary Ann Bradbury. There are signs throughout the diary that she struggled with jealousy, convinced that no one could love Charley as well as she. To spot the couple walking together, as she occasionally did, frustrated her to no end. Once, when Mary Ann was ill, Madaline gave her lover flowers to take home. The modern editor of her diary has concluded that the gesture was in fact insincere and manipulative.[4]

The next recorded dream was more chaotic than those preceding. Feeling "on the point of a miscarriage" after a "jolting" carriage ride, she wrote of her friend Buddington, a businessman, originally from New York, who had warned her about Charley's true nature: "I dreamed last night B rode a horse up and handed me a letter from dear C. I tore it open and it was dated three o'clock night all asleep." In the letter, Charley told her that he had heard a sermon preached by Mr. Clapp and had decided he would begin to take the sacrament. "I began to cry for I felt it was to Sever our connexion. . . . The letter contained two sheets but just as I read one I awoke, sadly disappointed. Oh will he not write to me? I am almost crazy and sick too." Ten more days passed. Her feelings were mixed. Dreams remained positive, but reality let her down. August 14: "Last night I dreamed that Mr Clapp presented me with some of the most beautiful flowers I ever saw. . . . No letter [from Charley] yet. My heart is almost wild with despair. . . . He cannot feel for me or he would write."[5]

Charley finally wrote to her at the end of August, but it only made things worse and justified the caution urged by her friends. "Recd a letter from C at last and I wish from my soul it had not come for it was as cold as marble and has put me in a state of mind that even his presence could not dissipate. . . . I have wept this day until I am not myself. I cannot get over Charleys coldness to me." She tried to bring up ethereal thoughts: "I have sat to night with one eye on Venus and the other on Saturn prying into the mysteries of the starry Heavens." Waiting grimly, impatiently, Madaline wrote an essay at this time, "Tale of Real Life," which was nearly an autobiography. In it, she surmised: "True there are not so many broken hearts in every day life as fiction represents, but there are more that are every thing but broken, or as Byron truly says 'though broken still live on.'" These were slightly misquoted lines from the canto of *Childe Harold's Pilgrimage* published in 1816, a stanza in which the poet describes forms of decay in the natural world to allegorically depict the ways of mourning, of surviving half intact: "The hull drives on, though mast and sail be torn . . . / And thus the heart will break, yet brokenly live on."[6]

On October 8, shortly before Charley's return to New Orleans, Madaline was moved when a male friend sat with her all evening and comforted her. "I wept from many emotions," she recorded, before turning in for the night. And then, "I . . . dreamed I was dressed in white floating on a wide muddy river and Charley rode on a white horse meeting me on the water and talked with me." As the anticipation of seeing him built, she had her most extravagant nocturnal vision: "I dreamed the firmament was all on fire and every thing and person in consternation for the day of judgment had arrived. I was with Charley. We clasped each other and fell on our knees. My final word was 'Thank God we are thus blest in dying together' and then both prayed but he could say little while eloquence was on my tongue and faith in my heart that all would be well." Some dreams do not have to be analyzed.

They reunited, but it did not take long for her to figure out that they would not live or die together. When Charley came to visit, he blew hot and cold. At the end of October, as she entered her third trimester of pregnancy, he sat with her one night for four full hours. She wrote in her diary: "I forgot pain and was happy." She read to him from her original compositions: "He was well pleased and that is all the recompense I ask. We talked of what should be done with my child if it should live and I die." "My" child, she wrote, curiously enough, not "our" child.[7]

In a somewhat didactic essay penned for publication a few days later, Madaline found ways to rationalize Charley's cruelty—by expressing resentment toward the unnamed Mary Ann Bradbury. "I say wives are more to blame for the neglect they and their home receives from the husband than he is," wrote the mistress. "She has it in her power by a thousand nameless attentions, of winning him to all her wishes." It was unfair that Mary Ann, who hardly appreciated what she had, had it all. Madaline denied the existence of sisterhood: "Men as husbands are unjustly called fickle." Here and throughout the piece, she pretended to be a wife, disguising her identity as a kept woman. More to the point, she portrayed herself as a woman who was capable of tremendous love and caring; if she lacked a real hearth, it was no fault of hers.

Next on her schedule was to write out an informal will, in case she died in childbirth. She played it up for Charley: "The time is close at hand that brings me a period of suffering and it may be death also." To her nameless, illegitimate child, in the same letter: "Oh what a crowd of reflections and agonizing emotions swell to my soul. . . . Oh! what have I not lost?" She feared that Charley would retain no feelings for the child once she was gone and forgotten, so she appealed to him with heightened pathos, asking that the child should be given precious keepsakes: "the little jewelry I wear . . . some of my pencillings and paintings . . . and a few, very few of my clothes." If a son, she proposed, "I trust it will be like his father, but yet teach it warmer feelings."[8]

But there was no child. The pregnancy was all in her mind. Though Madaline must have believed herself with child, her subconscious apparently devised a way to keep her lover attached to her and sustain her faith that they might one day be a real couple.

It was not until the spring of 1845 that Mary Ann Bradbury came to suspect the affair. On April 1, she confronted Madaline on the street, and Madaline maintained her composure. In her diary she wrote proudly: "April fool has not been made of me today."

She held on as long as she could. Finally, she faced up to the truth. The second stanza of a poem she wrote in March 1846, "To C.," tells all:

Two years ago, I did not deem
The bliss you had created
Should pass away, a bitter dream
And leave all hope prostrated.

She wrote a second poem that month, since lost, titled "Dream." And a third, the same year, called "Lines on dreaming that I was again at my Uncles in Tenn[essee] with whom I lived many years and at whose house I was married."[9]

Even after the dream ended, Madaline and Charley continued to see each other from time to time. In the first extant letter from him to her, in 1847, he addressed her familiarly as "Mad" and labeled her remarks as to his actions and motives "unkind, unjust, and altogether uncalled for." Four days after this, apparently in reaction to her reply, he admitted that "it was the Animal that first prompted me to seek an interview with you." But, he claimed condescendingly, his impulse immediately after was to "raise you up in the scale of human happiness as far as possible."

In the year of the Gold Rush, 1849, Madaline Edwards left New Orleans for San Francisco, where in the early 1850s she kept a boardinghouse. There she died, possibly of cholera, in the summer of 1854. Charles Bradbury continued on in New Orleans until 1880, when he expired quietly at home at the age of sixty-five.[10]

~∾~

Willie and Fannie were not a couple for long either, though under very different conditions. William George Scandlin arrived in Fannie's hometown of Meadville, Pennsylvania, not far from Pittsburgh, in 1850. He had been born in England in 1828, the youngest of fifteen children, and joined the Royal Navy when he came of age. Then he deserted and came to settle in Boston. With the assistance of the Seaman's Mission, he was sent to attend the Unitarian Meadville Theological School. There the increasingly devout student met Fannie, and after a short time, he proposed to her. They were married in December 1853. The marriage lasted only through the following April.

He recorded a conversation they had near the end.

Fannie: "My pains are not as severe now but there is nothing of me left. I feel as though I should like to die."

Willie: "All will be well in time, my dear."

Then they spoke of Heaven.

"When you go there," he said, "you must be my Guardian Spirit."

"O yes Willie—O yes Willie, I will be with & influence you all I can for good."

His diary for April 28, 1854, the day of her death, reads thus: "O My God My God this is a severe blow. . . . O Dear dear Fannie. My Father forgive the deep agonizing trouble of my overburdened heart. . . . Thou dost all things well but Oh! how deep & mysterious are the workings of they providence. . . . I have been a Husband & am now a Widower all in Four Months & fourteen days!!!"

A week later, struggling with his emotions, he marked the number of days "since the remains of my beloved wife were laid in the cemetery . . . how lonely the spots once so dear and hallowed." The day after this, he found the portion of her journal she had not destroyed. It was not much, but it would have to be enough. He rummaged around and tried to honor her memory as best he could. He wrote to a girlfriend of Fannie's who lived elsewhere: "My Dear

Friend," the letter began, "Though I have never enjoyed the privilege & pleasure of an introduction, let me assure you that your name is familiar to my ear." Its purpose was to tell Mary Hotchkiss what Fannie had requested he convey: "her dying entreaty to all her friends, 'Meet me in Heaven.'"

On July 15, two and a half months after his young wife's death, Scandlin beheld a vision of her, and it recharged him:

> Last night for the first time I was permitted in my dream to visit my dear dear Fannie—not in her spiritual home but in our earthly home at Meadville. I went into the front parlour. I found her laying on the sofa with Aunt Letitia sitting beside her. Oh what an embrace, what a kiss. It seemed we were just met after a long separation. How cheering is such a dream. Yes I went to visit her. God only knows how soon I may go to visit her.

When it came to a longing for love, dream worlds were not gendered. Willie Scandlin's visit with his departed wife on the parlor sofa is nearly identical to Louisa Park's dreams fifty-four years earlier, when her husband was away at sea. In general, when desperate dreamers reaped the intimacy they yearned for, it came not as sudden sparks but as faint glimmers, momentary glances at a better condition than present reality held. Scandlin allowed himself to believe that he had just touched heaven.

Graduating from Meadville Theological School, the young widower returned to Boston, where he served a Unitarian congregation. Eleven months after he saw Fannie in his dream, and scarcely more than a year after her death, Scandlin remarried. Eliza Foster Sprague was herself a young widow. Together they had six children. When the Civil War broke out, he enlisted as a chaplain in the 15th Massachusetts and was captured at Gettysburg. He was released after three months as a prisoner at Libby Prison, in Richmond, surviving the war only to die a few years later at the age of forty-three.[11]

~✺~

Caroline Clay Dillard was another who died too young. In her case, the enemy was consumption, the raging lung disease that destroyed untold thousands, if not millions, of lives in the eighteenth and nineteenth centuries. Shortly before she started coughing, breaking out in night sweats, and slowly wasting away, Clay, as friends and family called her, related a dream. It concerned her little nephew Tommy, who had died five years earlier, barely a year old. In her dream, she encountered baby Tommy as a "sweet little cherub boy" who took her by the hand and guided her through a "bright dazzling" dream city.

Despite her early passing, what makes Clay Dillard's life one worth knowing, and her dream especially poignant, is the dread of a loss of love that infuses the diary she kept in her late teens. After a childhood in Lynchburg, Virginia, she moved to eastern Tennessee with her parents and boarded at the Edgeworth Female Seminary in Greensboro, North Carolina, which she attended along with her older sister, May.

Edgeworth was a special community. It was the only female academy in North Carolina, its students drawn from across the tristate area. The school, founded in 1840, was named for the Irish author Maria Edgeworth. She is barely known anymore, but in the early American republic, "Miss Edgeworth" was far more popular than her English contemporary Jane Austen, the similarly inclined romantic novelist celebrated nowadays as a symbol of the age of gentility. Indeed, to judge by how many times her works were borrowed from the New York Society Library at mid-century, Edgeworth was every bit as popular as James Fenimore Cooper. She wrote morally accented novels about educated women and their emotional trials. She herself was a daddy's girl when she rose

Edgeworth Female Seminary (Greensboro, North Carolina) in the mid-1850s, which Clay and May Dillard attended, and where William Lafayette Scott taught.

to literary celebrity: it was *Practical Education,* the popular guide, that first made the Edgeworths, father and daughter, world-famous.

Maria Edgeworth chose to remain unmarried her whole life. She was seventy-three at the time the North Carolina academy was founded, and she died a few years before Clay Dillard's time there. In 1836, Caroline Lee Hentz of Florence, Alabama, the girls' school founder whom we met at the beginning of chapter 5, crooned in her diary as she was reading an Edgeworth novel: "Almost divine enchantress! who will ever wear thy mantle when thou art gone."[12]

Edgeworth faculty covered writing, grammar, geography, botany, chemistry, and mathematics; piano and guitar lessons were optional. Pupils were obliged to walk around the carriage circle in the front of the sturdy main building twelve times every morning before classes. So wrote Minna Alcott of Albany, New York, who came to teach at Edgeworth because her "constitution" was fragile and her doctor urged her to go where the climate would put less strain on her. A few years before Clay enrolled, Minna wrote home and described the campus, which lay within an oak grove, "luxuriantly planted" with flowering shrubs. She found herself mesmerized by the summer tanager: "its brilliant scarlet plumage makes an exclamation point when glimpsed against the sky." The "soft, mushy dialect" of Southerners was barely comprehensible to her, as was the constant presence of "Mammies," who served (and prettied up) the girls. One of her fellow teachers saw prospects differently, protesting the lack of political equality that held women back: "We should impress on our girls what an articulate and modern woman was Maria Edgeworth, and how we, as educated women, must try to improve the lot of women in the world today."[13]

That, in brief, was the environment in which Clay Dillard and her older sister May spent the middle years of the 1850s. Minna was still there as a singing teacher and harp instructor when the Dillards attended. May graduated first, so Clay spent her final year at Edgeworth feeling her sister's absence. Clay wrote of missing her parents and longing to rejoin May.

Glued to one of the first few pages of her intact diary is a card, two inches by four inches, on which is penned the signature "W. Lafayette Scott." Concealed on the reverse of the calling card, pressed against the page, and in Clay's hand, are the words "I'm dreaming. O! I'm dreaming." This is where the story of Clay Dillard really begins.[14]

William Lafayette Scott was her teacher. He had recently graduated from the University of North Carolina at Chapel Hill and came to Edgeworth that year to teach classical studies and mathematics. He was given his middle name, of course, in honor of the Marquis de Lafayette, who, as the last living general of the American Revolution, stole headlines throughout his tour of the twenty-four United States in 1824–1825.

In Clay's diary, below the calling card that she preserved, are these words:

> Here is Mr Scotts card, just as he sent it. . . . I know he thinks me so impolite, but I am afraid some of the girls will find it out and tease me. They are all the time at it now. They say he loves me, but I don't believe one word of it; though he does look at me so strangely often. What beautiful eyes he has—such a clear, liquid blue. . . . I often hate to move about the school room when Mr Scott is in it for I can feel his eyes on me.

The next day, Clay scratched out a sentiment she would live to regret: "I received the sweetest little card today from Hon' Thomas Rivers. I never saw him, but I love him dearly. He has completely won my heart. He is in N.C. from Tennessee, and is a beau of Sis May's so they say. I should feel sad to think Sis May was going to marry any one, but I know Genl Rivers is a noble line [i.e., lion] hearted man and we could entrust to his keeping the happiness of our darling Sister."

Brigadier General Thomas Rivers, in his late thirties, was an important figure in Tennessee. At that very moment, he was an attorney, a plantation owner, and a U.S. congressman representing the southwestern portion of the state.

Clay's entry for February 14, Valentine's Day, is even more emotional: "I received a letter from Sis May telling me she was to be married to Genl Rivers next month. I have cried until my head aches. How can I give her up! And I cannot be there either. I think they might wait until I come home."

But something else caught her attention on Valentine's Day: "Prof. Scott told me I was the most mischievous creature he ever saw. He tried to get my consent for him to show one of my compositions." She received an anonymous valentine. It was a picture of a pair of lovers and was signed, mysteriously, "Japonica." Though she doubted that her professor wrote it, she allowed herself to half imagine the possibility. "I think Prof. Scott talks like he knows something about the Valentine," she decoded, "but he could not have sent it."

Clay, at sixteen, was entirely smitten. Her teacher, twenty-seven, had singled her out—that much she knew. The Annual Catalogue of Edgeworth Female Academy for 1856 says that William L. Scott, A.B., graduated from the

University of North Carolina "with the highest honors of that Institution" and was "well known as an accomplished Classical and Mathematical Scholar." He was in his first year at the school. How careful he and his student had to be in expressing their feelings for each other (though she was of marriageable age and he, at least on paper, a perfectly plausible match) is reflected in the coy glances that, for some time, had to suffice. Edgeworth's Annual Catalogue for 1854 hints at the ambiguity, with "General Remarks" that read, in part: "Pupils are not watched, but sufficiently guarded for the detection of errors in conduct."[15]

During her final semester at Edgeworth, Clay and her teacher were kept apart by one continually disapproving faculty member. At graduation, Clay received an "affectionate grasp of the hand" from her restrained beau, but nothing more demonstrative than that. Will Scott stood at the door of the school building as Clay's carriage pulled away—their eyes remained fixed on each other, she tells her diary.

Finally, the young graduate arrived at her married sister's place and met the imposing General Rivers. "I dont know exactly what to think of him," Clay wrote with some foreboding. A package from Will Scott came in the mail: it was a leather-bound book called *Knickerbocker Gallery*. Tucked inside it was "a beautiful, tremulous little poem." Clay's expectations rose—she said she "dreamed over" the book. But it became apparent that her brother-in-law did not want her to marry a poor schoolteacher.

Will rode up in a carriage and met the family. He stayed an entire day. Clay was fixed on the delicate scent of jasmine and honeysuckle in the night air, as she wrote of the hours just past; otherwise she felt nought but her waning courage. "I was indeed loved by that noble, gifted man by my side," she scratched out, "and yet—how could it be?" All day long, she had wanted to tell Will she loved him, but she dared not. "We sat and talked for hours. I know not what was said—I answered like one in a dream."

Was it all a dream? After Will left, she was certain that her "abstracted" manner had left him wondering whether her feelings matched his. When she felt sad, she took out the lock of his "soft, silky, brown hair" that she had kept safe ever since a classmate had surreptitiously clipped it while Prof. Scott was helping someone else with an algebra problem. "He does not dream that I have a piece of his hair." Days and weeks passed, and she received a hopeful letter from Will. "My dreams tonight must be sweet," she wrote, "all soft and golden."

Though she blamed herself for holding back, the uncertainty about her future was not of her making. The unimpeachable General Thomas Rivers opposed a marital alliance with W. Lafayette Scott. He may have persuaded his absent in-laws, too. As Will Scott was writing "dearest" and "darling" to Clay, their engagement, which had lasted nearly a year, came to an abrupt end. So did all her happy dreams. Rivers—"Bro' Tom"—argued vociferously that Will did not really love her. "He does love me. I know he does," she told herself. The battle between Clay and her brother-in-law escalated when Rivers commanded her to write a letter releasing Will Scott from any and all obligation. "There is no such thing as resisting him," she wrote, unnerved. After "Bro' Tom" read and approved it, she hid the letter in the "secret corner" of a private drawer and only pretended to mail it. Clay thought she had won. But Rivers was sneaky. He rummaged through her drawers, found the letter, and carried it to the post office himself.

On her eighteenth birthday, July 26, 1857, a consequential piece of mail arrived. Clay delayed opening Will's letter, and her sister May and "Bro' Tom" took charge, stealing it from her "unresisting hand," reading it aloud. "I laughed wildly," wrote Clay. "I was upon the verge of madness, my brain was in a whirl—my heart like marble. They read on. He had loved me fondly—but the dream was over."

When she regained her composure, she returned his ring and all the love letters he had previously sent—standard procedure in any abortive romance. Tom Rivers insisted he would find her a wealthier, more suitable mate. Such words rang hollow. She went for long horseback rides, but neither this nor any other diversion worked. She simply could not forget Will Scott.

All she had left were her few tactile reminders of him. In addition to his calling card with her own "I'm dreaming!" on the reverse, she had his final expression of sadness and remorse: the note acknowledging receipt of the returned items. This note consisted of a single line: "Miss Clay:—Adieu, sweet lady, adieu!!! Will."

"Ah why cannot I forget, since I know I am forgotten," her diary reads. In September, darkness found her "committing to memory Young's Night Thoughts," the eighteenth-century epic verse we know for its constant drumbeat of mortal expectancy. Though in the light of day she practiced piano and guitar for hours at a stretch, she did not pick herself up and circulate in society.

Later, at her parents' new house, in Rocky Mount, North Carolina, the dutiful daughter was surrounded by people who cared. Her mother perceived

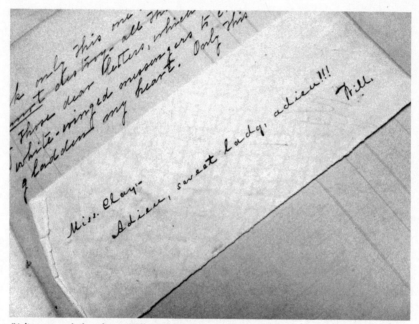

"O! I'm dreaming." Reverse of Will Scott's calling card. The secret words (in Clay Dillard's hand) are hidden on the back of the card, which she pasted into her diary. Much as she loved Will, her overbearing brother-in-law prevented them from marrying. Courtesy of the Southern Historical Collection, Wilson Library, University of North Carolina–Chapel Hill.

"Adieu, sweet lady, adieu!!! Will." A final souvenir in Clay Dillard's diary. Courtesy of the Southern Historical Collection, Wilson Library, University of North Carolina–Chapel Hill.

sadness beneath the gay exterior, half knowing the source of it: "She had reasons to think Genl Rivers was instrumental," Clay writes. "I did not wish to tell her, even my Mother." She did all she could to keep silent about the pain. "How could I hide my feelings from her who bore me—and such a dear, blessed Mother. She has but to look in my eyes, and she reads the workings of my heart."

The other parent was even more protective of her:

Sometimes when I am sitting on the ottoman by the side of Pa, with his arm resting caressingly around my shoulder, as I always do at night, I feel I am not a woman grown, with a hidden heart sorrow, but only a child. The past seems to me as some beautiful dream. Every one treats me so much as a child, I cannot feel otherwise. Pa's pet name for me is "Lap in Lay," and he so often knuckles me under the chin and says "If any of the boys come after my baby, we will shoot them with a pop-gun, wont we 'Lap in Lay.'" Then I hide my face in his bosom and tell him yes.

She had all but surrendered to a life of disappointment. Her plaint seems to be more than the gloominess after a breakup. The darkness inside had become so intoxicating that loneliness, resignation, and death whisper through the remainder of her diary:

January 1858: "Mortals are strangely constituted. They must have sorrow to make them feel the full value of happiness."

February 1858: "Those words from [Byron's] Childe Harold often come to me 'There is a pleasure in the pathless wood,' etc. Yes, '*there is society where none intrudes.*'"

March 1858: "Thoughts of one, loved and lost, whose name dwells ever in my heart, but passes not these lips. . . . He once said, 'Tis better to have loved and lost than never to have loved atal.' My hopes are blighted. Thus it is with life's golden hopes."

Her mother, bedridden for months, was by this time on the verge of death. To arrest the process of decay that the house reeked of, Clay attempted to restore to mind a better time, her "innocent and mirthful" childhood. "Memory will bring back the 'olden time,' with its wealth of smiles and hopes," she writes. But even this sentiment redirected her to the loss of Will Scott's love: "Yes there are times when Memory strikes cords too wildly mournful ever to be forgotten. In dreams comes back all the past—in dreams I see his face, and hear his voice Caress in a dream—'tis sweet to be bless'd. There is a void in my heart nothing else can fill. nothing."

Habituated to seeing in dreams the still-promising face of the man she loved, she turned her disappointment into something less costly, less immediate. But then, on May 7, 1858, Thomas Rivers, Jr., sister May's baby, barely a year old, breathed his last. "Little Tommy dead! Can it, Can it be?" This was the way of the nineteenth-century world. Christmas that year was quiet at the Dillard home, and Clay saw no better prospects. "I am in my room alone. No stockings hanging by the fire 'in hopes that St. Nicholas will soon be there'— nor mysterious parcels such as have often excited my curiosity when a child. Bright dreams, and happy illusions come not again."

All across the pages of her diary is the word "dream." Representative of many privileged girls in the mid-nineteenth century, the uninhibited Clay Dillard was raised with the expectation that if she studied hard and obeyed those who watched over her, she would find a worthy mate. In some ways pampered, in other ways restricted in what she could aspire to, she pursued a life that was modeled on Maria Edgeworth's upright women. The young were expected to dream now—that is, to consciously fantasize companionate love along with deep and devoted friendships.

It was in this manner that "dream" became a common noun and verb and exemplified the nineteenth century's retranslation of the Declaration's "pursuit of happiness." In Jefferson's day, "dream" most often described a "fallacious" or inconsequential thought, and the literal dream could be explained away as literally nonsense. The "pursuit" Jefferson had in mind in 1776 meant as much to society as to the individual. It meant working to build and defend a moral community. No dream of happiness could be realized except in the context of community. By the time Clay Dillard became socially aware, the pursuit of happiness more concretely embraced an individual's path to the future. The way to happiness was available to any person who was ambitious for love and social position.

Individual dreams were expressed without being thought a "somnium"; dreams of personal happiness were no longer automatically part of a cautionary tale associated with unlikely aims or unrealizable ambition. In Clay's diary, dreams refer to both her literal, nocturnal dreams and the larger dreams for life that she had been encouraged to cultivate. But all her hopes for a life in pursuit of happiness, a life that contained the love young women were now entitled to dream about, had dissolved into melancholy. All the education and all the literature—the power of awareness and discernment she was supposed to have acquired at the Edgeworth school—had not protected her. All that protected her was the infantilizing mirage created by a father who had formerly promised her a life as his "Lap in Lay."

We do not know what happened to her over the next few years, because the diary contains no more entries by her. But we do know how Clay Dillard's pursuit ended, and it was predictably tragic. In 1863, the one Clay called "Sis May" took over the diary and supplied a voice, because Clay's had gone silent. May's page was titled simply "A Dream," and it told the dream Clay had related to her a short time before her final illness took hold. It turns out to be a reprocessing of the old, familiar vision of a journey to heaven and back, punctuated by music.

> I had a deep dark abyss to cross on a narrow footway. After proceeding cautiously a few paces I was met by a sweet little cherub boy, who took me by the hand and conducted me safely over; when I stooped down and took him up in my arms to caress him, I found to my astonishment and delight "Little Tommy" whom I had loved so passionately, before he went with the angels. Soon a number of dear ones of other days met and welcomed me. I now heard strains of music and looking ahead saw a bright dazzling glorious City whence they proceeded. I listened as I approached and it proved to be Rock of Ages sung more exquisitely, more enrapturingly than any thing I had ever imagined or conceived. My friends said the inhabitants of the city spoke a strange language which I would not understand at first—I replied, you are mistaken, I have already learned it—and I awoke.

When her father died in 1859, Clay wrote that he had grieved over not seeing his little "Lap in Lay" in his last days: "Clay, God bless her, tell her to meet me in heaven." Now that Clay was gone, the surviving sister characterized the tender heart she knew by invoking one of Washington Irving's pathos-driven stories, one of the many that reminded their generation how hard it was for a broken heart to mend: "Like Irving's dove in the Broken Heart," May wrote of Clay, "she strove to hide from all the arrow that was preying on her vitals. I believe with that writer in broken hearts and that thus many lovely forms fade away into the tomb and none can tell the cause that blighted their loveliness." She had not been the same since Will Scott was taken from her.

In reviewing Clay's life of the mind, we see repeated the well-established literary symbols from which so many of the dreamers featured in these pages derived their inspiration: Edward Young's *Night Thoughts*, Lord Byron's *Childe Harold*, and Washington Irving's "Broken Heart." Interlocking themes of dream/death/memory persisted among those—especially educated women—who came of age in the nineteenth century.

Awake, we of the twenty-first century tell ourselves there is no reason to fear our dreams. We deny, disdain, and forestall the end of personhood with all the tools the modern world makes available. Actuarial evidence instructs us that we will experience only a very gradual physical decline. How much more "present" that feeling was in an age when the average individual died before fifty is difficult to qualify with any precision. But we know it was there.

That is what emotional history attempts to explain: qualitative differences between then and now. It is all meant to be presented in a detached, dispassionate manner. But when stories like that of Caroline Clay Dillard are placed before our eyes, and we imagine a time-bending communion, the emotionalism of those who came before is not so foreign seeming, so dead and buried. Their pathos reaches us. Still, we ask the question, first posed with cool objectivity: to what extent were they like us?

What we are able to grasp at this point in the narrative, with scarcely a doubt, is that their night thoughts contained strong passions, and their broken hearts were not just real, but like blinding sandstorms to them. They knew when they had agency in encountering life's end, which was certainly not often. They knew (as we do) that the imagination is much more than a limpid pool inside the brain, waiting to be stirred and stimulated—it actively creates events, good and bad.

In 1863, the same year Clay Dillard took sick and died, Brigadier General Thomas Rivers also died of natural causes. This must be some kind of poetic justice. William Lafayette Scott enlisted in the 21st North Carolina infantry when war broke out and was elected captain of Company M, the "Guilford Dixie Boys." He survived the war, only to die in 1872. To do the math, he outlasted by only nine years the heartbroken young woman who would have been delighted to marry him.[16]

~๛~

Missourian Spencer Brown would serve as a spy for the Union Army during the Civil War and forfeit his life because of it. But in 1858, he was a sixteen-year-old cowhand on a farm, and his diary had nothing more dramatic to report than the weight of a catfish someone caught. But on a couple of occasions that spring and summer, he dreamt of love. He did not give his fantasy a name. It was just a feeling: "I had a dream last night—truly a dream. I dreamed that I loved and was loved again." Gloom descended after he woke to a humdrum world. But at night, when he sat down to write, his mood changed: "I am cheered with hope." A few months later, a similar good feeling arose in his sleeping mind: "I have worked very hard to-day," he noted, and then explained why: "I had such a nice dream last night—I dreamed that I was loved. It made me work harder all day!" "Still," the teenager added glumly, "I wake to a sad reality."[17]

Francis Terry Leak was an attorney and plantation owner in North Carolina, born in 1803 and admitted to the bar at the age of twenty-one. In the late 1830s, he established himself in northern Mississippi. Much later, his diary would come to the attention of the author William Faulkner, who drew directly from it in some of his fiction.[18]

In the autumn of 1854, Leak wrote in his diary that he had dreamt of a Rockingham, North Carolina, friend, R. J. Steele. So he decided to write to him. Enclosing some "Java peas" from his plantation, he spelled it all out, telling Steele that "after looking at his daguerreotype a few evenings ago, I dreamed of him." In the dream, Steele had come down for a visit, "and very soon after walking in the house, he enjoined me not to forget to show him, before he left, the branch [of a river] I had been speaking to him about, when in North Carolina, in reference to its capacity for milling purposes. I promised, of course, to attend to the matter, being much gratified at the opportunity of getting his opinion upon the subject."

Here was a dream about forgetting and regretting, a familiar theme to any who have had the classic dream of arriving for a test unaware and unprepared. "Somehow or other," Leak went on, "I did let him slip off without showing him the branch. I regretted this very much upon awaking, & still regretted it, because I then thought, & still think, that had I taken him over to the stream I should probably have obtained some of his ideas upon the subject." So, in writing the letter to Steele, he made certain to ask for an opinion—precisely what he had neglected to ask in the dream. He explained, both to his correspondent and in his diary, "that I had often had ideas put into my mind in a dream which I could not account for by tracing them to any previous observations or reflections of my own." He was convinced that one function of dreaming was to hatch original, constructive thoughts.[19]

Mrs. George Thurston was the wife of a Mississippi riverboat captain and mother of a small boy named Webster. She lived in the Deep South. Her New York–designed "Pocket Diary for 1858" is only unusual in that, for a period of several months, she jotted a brief, almost daily summary of her dreams. Only Ichabod Cook devoted more time in a single bound journal to regular notations of raw dream content.

June 28: "Dreamed was in the Catholic Church. Seen Some Girls dressed in white, knitting—awoke feeling bad."

July 6: "Dreamed Riding on horseback and dancing."

July 7: "Dreamed I seen [her deceased] Father. Seen some wonderful manifestation in Spiritualism."

(Across the United States, the 1840s and 1850s saw a flowering of interest in Spiritualism, an offshoot of Christianity readily identified with séances, mesmeric trances, and especially the teachings of Emanuel Swedenborg [1688–1772]. Biographies of Swedenborg rolled from American presses. In the words of one, the Stockholm-born philosopher considered "the brain and nerves, or spirit vessels" as "channels of a transcendent or spirituous circulation." Questioning traditional assumptions about heaven and hell, Swedenborg treated Judgment Day as a decision about the quality of a person's spirit, unrelated to his or her adherence to sectarian principles. In Swedenborgian terms, all who yearned to communicate with the dead, all who thought that ways could be found to contact spirits, accepted dreams as a possible source of extraordinary knowledge.[20])

Back to Mrs. Thurston:

July 10: "Dreamed of having something to do with chickens."

July 11: "Slept Sound last night. Got up with the headach."

("Slept sound" meant that she did not dream. Periodicals of the 1850s upheld the dictum "perfect health insures dreamless sleep." Personal dream records had heightened in complexity and deepened in self-discovery, but the public discourse had hardly budged: dreaming still indicated the existence of an internal problem—either a person had not been eating right or was suffering from an identifiable medical condition, as doctors since Benjamin Rush's day had claimed. For Mrs. Thurston, though, sound sleep did not prevent a morning headache.)

July 14: "Dreamed Something about talking with B. about buying a woman" (a slave to do household chores).

July 15: "Had bad dreams about sick Babys. Webster is very sick, sent for the Dr."

July 16: "Dreamed about putting out fire, killing a bird."

July 17: "Dreamed about Dr. Davis thought he had grown so ugly."

July 19: "Dreamed something about a letter."

July 21: "Dreamed of having 4 different kinds of Birds in one Cage + caught another large one. Had some notion of giving lessons in painting."

July 22: "Dreamed I seen . . . a strange Bird gave away half a hog then helped cut it up."

July 25: "Had disagreeable Dreams, got feeling low, got the headach."

July 26: "Dreamed I slept on my scissors & broke them."

July 27: "Dreamed I had a difficulty with Mrs. Weed about a Servant & beat her."

July 28: "Dreamed a man gave me a piece of a Tarantula."

August 3: "Dreamed of being in a hotell."

August 5: "Dreamed of having Some very large Strawberries."

August 6: "Dreamed of climing up a [?] verry high to fly, then let all holds[?] go to see if I could not fly but I would come down again."

Her husband, George, returned home on the morning of the sixth, after a long absence plying the Mississippi. He had been ill. We have none of George's dreams to compare, but if Robert Stuart, another American seafarer at virtually the same moment, can serve as a stand-in, it is easy to imagine what the long absences must have produced in George's mind. Wrote Stuart to his wife: "How strange it is that I so constantly dream of home, either yourself or one of the little darlings invariably appearing to me." With her husband once again sharing her bed, Mrs. Thurston stopped recording her dreams and did not start up again for weeks:

September 1: "Dreamed I was in a strange place, a hotell. Seen deep water, rode horse back. had a dispute with Mr. Thurston a bout going Somewhere after Money."

September 2: "Dreamed of having trouble Seperating with Mr. T. Thought after it was all over I felt comfortable."

September 3: "Dreamed of seeing large trees that had been taken up and replanted close to a house."

September 4: "Had disagreeable Dream."

September 5: "Dreamed of spending most of our Money."

September 6: "Dreamed I had a new bonnet, was trying it on."

September 8: "Dreamed of broken Eggs and haveing to work hard."

September 9: "Dreamed of being nearly to the end of the world and Seeing Some large Osien [ocean]."

September 10: "Dreamed I was in a Hotell. Seen Some dead men's bodies covered up with a dead dog's carcase. Went in the wash house and in the Soap house."

September 11: "Dreamed I was making a pair of Pantaloons for a Tailor. Sewed them with a Shuttle. . . . Had on a dirty Dress. Seen some ugly men and women."

September 12: "Dreamed of being in a boarding house. Stole a glove. Seen a floor painted with many colors, verry bright. Had Something to do with a Baby."

September 13: "Dreamed of seeing Father. and I fear Some of us is going to be Sick."[21]

There is considerable variation in Mrs. Thurston's dream symbols—birds, babies, ugly faces, broken things, household tasks, money spent, strange hotels—but what they all have in common is an emotional reaction to disorganization or the reorganization of her environment. Most of the dreams contain negative features, and none appears to suggest anything enduringly positive. Of the two wherein she saw the image of her deceased father, the first was hopeful, as it was accompanied by "some wonderful manifestation" of Spiritualism; the second struck her as a bad omen, predicting illness in her household. With her husband away for long stretches, adaptation to two distinct routines must have presented significant challenges, making stress unavoidable.

Mrs. Thurston's pocket diary is informative in its listing of the incongruous household items that appear in her sleeping mind and the impulses they relate to. We can say with some assurance that these dreams, consisting of odd conjunctions (birds and hogs; broken eggs and hard work) and odd disjunctions (dead men covered up with a dog's carcass), brought more dismay than conscious clarity. In a society absent of professional therapists, shamans, or an Ichabod Cook in the neighborhood to explain and soothe, there was no reliable cure for troubling dreams.

~∂~

Mollie Dorsey was unusual. She accepted her visions, unorthodox though they were, and held her head high wherever she went. She persisted in expressing her mind, projecting her thoughts.

Mollie was not a witch, though people called her that. She began her journal in March 1857, at age eighteen, as she left Indianapolis with her large family and trekked west. When her father, William, brought them into Nebraska Territory, the area had been open to white settlement for only a few short years. They were real log-cabin pioneers. Mollie, with a venturesome spirit and a vibrant pen, wrote every few evenings by candlelight. She liked the prairie, and she always looked forward to sleeping and dreaming.

The land on which the Dorsey family settled was remote. Mollie described the view along the Nemaha River, "where myriads of tiny fish sport, and whose banks are overhung with creeping vines and flowers." Aside from the occasional rattlesnake, which the other young people lived in fear of (and she, less timorously, kept an eye out for), her surroundings were pristine.

On June 29, 1857, she met blue-eyed Byron Sanford, who was twelve years her senior. "It is refreshing to meet a fellow like him after seeing so many flattering fops," she wrote, all too aware that the rarity of marriageable women in the territory meant that word of her arrival was spreading quickly. In other respects, she seemed to adapt easily to this new life.[22]

That August, William Dorsey had just set out on a trip, and "a queer experience" occurred that Mollie felt compelled to relate. "I had gone to bed one night, but could not sleep," she began. "My father was constantly on my mind." She sensed that he was coming home, though he had been gone only two days and was not expected back for weeks. She rose from bed in the middle of the night and lit a fire to keep warm. Her mother awakened and came out to see what was wrong. "I told her I was looking for Father," writes Mollie. "She thought I was losing my senses."

But the impression in her mind continued to grow. "Hardly aware of what I was doing, I ground up and made some coffee. Mother was about to get up and shake me, when we heard the dogs bark, the voices, and soon Father was at the door." He was accompanied by his traveling companions, Byron Sanford and a Mr. Holden. "Mr. Holden is a spiritualist," she records next, "and readily accounted for it by saying I was a 'medium.'" It was hard for her to believe, though she knew something extraordinary had just occurred. "I hope if I am controlled by any spirit," she concluded, "it will be for good." The day before, her brother was bitten by a rattlesnake. Unfortunately for young Sam Dorsey, Mollie didn't see that coming.[23]

"Guess I'm going to be a 'mejium' or spiritualist whether I want to be or not," she wrote in September 1857. The girl from Indiana did not know what the Great Plains, or as she put it, "this wild life," held for her, but she was remarkably unafraid. She sensed there was something special about her, and that her powers of mind obliged her to look out for those she loved.

It was at this time that dream life first directed her actions. Her father had given her a pair of shell puff combs to wear in her hair. One day, she went off on a "long tramp hunting plums" with several other girls and boys and realized only when she returned home that one of the combs was gone. "It worried me half the night," she wrote. "But I dreamed that I saw my comb on the limb of a certain plum tree I remembered, because it was close to an old deserted cabin a mile from the house." After she had the dream a second time, she resolved to test its power. "I went to the tree, and there sure enough! just as I had seen it in my dream, hung my comb! My hair seemed to rise upon my head and my knees knocked together, but I had my treasure, and had also demonstrated the fact that there was something in my dream."

Family members starting calling her "prophet" and "witch." Not long after came the most amazing of all her night visions: "I saw in a dream a closed carriage drive to the door, containing a man and a woman, the woman wearing glasses, and a green veil, and the man driving one white and one bay horse. The advent of a female occurs so seldom that we never look for them any more." Mollie proceeded to inform her family that they were going to have company at their log cabin home, come breakfast. She described the woman. Only one of the Dorsey clan believed in what Mollie now called her "prognostical spasms," and she was filled with anticipation, "perched by the window to watch the road." Soon enough, "an excited exclamation brought us to see the identical carriage, the white and bay horse, the man, and stranger yet, the woman with the glasses and the green veil." It was a couple who had come to visit relatives in the area.

Mollie finished telling her tale. At nightfall, the travelers had stopped six miles away at a "bachelor's cabin," where the woman in the green veil was assailed by bedbugs and then refused to stay for breakfast with the unclean bachelor. So the party started out early and arrived at the Dorseys in time for breakfast. When told of Mollie's dream, the woman in green said: "There's no use talking—you are a medium." Mollie accepted who and what she was, writing: "I cannot explain, nor do I try to."[24]

The next spring, she moved to Nebraska City and took up work as a dressmaker. In the intervening months, given her eligibility, she had several suitors. She told herself she would not make a choice of husband until she turned twenty-one. There are no dream entries for the year 1858, though Mollie did continue to ruminate on her natural abilities: "I have many seasons of sublime and poetic thoughts, and often soar above the cares of life into a world of my own, into whose portals no one may invade. It is well perhaps that I have to battle with stern realities. I might become an idle dreamer, for I have not talent enough to make much of myself. I used to dream of being an author. . . ." She is slightly older, and sounds it. She has also resolved that "By," as she called her new beau, Byron Sanford, was "a good match for me. He is so thoroughly matter-of-fact and practical that it will help equalize my romance and sentiment." She declared to her diary that she loved him.[25]

At nineteen, with thoughts of marriage entering her mind, Mollie apparently considered her prophetic visions to belong to the past. She was no longer a "mejium," no longer living through dreams. Except that on the last day of February 1859, while staying with a family an hour outside Nebraska City, she was again startled by a vision, and a deeply disturbing one. It came to her not long after she had learned that her cousin Mary, in Nebraska City, was unhappy with her new stepmother. Mary's widowed father had married "suddenly," and it seemed to unleash a season of ill fortune.

"I feel sad and depressed today from the effects of one of my dreams last night," Mollie recorded. "All night long when I slept I could see Cousin Mary first a bride and then in a coffin, and waking, I seemed to hear her calling me. Mother says I am morbid and must have a change, but no! There's something wrong and I fully expect before night to hear bad news."

There was a hill where one always caught a first glimpse of teams of horses approaching the little town, and Mollie found herself looking anxiously in the direction of that hill. "I wish I were not this way," she wrote, "and maybe after all I am morbid or something else. I do not dwell on imaginary or impending evils, and these impressions come unsolicited."[26]

But just as she predicted, that very night her Uncle Frank rode up on horseback and delivered the news: "The moment I saw him my heart beat faster. I said, 'Uncle, you bring bad tidings?' He looked surprised and said, 'Who told you?' I said, 'What is it?' He said, 'Your Cousin Mary has had a hemorrhage and cannot live, and is constantly calling you.'" There is nothing in the analytical character of her writing, at this or any other time, to suggest Mollie was lying or allowing an admittedly rich imagination to get the better of her. In fact, except for those occasional reflections on her gift of prophecy, her writing is marked by utter earnestness.

She returned to Nebraska City and cared for her cousin. This meant, too, that she had to tangle with the evil stepmother, who seemed to her strangely jealous of the dying girl: "She has a natural antipathy to Mary," Mollie wrote.

The pathos of the deathbed scene, a staple of early American literature, was replicated in Mollie's diary. "O! Mollie," Mary cried out to her. "I shall be soon where flowers never die." It was on May 4, 1859, after Mollie had begun a new job as a schoolteacher, that she recorded her personal loss: "I come with saddened heart and tearful eyes today, my Journal. This afternoon Mary was laid away. She called for me the eve before she passed away. Through the stepmother's misrepresentations I did not get the message, and only heard of the event in time to reach the house for the funeral services."[27]

She and By were married on St. Valentine's Day, 1860. When the snows melted, the newlyweds moved farther west, to the rugged metropolis of Denver. Mollie's portentous dreams stopped, or at least she stopped recording them in her journal. Other things were happening that took precedent. She delivered a baby who did not survive, and she and her husband got to know the Colorado governor and played cards with the Indian agent Albert Gallatin Boone, grandson of the trailblazing Daniel Boone. The Sanfords were upstanding citizens of the territory.

With the outbreak of war, Byron Sanford enlisted in the Union Army, assumed the rank of lieutenant, and in the spring of 1862 saw action at the Battle of Pigeon Ranch, New Mexico. Mollie waited nervously for word of the fighting and word from her husband. And then there was this journal entry: "Last night while brooding over my troubles I had one of my impressions that By was coming home . . . and sure enough! this morning the advance guard arrived, and as Col. Slough shook hands with me he said, 'Let me congratulate you, Madam. You will soon see your husband.' And so my dream came true."[28]

—⁓—

The decade of the 1850s produced an astounding number of dream vignettes—those recoverable from personal diaries and those featured in the public papers. Children's literature of this decade featured dream-based tales, often the sort in which an angel led the sleeper through "liquid realms" of heavenly firmament. The didactic *Sunday School-Teacher's Dream* took its author to the world beyond, allowing him to watch a drama play out between a former colleague and the delinquent student he had failed to inspire—both, as a consequence, were troubled souls. On waking, the afflicted teacher resolved: "I have never met my class since that memorable night, without a vivid recollection of every circumstance of my dream."[29]

Many deeply religious people would store up a dream so powerful that it became part of a devotional. Priscilla Munnikhuysen held fast to one in particular, which she felt protected her soul from degradation. The twenty-year-old daughter of a Dutch immigrant merchant, she lived outside Baltimore in the late 1850s and attended the Methodist Church, where she enjoyed a good sermon. "I once had a dream which has left a lasting impression on my mind," she wrote in her diary. "I dreamed I was walking along a road leading from our house to one of the neighbors', and I came to a run where I had to cross before I could reach the house I was going to, and when I looked I found there were no stepping stones or any other way of crossing that I could see." The obstacle was great, but so was her faith. "On looking up very far I saw a log, as it were fastened up by bushes, and seeming to be almost entirely suspended in the air. But I thought I had to go, and although the way looked dangerous, I had to cross over. On looking up I beheld our Savior looking down at me with a halo around his head, more like the sun, and as I looked up He said, 'have faith in God.'" It had been some years since she had had this dream, and yet, "it is as fresh in the halls of memory as when I dreamed it."[30]

Then there was Martini Brandigee of Detroit, who spent the night at the home of a family friend and came to breakfast with a dream to report: "Oh, Mrs. S., I have a sweet Heavenly vision—I could not sleep for excitement." She had found herself in the girlhood home of a friend they shared, who was now deceased. Their friend was not shrouded in mist, but appeared as her earthly self—yet "surrounded by a halo of light." She whispered to the dreamer, "Martini, is it you?" Martini could not speak, which the deceased seemed to understand, and proceeded to sing a tune for her that they had formerly sung together.[31]

Mysteries of science were as popular as mysteries of faith. In 1859, *Harper's Weekly* published "A Physician's Dreams." The author, English, had observed a patient whose brain was exposed as a result of an accident. Adopting a metaphor of modern communications, the doctor laid out what the naked brain had revealed to him: "In a waking state, the brain had intelligent . . . telegraphic motions, correspondent to the thoughts which it was printing off. . . . But in a state of sleep the patient's brain worked and telegraphed no more. It became a mere pulse, like that at the wrist." From this, he concluded, sleep was "quietude," and someone unable to get a night's rest could not but "drown the busy brain in a kind of artificial apoplexy."

Good men have bad dreams. One was not to judge character on the basis of dream content. The doctor could only conclude, as his eighteenth-century predecessors had done, that external (physical) or internal (physiological) disruptions made dreams what they were. With epigrammatic force, he proclaimed:

"Indigestion, both in its labor and its fatigue, is a prolific hag-mother of ugly dreams."

He tried not to address his reader in absolutes. "I imagine that a dream of sound is caused by an actual sound . . . , perhaps nothing more musical than a London cry." (Perhaps this is what he would have told Dr. Rush about his Final Judgment trumpet.) The sleeping mind was too "idle" to create elaborate theater by itself, and so if "some stray memory, some throb in the blood, makes us wish to hear a singer," a fractured effort on the part of the brain, a "momentary volition," might produce a facsimile of it, but a weak facsimile. And this, in a phrase, explained the bizarre imagery that dreamers experienced.

Undertaking a self-examination, the doctor found that a little too much wine with dinner could bring on a nightmare. "I imagined myself to be in some unknown country, arriving at a mysterious hotel. I was put to sleep in a mysterious room, which resembled the hall of an old castle. . . . I was lying in a dim, shadowy bed." Standing imposingly in all four corners of the room were statues of men in armor, which before long came alive and began to move toward him. "The sense of the supernatural now became in me horrifying and intense. . . . I struggled to get up, but could only utter faint cries." All at once, as the men in armor neared his bed, "a sudden change came over me. I felt loosed from my nightmare bonds, and by a prodigious effort leaped out of bed."

Once awake, he gradually realized that there was no flesh-and-blood thief in the house, only a terrible dream in his head. With this reassurance, he returned to bed and fell asleep easily. The dream renewed, but instead of a nightmarish attack, it morphed into "a pleasant tour." He was still traveling to unknown places, but the haunted inn was left behind, and a lighthearted feeling replaced fear. Having battled past the effects of wine midway through the night, he was able to pass several good hours: "I awoke with a feeling of mingled amusement and comfort."

In the 1840s and 1850s, dream books and itinerant seers tapped into common anxieties more than ever before. Dream books held the key to instant salvation, promised an end to chaos, and offered a means of reversing the hopeless spiral into which the financially strapped were sinking. While better-educated people arranged séances or turned to Transcendentalism or Swedenborgian mysticism, more ordinary folks found themselves led into the "vernacular divination" provided by dream books, where supernatural messages were hidden in dream symbols. There was no clear winner in the competition between popular science and popular religion.[32]

This was also the era of Joseph Smith, the martyred visionary, and his successor, Brigham Young, who journeyed west to establish the Mormon Church in Utah. In Mormonism, dreams and visions carry great weight. Many are archetypal, involving a glimpse of heaven and loved ones who await the dreamer there. But while going west with Brigham Young in 1847, thirty-three-year-old pioneer William Clayton recorded a dream about his Mormon fellows that contains those raw elements, free of religious sentiment, that speak to the cultural project we are addressing.

Clayton dreamt that the traveling party had stopped beside a deep river. "Our horses and cattle were tied to stakes all around the camp to the distance of a quarter of a mile, some good timber thinly scattered around." He thought he spotted Brigham Young and others moving away from them, heading up the river in a flatboat. "When they had been gone some time I thought a large herd of buffalo came on full gallop right amongst our horses and cattle, causing them to break their ropes and fly in every direction. The brethren seemed thunderstruck and did not know what to do." This was when the dreamer found himself taking charge and arresting the panic: "Seeing a small skiff in the river, I sprang into it, and a paddle lying in it, I commenced rowing in pursuit of the President [Young]. It seemed as though I literally flew through the water." He succeeded in overtaking the leadership, and as he brought the skiff to shore, he suddenly realized that it was full of cracks and incapable of having gone upriver without sinking. "The paddle," moreover, "proved to be a very large feather." In the end, the party he had chased after thought nothing of the incident back in camp; they "seemed no ways alarmed." It was at this moment in his dream, with the impossible coming close to believable, that William Clayton awoke.[33]

One can only assume that as American families migrated west, crossing rivers and fording streams, many people experienced this same species of dream. Physical exertions in one's daily life could translate easily into physical challenges within the dreaming mind.

∽෴∾

"Dreams," says a writer, "are the novels which we read when asleep." This is one of the gems in an anthology of wisdom and verse relating to dreamscapes. *The Poetry and Mystery of Dreams*, published in 1856, declared itself to be a poetic refrain, not a prophetic guide. Dreams were no longer "sources of hope or fear," according to the book's compiler, "but they are still recorded as mysterious or pleasing fantasies, still narrated at the breakfast table, and still quoted by lovers as affording involuntary illustrations of a passion which dares not declare itself in more direct terms."[34]

When literal dreams were voiced unreservedly at the breakfast table, something meaningful was going on. Mollie Dorsey was never thought afflicted, though her mind wandered into the occult. Where book reading was a rich pleasure within families, vivid, psychologically drawn characters translated into ever more demonstrative diaries. It was reaching the point where the animated individual exuded an energy that had physico-chemical properties. "Of physiology from tip to toe I sing," penned Walt Whitman, who published *Leaves of Grass* in 1855 and assimilated the song of nation into the song of self. "Of Life immense in passion, pulse, and power," he hummed, "Cheerful, for freest action form'd under the laws divine, The Modern Man I sing."[35]

Science is now saying that we are wired in favor of optimism, no matter how much we police morality or dwell on our mortality. Recent studies show that narrative consciousness collects and distributes our visual stories in convenient ways in order to feed a built-in sense of our resilience. Humans are adaptive, meaning we take our traumas, our living nightmares, and try to construct scenarios around them so that they do not impede progress toward the future.[36]

That optimistic undercurrent may be what we are seeing as the nineteenth century moved along. Yes, nineteenth-century lives were strewn with death. In and out of dreams, they knew a more profound helplessness than we do. Among the individuals whose stories have been collected in these pages, morning consciousness seems most positive when dreams removed the dreamer to a childhood scene or to a place far away. Nostalgic or utopian visions were the easiest for them to express.

None of this meant that conformity had come to an end in America. We see, despite the increased appearance of odd objects and unique configurations, that dreams such as Clay Dillard's were populated with angels and dead loved ones. What the record does show, at least, is that the middle decades of the nineteenth century witnessed an upsurge in dramatic encounters within dreams, without stuffy rationalizations.

For the heartbreak kids, if we might dub them that, dreams produced just enough of hope to offset the omnipresent prospect of devastating loss. In Madaline Edwards's case, dreams of love were brief interruptions in a life of emotional betrayal. Clay Dillard, her father's "Lap in Lay," was never allowed to grow up. Her dreams symbolized what she was deprived of in reality and could not acknowledge to her family; they were her passage to freedom and independence, to an alternative life where she could live out the desire to know and enjoy love. In contrast to Madaline and Clay, the self-assured Mollie Dorsey dreamt and prophesied as a means of coping with ambiguity, thereby obtaining mastery over her emotions.

Their stories detract from the typical narrative requirement of charting progress over time. Aside from Mollie, whose "sixth sense" made her as much a seer as a dreamer, the other individuals we met in this chapter whose lives can be reconstructed with emotional complexity were fated to lose love and die before they had a real chance to make a mark on society. One would only expect that the Civil War, America's first modern war, stood to intensify the tragic dimension in dream telling. But that is only partly true.

PART THREE
1861–1900

SEVEN

LINCOLN DREAMS
HE'S DIED

Dreamed of home last night. O Dreams! Visions! Shadows of the brain! What are you? My whole consciousness, since I heard of President Lincoln's assassination, seems nothing but a horrid dream.

—Alexander H. Stephens, vice president of the Confederate
States of America, June 1865. He penned these words
from prison, three weeks after his arrest.

John C. Calhoun was twice an unhappy vice president, and for years afterward a magisterial, if, to many, a chilly presence in the U.S. Senate. In the 1820s, the Yale-educated South Carolinian defected from John Quincy Adams's administration to support Andrew Jackson, only to fall out of favor with Jackson. As a senator, he gave early voice to a theory of disunion, and his sturdy defense of slavery added to his luster in the South as war loomed.

A couple of months before he died, Calhoun had a "singular dream," if one is to accept the inventive George Lippard. In January 1850, the story went, the senator sat down to breakfast with Congressman Robert Toombs of Georgia and exhibited tremendous agitation. Toombs noticed that Calhoun was looking down at his right hand. He asked whether the senator was in any pain. "It is nothing!" Calhoun exclaimed. "Only a dream I had last night."

In the hours since dawn, he had continued to see a black spot ("like an ink blotch") on the back of his hand. George Washington had come to him, dressed in Revolutionary garb, and pressed him about his intention of signing a "Declaration of Disunion." It was as Washington was speaking that the black first appeared on Calhoun's hand. Said Washington gravely: "That is the mark by which Benedict Arnold is known in the next world."[1]

In March of that year, as Calhoun lay dying in Washington, D.C., word began to get around. The *Wisconsin Democrat* prefaced "Calhoun's Dream—The Union" with an editorial tease: "The Washington correspondent of Lippard's paper the Quaker City, communicates the following curious account of a recent remarkable dream of Mr. Calhoun's. The allegory is certainly well carried out."

Even when presented as an allegory, however, some were persuaded that Calhoun did actually have some sort of prophetic dream. The senator's daughter-in-law, Margaret Green Calhoun, was credulous enough to write from Alabama's cotton-rich Black Belt to her sister, then in Washington, asking about its authenticity. "The dream you speak of in your letter I had never heard of," replied Eliza Green Reid. "I have inquired however & learn that most persons think he never had such a dream as the one in the papers[;] he had a dream but I cannot get the correct account of it. I have heard several, all different, as soon as he is well enough I will see him and get his own version of it." But of course, Senator Calhoun never recovered, so whatever dream he did have eludes the historian.[2]

Before inventing Calhoun's dream, George Lippard had earned renown as the author of a nightmarish book about urban vice and violence. Though a devoted fan of Edgar Allan Poe, Lippard chose to dedicate his novel *The Quaker City* (the same title he later gave to his weekly) to their long-dead predecessor in the gothic arts, Charles Brockden Brown. Lippard's sadistic character Abijah K. Jones, better known as "Devil-Bug," is so warped that he longs to live among the phantoms of those he has murdered. As his story unfolds, Abijah has a dream in which his victims rise before him. Blood drips and confusion reigns amid groans and whispers and grotesque laughter. Coffins float by the dreamer's inward eyes. The sun assumes the shape of "a grinning skeleton-head," dancing stars gleam "through the orbless socket of a skull" (recall the dream in *Richard III*), and a blood-red crescent moon rises. The haunted heavens disappear at once into a "thick and impenetrable darkness," and Devil-Bug is treated to the shrieking sounds of "the Orchestra of Hell."

Lippard wrote the sequence of sudden movements in a way that reproduces the emotional battlefield of a literal dream, capturing the cool, cruel concoction of a nightmare. But if Devil-Bug got what was coming to him, so did Lippard: the prolific young author turned out to be another heartbreak kid, dying of tuberculosis at thirty-one, in 1854. His work and his abbreviated life serve to remind us again that even before the photographed bloodshed of the Civil War, Americans were witness to disturbing images and inescapable personal tragedy.[3]

Whether or not the dying John C. Calhoun had a dream worth telling, he no longer believed in 1850 that North and South could coexist as one nation. In words he dictated to his private secretary, a New York City journalist, he said ominously that "the time had come" for the two sections to settle the slavery question "fully & forever." Planting seeds of discontent, the South Carolinian made many of his peers nervous. "Mr. Calhoun's death has deified his opinions," one northern judge noted, "and he is therefore more dangerous dead than living." And perhaps he was. South Carolina, the first state to secede, went its own way in December 1860; within three months, the rest of the Deep South had joined in rebellion, awaiting only Virginia, North Carolina, and Tennessee to make the Confederacy complete.[4]

Only the South's final defection enabled the northern states to find common cause. In 1860, even the dreamy Transcendentalists of the 1840s were disoriented and divided. Nathaniel Hawthorne returned from seven years abroad as a diplomat to find his old comrades Emerson, Thoreau, and Alcott viewing the coming war as the culmination of a moral crusade to open minds and save souls. Hawthorne bristled.

An event of October 1859 had put the final nail in the coffin. John Brown's bloody, badly organized raid on the national armory in Harper's Ferry, Virginia, had been designed to spark a race war. In its wake, an unrestrained Emerson called the violent abolitionist a "saint"; Thoreau uttered a plea on behalf of the convicted terrorist on the eve of his hanging (and martyrdom). Months later, Concord's schoolmaster brought two of John Brown's children to the town; they stayed with the Emersons and went to school with Hawthorne's son Julian.

When war broke out, Concord sent a company of volunteers to the Army of the Potomac. Gloomy Nathaniel Hawthorne did not join in the celebration. The bestselling author of *The Scarlet Letter,* a story of dark secrets, took solace in the fact that Julian, though old enough to have his eye on Harvard, was too young for soldiering.[5]

On the other side of the Mason-Dixon Line, a dreamer with dark secrets wrote in her diary on the day after Fort Sumter surrendered to the Confederacy: "O Lord let the N. & S. compromise & shed no more blood. . . . I never believed I should live to see my Country severed." She was Keziah Hopkins Brevard, a fifty-seven-year-old widow living alone with her numerous slaves on a six-thousand-acre plantation outside Columbia, South Carolina. Her late husband had been a state legislator during the first year of their marriage, but he was also a heavy drinker. He became so obsessed with his wife's fidelity that he went around monomaniacally hunting for her paramour, until he was finally hospitalized and then, after a few short weeks, pronounced cured.

Keziah, or "Kizzie," as she was known, recorded a series of dreams in the second half of 1860. The coming of war deeply affected her, and its disruptive prospect fed her dreams. July 31, 1860: "Last night I dreamed there was to be a commotion of some kind in Columbia. . . . I do hope there will be nothing to correspond with this dream—I don't wish to be superstitious." Five days later, she dreamt that James Hopkins Adams, the only son of her half sister, had returned home. He was a Yale graduate and a recent governor of South Carolina, and he would shortly sign the articles of secession. "I thought I was up a stair—I know not where," Kizzie wrote. "I saw J.H. comeing up slowly & looking wearied with a complexion of death—I thought I clasped his hands in mine & exclaimed My God! My God! I thought he said to his wife 'Oh you don't know how you cheer me.'" Adams, father of eleven, died the next year.[6]

The final day of December 1860 yielded to a particularly dreary night of rain and wind, and Kizzie was roused from sleep several times. "I woke dreaming an alarming dream—thought singular clouds were flitting over my head while I stood near an old brick oven of my mother's—while these clouds were fearful over my head—I saw in the S.E. corner of the yard two raging, smoking fires, the flames bursting high at intervals." (Recall the conflagration dreams of Washington Irving and Ichabod Cook, the latter of whom also denoted the direction of the fire.) Under threat, Kizzie imagined that she was urgently calling to her slaves and ordering the fires to be extinguished. "Lord save me from trouble," she wrote next. But it wasn't war she was concerned about: "This is the last day of 1860—am I nearer my God than I was one year ago?"

As the political times worsened, the widow Brevard continued to note down her troubled dreams. On April 2, days from the fall of Fort Sumter, she dreamt she was in the Presbyterian church in Columbia, sitting "either in or near" the pew of another planter's wife. "I thought Old Mrs. Bell sat at my right & young ladies at my left—I soon missed Mrs. Bell—I turned to my left & saw Mrs. B. M. Palmer [the former pastor's wife] going from the pulpit up the aisle to the door—she was dressed in deep black with a bonnet trimmed very much. Some one told me she had been up to the pulpit taking some bandages from Mr. P's face—his health was feeble & he had to use them." The odd thing about this picture is that Benjamin M. Palmer had not been the pastor at her church for five years, having relocated to New Orleans.

"I thought Mr. P looked sunken near the eyes," Kizzie continued. "Then immediately I found myself alone—looking around, every one had left the church & gone out doors to hear the preaching." So she followed and on the way out spotted an "old neighbour" of her mother's, long since dead. The neighbor was "sitting on a chair looking very cheerful & happy." So she proposed accompanying her, and the woman said: "Not while Mr. P was there." And that was as much as the dreamer remembered. Nothing made sense to her. "Is there any thing in dreams?" she posed. Later in the day, one of the slaves ran up to her and told her that one of her fields was ablaze.

Keziah Brevard repeated the cheerless refrain of so many: that she lived in a world of uncertainty. The day after her church dream, she said she was willing to give up her wealth if only North and South would reconcile. Referring to her home state of South Carolina, she wrote bleakly: "I do not love her disposition to cavil at every move—My heart has never been in the breaking up of the Union."[7]

Freud's theory that dreams often involve unacceptable desires and preoccupations seems entirely apropos at this turning point in history. As the abolitionist press was calling for across-the-board emancipation of the slaves, future secessionists printed anti-miscegenation engravings, hard-nosed editorials, and fanciful novels celebrating—we might call it daydreaming—the happy extended southern family. From *The Partisan Leader* (1836) to *Wild Southern Scenes* (1859), dreamy novels of southern independence, obtained bloodlessly, painted the North as overbearing and dictatorial. When the South finally went its own way, taking its chivalric dreams to the battlefield, it was persisting in a long-cultivated style of wishful thinking, hoping it would never have to wake up.[8]

～რ

In the North, too, the general feeling was that the Civil War would not last half as long as it did. But not everyone held this view. Calling the war "unsurpassed in the history of Christendom," Henry Boynton Smith of Maine predicted a long and bloody conflict: "I apprehend that few yet realize the sacrifice it may, must cost." Smith was the founder of a short-lived magazine, *The American Theological Review*, which published its first number in 1859 and its last in 1863. He proclaimed his periodical to be nondenominational, with theological, not ecclesiastical, objectives. "God's good providence," he said, would decide whether slavery outlived the war. Smith had become acquainted with New England Transcendentalists in the 1840s: "A strange set they are, full of what they call inspiration . . . but their belief yet shrouded in dreams and phantasmagorical shapes." He heard Emerson lecture and adjudged his theories "partial truth and total error." Beyond Henry Boynton Smith's religiosity, he was a fervent patriot who attended the inauguration of Abraham Lincoln in Washington.[9]

Tayler Lewis was for several decades a professor of Greek at Union College in Schenectady, New York; and he was the author of *The Divine Human in the Scriptures*. In January 1862, he offered up a deeply humanistic meditation on the soul's affections for the *American Theological Review*, building on the themes of his book. He told of an old gypsy, an unschooled centenarian, who asked an English-speaking friend whether he had ever thought that the "outer world"—what we take for reality—existed only in our minds, "and that each man, in fact, made his own world." His solipsistic dream had haunted the gypsy throughout his life. Buddhist doctrine held that "All is a Phantom," noted Lewis. Maybe, just maybe, our musing was as real as the rest of existence.

After weighing the gypsy's notion, Lewis pondered whether "the senses that God has given us" could deceive. Humans appeared to him to dream in a "hard material world," doing so purposefully. Yet the professor would not dismiss the possibility that an intense reality without materiality was also possible. A nonmaterial sensory reality.

He was defining dream as feeling. External and internal forces operated upon every person differently—"such has ever been the language of the musing mind." The science of invisible effects was still very young, and Professor Lewis would only say that he believed there was common ground between science and faith, between their two perspectives on the nature of the mind.

Narrowing his focus, Lewis addressed what dreamers since Dr. Rush had known as a register of inner life: the faculty of hearing. "The rational soul alone perceives music," he philosophized. "The sense only feels, and what it feels is only noise, a roaring in the ears, until the intelligence sees (we were going to say hears) its own ideas, its own harmonies." The rational soul, that which separated men from animals, had a nice ring to it. Music helped one understand spirit. The strings and vibrations of what Lewis called "musical science" needed no external confirmation to register the emotion of joy, any more than an inward vision needed external confirmation to create a comparable effect. Spiritual perception arose from some nonmaterial place, and that was that.[10]

In 1860, putting his own twist on the mystery of dream life, the opiated French poet Charles Baudelaire published *Les paradis artificiels*, in which he wrote:

> Man's dreams are of two classes. The first kind, filled with the details of his ordinary life, his preoccupations, his desires, and his vices, combine more or less bizarrely with objects seen in the daytime. . . . But as for the other kind of dream! the absurd, unexpected dream, unrelated and unconnected to the sleeper's character, life, and passions! This dream . . . represents the supernatural side of man, and it is precisely because it is absurd that the Ancients thought it divine.

~~~

Abraham Lincoln, who steered America through its national nightmare, was a very active, suggestible—even superstitious—dreamer. As president, he repeated his dreams to those close to him: an entire chapter in the memoir of Ward Hill Lamon, Lincoln's personal bodyguard and confidant during the war, is devoted to "Dreams and Presentiments." Born in Virginia, Lamon arrived in Illinois at the age of nineteen, in 1847, and passed the bar four years later. He was six feet two inches tall, nearly as tall as Lincoln. As a trusted friend of the president-elect, he accompanied Lincoln by train from Springfield to Washington, organized and commanded a regiment of volunteer infantry in 1861, and for the balance of the war served as marshal of the District of Columbia as well as Lincoln's personal assistant in several capacities—most particularly in guarding the president from physical danger.

Colonel Lamon explains in his memoir that Lincoln, an avid, gifted storyteller, found various ways to communicate a sense of foreboding. For example, he told Lamon of the night he broke free from imprisonment in the White House and went for a ride, alone, on "Old Abe," a favorite horse. "Immersed in deep thought," the president was shocked into a hypervigilant state by a rifle shot, courtesy of a "disloyal bushwhacker" who stood not fifty yards from him. In Lamon's retelling, the president narrowly escaped a sniper's bullet, lost his hat in the confusion, and chose to convey the nearly deadly story in a light, informal way. That was how Lincoln operated. Years before, he had informed his law partner, Billy Herndon, that he expected his life to come to an unfortunate end. But even these words were not spoken with sullenness or the least irritability. Lincoln lacked the capacity for self-pity. He was simply a superstitious man who tested the fate he prophesied for himself.[11]

In an antiwar speech Lincoln gave before Congress during the Mexican-American War in 1848, he compared one of President Polk's bellicose messages to "the half-insane mumbling of a fever dream." Obviously, scoffing at one species of dream did not mean the future president was a scoffer of dreams in general. In the 1850s, friends sometimes saw him enter a trancelike state, unmistakably lost in reverie. And before that, as a young lawyer in the 1830s, he had a distinct fondness for the faraway poetry of Lord Byron. One of his favorites was the one that opened: "I had a dream that was not all a dream." Lamon often heard the president repeat lines from that poem of Byron's titled "The Dream":

> Sleep hath its own world
> A boundary between the things misnamed
> Death and existence. Sleep hath its own world
> And a wide realm of wild reality.

As Lincoln scholar Douglas L. Wilson points out, Byron's poem "underscores the importance of the submerged half of one's being." Indeed, Lincoln's brooding side was no less a hallmark of his personality than his famous wit.[12]

He spent his younger years in Kentucky and Indiana, among plain people who, Lamon writes, "believed in the marvellous as revealed in presentiments and dreams." Lincoln imbibed these notions. He could be encouraged or he could be undone by his dreams, convinced that there was much to be made of them. At the time of his renomination in 1864, he flashed back to "an ominous incident of mysterious character" that had taken place in the fall of 1860, upon his election as president. It was, Lamon says, "the double-image of himself in the looking-glass, which he saw while lying on a lounge in his own chamber in Springfield." One image was full of life, the other reflecting a "ghostly paleness." Lincoln could not exorcise the vision from his mind, and the meaning of it was plenty clear to him: "safe passage" through his first term, death before his second was completed. Of Lincoln's concern with this presentiment, Lamon was insistent. He blasted Lincoln for his carelessness in exposing himself to unnecessary dangers. It seemed that the president could not hide from (nor would he take action to evade) the torments his mind was prone to.[13]

In 1861, as the sixteenth president was just getting accustomed to being the occupant of the White House, First Lady Mary Todd Lincoln received a curious letter from a woman in Rochester, New York. It began with an apology to "Mrs. President Lincoln" for the intrusion on her time. Then, lest her foreign surname cause confusion, the writer attested to her parents' homely origins in Vermont and her own previous work at a New York City weekly newspaper, where she met her "sober honest industrious" German-born husband, who shared her admiration for the new chief executive. Then, Helen Rauschnabel got to her true purpose in writing, which was to relate "a remarkable dream I had last night about Mr. Lincoln which I think has a significant meaning."

> I dreamed it stormed & thunderd & lightned terribly, it seemed as tho the Heavens & Earth were coming together, but it soon ceased, still there seemed to be very dark clouds sailing thro the horison, I thought I stood pensively viewing the scene, when a man resembling Mr Lincoln appeard standing erect in the firmament with a book in his hand, he stood as near as I could calculate over the City of Washington, his head seemed reard above the lightnings flash and thunder bolt, the sun seemed to be just rising in the East. . . . I saw him walk thro all the Southern part of the horison with a book in one hand, & a pen in the other.

As the Lincoln of her dream turned west, he was "crowned with honors & coverd Laurels, and looked very smiling." The dream ended, but not before Mrs. Rauschnabel thought she clapped her hands and sang a song that contained the lyric "Slavery is ended & Freedom is born."[14]

～∽～

The war began in earnest, and General George McClellan was put in charge of the Army of the Potomac. A broadside appeared in late 1861 or early 1862, titled "General M'Clellan's Dream," meant to describe "something supernatural almost" in the commander's troop movements. As a dream narrative, it bore striking similarities to the invented dream of John C. Calhoun, once more featuring the superintending spirit of George Washington.

Here is how the mysterious, morale-boosting McClellan dream unfolds:

"'I could not have been slumbering thus more than ten minutes,' said the General to an intimate friend."

Someone bursts through the door to his room.

"General McClellan, do you sleep at your post?" The voice addresses him in a "commanding and even terrible tone," paralyzing the dreamer, and the voice repeats the question. The paralysis slowly lifts, and McClellan rises to find a map spread before him. He calls it "a living map," which presents an "immense scene": the whole of the United States, from the North Atlantic to the Gulf of Mexico.

The voice, now called "apparition," approaches to within six feet of him. The dreaming McClellan strains to recognize him, but perceives no more than "a vapor, a cloud, having only the general outlines of a man." Next, he receives his orders: "Look to the Southward!"

The "living map" reveals a blockading squadron "looming up" under a bright moon. The general follows with his eyes the harbors and forts, hills and valleys, "every sentinel, every earthwork." In revealing all, the ghost is giving him a decisive advantage over the rebel forces. As he takes in the prospect and conceives a counterstrategy, McClellan hears: "Tarry not; your time is short."

The "vapory mentor" at last reveals himself as "the glorified and refulgent spirit of Washington, the Father of his country, and now a second time its saviour." McClellan, as the yet untested general, can hardly believe who it is he is seeing: "Like a weak, dazzled bird, I sat gazing at the heavenly vision." General Washington, with his "saving arm," had come to "raise up" his embattled country, anointing McClellan as the man to enact his will. Lest providential purposes be deprived of their full mystery, the broadside concludes: "The future is too vast for our comprehension; we are the children of the present."[15]

One member of McClellan's staff, twenty-two-year-old George Armstrong Custer, helped draw up maps and occasionally ascended in a reconnaissance balloon over the Virginia countryside. "I am not a believer in dreams," he wrote to family in Monroe, Michigan, echoing the skepticism of so many others. "However I must tell you about my dream last night." Someone had called him from his tent to view a balloon in flight. He took field glasses and focused them on a pair of ladies from Monroe, who were seated in the basket of the balloon. "I told the men who had charge of the balloon to 'let me go up too.' They consented. I reached the balloon in some manner unknown to me but my friends had gone, much to my disappointment." Custer's was that species of dream in which thought travels back in time to a lost familiar setting—compelled by desire for a happy reunion with loved ones, yet bound by the exigencies of the moment.[16]

George McClellan was all over the news for the first year of the war. It is not surprising, then, that an aging Bostonian, in no shape to serve in the army, spent a troubled sleep "carrying important despatches to McClellan, of which the bitterness in his mouth formed a part." McClellan's demands gave the man a headache that would not go away.[17]

The same was true for President Lincoln, who found himself verbally abused by the real George McClellan—an overconfident underperformer who did not live up to all the hype. Lincoln, who had hired him, now fired him. It could also be said, of course, that the saintly Washington had erred in choosing General McClellan, instead of Ulysses Grant, to visit in the night.

Like the unnamed Bostonian, nearby Concord's number-one celebrity, Ralph Waldo Emerson, read and reacted to war news. In September 1861, after learning of an early Union success in North Carolina, he had what he called "a pictorial dream fit for Dante." In it, he was delivering a talk somewhere. But for no particular reason, he had trouble staying awake during his own address, at which point he somehow found himself in a house he did not recognize. It was a new house, "the inside wall of which had many shelves let into the wall, on which great & costly Vases of Etruscan and other richly adorned pottery stood." The wall was unfinished and seemed about to fall apart. "Then," Emerson records, "I noticed in the center shelf or alcove of the wall a man asleep, whom I understood to be the architect of the house." The dreamer called out to his brother and pointed to the sleeping architect. At this, the architect arose, "& muttered something about a plot to expose him." When Emerson awoke, he compared the interlocking dreams and posed wryly: "What could I think of the purpose of Jove who sends the dream?"

This one was a highly individualized drama with plenty of bizarreness, the dreamer frustrated by the sapping of his energy. He is unhappy to discover that the unfinished house is not as solid as it appears on first inspection. One who might supply answers—the dozing architect—is in his sights. But having the man cornered (or shelved) doesn't seem to get Emerson anywhere. He is diverted from his purposes, cannot ensure that the valuable art will be preserved, and is basically prevented from accomplishing anything of any meaning. Whether or not it is connected to news of the war, the dream has taken him to a battlefield in the mind, where he is unable to obtain tactical advantage. The Etruscans had a rich warrior tradition, as well as an aesthetic one, which Emerson had written of before.

Emerson's next journal entry contained a further rumination about present danger: "War the searcher of character, the test of men, has tried so many reputations, has pricked so many bladders." Generals came and went, were lifted up and measured, tested and tried. Emerson put them in the company of bankers, whose value to the economy was considered only in times of crises. They were really minor actors, pawns, and what they did bore little relation to the natural world. If dreams were absurd, temporally out of step, confused and unmanageable, then warrior chiefs were bred for nightmares; they were prisoners of broken time and manufactured not to last.[18]

It was hard for Emerson, despite his abolitionism, to make sense of this or any war. For him who wrote in the essay "Nature" that "a dream may let us deeper into the secret of nature than a hundred concerted experiments," war brushed aside all abstraction. It required too much calculation—it did not tap inspiration.

So he returned to the invisible, where he was more comfortable. Of the mystery of human memory, he wrote early in 1862, "drop one link" in a chain of thoughts, and there is no recovery of the ideas or pictures that preceded in the activity of the mind.

> When newly awaked from lively dreams, we are so near them, still agitated by them, still in their sphere;—give us one syllable, one feature, one hint, & we should repossess the whole;—hours of this strange entertainment & conversation would come trooping back to us; but we cannot get our hand on the first link or fibre, and the whole is forever lost. There is a strange wilfulness [sic] in the speed with which it disperses, & baffles your grasp.

Today's dream researcher would probably say that it was never the brain's job to retain visible dreams in memory. But for Emerson, a desire to recover what he assumed were "hours" of dream narratives merely underscored his lifelong frustration with their disappearance from the relative certitude of forward consciousness. The more stories he had full access to, the closer he might approach a godlike knowledge of the extent of the mind. That, as much as anything, was Emerson's pursuit of happiness in a nutshell.[19]

Unlike Lincoln, who dwelled on the suspicions his mind's eye produced, Emerson wanted to design a path to knowledge. Implausibly, he hoped to find some way around the process of decay and disrepair. As it is for most of us today, the fragments of those dreams Emerson remembered invariably delivered more questions than answers.

～ⁿ

I n their letters and diaries, enlisted men, wives and sweethearts, families caught between the warring sides, and hapless prisoners enduring miserable conditions all contributed errant dreams to the emotion-packed literature of these years. To stack up dreams written down on rough paper, to read the passionate appeals of lovers and fragile words of remembrance, is to feel the weight of the war years in a different way.

Adelaide Case of Mecca, Ohio, east of Cleveland, had dreams any teenage girl might have. When she promised herself to a Union soldier, she hoped for a love that would endure. Her beau, twenty-year-old Charlie Tenney, had enlisted in the 7th Ohio in the first year of the war. At the time he went off, the two had not shared intimate thoughts. He had vowed to write, and she to write in turn. But neither had dared to suggest that they would ever be to each other more

Adelaide Case and family. Addie is on the far right. Courtesy of the Albert and Shirley Small Special Collections Library, University of Virginia.

than a brother to a sister. The spark was lit through the mails in the early months of 1862, when the lonely soldier worked up the courage to take a chance.

"Dear Addie," he addressed her on New Year's Day, 1862, from camp in Romney, Virginia (soon to become part of the new state of West Virginia). His first letter was informational. He wanted her to know something about soldiering without vulgarizing the experience. "Some times it happens that inefficient men are placed on a dangerous post," he explained after a watchful night. "A man was placed on a post near mine, and towards daylight he fancied he saw a man, preparing to make a hostile movement; frightened nearly to death he drew up his musket and fired." It turned out to be a deer.

In the next letter, he focused on self-improvement. He wanted her to know what kind of man he was. "Over two months ago, I eschewed the use of tobacco," he wrote. "While at Green Run [on the Virginia side of the Ohio River] I foreswore the practice of playing cards. This I did for my own benefit and character hereafter. Is Addie satisfied with this statement?" He wanted to impress upon her that he would not succumb to the temptations for which soldiers were known. He then ventured cautiously: "Have you passed a happy new-year's day? and did your thoughts revert once to 'Soldier boy' Charlie?" He had shed tears thinking of home, he confessed, reassuring her one last time (in the third person) "that Charlie never was intoxicated in his life."

"Darling Sister!" was his salutation a week later. "What emotions the writing of that word causes in my heart!" The occasion was his receipt of Addie's first letter. Whatever it contained showed that she was in no way disappointed with his insinuating tone. She had deemed Charlie's profession of moral rectitude credible. With her apparent consent, he had graduated from "dear Addie" to "darling sister," hoping, with Heaven's help, "that I may be worthy of your love as a brother ought."

Four days later, he picked up his pen again, already pushing for something stronger than brother-sister. And with hardly a prefatory statement, he declared his love outright. "Do not think me presumptuous, Addie if I say I love you. Do not discard me from your thoughts." The young soldier laid his heart bare: "With you now rests my happiness. Shall I be happy or the reverse? Do you ask me to wait until you become better acquainted with me? I do not ask or expect that on so short acquaintance you shall decide forever." Later in the month, with no answer as yet received, he appealed a second time: "Allow me to love you." And he signed the letter, "Your Charlie."[20]

Most of this had transpired within the single month of January. By Valentine's Day, she was his. He called her letters "angel visits," and she did the same. In her tiny handwriting, he became "Charlie my darling." He asked her to send a photograph. When too many days passed between letters, she, as much as he, grew despondent, until the "messenger of love" arrived at her front door in Mecca. Addie was still in school. It was a single classroom containing fifty "scholars," as she called her classmates, who ranged in age from four to twenty. She had turned eighteen. When the teacher wasn't paying attention, Addie stole time to write to her soldier boy. And when she counted on a letter and one did not come, she feared he had fallen ill.

Pretty soon, her imagination spiraled out of control. "Oh! I had such a strange dream last night," she told him. "I shudder even more when I think of it. You were lying ill and delirious where I could both see and hear you. You were calling for me and yet I could not go to you. I struggled long earnestly and in vain but there seemed some great obstacle between us which I could not surmount." The obstacle, we can assume, was the irregularity of mail delivery in a time of war; but in a dream the rational explanation is replaced by the fantastic—in Addie's case, it was the presence of personal enemies:

> There were all whom I had ever had the least feeling of anger toward mocking me. One thing makes it almost laughable. Col. Tyler [Charlie's unpopular commander] was one of them. I awoke completely exhausted and—do not laugh, dearest—weeping. Be assured my darling, there was no more rest for me. Why bless you dearest. I have not recd a letter from you for two weeks, and it is no wonder that such dreams as the above come to disturb me, when you, before, have written so often. Why: I believe the tortures of the rack can be nothing to the imaginings of such dreams.[21]

Swearing love for each other had taken place in an instant and then escalated quickly, making Addie sensitive to the point of obsession. On March 1, she penned a panicky note: "Have I offended you the reason that you do not write?" Again, on March 23, "Do I not deserve—am I not worthy of a letter from my idol?" Her stationery was marred by a round, dark stain: "This is not a tear," she assured him, adding: "I hope my tears are not quite so black as that ugly spot." It turns out he had taken part in the Battle of Kernstown, in Virginia's Shenandoah Valley, on the twenty-third, where he was wounded in the only action that saw Confederate General Thomas J. "Stonewall" Jackson suffer defeat. Charlie recovered and went back to active duty.

On Independence Day, 1862, from Alexandria, he informed Addie that he had tried and failed to secure a leave of absence. He would not be able to return to Ohio to see her. It was not only his request that was denied—all furloughs were prohibited. He urged her to take heart. "I have a definite foreknowledge," he said, "that your prayers shall be answered." Though "the green earth in many places is saturated with the blood of the thousands who have fallen," he would return to her.

They wrote at least one letter per week, generally more than that, for the balance of the year. "I am loved. Thou art my betrothed," he gleamed that fall. In January 1863, having just heard from another Ohio soldier that Charlie had "suffered a relapse" under primitive camp conditions, Addie sent him one more dream, and as an interrogation of her emotions it was a predictable one:

> In my dreams I was with you last night. I went to sleep wishing that I could fly to you. I had no sooner fallen into a gentle slumber, than I was lifted from my bed, and wafted far far away, over mountains, hills, rivers, cities and so on on on till at last I found myself in a dark comfortable room surrounded by men. Some were lying on rough beds others walking around as if tired of life and wished to walk into eternity.

She asked about, attempting to gain a better sense of her surroundings. A man explained to her that she had come to a military hospital. She was surrounded by badly wounded soldiers.

> Mentally I asked if Charlie was there and began searching. Earnestly I gazed in each face hoping to see one familiar glance one loving one but vainly, until I looked in one corner and noticed a rude couch of straw occupied by my Charlie. It needed no second glance to convince me . . . his face animated and his blue eyes beeming with joy as he asked, "Have you come?" I flew to thee darling and awoke.

Letter after letter, they tried to sound confident. She told him that she trusted "a bright and happy future is before us." He guaranteed his safe return, if she just trusted in God. But on June 14, 1863, as Robert E. Lee was clearing the Shenandoah Valley and heading north toward Pennsylvania, Private

Charles Tenney of the 7th Ohio Infantry died at Harper's Ferry. His comrades would move on to Gettysburg and perform poorly there. Back in Mecca, Ohio, barely nineteen, Adelaide Case became another of the heartbreak kids.[22]

Louisa May Alcott did not have to dream of visiting the wounded. Toward the end of 1862, she volunteered at the Union Hotel Hospital in Washington, D.C. On any given day, the unmarried thirty-year-old nurse was surrounded by hundreds of men, more of them made worse by the noxious air and circulating disease than by the gaping wounds they received on the battlefield. She sponged clean these maimed male bodies, wrote letters on behalf of some of the convalescents, and did whatever else was expected of her as a never-ending stream of groaning, mud-soaked patients arrived in horse-drawn ambulances.

After just a few weeks, the nurse herself took ill with what was later determined to be typhoid. In her delirium, she experienced "strange fancies," as she called her dreams, the most peculiar of which Louisa May recorded in her journal. In one of these, she had married a "stout, handsome Spaniard" with "very soft hands" who urged her to "lie still" and was otherwise uncivil toward her. In another, she found herself visiting heaven, "a twilight place with people darting thro the air in a queer way. All very busy & dismal & ordinary." In a third vision, she was "hung for a witch." And least improbably of all, she saw herself "tending millions of sick men who never died or got well."

It was while she was at the Union Hotel Hospital that Louisa May Alcott received word from Frank Leslie's *Illustrated Newspaper* that she had won a $100 prize for her short story about a strong-minded woman who aimed to avenge herself after the man she loved had withdrawn his affection. Publishing under the pseudonym of A. M. Barnard, the war nurse kept her authorship of this fantasy piece a secret from Bronson Alcott, her emotionally demanding (some have said emotionally abusive) father. In mid-1863, she published *Hospital Sketches* in the abolitionist press and earned high acclaim. After struggling for years, and acting the supplicant to editors, it had taken nightmares to establish her in publishing circles. The deeply committed author would then be catapulted to greater commercial success after the war with her breakout book, *Little Women*.[23]

⤳

As the rebel government was first assembling in Montgomery, Alabama, another committed individual, Thomas R. R. Cobb of Athens, Georgia, had a peaceful dream. The younger brother of President James Buchanan's secretary of the Treasury (who was just then helping draft the Confederate Constitution), Cobb was one of the most ardent of fire-eaters in the lead-up to war and the author of a treatise on slavery law. Awaiting the inauguration of Jefferson Davis and ecstatic about the South's prospects, he wrote home to his wife, Marion: "I dreamed a precious dream about you last night and you were so good, so kind, so sweet, but when were you otherwise?"

Cobb believed in southern values and in the southern family. He slept easily at night. But as a brigadier general in the Army of Northern Virginia, his gentle dream of a future of quiet domesticity faded fast. He saw plenty of death and destruction before his final engagement at the Battle of Fredericksburg in December 1862, where an exploding artillery shell tore up his leg. As Louisa May Alcott tended to Yankee soldiers wounded at Fredericksburg, Cobb bled to death, shy of his fortieth birthday.[24]

"A Singular Prophecy," declared the *Mobile Advertiser* in the early spring of 1862. "Its truth is vouched for by a reliable officer in the army." The story was pretty straightforward: in Pensacola, Florida, "a soldier in the Confederate service fell into a long and profound sleep, from which his comrades vainly essayed to arouse him. At last he woke up himself. He then stated that he should die the next afternoon at 4 o'clock, for it was revealed to him in his dream." But the dreamer did not stop there, informing his hearers that a massive battle would take place in April of that year, and by May, miraculously, "peace would break upon the land." His prophecy attracted the newspapers of the region when the soldier died on schedule, leading the *Advertiser* to ask whether the balance of the prophecy would soon be realized. The last line of the article was a simple suggestion: "Let believers in dreams wait and see."[25]

The Confederate soldier's "singular prophecy" turns out to be plural, because as the fighting intensified, newspapers on both sides regularly featured stories of soldiers dreaming of specific dates when the war would conclude. As though it had a legitimate news item on its hands, the *Saturday Evening Gazette* of Boston matter-of-factly stated on April 25, 1863, that "the dream which an artilleryman at Fort Warren [Boston] and a member of Hawkins' Zouaves [a New York outfit] both had six weeks ago, fixing April 23 as the date of Peace has not been fulfilled." The long-running *Richmond Examiner,* alluding to the "old women, old men, and young maidens telling their dreams and prophesying the close of the war," added to the existing stock of rumor with the dream of a soldier in General George Pickett's division: "He dreamed that he laid down and slept for twenty years—seven more than old Rip Van Winkle snoozed—and that when he woke up, he was lying near Hanovertown [Virginia], General Lee in front of him, with a corporal and four men, waving his sword and crying out, 'Come on, men, let's finish up this fight anyhow.'"[26]

We do not know the fate of the soldier who saw the war continuing another twenty years, but we do know that General Pickett himself wrote home to his wife about "a beautiful dream" he'd had, and apparently the missus was of a similar bent. It pained him to have to instruct her in bearing up to the reality each love-filled dream tried to deny. "While its glory still overshadows the waking and fills my soul with radiance," he wrote of his own, "You know, my darling, we have no prophets in these days to tell us how near or how far is the end of this awful struggle."[27]

Where were people in the Deep South getting their ideas about dream life? To judge by newspaper coverage, one regular reference work was *The Anatomy of Sleep* by Dr. Edward Binns, first published in 1842 and still considered a highly reputable source twenty years later. At the outset of his book, Binns described sleep as "the art of escaping reflection." Under normal functioning, he said, imagination, memory, judgment, locomotion, and voice were all "suspended" in sleep. At other times, imagination, memory, and judgment remained active, while locomotion and voice expressed themselves in a sleep "agitated" by dreams.

Retreating ever so slightly from the traditional insistence that dreamless sleep was perfect sleep, he wrote: "Sound, or heavy, or dull sleep is not always an indication of health." Having studied the dreams of historical figures, and the interpretive use to which they were put, he concluded that great men had great dreams (and knew what to make of their content). He counted on his readers to recognize familiar faces in their dreams: angels and devils, and past giants such as Julius Caesar. Binns allowed that certain dreams accurately predicted. In late 1860, the *Baton Rouge Daily Gazette and Comet* printed "A Strange Dream," citing chapter and verse from one that ended in shipwreck—a dream extracted from Dr. Binns's *Anatomy of Sleep*.[28]

Binns, like Professor Lewis, took an interest in thought that came to the dreaming mind in musical form. "Who has not dreamed of listening to beautiful and melodious music?" he posed. If dreams were "a sort of delirium," he went on, defaulting to medical theorists of the prior century, nightmares were warning signs of danger, an automatic association triggered by the body to isolate an ill or defective organ.

Feeling most comfortable when he went over old territory, Dr. Binns re-affirmed the neurological alliance between dreaming and insanity. Only his descriptive vocabulary sounded different: "Maniacs are inundated with a flow of thoughts, a superabundance of ideas, and a catenation of impressions which invert order, escape arrangement, and defy control, exactly similar to images in dreams." If the reading public was amenable to lively language, the medical establishment continued to behave conventionally through the Civil War era. When it came to dreaming, the issue that seemed to divide the early nine-teenth century's pious doctors from their mid-century successors was the extent to which they entertained their prophetic potential. Nearly all subscribed to prophecy when it pertained to biblical times, but the verdict had yet to be rendered on the supernatural in their present.

Dr. Binns ended his book where he began, defining sleep as the body's way of "escaping reflection," giving needed rest to the thought process. "Sleep," he said, "is not a negative, but a positive state of existence; and differs from death which is a negative quality, in this: that death is the total absence of sensation, voluntary motion, assimilation, and all the vital phenomena." Civil War soldiers spoke of angels and comforted themselves by believing that God was the author of a plan for all human experience; meanwhile, noncombatants across the country fought isolation and disillusionment with the tools at hand. In trying circumstances, pleasant dreams could be counted among the divine mercies.[29]

~~∽∽~~

When the war began, sixteen-year-old Clara Solomon of New Orleans was a staunch supporter of the new Confederate government. Her father, Solomon Solomon—"the dearest and best of fathers"—was a merchant supplying clothing to the army. In June 1861, when he was away on business, Clara worried for his safety. One night, after their household slave, Lucy, "lowered the gas and bade me good night," she lay in bed trying to lull herself to sleep. She heard her father's voice, and she pictured her older sister and herself on board a steamboat, accompanying him to "some distant place." Then, sitting on a sofa, Clara was accosted by some drunken men. She fled their presence, but in evading their clutches, she was, she said, "so exhausted that I fell down, and the shock awoke me."

At four in the morning, she heard screams coming from Lucy's room. Clara roused her mother and sisters, and they all went in to check on the servant, who protested that it was not a nightmare at all, but menstrual cramps that had prompted her outburst. "Ma administered the available remedies, which afforded some relief," and they all enjoyed a long moment of laughter at Lucy's expense.

The train of events is informative. An anxiety dream, remembered because a slave cried out in the depths of night, offers a glimpse of the moving images and voices in the diarist's head. Clara invokes words of fear—"pursuit," "evading," and "accosted"—in her dream telling. In the same diary entry she repeats the words "scream" and "frighten." A friend's young daughter had recently died a shocking death from a "pernicious fever," which led Clara to write of the "spotless little soul" having "winged its flight to another world."

The lexicon of this young diarist is representative of the mid-nineteenth century, when the "winged flight" metaphor was repeated in multiple dream descriptions. Dreams were seen as a kind of flight that spirited the dreamer away and opened up another world. The associated realms of death and dreams were awe inspiring and remained beyond human comprehension—ill defined and unresolvable for assimilated Jews like the Solomons as much as for their Catholic neighbors.

The year 1862 brought the war to Clara's doorstep. Of the relatively few dreams she recorded, one that summer was the bearer of unmitigated pleasure. In it, two "dear persons," both male, "figured so conspicuously" that she refused to confide, even to her diary, what had transpired in her mind. "Oh! dreams are unpleasant in whatever aspect we near them," she wrote, complaining that her hopeful fantasies caused almost as much sorrow and disappointment as her scarier dreams did. "How sad I was to wake & contrary to my thoughts find myself in my own bed!"

She turned to the approaching Fourth of July, which she hoped to celebrate—"but oh! how differently from former years." The Confederate cause was sinking in the bayou, as Union forces under the iron hand of General Benjamin Franklin Butler occupied the South's most vibrant commercial port. "The Beast," as some called Butler, had just ordered the hanging of a Confederate patriot for hauling down a U.S. flag. Beyond this, he was hated for treating uncooperative southern women much as prostitutes were treated, decreeing a night's imprisonment for any female who was so unladylike as to insult a Union officer.[30]

Bald and pudgy, Butler was a family man as well as a warrior, a husband who made fun of the dream-book genre and his wife's credulity when he felt

like needling her: "How do you do this fine morning?" he gaily taunted in a letter home. "You are not yet up, eh! Have you slept well? Did you dream of me?
Or did you dream of snakes, having eaten salad over night?" Evidently, he knew
how to strike a nerve, to judge from letters later in the war, when the "Beast's"
wife, Sarah, wrote to their daughter with inauspicious premonitions regarding
the family: "I am worried every night for fear something should go wrong at
home. One night I dream that Paul is drowned, another that Benny is dead.
Nothing as yet, that is wrong with you. But tonight I may have some fearful
dream of you." And then, after a pause: "I have done eating their odious soups,
and various other abominations. Coffee, bread, eggs and milk make up my
diet. This will do away with dreams." The old notion that indigestion caused
nightmares remained standard thinking. Evidently, General Butler could not
dissuade his wife.[31]

As Clara Solomon and the rebels of south Louisiana were dealing with the
reverses of war, another young woman, Lucy Breckinridge of Grove Hill plantation, near Fincastle, Virginia, worried for the safety of her several brothers who
were away fighting the Yankees. Johnny, the younger brother who was closest to
her in age, died in June 1862, at the very bloody Battle of Seven Pines, outside
Richmond. The image of him in life, and the pain of his untimely passing,
returned to her mind often.

One winter's night, early in 1863, after a week without caring to compose
her thoughts, Lucy was lured to the blank page of her diary ("this dear, stupid
old book," she bemoaned) in order to debate a vision. "I dreamed of peaches
last night," she wrote, "and upon waking lay in bed thinking of Dolly's mournful interpretation: 'to dream of fruit out of season is trouble without reason,'
and in my own mind trying to establish the fallacy of it." Dolly was her slave,
and Lucy willed herself to resist superstition gleaned from dream-book notions,
to which many of the slaves were drawn. A second brother, the aptly named
Peachy Gilmer Breckinridge, rose to the rank of captain and not long after died
in battle, his body never recovered.

Dreams fade in the daylight, and she never wrote in her diary but at night,
so we cannot go deeper. As the war ended, and only a few months into her marriage to a Texan, Lucy Breckinridge, of an old and respected Virginia lineage,
died of typhoid fever. Life was short and her Civil War a sad tale of peaches
and dreams.[32]

Here's what does come through, at least. When she told her peach dream
to her slave Dolly, Lucy had gotten in return a simple formula for interpreting

it. In a similar manner, an Arkansan, born a slave, told an interviewer later in life: "When you dream of the dead there's sho' gonna be falling weather." To this day, among eastern North Carolina's African American communities, belief has persisted (if in a less structured way than in West Africa) that ancestors communicated directly through dreams, especially at moments of emotional crisis. Said one black North Carolinian: "The night before I had a mild heart attack, I dreamed of my grandmother." Her voice was loud and firm, and commanded, "Get control of yourself boy." Ancestor dreams brought news of impending death and at other times served to allay fears and calm the nerves. The common denominator was the strong sense that no one is entirely self-made, that human beings are products of the past and cannot be detached from those who came before.[33]

As one might imagine, the dreams of the enslaved carry a special poignancy. Under the institution of slavery, families were routinely torn apart, fathers and mothers separated from their children, if not as punishment then simply owing to perceived economic necessity. Charles Ball, sold by his Maryland owner and brought south to Georgia, had a dream en route:

> I thought I had, by some means, escaped from my master, and through infinite and unparalleled dangers and sufferings, had made my way back to Maryland; and was again in the cabin of my wife, with two of my little children on my lap; whilst their mother was busy in preparing for me a supper of fried fish, such as she often dressed, while I was at home. . . . Every object was so vividly impressed upon my imagination in this dream that, when I awoke, a firm conviction settled upon my mind, that by some means, at present incomprehensible to me, I should yet again embrace my wife and caress my children.[34]

While it may be that songs inspired by biblical lessons kept hope alive, literal dreams tended to keep slaves on edge. Francis Federic, held in bondage in both Virginia and Kentucky, had a dream shortly after his escape across the Ohio River to freedom in 1855. He could not accept that the nightmare was over: "Two or three nights in succession I dreamt that I was taken by my master, and all the details of the capture were so vividly depicted in my dreams, that I could scarcely, when awake, believe it was all a vision of the night."[35]

Masters and slaves were often traveling companions, and every once in a while, a white man of privilege revealed just how intimate their conversation could be. "My faithful servant Juba is sick," the irrepressible Virginia congressman John Randolph, a master of the Old South, wrote to a friend. "I heard him in his sleep cry out 'I wish I and master were at home!'" Dream or delirium, the incident reminds us of what happens when we convert the clash of cultures into a simple story of good versus evil. The paternalism Randolph lived by fed arrogance, but it also required kindness. He and Juba slept within earshot of each other, and in his own way, he believed they had made common cause.[36]

The cult of the "good master" married to a sense of southern honor thrived because slavery could not otherwise be defended. In dream terms, one telling symbol of the underlying trauma appears in a book published in Philadelphia in the mid-1830s, as tensions between North and South were rising, but not yet full-blown. In *A Concise View of Slavery,* a chapter with the heading "The Slave Whipped to Death for Telling His Vision" related the shortened life of a slave named Ajax, living in Leesburg, Virginia. According to the author, Ajax had had "a very remarkable dream or vision, which of the two I cannot pretend to determine . . . , the substance of which was . . . he conceived himself transported into the midst of the infernal regions [and] saw his master and overseer . . . suspended by their tongues." Ajax's master "hated him for his dream" and reacted impulsively. Either unwilling or unable to distinguish between unsuppressed imagination and active subversion of power, the slave owner gave his slave the ultimate punishment.[37]

Just after President Lincoln delivered his immortal Gettysburg Address, one of his generals, James A. Garfield of Ohio, spoke in Baltimore about the fighting spirit of the men under his command, and he left no doubt why the war was being waged. "Slavery is dead," he proclaimed, "and only remains to be buried." He had read Harriet Beecher Stowe's *Uncle Tom's Cabin* in 1852; three years later, while he was courting his wife, Lucretia, she wrote to him of the effect that Stowe's "sad thrilling story" had on her spirit—it framed a passionate correspondence in which both parties recurred often to the language of dreams and reveries. He posed to her, for instance: "Did you ever dream in a winter night of the lovely summertime?"

Garfield was a man of action who devoured adventure stories and biographies and would later become himself an exemplar of self-made American manhood. Portraying the slave-owning generals of the South as pampered boys born with silver spoons, the brigadier general roused Baltimoreans with the boast that his "mudsills," common farmers and shopkeepers of the New West, were crushing the fatuous "dream" of those "frantic men" of the effete South who had divided the nation. So, in romancing his future wife, he approved of literal dreams; and in firing up his men and their supporters back home, he applied the old, derisive epithet of dreamers as losers. A bit later in the war, as we shall see, Garfield was to have less success convincing his wife that her dream of him cavorting with other women was a mere figment of her sleeping imagination.[38]

~*~

"The Soldier's Dream" was a poem that made the rounds often and from early in the war. Originally penned by the late eighteenth-century Scottish poet Thomas Campbell, it told of a war-wearied husband and father who transported himself home in a dream that repeated three times in one night. His loved ones were there to embrace and console him and to beg him to stay. All was well for the soldier until sorrow returned with the dawn, all his nostalgic feeling dissolving into the ground where he lay—as "the voice in my dreaming ear melted away."

The old pastoral dream was a potent anthem for the romantic youth who put themselves in harm's way in order to defend their ideals. Ohioan Charlie Tenney composed a love letter to his "dearest Addie" on stationery that reprinted Campbell's poem. Above its title, the doomed private scrawled: "Is not this beautiful."[39]

Soldiers' dreams ranged from hot pursuit of a visible enemy to sweet fantasies of being back home with family. As often, they deplored not being able to dream at all, mired as they were (often literally) in the places where their flimsy tents were pitched. A Union lieutenant who was part of an amphibious landing on the northeast coast of Florida in 1862 spoke clearly in his sleep, and his comrade reported him "evidently chasing a rebel in his dream." A Massachusetts man involved in the long siege of Vicksburg wrote in his diary on July 6, 1863, two days after the city fell to Union forces, that to "lie down to pleasant dreams" was too much to hope for, especially after an overnight thunderstorm, with no shelter but a rubber coat. Twenty-year-old Thomas Christie of the First Minnesota Light Artillery, stationed in the same Mississippi River town some months later, dreamt about his day job: "I ought to have been quietly sleeping last night," he wrote home, "but according to my tent-mate this is what I was saying: 'By detail, load; two, three, four! Sponge; two, three, four! Ram two, three! Ready, fire!'" And then, turning to a soldier he was in charge of, he continued issuing orders: "Bend that knee a little more; hold your shoulders square to the front." He told his father: "Nothing is so exciting as working a gun in action. The sound of the discharge almost raises us off our feet with delight."[40]

Post-traumatic stress disorder was not part of the Civil War vocabulary, but it is suggested in the account of a soldier who had been wounded in the foot and was recuperating in Philadelphia. As he was waiting for a furlough to visit his sick wife and children in Maine, he had two related dreams: in one, he lost an entire leg and his face was badly scarred; he feared his family would not be accepting of him, but as the changed, crippled man hobbled up to his front door, he was wildly embraced by his wife and welcoming neighbors. In the second dream, the war was over and he was coming home a hero, but when he arrived, his wife greeted him coldly, and even his children looked sad and disappointed. He asked his wife for an explanation, and she "looked me right in the face but wouldn't say a word." Somehow he figured out that she was perturbed because he had fallen in with some unprincipled men and had neglected to write to her. "While she was looking at me this way, and I was trying to hide my face," he concluded nervously, "I all of a sudden waked up."[41]

One of the most bizarre of violent dreams reported during the Civil War did not have anything to do with the fighting. In Medina, Ohio, around the time of Gettysburg, newspapers reported that "a boy in the village" dreamt of a nearby triple murder. At first, when he woke his parents in the middle of the night, his father laughed it off. By morning, as news of the actual slayings circulated in Medina, "the boy dreamer," as he was known, supplied authorities with details not only of "the disposition of the contents of the room" where the victims were, but also the face of the killer, which he described "minutely." A man who fit the description, twenty-three-year-old Frederick Streeter, originally from Vermont and a Union Army deserter, was arrested. But the story did not end there: after escaping from prison and eventually being recaptured, he was found guilty of the crime and swung from the gallows in early 1864.[42]

Women on the home front had their share of prophetic dreams. Georgia-born Sarah Wadley relocated to Vicksburg before the war and was living in Louisiana when, in the summer of 1863, she had a dream, "beautiful and as vivid as reality," in which a brilliant star, "as large and round as the moon," rose above the trees outside her home. It sparkled like a diamond and expanded to spell the word Nebraska, standing out clear and distinct against the dark blue. She thought that her visionary experience related somehow to the future of the country. Next the word "Massachusetts" was spelled out, and below, the French word "epouvantee," which Sarah somehow found uplifting. As her visions dissolved, she felt it was near dawn, and "the whole yard was crowded with negroes gazing awestruck"; they began to disperse, and her grandmother's pastor from Savannah, though already "three years in the silent land," drove up to where she was. "Without speaking I put my arm in his and walking into the house . . . , I spoke to him of the marvellous sight which he had also witnessed." Then she awoke, went to her bookshelf, and looked up the French word she had seen in her dream, the meaning of which—"terrified"—she had not known until that moment. She thought it might signify official French recognition of the independence of the Confederacy. Underscoring a proneness to wishful thinking, Sarah concluded: "This vision gives me new confidence, it seems to me that God has revealed to me that we will prevail through his mercy."[43]

Of this species of dream, we can add that of seventy-eight-year-old Eleanor Meigs, a member of a pacifist Shaker community in southwestern Kentucky that was caught between the northern and southern armies and strove to maintain friendly relations with both. In April 1864, as General Grant was gearing up for his devastating campaign against Lee in Virginia, she woke from a dream around midnight: "I appeared to be traveling with my guide who took me to Washington City & into the White House. I saw a number of soldiers, my guide who was a brother [Shaker] spoke to them in a loud and commanding Voice—told them to be wide awake. He then told me that there were ten times as many soldiers around the City of Richmond as were here. . . . I marveled at this and began to look at how many there were." She was predicting the fall of the Confederacy a year ahead of schedule.[44]

Not surprisingly, sweet dreams filled letters to and from the battlefront. At times, men hardened by army life found themselves amazed by the sense of transport as they slipped from a resolute, watchful consciousness into the blissful abstraction of the night's memory probe. From Meridian, Mississippi, a twenty-three-year-old Confederate soldier wrote to his cousin and future wife, thanking God for a hopeful vision he received while asleep: "Oh! I had a dream last night," he cried, "a dream of happiness without alloy, and its spirit breathings linger around me yet. My soul thanks the great Giver of all good that He has endowed us with the faculty of dreaming, that the overwrought, wearied soul may wander a season, through the mystic regions of the Dream-land . . . of another and happier world. I thought it was spring-time."

Virginian Willie Brand wrote to Kate Armentrout, the woman he was courting, with understandable apprehension, given the extent of his deployment: "I had a very strange dream the other night[.] I drempt that me & you had fallen out & Rachel Crobarger was interseeding for me." Below his signature, the insecure soldier, doubting how long his girlfriend's patience would last, exhorted: "You will please never show this to anyone." She must have replied in a thoroughly soothing way by deploying a dream of her own, because he wrote back to her: "My darling Kate you said your face could not ware a joyous smile, untill you could behold my face. . . . That dream of yours oh that it was a reality."

From east Tennessee, Lieutenant Colonel William McKnight, a cavalryman who hailed from Ohio, wrote to Samaria, his wife of eight years, of the world that stared him in the face in the light of day: "The Rebs are about ten thousand strong in front of us . . . , creeping up on our pickets & fireing." But all this disappeared from his mind when he fell asleep: "I dreamed a sweet dream about you," he purred. For that short time he saw her and their children sitting before him "on bended knee," only to wake to the realization that it was all a "Delusion," and he could do no more than bid her kiss their little ones and pray that he would make it back. "Let the memory of the past and hopes of the future sustain you," he wrote in more than one letter home. McKnight was killed in action in Kentucky only months later, age thirty-two.[45]

Such pathos was not missed by the columnists of the day. Under the heading "A Beautiful Picture," the Cleveland *Plain Dealer* offered a painfully simple, and very visual, example of the true cost of war to thousands of families. The story centered on an ambrotype—a photograph, related to the daguerreotype, in which the image is exposed on a glass sheet and encased in a protective folder. There were "three charming little children" in the picture. They were nameless, and all efforts to locate them came up empty. What mattered, though, was where the ambrotype was found: "Amidst the awful debris of the Battle of Gettysburg, a soldier was discovered, in a half sitting posture, stricken with death, grasping in one hand the ambrotype. . . . It was probably taken out by the dying soldier after the fatal bullet had struck him down." As an antiwar symbol, this one hardly needed a caption.[46]

Americans received no real respite from the carnage, as the frozen, faded images produced by the likes of Matthew Brady attest. But a different death stared prisoners of war in their gaunt faces. The notorious Andersonville camp in southwestern Georgia was not constructed until after the tide had turned against the Confederacy. But conditions fast deteriorated, and nearly 30 percent of the thousands of Union men interned there died of starvation or disease before war's end.

Two imprisoned diarists, who lived to tell their tales, give some hint of the nature of their dreams while in confinement. John Northrup related a gruesome chronicle of mass deprivation, of hungry men exhibiting symptoms of scurvy ("the flesh of their limbs has become lifeless"). He detailed the "strange dream" of one of his fellow sufferers, who first glimpsed a hellish foreground and then a better beyond. In the diarist's words, he "beheld immediate conditions, and the blackness and terror of the supposed 'river of death' which soon brightened into a bordering stream, before which all misery, terror and darkness vanished, and he beheld the mystic world. He regarded this as a prophecy of change soon to come to him and said he had no terror of what might come; it had given him strength ineffable." Theirs was a cheerless (if not friendless) death camp, and the dream was this prisoner's saving grace.

In December 1863, Andersonville prisoner John Ransom, a Michigander captured in east Tennessee, wrote: "Dream continually nights about something good to eat. . . . A man froze to death last night where I slept." The counter positioning of ideas proves that the absurd in life will come into dreams just as easily when life is barely life at all. Still at Andersonville six months later, Ransom pursued a deeper understanding of the absurd. It was "funny" to him that men were attempting to escape by pretending to be dead so that they would be carried beyond the prison walls with the other dead, only to "jump up and run" as night fell. It had worked for some, because "dead men are so plenty that not much attention is paid." The next day, he found something else "funny" that might not have been under other circumstances: "Had a funny dream last night. Thought the rebels were so hard up for mules that they hitched up a couple of gray-back lice to draw in the bread." Surprised by how robust he was after a half year of incarceration in sandy soil "alive with vermin," the diarist thought ahead to the hottest months and simply shrugged: "Every man will die, in my estimation."[47]

~∞~

When General Ambrose E. Burnside disobeyed President Lincoln's instructions in September 1863, the president replied incredulously, "Yours of the 23rd is just received, and it makes me doubt whether I am awake or dreaming." The war had acquired such surreal ugliness that the commander-in-chief vied as often with his own contradictory emotions as with the actions of his general officers.

He found he had to. Lincoln, so often referred to as "brooding," was a realist who turned to books and educated himself on military strategy. He presided over the deaths of hundreds of thousands he did not know; and in the midst of it all, his outgoing eleven-year-old son, Willie, wasted away and died of an illness related to poor sanitation. The end of the war did not come until Grant threw his troops against Lee's for weeks on end, whittling down the rebel army. Lincoln saw a sample of this effort when he crossed into Virginia to view a Union bombardment of the Confederate position toward the end of March 1865.

His secretary of the navy, Gideon Welles, kept a comprehensive diary. On April 3, while all were awaiting the Confederate surrender, Welles recorded what Secretary of War Edwin Stanton said in a cabinet meeting about the behavior of Lincoln's predecessor, James Buchanan. As a lame duck president in early 1861, waiting for Lincoln's arrival in Washington, Buchanan (Stanton could not resist calling him "a miserable coward") believed that the tall, unmistakable Illinoisan was a walking target who would not live to take the oath of office.

On April 10, Welles noted, guns fired a salute to announce the final capture of Lee's army. On the evening of the thirteenth, fireworks filled the skies of Washington as celebration continued. The next day, the president's last, General Grant attended a meeting of the cabinet, and Stanton put forward his plan for Reconstruction. Welles noted that Lincoln now expected to hear more good news from General Sherman, still in the field, "for he [Lincoln] had last night the usual dream which he had preceding nearly every great and important event in the War. Generally the news had been favorable which succeeded this dream, and the dream itself was always the same." Welles asked what the dream consisted of, and Lincoln explained that it related to the element water. As Welles put it: "He seemed to be in some singular, indescribable vessel, and that he was moving with great rapidity towards an indefinite shore." He had had the same dream before the firing on Fort Sumter and the Battles of Bull Run, Antietam, Gettysburg, and Vicksburg, as well as Stone River (in Tennessee), which, Grant reminded him, was not a victory. Lincoln's response was to shrug and suggest that Stone River might be an exception, but the fact was, on April 12, he had had the same dream then that ordinarily presaged positive war news.[48]

According to the president's great friend Ward Hill Lamon, a few days before this, Lincoln had said, "in slow and measured tones," and in the company of Lamon and Mary Todd Lincoln: "It seems strange how much there is in the Bible about dreams." He had counted "some sixteen chapters" in the Old Testament, and "four or five" in the New, that contained dreams. "If we believe the Bible," Lincoln said, "we must accept the fact that in the good old days God and His angels came to men in their sleep and made themselves known in dreams." This more or less coincided with Benjamin Rush's rationale that dreams were once, but no longer, messages from the divine. "Nowadays," Lincoln reputedly added, "dreams are regarded as very foolish, and are seldom told, except by old women and by young men and maidens in love."

In Lamon's telling, "Mrs. Lincoln here remarked: 'Why you look dreadfully solemn; do you believe in dreams?'"

"I can't say that I do," Lincoln is meant to have answered her. "But I had one the other night which has haunted me ever since."

As he began to explain the dream, his wife grew more concerned, and he regretted having broached the subject. While outwardly denying the significance of dreams and visions, she forced him to provide as much of the detail as he could recollect. He dreamt, he thought, very soon after falling asleep. He was passing from room to room in the White House, trying to track down a disturbing sound he was hearing—the "pitiful sobbing" of invisible mourners. Arriving at the East Room, Lincoln narrated, "I was met with a sickening surprise." There lay a fully decorated coffin on a raised platform, surrounded by a military guard. "Who is dead in the White House?" the dreamer asked one of the soldiers. "The President," came the reply. "He was killed by an assassin." The mourners again cried out, and this awoke the president from his dream. Or so Lamon assures us.

Lincoln was convinced of the prophetic nature of dreams, but only some dreams. This one, in describing his impending death, may be an embellished version of what actually took place, given the unlikelihood that Mary Todd Lincoln would have to ask her husband at this stage in their marriage, "Do you believe in dreams?" The reader must decide whether the entire vignette should be dismissed on the basis of one tiny clue to its inauthenticity. After relating the assassination dream, Lamon says that Lincoln recited for him Shakespeare's famous line from Hamlet's soliloquy: "To sleep, perchance to dream: ay, there's the rub!"

Regardless of how true to life these sketches are, they make Lamon's final apologia all the more dramatic. He insists that he specifically warned his old friend not to attend the theater on the evening of the fourteenth. Lamon was leaving Washington for Richmond and obliged Secretary of the Interior John

P. Usher of Indiana, another old acquaintance of the president's, to join him in urging Lincoln not to leave the White House while Lamon was away. They had their audience with Lincoln, who turned to Usher and said of Lamon: "This boy is a monomaniac on the subject of my safety. . . . He thinks I shall be killed."

If Lincoln truly experienced the disturbing dream of his own corpse lying in the East Room, and not long after jokingly complained to Usher about Lamon's concerns, some crucial connection has to be missing in Lamon's narrative. The author frustrates the modern historian by repeating conversations at length, yet failing to provide a proper explanation for the president's different faces and irreconcilable attitudes. It seems only fitting that we should be left with a mystery.

Lincoln remains endlessly fascinating to students of history for obvious reasons. He was a man of many moods, of good humor and grave prospects. He said "howdy" to visitors in his Midwest folk dialect, but he also adored Shakespeare, and his speeches were laced with Byronic eloquence. As the late historian Kenneth Cmiel has explained, his power as a communicator had as much to do with dramatic cadence as chosen vocabulary: the folksy Lincoln was selective in deciding to insert a formal phrase ("shall not perish from the earth") in order to dignify an occasion.

Echoes of the Civil War reverberate even in our present. But good history ought not submit too easily to the allure of a Lincoln cult. The martyred president repeatedly dreamt of an "indescribable vessel" heading for a safe port, and it said to him that the war was going well. Maybe—just maybe—he also dreamt he'd died.[49]

~∾

When he first glimpsed Lincoln in February 1861, future President James A. Garfield wrote of the president-elect in a letter to his wife Lucretia, back in Ohio, saying that, notwithstanding the "beautifying effects" of his new whiskers, Lincoln was "distressedly homely." "But," he went on, "through all his awkward homeliness there is a look of transparent, genuine goodness, which at once reaches your heart and makes you trust and love him."

Garfield had been a hard man to drag to the altar. He met Lucretia ("Crete") Randolph in the early 1850s, before he went off to study at Williams College in western Massachusetts. They had their first kiss in February 1854, as Crete reminded him on its one-year anniversary. "Jamie" was then a responsible, caring suitor, nervously appealing to her after a long stretch without a letter for some-thing to allay his fear that "some one of the ten thousand evils of which the dreaming spirit conceives had befallen you." She had no difficulty telling him she loved him and made a practice of writing to him at bedtime: "I fancied my dreams would be sweeter, and visions fairer would rise before me if but a few lines were traced for your dear eye ere I slept."[50]

Between academic years, he returned to the small town of Hiram, Ohio, and when he did, he openly revealed his doubts to his intended. Like other men who were to become powerful figures on the political scene, he sensed where his weakness lay. Taking a job teaching at the Hiram Eclectic Institute after graduation, he became enamored of another woman, and relations with Crete took a turn for the worse. But she refused to let him go, writing him after their reconciliation, in language laced with ghostly imagery, that she was convinced "the darkness" had been lifted from his soul. The couple finally married at the end of 1858.

When the war began, Garfield formed a regiment, built around his former Hiram students, and they fought well. Dysentery sidelined him for a time, which was when he turned from soldiering to politics—entering Congress in the spring of 1863. Crete made the best of their long separations, resolving to trust in his fidelity. "James, I do love you with such fondness and nearness I have never known before. I have dreamed of it, have thought about it and hoped for it."

At the end of 1863, their daughter died. A few months later, Garfield had an affair with a widow in New York, confessing to his wife what he had done. To police him better, she came to Washington for a time, though in April 1865, she was in Ohio again. On the tenth of that month, she wrote to her husband: "I dreamed of you last night, a dream that made me so unhappy that I awoke and could not sleep again for a long time. I will tell you nothing now. . . . To me you said not long since, 'be gentle' to you; allow me to say 'be prudent.'" And then, switching gears: "The glorious news of Lee's surrender has reached us. I have no words to tell you what my heart feels that the end draws so near."

Events overtook one another. On April 14, the day Lincoln was shot, Gar-field was in New York City. It was three days after this that he replied to his wife's letter of the tenth and the jealous imagery that her dream had left her with: "My heart is so broken with our great national loss," he bewailed, "that I can hardly think or write or speak." In closing, though, the philandering hus-band assured her: "Your dream had no basis in reality. Ever your own James."

Dreams coursed through their lives, accenting their epistolary conversations either as literal recitations or metaphorical constructions of the world seen through their two pairs of eyes. In a way, the awkward variability of dreams symbolized the uncertain balance within their marriage. Congressman Garfield continued to represent Ohio for another fifteen years, after which, in 1880, he was elected president. A month before the inauguration, he recorded a ship-wreck dream in which he and a friend escaped, but his vice president, Chester Alan Arthur, who had failed to lift himself from the couch he lay across, drowned. In the dream, Garfield attempted to save Arthur, but his friend, a fellow Ohioan and Civil War officer, held him back, saying: "You will perish if you attempt it."

After her husband's swearing-in, First Lady Lucretia Garfield expected some sign as she prepared for bed on her first night's sleep in the White House. But, she wrote in her diary, she "slept too soundly to remember any dream." And so, she concluded, counting back to John and Abigail Adams, the first occupants of the White House, "our first night among the shadows of the last 80 years gave no forecast of our future."

It was just as well. The new president, as cavalier about the possibility of assassination as Lincoln had been, carried out his duties. On July 2, 1881, only four months into his presidency, he was preparing to go back to Massachusetts for a college reunion when he was shot twice at close range by a mentally unbalanced man at the Washington train station. Infection spread. The wounded president held on until September, when, shy of his fiftieth birthday, James A. Garfield became the second U.S. chief executive to fall to an assassin's bullet. His talent-deprived vice president, Chester Arthur, served out Garfield's term, proving the lie to his earlier dream; his widow Crete survived until 1918 and was buried by his side in Cleveland.[51]

~~~

One of Garfield's closest political associates was fellow Ohioan Salmon Chase, who had sought the presidency in 1860 and served as Lincoln's Treasury secretary from 1861 to 1864. We encountered him in chapter 5 as a young widower in the mid-1830s straining to reconnect with his late wife in dreams. He remarried twice, burying both his second and third wives. And so, although he was no stranger to untimely death, he refused to believe on April 14, 1865, that Abraham Lincoln would die of his head wound.

That day, while Garfield was in New York, Chase was in Washington. He had intended to pay a call on the president in order to discuss how far it was wise to go in restoring southern citizens' rights. Prior to this, as a member of the cabinet, Chase had openly taken issue with Lincoln's decisions on enough occasions that he opted to put off his White House visit, "lest my talk might annoy him & do harm rather than good." Learning that night of the attack at Ford's Theatre, and while Lincoln lay unconscious, he held back from going to the dying man's bedside, slow in accepting reality. He felt he could wait till morning to seek "further intelligence."

A few months earlier, Lincoln had named him chief justice of the Supreme Court. He was just the sixth chief justice in the nation's history and would remain on the bench for seventeen years, until his death. It was Chase, then, who administered the oath of office to Lincoln's vice president, Andrew Johnson, only to preside, before much longer, at President Johnson's impeachment trial.

Flash forward to the summer of 1870. Thirty-five years after Salmon Chase first sought emotional healing through dreams, he remained watchful as to their effects. At sixty-two, Chief Justice Chase suffered a stroke and began to note in his journal how he slept, whether his body was cooperating, and occasionally, nonspecifically at first, any appearance of "unpleasant dreams." His record-keeping in these, his final years, was clinical. For example: "wakeful night—frequent urination, say three times—unpleasant dreams—breakfast—beef, steak, eggs—hominy—oat meal porridge. . . ." Whether or not it means anything here, Dr. Rush, all those years before, had his own theory about urination: that "the stimulus of this liquor in the bladder" was a primary cause of dreams among older people. It made sense to him because people tended to remember those dreams that occurred just prior to waking, when the bladder was most full.

On July 29, 1872, seven years after Abraham Lincoln's assassination and ten months before he died, Chase was in Narragansett, Rhode Island, where his accomplished daughter Kate and her husband, U.S. Senator William Sprague, lived. On that date, he wrote down an extraordinary dream that returned him to Civil War politics. He told it to his Harvard-trained physician, John Perry:

Last night or this morning singular dream which I related to Doctor / Lincoln—Davis—last battle—D beaten & prisoner—L resigned—D President—Congress met & [only 11] members of Conf[ederate] Congress–Constitution

amended and slavery abolished—Suffrage made universal—Davis resigned—
Lincoln elected / Universal Amnesty—Members of Congress elected in all [the]
insurgent states—general harmony & reconciliation—finis."

General harmony and reconciliation. Lincoln was alive again. He had defeated Jefferson Davis and taken him prisoner, only to yield back the reins of
government to the Mississippian. Thus Reconstruction, the topic Chase never
got the chance to discuss with Lincoln on the day he went to Ford's Theatre,
was realized through a dream. Also striking is the fact that Chase's dream of
Lincoln and Davis is the obverse of Benjamin Rush's of Adams and Jefferson:
in that dream, the dreamer was fated to die before the dream came true; here,
instead of the dreamer writing history before it happened, he rewrote history,
counterfactually, after it had resolved itself. Rush's dream was wish fulfillment,
Chase's a creative experiment.

At least one element in the chief justice's reconciliation dream could be
considered precognitive. At the time, the Thirteenth Amendment, abolish-
ing slavery, had already been incorporated into the Constitution, as had the
Fourteenth, guaranteeing full citizenship and equal protection under the law to
all U.S.-born (white or black) as well as naturalized Americans. The Fifteenth
Amendment, guaranteeing voting rights to all, regardless of "race, color, or
previous condition of servitude," took effect in 1870. But in February 1872, at
the time of Chase's last recorded dream, the Amnesty Act, returning to former
rebels the right to vote and hold office, had yet to be enacted. And that is what
the chief justice dreamt was happening.

An early champion of racial and gender equality, Salmon Chase did not
live to see the full wrath of the postwar white southerner. On one of the very last
pages of his journal, in 1872, he noted, albeit with some ambiguity: "Frightfull
dreams from lunch." The final chapter in an eventful life was unfolding for the
statesman who probably never dreamt that he would be posthumously honored
by having his name appended to one of the nation's largest banks.[52]

~∿∂~

Postwar America would reassess the costs, personal and collective, of the
fighting. While the onslaught continued, romantic thoughts of home were
bolstered by fantasies of reunion and recovery. With General Lee's surrender
at Appomattox on April 9, 1865, some soldiers' dreams and reveries could be
realized. On April 30, three weeks to the day after the signing took place, a

cavalryman stationed alongside the Potomac, in Maryland, closed a letter to his sweetheart, written under candlelight: "I think I must quit and take a sleep and perhaps dream of you for that would be nothing uncommon—you would not believe how the Yankee ladies haunt the soldiers pillows."[53]

Changes were coming, though certain battles would continue to be fought. The Civil War grew into an industry in books and film, as a market arose for the more tactile remains of the war, its memorabilia. Collective memory became contested ground, just like the war itself. What seems remarkable, therefore, given the monumental loss of life that Americans witnessed from 1861 to 1865, is how few actual nightmares were recorded by the men who fought, and how many more sought to discover their feelings through the sentimental strains of Alexander Campbell's "The Soldier's Dream."

And yet, amid the sober and symbolic commemorations of men and battles destined to take place in the coming decades, it was the extravagance of nineteenth-century sentimentalism that disappeared as ground was ceded from the divine to the human. The world, thanks to Charles Darwin, was still evolving, and American literature gravitated in two very different directions at once: toward the colorfully ironic and the pointedly real. A new version of observed life would replace the genteel tradition in literature, making it that much harder for old-fashioned dreams to hold on. But nature's secrets were not about to surrender to science.

The next phase in dream life was to reveal less about conscience and more about impulse. The inner space where people did their striving and played with fire was about to open wide.

EIGHT

MARK TWAIN CAN'T RESIST A MUSHY APPLE PIE

Even the wisest is sometimes a fool. For example, the philosopher who wore his spectacles when he was asleep that he might recognize friends he might see in his dreams.

—"Lagniappe," in the *Daily Picayune* (New Orleans), 1880

"I had such a droll dream last night, I must tell you," Louisa May Alcott, the celebrated author of *Little Women* (1868), wrote to her sister Anna in the summer of 1870, from Lake Geneva in Switzerland. "I thought I was returning to Concord after my trip, and was alone." She had negotiated a corner in her dream and found herself in a place she no longer recognized. "Our house was gone, and in its place stood a great gray stone castle, with towers and arches and lawns and bridges, very fine and antique. Somehow I got into it without meeting any one of you, and wandered about trying to find my family. At last I came across Mr. Moore [a neighbor], papering a room, and asked him where his house was. He didn't know me, and said—

"'Oh! I sold it to Mr. Alcott for his school, and we live in Acton now.'

"'Where did Mr. Alcott get the means to build this great concern?' I asked.

"'Well, he gave his own land, and took the great pasture his daughter left him—the one that died some ten years ago.'

"'So I am dead, am I?' says I to myself, feeling so queerly."

Mr. Moore proceeds to inform Louisa that her father, despite his historic inability to make any sort of fortune, had established a "fine" college there. At which point the dreaming "Lu," as she signed her letter, looked for her reflection in the glass, to see how she appeared in death, and discovered that she was now "a fat old lady, with gray hair and specs."

Rather than feel bad, this vision actually made her laugh. She turned and peered out at the lawn, where she saw "hundreds" of strangely clad young men. Then she spied her own father. He looked to her as he had thirty years earlier, when they had just arrived in Concord, "with brown hair and a big white neck-cloth, as in the old times. He looked so plump and placid and young and happy I was charmed to see him, and nodded; but he didn't know me; and I was so

Louisa May Alcott (1832–1888).

grieved and troubled at being a Rip Van Winkle, I cried, and said I had better go away and not disturb any one—and in the midst of my woe, I woke up."

Having this dream in Switzerland spoke to the disadvantage of distance. She was far from home and long out of contact, a problem she manifested as time displacement (precisely what the story "Rip Van Winkle" entailed). Her dream, like Rip's, united youthful fantasy with an adult capacity to appreciate tenderness.

The dream also reconfirms what biographies of the author uniformly state: that she wanted to see her difficult, quixotic father, who was an idea man only, professionally successful. Lu was convinced she knew what would make him happy; as it was, her earnings as an author already contributed substantially to his material comfort. It is surely not overreading to suggest that the warm-hearted (if not always sunny) Louisa wanted to come back to a place where she felt welcome. And how better for the middle sister to express her feeling for home—that emotional world from which she was removed—than to share a revelatory dream with the sister who was only a year and a half her elder.

"It was all so clear and funny," she wrote, lightheartedly evaluating the dream. "I can't help thinking that it may be a foreshadowing of something real. I used to dream of being famous, and it has partly become true; so why not Pa's college blossom, and he get young and happy with his disciples? I only hope he won't quite forget me when I come back, fat and gray and old."

For now at least, it was only by communicating with Anna that sister Lu could entertain the fantasy of Bronson Alcott's success. "Perhaps his dream is to come in another world," she wrote, "where everything is fresh and calm." Her dream was more prophetic than she knew: her father did not have to wait for the afterlife to claim his college. Nine years after Louisa's dream, owing to the generosity of Bronson Alcott's admirers, the unconventional patriarch got the chance to end his years maintaining a school for philosophy in Concord. However, Louisa certainly did not foresee that as her father was being lowered into his grave, after living to the ripe age of eighty-eight, she herself would be just moments from succumbing at fifty-five to a history of ingesting medical mercury.

As to the old man's failure to recognize her in the dream, the practical-minded daughter had a ready-made explanation: "because I was still in this work-a-day world, and so felt old and strange in this lovely castle in the air." Shifting back and forth from the existing world to a hoped-for state of immortality, she added wistfully: "The daughter who did die ten years ago is more likely to be the one who helped him build his School of Concord up aloft." That was Beth, whose slow, horrible death was a moving event in *Little Women*.

Lu could now complete her self-analysis: "I can see how the dream came." The day before, the "dear little lads" she had been traveling with were playing in nearby gardens; she had been to the barber's and spoken about her gray hairs. She was carrying a picture of her father on her journey, too, and had shown it around. And yet, even in listing these logical associations, she could not surrender entirely to reason. So she said it outright: "I believe in dreams."[1]

Louisa May Alcott's longtime hero, Ralph Waldo Emerson, continued to keep a reliable journal in the postbellum years. Memory, imagination, and the nature of dreams never ceased to engage his interest. Writing in 1868 about the role of the poet in society, he directly linked the one with the other:

> The distinction of the poet is ever this force of imagination which puts its objects before him with such deceptive power that he treats them as real, he talks to them as if they were present, he puts words in their mouths such as they should have spoken, & is affected by them as by Persons. As in dreams we create the persons, then talk with them, are surprised at what they do,—we putting, of course, the speeches into the mouths of the actors.[2]

Ever the idealist, Emerson marveled at the mind's capacity to create. He laid out his questions and let them sit in order to watch them ferment. His life was one of observing and remembering and observing what he remembered. In 1870, at the age of sixty-six, and more intrigued than troubled about the state of his own memory, he came up with this outline of a thought: "Compensation of failing memory in age by the increased power & means of generalization."

It was but a short while later that he became privy to the experience of Boston-area teacher Charles P. Ware. Five years prior, Ware had arisen from a dream, the outlines of which he could not recover, retaining a single sentence in his mind: "And what they dare to dream of, dare to die for." Later that day, he attended a dinner at which the poet James Russell Lowell read from his work. Lowell reached the line "Those love her best who to themselves are true" and, to Ware's astonishment, completed the couplet: "And what they dare to dream, dare to do." The unspoken question, of course, was whether this was coincidence or something else. Emerson deliberated, but chose not to comment.[3]

His next dream-related journal entry, six weeks later, was reminiscent of those of his early years that condemned "the gods" for their "jealousy" in refusing to allow memory to hold on to each "impressive dream" that was spun in sleep. "There is an air," he wrote, "as if the sender of the illusion had been heedless for a moment that Reason had returned to its seat, & was startled into attention. Instantly there is a rush from some quarter to break up the drama into a chaos of parts, then of particles, then of ether, like smoke dissolving in a wind." If the dream's origin was supernatural, whatever "god" had wrought it was puckish, evidently using the visions of sleep as a less-than-serious art form—a doodle, if you will.

Almost by definition, an Emersonian explanation was elusive: something more than a wild wish, something less than a real judgment. For Emerson, the human mind was suffering from battle fatigue, and the gods were deceivers, toying with those who went in search of truth. "The waked watchman" tried to reconstruct his dream, at first confident that he would succeed; but the "disappearing parts" could not be recaptured, and "the last fragment or film" melted away "before he could say, I have it." In 1871, Emerson left one more hint about what amounts to a lifelong concern: "Dreams are jealous of being remembered: they dissipate instantly & angrily if you try to hold them." In the end, it was he who was angry at his dreams; for they coalesced without ever lodging.[4]

~ɔ~

If there was one member of the literary community who spent as much time with his dreams as Ralph Waldo Emerson, it would have to be that amiable trouble-seeker from Hannibal, Missouri, Samuel Langhorne Clemens (1835–1910). In 1868, the man best known by his pen name Mark Twain wrote to his future wife, Olivia Louise ("Livy") Langdon, with an Emersonian complaint: "Last night I dreamed of you—but you were only with me a single moment & then instantly the vision faded & passed away." This motif extended as the months went by, when, upon hearing a particular song, he wrote: " . . . then my darling you seemed almost present in the flesh. And as the rich chords floated up, the air seemed filled with a mysterious presence, & I fancied it the soul of Livy wandering abroad on the invisible wings of a dream while the sweet body slept. Oh you visit me, even when you do not know it yourself."[5]

He had met Livy's brother Charley while traveling in Europe in 1867 and allegedly fell for her as soon as he glimpsed her photograph. The Langdons were the children of a wealthy coal merchant from Elmira, New York, and had grown up in a religious household. During their lengthy courtship, Sam wrote numerous chatty, adoring letters to Livy, on the order of the above. It was not unusual for him to sign off, "Pleasant dreams, sweetheart" or "Happy dreams to you, Livy darling." In one of these, he compared the women of his past unfavorably to her, saying that he had become increasingly "critical & hard to please, as in the way of old bachelors—but behold, I have found you at last." In fact, though, whether or not he ever told her, the doting husband continued to see previous girlfriends in his dreams throughout his long life—learning that dreams cannot easily be censored or controlled so as to erase the faces of former girlfriends.

Courting Livy, Clemens sentimentalized his dream vocabulary, as in "the lovely impalpableness of a dream-spirit in the twinkling of an eye" or "I had not dreamed that there was such a Livy." Yet he was not afraid to confront his unpleasant visions. The same letter (in the spring of 1869) that contained the preceding effusions led eventually to: "Life is short & uncertain (I had dreadful dreams last night) & do let us be together all we can. We do not know at what moment Death may invade our Eden."

Once aboard, it was hard to get off. "Little sweetheart," he addressed her ten days later, "I had a scary dream about you last night. I thought you came to me crying, & said 'Farewell'—& I knew by some instinct that you meant it for a final farewell." She had spurned him, and he could not fathom why. "It made me feel as if the world had dropped from under my feet!" He put his arms around her and tried gentle persuasion. It had the desired effect. "Bye & bye your tears ceased & your eyes brightened, & your hand sought mine & nestled in it." He now read trust on her face and relaxed. But as he awoke from the dream, "in a bewildered way, & half doubting," he could not be sure whether the first or second part of the dream was his present reality. He spent the next day feeling "jolly," as if he had somehow dodged a bullet, at the same time aware that he arrived at "jolly" only by repeatedly telling himself, "it was all a hideous dream & she is my darling yet." He concluded: "If anybody were to tell me now that a dream is able to turn the hair gray in a single night, I would believe it."[6]

At the end of 1869, barely a month before their wedding, he wrote Livy with another unpromising report. "And honey, I had such a vivid, vivid dream! I thought that you had discarded me." This time, the dream presented the lovelorn fiancé with a visible rival. "He was always with you, & I seemed to understand that he was an old rejected lover of yours, who had patiently waited, knowing that he could regain his place in your love if he could but get with you in my absence." The jealousy built as he looked into Livy's eyes and saw how glad she was to be near the other man. Sam appealed to her, and she admitted that she did not wish to destroy what they had, and yet she could not help what was happening. "And you fled away & left me prostrate upon the floor," he grieved. "Livy, for an hour after I awoke this morning (but had not yet opened my eyes), I lay in unspeakable misery."[7]

This species of dream is inter-generational. We have seen it several times before, notably among soldiers and prisoners of war. Given what we know about the power of attachment, and knowing that time and distance do many things to the feeling brain, it makes perfect sense that worry and insecurity should be articulated in that space—dream space—where life's transience is dramatized and tested. In Twain's abandonment dream, a universal instinct for self-preservation is engaged, while an interior urge is exposed.

Sanity requires us to rein in fantasy. We sustain emotional balance only by recognizing what life is and is not. Dreamers of old, dreamers near and far, have all learned how hard it is to will dreams to submit to our waking desires. This must also be why rational writers throughout history have prejudiced the word "dream" with its ironic usage, a synonym for unreality, flightiness, or an untamed mind; and why poems and songs and stories—the novel, the whimsical, the sensational—are the forms through which the world imagines the fairy-tale dream-come-true.[8]

In the 1870s and 1880s, while he and his wife resided in Hartford, Connecticut, the dream-plagued Clemens belonged to a gentlemen's group known as the Monday Evening Club. In his autobiography, he writes of a particular gathering at the home of one of its members, an Episcopal clergyman: "The subject under discussion was Dreams." Even in narrating his own life, the author does here what he does so well in stories: he lights upon personalities and makes each vignette an occasion to play with words in a series of digressions, going on for pages about everything but the participants' opinions on "the Dream question." Apparently, he did not remember their various theories about dreams in sufficient detail to include them. His purpose in telling the story was something else anyway: to pick at each of the club members' tendency to close his remarks with some "misplaced piety."

Twain had endured these upright men's "intolerable and inexcusable exudations" for a considerable amount of time, he tells us. It was attorney Charles E. Perkins, "the dullest white man in Connecticut," as Twain terms him, who finally crossed the line with such "wandering twaddle" that the famous author could stomach it no longer. Perkins insisted, as the learned had for many decades, that "Dreams merely proceed from indigestion—there is no quality of intelligence in them—they are thoroughly fantastic and without beginning, logical sequence, or definite end." Only the "stupid" found any value in them. And from here, Twain's antagonist "blandly and pleasantly" asserted that dreams "once had a mighty importance, that they had had the illustrious honor of being used by the Almighty as a means of conveying desires, warnings, commands to people whom He loved or hated—that these dreams are set down in Holy Writ; that no sane man challenges their authenticity."

These words would have been swallowed easily in Benjamin Rush's day, but that America was long gone, and for Twain they had the taste of a poison pill. Here and in his books, the author's disgust with sanctimony is anything but subtle. It was his turn after Perkins, and as he writes in the autobiography, he suggested (sarcastically, of course) that they move their future meetings to "the garret of some church," where prayer meetings belonged. The club "always had more clergyman in it than good people," he adds bitingly, in reconstructing that night.[9]

"I do not now remember what form my views concerning dreams took at that time," he picks up. "But I do remember telling a dream by way of illustrating some detail of my speech. . . . I was probably engaged in trying to make those people believe that now and then, by some accident, or otherwise, a dream which was prophetic turned up in the dreamer's mind."

The dream he told the assembled club mates was not just unforgettable, but life-altering. It dated back to the year 1858, when, as a Mississippi riverboat hand, Sam lost his brother Henry in a tragic accident. "I was a steersman on board the swift and popular New Orleans and St. Louis packet," he relates, adding parenthetically that he had resisted the temptation to publish this dream in his mother's lifetime because of the hurt it would have done to her. The boat was called the *Pennsylvania,* and on what would prove to be her final run, he had found a job for Henry as "mud clerk," which paid nothing but offered some prospect of gainful employment in the future. A few short weeks before that fateful night, Sam dreamt so vividly that he could scarcely separate the vision from reality. "In the dream I had seen Henry a corpse. He lay in a metallic burial case. He was dressed in a suit of my clothing, and on his breast lay a great bouquet of flowers, mainly white roses, with a red rose in the centre." The dreamer considered entering the chamber, but then changed his mind.

He knew where this house was. It was at Thirteenth and Locust in downtown St. Louis. As Twain saw himself walking up the street, he became aware that he was dreaming and awoke. He dressed quickly and rushed over to the house in question, ran up the stairs, and saw to his satisfaction that no casket lay there. He had needed proof that the dream was just a dream.

By the time he and Henry began their transit to New Orleans, Sam had forgotten his concern—easy to understand, given the transient nature of dreams in general. At night, the brothers walked the deck together, and Sam exhorted Henry, in case of a disaster, to keep his head and follow the orders of the first mate to ready the lifeboats. When they were below Memphis, the boat's boilers exploded. It was a messy scene. Sam found his brother's scalded body stretched across a mattress alongside a score of badly injured men. He was alive but despaired of; only through the sympathetic attention of one well-established physician did Henry start to turn the corner. Sadly, though, when he was subsequently attended to by an inexperienced doctor, the lad was administered a dose of morphine that proved fatal.

Twain narrates the rest of the story:

> He was carried to the dead-room and I went away a while to a citizen's house and slept off some of my accumulated fatigue—and meantime something was happening. The coffins provided for the dead were of unpainted white pine, but in this instance some of the ladies of Memphis had made up a fund of sixty dollars and brought a metallic case, and when I came back and entered the dead-room Henry lay in that open case, and he was dressed in a suit of my clothing. He had borrowed it without my knowledge during our last sojourn in St. Louis; and I recognized instantly that my dream of several weeks before was here exactly reproduced.

An elderly lady came into the room where Sam stood. She placed a bouquet, "consisting mainly of white roses," on Henry's chest. In the center of the bouquet was a red rose. Concludes the mystified survivor decades later: "I told the dream there in the Club that night just as I have told it here."[10]

While believing in such possibilities, Mark Twain otherwise maintained a witty, discursive pose in speculating about dreams. When his daughter Susie was six, in 1878, he wrote to his friend and fellow author William Dean Howells: "She is sorely badgered with dreams; & her stock dream is that she is being eaten up by bears. She is a grave & thoughtful child." He was prompted to relate Susie's repeating nightmare because she had awakened that day and innocently, plaintively wondered about her situation. "The trouble is," she remarked with the precious insight of a child, "I am never the bear, but always the person." To the father, Susie's point was well taken.[11]

Buoyed by the levelheadedness of an affectionate wife, Sam took pure delight in the life of the mind whenever he could. It may be that sexuality is never overt in the published writings of Mark Twain, but commentators have found in his books and in his recorded dreams a measure of inner conflict, inhibition, and evidence of unfocused guilt. He repeatedly experienced the familiar dream of being naked, or nearly naked, and in search of clothes. In one striking instance, he dreamt that he was propositioned by a "negro wench," who beckoned to him from a lounging position on a "long park-sofa" in an open field. He pegged her age as twenty-two and described the shape of her face, her smile, and the texture of her coarse linen shirt. He rejected the proposition, but accepted from her "a mushy apple pie—hot." One can read erotic symbols as one chooses, of course, but no one denies the linkage between drippy food (honey, sugar, pudding, pie) and the sensual mouth. Clearly, Sam Clemens had tasted sexual temptation somewhere along the road of life.[12]

Two years after he died, *Harper's* published a previously unknown story of Twain's, written in 1898, called "My Platonic Sweetheart." Introducing the piece to his readers, the editor commented that its author "was always interested in those psychic phenomena which we call dreams." "My Platonic Sweetheart" features a recurrent dream, inherently amusing, that leads Twain to philosophize more broadly about the phenomenon.

Here is how the story opens:

> I met her first when I was seventeen and she fifteen. It was in a dream. No, I did not meet her; I overtook her. It was in a Missourian village which I had never been in before, and was not in at that time, except dreamwise; in the flesh I was on the Atlantic seaboard ten or twelve hundred miles away. The thing was sudden, and without preparation—after the custom of dreams. There I was, crossing a wooden bridge that had a wooden rail and was untidy with scattered wisps of hay, and there she was, five steps in front of me; half a second previously neither of us was there.

Twain's actual dreams involved pursuits of one kind or another and a desire to capture beauty or balance or permanence. As we have seen, he was very much aware that encounters in dreams could be as cruel as they were romantic, enlarging and diminishing the self in turn. After finishing "My Platonic

Sweetheart," he wrote down a literal dream that captured the same sort of creative confusion: "Dreamed of a whaling cruise in a drop of water. Not by microscope, but actually. This would mean a reduction of the participants to a minuteness which would make them nearly invisible to God."

Through the various forms of his writing, Mark Twain serves as an indicator of the changes taking place in Americans' dream lives. Unprecedented levels of absurdity are revealed in his work, as the psychic possibilities in dreaming move beyond the reach of antebellum dreamers (even one so enterprising as Ichabod Cook). One wonders whether it was the relationship between humans and technology that stimulated this new kind of dream, or perhaps it was the sort of literature popularized by science fiction pioneer Jules Verne, the Scottish physician and paranormal enthusiast Sir Arthur Conan Doyle, and others of their ilk. The political world was beginning to experience riots and strikes stemming from indignation toward the excessive power of multimillionaire businessmen. Where was faith to lodge, when individualism resulted in such social disharmony?

It is hard to know precisely where the emphasis belongs, but we begin to see in the postbellum years a more familiar (modern) expression of dream disorientation. It does not require opium, or even poetic engagement, to sense the new uncanny. A dream is a thief, raiding the home body; and even if it does not wreak havoc, it subverts all expectation of calm.

Wandering whimsy is tempered by an almost philosophical sense of resignation in Twain's later work. In notes for *The Chronicle of Young Satan,* first published in 1916 as *The Mysterious Stranger,* he wrote: "each human being contains not merely two independent entities, but three—the Waking-Self, the Dream-Self, and the Soul. The last is immortal, the others are functioned by the brain and nerves, and are physical and mortal." It is noteworthy that the author meant for his main character in this tale to be an invisible soul, "able to exhibit forces, passions, and emotions of a quite tremendously effective character." This was a godlike hero (in the Emersonian sense) with psychic powers that could become mischievous. As one modern commentator has observed, the "fleshing" of the "dream-self" was, in typical Twain fashion, mysterious and comic at once.

In a life of ample disappointment and pain, punctuated by the shocking loss of his talented daughter Susie from meningitis, Sam Clemens found that dreams intensified what it was that humans ordinarily felt. To take "My Platonic Sweetheart" as one example, he wrote: "For everything in a dream is more deep and strong and sharp and real than is ever its pale imitation in the unreal life which is ours when we go about awake and clothed with our artificial selves in this vague and dull-tinted artificial world." His agonized character in "My Platonic Sweetheart" (presumably Twain himself) was convinced that no bad dream could be as bad as the real tortures of emotional life; he described the promise of a postcorporeal existence as the chance to "go abroad in Dreamland clothed in our real selves," enriched by the "mysterious mental magician" that is the truer selfhood composed in dreams.[13]

Clemens had a long and abiding interest in psychic phenomena. He was an early member of the Society for Psychical Research (SPR), a group formed in England in 1882, which studied occult incidents without fear or favor. Just because some mediums were frauds did not mean all were. The SPR quickly expanded to the United States, where greater skepticism of the organization's value came from the suggestion that its members were exposing impostors more than they were substantiating incidents of clairvoyance. Twain was one who hoped for more investigations of "the possible," which meant collecting and evaluating precognitive dreams, bridging past and present.

Prior to this moment in his career, Twain's narrative strategy was fairly traditional—linear, that is. But in the mid-1880s, something else took over him. In 1884, he woke one morning from a dream in which he had found himself "a knight errant in armor," and with *A Connecticut Yankee in King Arthur's Court* (1889), he translated that dream into a time-travel adventure of epic proportions. Once again, its burlesque humor does not negate its occult quality.

In Twain's delusional Camelot, past and present collide. Protagonist Hank Morgan of mid-nineteenth-century Hartford wanders, in his unconscious state, through sixth-century England. As he endeavors to make the impossible seem possible, Twain repeatedly places Hank in harm's way and pits him against the wizard Merlin. In effect, the novel is one long dream.

The trend in time bending does not begin or end with Twain, of course. Edward Bellamy's highly successful *Looking Backward,* published in 1888, catapulted his sleeping protagonist to the year 2000. H. G. Wells gave the world *The Time Machine* in 1895. Stage actor Joseph Jefferson's portrayal of Rip Van Winkle over several decades made him a millionaire, as the dream-inspired American literati responded to reports of unexplained phenomena—of minds unleashed. And in American Protestant circles, the practice of faith healing was given new life in the 1880s.[14]

~~❧~~

N ew Englander William James (1842–1910), another active member of the Society for Psychical Research, got to know Twain personally. The son of a Swedenborgian spiritualist and older brother of the novelist Henry James, he was exposed to Emerson, received extensive training as a physician before turning to philosophy, and lived long enough to witness up close the success of Sigmund Freud in America—albeit harboring suspicions about the Viennese doctor's dream theories. Julian Hawthorne, William James's companion in youth, wrote that as a Harvard professor in the 1870s, James appeared "nervous, worried, with bright troubled eyes. He was diving into the depth of his soul, but he had not found peace." It was an astute remark.[15]

James spent his entire career at Harvard, ranging in what he taught from physiology to philosophy to psychology. He hoped, above all, to establish a proper relationship between the worlds of science and faith. One of his students, G. Stanley Hall, who started out life as a preacher, became America's first Ph.D. in psychology and founded the *American Journal of Psychology* in 1887. When Hall was named president of Clark University, in nearby Worcester, James was envious. For his part, Hall criticized his former teacher for going overboard in his engagement with the paranormal. To believe in dreams was, he insisted, self-deception. Undeterred, James persisted in studying the biology of consciousness, entering into long conversations with his scientific peers about dreams, prophecies, and myriad mysteries of the mind. He came to accept the idea of a subconscious, that is, coexistence of the waking personality and a hidden self.

His commitment to the American Society for Psychical Research led James to take particular interest in a strangely gifted Boston shopkeeper's wife. Leonora Piper was born in the late 1850s, the decade when "mejium" Mollie Dorsey was inexplicably seeing events at a distance in sparsely settled Nebraska. Beginning in her childhood, Piper received communications from people at the moment of their deaths. In 1885, as a young mother and reluctant telepath, she came to James's attention. For years thereafter, she delivered insights that were never rationally explained, frequently tested by professional skeptics, and never shown to have been fraudulently obtained. As it turned out, Mrs. Piper was less enthralled by what she could do than her patron William James was.[16]

The year 1885 sorely tested James. As his involvement in psychical research began to blossom, his wife contracted scarlet fever and closed herself off from their three young children while she fought it. As she began to get better, she reentered her children's lives, only to come down next with whooping cough, which their one-year-old, Herman, also caught. This meant the family was split up again, and for all the family physician's efforts, nothing could save Herman, the youngest child, whom James called "the flower of our little flock." While tending to the older two some distance away, he closed a letter to his wife, who remained with the baby: "I dreamed last night that poor little humster [their pet name for Herman] had a hooked nose and was moribund!" Perhaps the unrecognizable feature on his face meant that James felt some separation from the boy already, as if he was preparing himself for what impended. A week later, the child died and was buried in a flannel-lined wicker casket. James wrote that the experience was "one more taste of the intolerable mysteriousness of this thing called existence." Thus it was, as the couple grieved, that the philosopher James paid his first visit to Leonora Piper, open to the possibility that the medium could tell him and his wife something meaningful.[17]

What other kind of American belonged to the Society for Psychical Research? Isaiah Thornton Williams was a successful Manhattan attorney who shared Sam Clemens's and William James's deep curiosity about mental telepathy, which was at this time better known as "thought transference." Before he became attached to the SPR, Williams was attracted to Swedenborgian mysticism and functioned as a lay preacher. His openness to new ideas is reflected in a letter from a friend who fed him with information about a Chicagoan who was freed from her physical ills by the "mind cure" and was convinced that "all sickness is simply a belief—there is no life in matter except as the spirit gives it life." A while later, a newly formed "Cosmic Club" invited Williams to attend a meeting to discuss the origins of the universe, to "penetrate the latent arcana of omnipotent infinitude . . . , suppressing dogmatical creeds." They were seekers, all.[18]

Isaiah Williams's most reliable correspondent was a relative in Maine named Martha Osgood. From 1878, the pair corresponded regularly about the mind and ways to address unanswerable questions about the nature of the universe. In almost every one of her letters to Williams, Osgood invoked dreams, either directly or by metaphor. "You dream of pleasant things and never do them," she coached him. "But I am inclined to think there is much pleasure to dreaming as in doing with an enthusiastic imagination, for the dream has an ideal quality which can never be realized in actual experience." She copied out an obscure poem "by an English Seamstress," titled "The Dreamer." It reads a lot like Edward Young's *Night Thoughts,* combining dreams with flashes of mortality. The poem concludes: "Dream of a sleep whose dreams no more shall come, / My last, my first, my only welcome home!"[19]

It was the decade when the Ouija board was introduced and mass-marketed. It was, no less significantly, a time when one breed of scientist could insist that even a detailed dream of impending death (as Sam Clemens had of his brother Henry) could be chalked up to coincidence or an overactive imagination, and a different breed of scientist could acknowledge that there were still unsolved mysteries of the mind. Science held that the transport of thoughts from one mind to another, at the moment of death or at any other time— telepathy—was a natural event.

~ಿ~

More or less from the day the Civil War ended, both published and unpublished dream reports took on an increasingly sensational character. It was not by chance: they were meant to be deliberately shocking. Save for the disappearance of angels, guides, and obvious religious symbolism, the prophetic quality of dreams was no less prized than it had been before the war.

A San Francisco newspaper, *The Elevator,* printed a story from Paris that had been "authenticated" by multiple sources. A mining engineer awoke after a "frightful" dream to find that his hair had turned white overnight. He had eaten a large quantity of pork at dinner and dreamt of being lowered into a deep mine, only to see on his way back up that the rope was nearly severed. As it gave way, "he uttered a fearful shriek, which aroused the inmates of the house, and when they burst open the door of the dreamer's room, they found a white-headed man in place of the black-haired young gentleman." It was, the story concluded, "the first instance on record" of a dream changing the dreamer's hair color. Unlike the case of Mrs. Drinker's choking dinner guest, the role that pork played—indigestion?—was not explicitly given here.[20]

The press carried many of this stamp, ranging from *Twilight Zone* dreams to straightforward sixth-sense dramas. In "Her Dream Was Verified," Mrs. Lawson Valentine, a high-society woman connected to the nationally prominent Beecher clan, was at her home in Brooklyn when she woke from a dream in which her summer house upstate had been robbed. She could not be dissuaded and the next day received a telegram informing her that the place had been looted of valuable jewelry and "ransacked from top to bottom." Given that the story was conveyed by a family of prominence, the *North American,* a respectable journal, did not doubt its veracity.[21]

People were always moved to record the dreams of the dangerously ill, half expecting some supernatural revelation. Recall Clay Dillard's pre-death vision of her little nephew in heaven or even Eliza Way Champlain's urgently writing home to see whether her morbid dream foretold a death in the family. During his final sickness late in 1876, steamboat magnate Cornelius Vanderbilt, one of the richest and most powerful men in American history, had "queer dreams," according to his wife. He dreamt of being cast down to the ocean floor, needing "all the power of the steamer Vanderbilt" to pull him back up. In the dream, it did so successfully. Once dubbed "the leviathan of the deep," *The Vanderbilt* proved its extractive might; Vanderbilt, the man, rallied at first, but soon thereafter proved mortal.[22]

Another example of the phenomenon, this one blatantly fed by superstition, comes through the testimony of a woman named Margaret Dickins, who advised her adult son Francis to mark the date, October 27, every year of his life. For it was on that day, in 1872, that her late husband recorded a dream in his journal, a dream "so wonderfully fulfilled" (she meant "wonderful" in the old sense of "astonishing") six years later. She copied it down for Francis so he would retain it:

> Had a dream that Margaret and I were in a desperate situation and the only possibility of escape was to make the horses we were on jump off a high precipice into a stream of water. It appeared hopeless. Margaret said, "dont do it" but I said God have mercy on us and dashed over. Fell much hurt, saw Margaret a short distance bleeding found that she was much but not sensibly hurt and awoke.

Although it was on November 16 (not October 27), 1878, that the accident her husband had dreamt of occurred, she had convinced herself that the two dates were suspiciously close. And nothing could change the fact that Francis's father had breathed his last on October 27, 1879, seven years to the day after his remarkable dream.[23]

Horror was a drug that could be easily abused and as easily reconstituted in novel ways. In the 1820s, one could read about the Indian in Georgia who was so spooked by a dream that, as he woke, he grabbed his rifle and shot his uncle in the head as he slept nearby. In the last decades of the nineteenth century, that tale had morphed into an entirely new subgenre of the macabre news story: the murderous dreamer. The *Philadelphia News* reported on a railroad man who had to give up his calling when he nearly strangled his wife to death. The whole thing started out innocently enough: "I began to dream, and I thought I was a boy again, climbing the hills of my father's farm in Lancaster county, with my brother's hand in mine." Then, something possessed him. It began with sounds in the air, winds moaning and birds shrieking, and suddenly he was behind the engine of a locomotive. "The exhilarations of the midnight ride made the blood in my veins tingle." The next thing he heard was the voice of his wife: "You meant to murder me!" she cried, showing him where his fingers had pressed into her throat. And so, at her insistence, he gave up railroading as he would flee the Devil.

There were murderers, and there were victims. A man named Porter, a "member of a traveling dramatic company," was in Marshall, Texas, when he awoke from a bad dream and told his fellows that it involved a "mangled, bleeding corpse." Soon after, he fell victim to murder, which made his story newsworthy as far away as St. Paul, Minnesota.[24]

As the popularity of dime novels attests, late nineteenth-century Americans loved to relate "amazing true tales," and the press loved to circulate them. In the columns of America's newspapers, the "singular" dream of the early decades of the century largely yielded to the "amazing" dream. Nor would this trend cease, as anyone who has read a daily horoscope well knows. The line between truth and fiction is regularly bent in the interest of mass entertainment.

Advertisers in the postwar decades could sell products as pleasant dream producers or bad dream inhibitors—there were always ways to tap dream lore in order to make a buck. Among the nation's classic hucksters was a New Yorker named Pierce who boasted a medicine with multiple uses. The *Chicago Times* ran the following ad:

> *The spooks and goblins that delight*
> *To fill with terror all the night;*
> *That stalk abroad with hideous dreams*
> *With which dyspepsia's fancy teems,*
> *Will never trouble with their ills*
> *The man who trusts in Pierce's pills.*

The purveyor of the pills, as it turns out, was not only a trained physician but a U.S. congressman from upstate New York. Dr. Ray Vaughn Pierce graduated Eclectic Medical College, in Cincinnati, in 1862. He served in Washington briefly, alongside such brighter lights as James A. Garfield and William McKinley, before returning to the more lucrative profession of hawking his unproven remedies, which he kept alive into the twentieth century. Eclectic, indeed.[25]

A lot of old thinking about dreams persisted into the industrial age. The folks of Dodge City, Kansas, were putting in their crops during the spring of 1880, as the *Dodge City Times* reported: "People have dreamed of spending the severest winter in Siberia—simply because the bed-clothes have been thrown off during sleep. It is said that a moderate heat applied to the soles of the feet will generate dreams of volcanoes." In "Hints from Beyond," the *National Republican,* of Washington, D.C., made fun of the whole enterprise. Interpretation guides could be found "wherever books are made," a truth that extended to the Chinese, "with their 40,000,000 or less years of recorded existence." According to the *National Republican,* for as long as dream books had been in print, no one ever explained how and where the ideas contained in them had originated.[26]

Mainstream newspapers often positioned peculiar tales prominently on the page. That is how one Kentucky paper in 1889 reported a dream within a dream, in which a man asleep tried to stop a friend, whose beloved had just died, from jumping off a bridge to his death. The dreamer failed in his mission and tumbled over the side with his friend. Hitting the water, his sleeping self broke out in a cold sweat. Someone threw a rope, and as he found his way ashore, he tried telling bystanders that it was all a dream. They scoffed at him: "You ain't got no more nerve 'n a rabbit!" At which point he was taken by the police and brought to the station, where he was introduced around as the "blank blank fool who jumped in the river and then changed his mind and called for help." He knew he hadn't called for help. Then, as he was being led to a cell, he struck his head. And that is when he really awoke![27]

By now, traditional understandings about dreams were regularly being employed to raise a smile. The *Daily Picayune,* in New Orleans, published the following squib in 1880: "A tramp woke up suddenly with cold sweat standing in great beads upon his forehead. 'What's the matter?' asks his companion. 'A frightful dream! I dreamt I was at work!' 'I told you that that last piece of mince pie would give you a horrid nightmare.'" Two commonplace notions

"The Dreamers Dine." From John Kendrick Bangs, The Dreamers: A Club *(New York: Harper & Brothers, 1899). In the final decades of the century, dreaming was easily burlesqued. The make-believe club was made up of writers whose "masterpieces of fiction had their basis in actual dreams." Comically overturning the long-accepted explanation that associated dreaming with indigestion, the club met monthly to eat and drink "such stuff as dreams are made of."*

are at work here, of course. First, the very thought of gainful employment is a nightmare to the good-for-nothing tramp. Second, the belief that indigestion causes bad dreams just won't die.[28]

There were those who giggled over their dreams and others who taunted their loved ones over them. "They say you must remember what you dream when you sleep in a strange bed, for it will come true," wrote a single girl who spent the night at a friend's. "I have dreamed about you every night," wrote bride-to-be Emily Beale to the man of her dreams, twisting the romantic commonplace into a gently mocking quip: "I hear your voice in the evening wind, & also in the gobbling of turkeys." The same Emily was scheduled to attend a relative's wedding and dreamt that the groom had turned out to be someone other than the woman's fiancé. And as this man was Roman Catholic, he brought his priest to officiate in the Protestant church. Instead of taking wedding vows, the couple performed a ritual square dance. Then the virgin bride retired behind a screen, only to be observed nursing her three-month-old baby! "So mixed up," Emily acknowledged giddily the next day. Another woman's dream of wedding jitters was more classic. "I woke from a very disagreeable dream about you," she told her intended. "I thought it was the day after the wedding and my friends were asking for you, but strange to say I did not know where you were, or when you went away."[29]

Many in the popular press took to the study of dreams as a means of fathoming the human condition. In 1882, the *National Tribune,* a Washington,

D.C., paper, tried to get serious without slipping too obviously into science fiction. Its columnist built his piece around a dream scientist who had recently hypothesized that "the time would come when dreams might be controlled." Sleep, the specialist thought, "could be utilized, so that during the still hours of the night the human subject could be made pleasantly conscious, of an ideal, if not a real existence." Dream therapy did not exist, but belief in the power of suggestion had arisen alongside an improved knowledge of the power of narcotics and stimulants and their effect on the nerves. What made this newspaperman different was that, instead of simply combining past generations' testaments with the most recent dream reports in "Ripley's Believe It or Not" fashion, he offered his audience something that might one day become "true and amazing" and life affirming.

Then the *Tribune* writer got more intimate: "A common dream with reputable men and women is to find themselves in strange places with very little clothing on. They undergo intolerable agonies of shame and distress to reach some place where they can be arrayed in fitting garments." The writer would not hazard a guess as to what such dreams meant, nor would he explain how he had concluded that "very unimaginative persons often have highly poetic and fanciful, as well as fantastical, dreams." Waiting for science to come up with real answers, he speculated that "the fantastic images which flit through the visions of the dreamer" indicated the presence of a sense of humor in the sleep state.

Finally, in identifying sleep as seven or eight hours passed each night in "mock death," he catalogued the latest intelligence gleaned from neurophysiological research: "Every part of the body lives and carries on its functions, with the single exception of the nerve centers. These succumb to unconsciousness." Therefore, the writer judged, with an eye toward the future, if a scientist, a "dream-inducer," should arise who could inject pleasant thoughts and use the dream state to promote mental health, he would be "the inventor of a kind of eternity protein!" Set against the banal and formulaic, the deliberately shocking and sensational, the *National Tribune*'s account was perhaps the most unusual, most optimistic take on dreams before the 1890s.[30]

More and more people saw the future getting closer. In 1885, an Iowa woman in her mid-forties could not get out of her head a dream she had some fifteen years before, in which she had invented a perpetual motion machine— she even felt its weight and the pressure on its springs. She said (in her diary) that she could imagine nothing so wonderful as living two hundred years in order to see what science would come up with: that was the only way she figured she would be able to see the amazing device she had conjured in her dream. Better this, she thought, than to relive the most recent of her sleep visions, that of "a great snake wrigling & twisting every way near me . . . in a sky of waves." Late nineteenth-century Americans marveled at the originality, as well as complexity, of their dreams. They were coming to expect real answers from science.[31]

Whenever the old impression of sleep as a "mock death" was revived, the matter was now being raised with greater purpose. In 1890, under the headline "Sleep, Death, Dreams," the *Wichita Eagle* examined the common comparison, affirming that sound sleep was actually "a counterfeit and exact counterpart" of death. People had convinced themselves that dreamless sleep was "restorative," but, this writer taunted, "Have they any reason for thinking that death is not good for them, even better than sleep, since it is eternal?" To the ancient Greeks, Sleep and Death were the twin brothers Hypnos and Thanatos, offspring of the goddess of Night. "We imagine that we comprehend sleep," the piece continued. "Death we account a mystery, and, being mysterious, it is alarming." Obviously, "mock death" was less worrisome than the real thing, although it must also be said that Morpheus, the god of Dreams and son of Sleep, was never as well understood as his father.

The *Wichita Eagle* piece was provocative in declaring dreams to be "far more unintelligible than death," in fact, "a sort of life." And yet the writer recurred to the vague prognostications of others of this era in stating that "we appear to share the same feelings, to cherish the same passions, to perform the same acts as in our waking hours." Psychological interpretation was still off-limits or at least poorly focused. But the unnamed author went beyond the comfort zone of many when he claimed that, despite our knowing that "we are not our actual selves" in "dream-land," something inside, something integral, must change as a result of dreaming: "our principles, our morals, our judgments." Though this was the same conversation that eighteenth-century thinkers were having among themselves, this one local authority, at least, was saying that change was not to be feared. As the *National Tribune* piece had put forward, dreams were a good and alluring mystery of the mind—emphasis on good.[32]

Change was in the wind. For one, the separation of the new laboratory-based science of psychology from the traditional discipline of philosophy was having lasting implications. As G. Stanley Hall was in the process of establishing the American Psychological Association in 1892, a new edition of James

Sully's *Illusions: A Psychological Study* was published in New York. As the author of *Sensation and Intuition,* Sully had already established a reputation for clarity, and he privileged rational recourse over speculation about the soul. He and William James were on familiar terms, and *Illusions* would prove valuable to Freud as well.

In this work, beginning with the "reception, discrimination, and classification of an impression," Sully demonstrated how degrees of attentiveness modified that impression and caused the "timid" to see ghosts. In his chapter on the "unfamiliar world" of dreams, he described sleep narratives in evolutionary terms: the primitive believed in a "second self" that commingled with dead ancestors during sleep; a somewhat more developed society understood night visions as "symbolic pictures unfolded to the inner eye of the soul by some supernatural being"; modern science could now remove nearly all the mystery by describing the "intimate union" of the operations that joined mind to body. "Our waking consciousness acts in numberless ways on our dreams," Sully wrote, "and these again in unsuspected ways influence our waking mental life." In short, dreams could be made intelligible.[33]

~ɔ

We all know what it means to be human. It is to generate hope and mark moments of happiness, while navigating between fear and acceptance. It is why our literal dreams are sometimes as compelling as our consciously spun dreams. It also helps explain why it is that questions of coincidence and psychic connections always attach to dream lore. The impulse is the same as that which makes instances of ghost sightings, UFOs, and concepts of fate or luck eternally of interest to all but the most rationally impelled among us.

In 1889, the *New York Evening World* held a national contest. It was a newspaper owned by Joseph Pulitzer, which claimed at that time a circulation of 286,000. It asked readers to submit dreams they had had that they considered extraordinary. From among the entries, one would emerge as the best dream.

The judge of the contest was Julian Hawthorne. He had attended Harvard in the 1860s and went on to be a writer of some renown, always able to trade on his family name. In 1884, he published a book about his parents, *Nathaniel Hawthorne and His Wife*; in 1888, he came out with the title that explains his selection, a few months later, as judge in the *Evening World's* "best dream" contest. It was a clever little morality tale called *A Dream and a Forgetting*.

The apple did not fall far from the tree. Taking up his pen, as his father had, at the crossroads of morality and psychology, Julian found ironic juxtapositions hard to resist. In the memoir that was published at the end of his life, he related an unsettling coincidence that occurred on May 18, 1864, while he was at Harvard. "I was initiated into a college secret society," he wrote, "a couple of hours of grotesque and good-humored rodomontade and horseplay, in which I cooperated as in a kind of pleasant nightmare." Blindfolded and led into a crypt, he was placed in a coffin, "to lie until the Resurrection." After testing out death for some length of time, someone came to fetch him, he was led away, and the blindfold removed. He was thus "reawakened" in a brightly lit room, surrounded by his mates. The very next day, though, Julian received news that his famous father was dead, a freshly made coffin being readied for him.[34]

The younger Hawthorne almost certainly borrowed his title, *A Dream and a Forgetting,* from William Wordsworth, who wrote: "Our birth is but a sleep and a forgetting." The line appears in the middle of a well-known ode, "Intimations of Immortality from Recollections of Early Childhood," in which the poet marvels at his own long-ago sense impressions. No person was empty of substance at birth, Wordsworth contended, because the soul "cometh from afar" (that is, from God). We enter life as already something, and "not in entire forgetfulness." In the poet's words: "Heaven lies about us in our infancy."[35]

The larger message in Wordsworth's ode is that memory disappoints. The purity of early visions are lost as the child becomes a man. It is a theme that every generation can relate to. By exchanging "sleep" for "dream," while retaining Wordsworth's "forgetting," Julian Hawthorne seems to have highlighted the connection between dream and soul (or essence). In dreams, he would have us believe, clues are present that are designed to bring a person's destiny forward.

A Dream and a Forgetting is the tale of Fairfax Boardwine's courtship of Mary Gault. He was a farmer's son and she, as she understood herself, the offspring of "very commonplace people." But Fairfax aspired to be a great poet and asked Mary whether she would look upon him differently if he were to skyrocket to literary fame. She answered simply: "I love you. I don't know whether I can love a great poet. He will seem like another person for a time." When he proposed marriage, she selflessly declined, at least for the moment, fearing that a wife would only drag him down. He tried to understand her decision.

Next, praying for the power to help Fairfax sell his poetry in New York, Mary fell asleep and was "visited by a vivid and consistent dream, which remained distinctly in her memory when she awoke." She wrote it down from start to finish, giving it the eponymous title "A Dream and a Forgetting." He stopped by her house and perceived that the woman he loved suddenly exuded a strange emotional power. She folded the paper and handed it to him, saying: "I did not make it up—it came to me." He read it eagerly, saw every person and event "in living colors," and gleaned the rich meanings she intended for him. But "the longer he dwelt upon the matter, the less it affected him as something communicated from an extraneous source, and the more as if it were generated by his own brain." In short, he stole Mary's idea, convincing himself that "without his genius to develop it, her dream would have availed nothing."

Fairfax, of course, named his poem "A Dream and a Forgetting," too, and the New York literary crowd delighted in the farmer-poet's native genius. Taken with success, he recast his work as a play, eagerly awaiting the greater fame he now expected was imminent. Ever-faithful Mary came to New York, excited to see the opening performance, only to be shunned by the egotistical playwright who had, until fame descended, worshipped her. He had since wronged her by taking up with another woman. It was most shameful. Mary had inspired his art, and in no time he already had eyes for another.

The curtain lifted, the actors performed, and the audience booed and hissed and mocked Fairfax with "ironical applause." He tried to turn his luck around by coming from backstage and taking a bow, pretending that he had composed a satire and had fully intended for the crowd to react this way. Nevertheless, his display of self-possession backfired. No one bought his excuses. Someone threw an orange, and it splattered all over his new suit.

It was, Hawthorne's narrator explains, "an ignominious spectacle to gods and men," to watch as the defeated poet "staggered back, nerveless and bewildered." Though his new girlfriend was nowhere to be found, Mary remained to witness her errant lover's failure. Fairfax finally came to his senses and realized the meaning of honor and sacrifice: he had rediscovered his soul. The couple quietly returned to the countryside and married, "with starvation staring them in the face." Fairfax abandoned his dream of writing and worked his farm with splendid success, while Mary grew roses for the New York market. The novel ends with the moral: "To dwell in heaven before your time may not be happiness."[36]

After surveying the many dreams submitted to the *Evening World*, Hawthorne awarded first prize to J. E. J. Buckey, of Cumberland, Maryland. The winning dreamer had been a professor at a junior college for women in North East, Pennsylvania, where he met, and in 1873 married, a well-traveled,

> *A Dream and a Forgetting.* 57
>
> ---
>
> she fell asleep; and in her sleep she was visited by a vivid and consistent dream, which remained distinctly in her memory when she awoke in the morning. And so much was she impressed by it, as being a thing specially sent to her in response to her passionate desire, that she sat down at her table and, before leaving her room, wrote out the story of her dream in full. The title she gave the story was the same as that which I have given to this narrative "A Dream and a Forgetting."
>
> When, later in the day, she met Fairfax, she wore a serene and smiling countenance,

A page from Julian Hawthorne's novel A Dream and a Forgetting (1888).

college-educated administrator. After they settled in Maryland, Buckey sat on the State Board of Education, clearly a man with a sound reputation. Without explaining precisely how one could test the veracity of a man's dream, the newspaper printed, below the text of the dream he had sent in, an "Affidavit as to its genuineness," provided by Buckey. The Maryland educator was ceremoniously billed "Champion Dreamer."

Here was Buckey's winning submission: He dreamt that he had shot a man in the neck, a short man with a "heavy black mustache." He stood as blood spurted from his victim and stained the dreamer's white vest. The following morning, wide awake, Buckey dressed for work, left home, and was turning a corner when he suddenly spotted his "dream man"; and at that very moment, the man before him unexpectedly yelled at Buckey: "For God's sake, don't shoot me!" As the Marylander tells it, "We were both too much shocked to speak. . . .

The World

Published by the Press Publishing Company.

TUESDAY EVENING, MARCH 5.

SUBSCRIPTION TO THE EVENING EDITION
(Including Postage),
PER MONTH..............................30c.
PER YEAR..............................$2.50

VOL. 29.......................NO. 10,059

Entered at the Post-Office at New York as second-class mail matter.

BRANCH OFFICES:
WORLD UPTOWN OFFICE—1267 Broadway between 31st and 32d sts., NEW YORK.
BROOKLYN—359 FULTON ST. HARLEM—News Department, 150 EAST 125TH ST.; Advertisements at 237 EAST 115TH ST. PHILADELPHIA, PA.—Ledger Building, 112 SOUTH 6TH ST. WASHINGTON—610 14TH ST.
LONDON OFFICE—32 COCKSPUR ST., TRAFALGAR

CHAMPION DREAMER.

Judge Hawthorne Awards the Prize to J. E. J. Buckey, of Cumberland, Md.

The Successful Dream and an Affidavit as to Its Genuineness.

Very Interesting Report on the Competition from Julian Hawthorne.

THE SUCCESSFUL DREAM.

I dreamed one night last Summer that I met a man of small stature, dark complexion, black hair and heavy black mustache, fashionably dressed, on the corner of Centre and Baltimore streets, in this city. Some quarrel arose, and I shot him in the neck. Some of

"Champion Dreamer." In 1889, J. E. J. Buckey shoots a mustached stranger in his dream and then sees him on the street the next morning. His dream is certified "genuine" and taken for the nation's best.

We had both dreamed the same dream." As if that were not enough, upon looking at his vest later in the day, Buckey found "a smear of something red on it about the size of a quarter." To satisfy his curiosity, he took it to a chemist, who removed the stain and confirmed it to be human blood.[37]

Buckey's "champion dream," authentic and legally certified though it may have been, was less original than it appeared. In the *London Magazine,* way back in 1765, a young man who signed his name "Josephus" attested to having a dream that another person dreamt at the same time. He imagined that he had gone home to visit his parents, tried the front door, found it locked, and entered from the back. Upstairs, he discovered his father fast asleep and his mother "broad awake." He said to her, "Mother! I am going on a long journey," to which she replied: "O dear son, thee art dead!" Hearing this exclamation, "Josephus" awoke.

A few days later, he received a letter from his father, informing him that his mother had heard someone entering their home through the back door in the middle of the night and soon after encountered him at her bedside. The father repeated, word for word, what his wife said she heard, which were, of course, the very words the son had spoken, adding that she feared he was dead. Fortunately, the magazine explains, it was all a dream, and "nothing extraordinary turned up, on either side."

As Pulitzer's newspaper would do in 1889, a commentator in the *London Magazine* in 1765 evaluated this "authentic" dream, investigating the mother and finding her to be "a woman of undoubted veracity." The magazine resolved that the son's dream, on the face of it, was "not a whit more wonderful [i.e., astonishing] than what is found coming out in a hundred instances of dreams that occur every day"; but the mother's complete apprehension of the dream at the same moment was so amazing that the magazine decided to invite "ingenious and learned persons" to conduct a further study and report on its true implication. A dual dream was so unprecedented in 1765 that it required the best minds to undertake a solution. The editors of the *Evening World,* on the other hand, did not call on modern science to explain what it all meant; rather, they decided to leave well enough alone after claiming readers' attention, washing their ink-stained hands of the matter and moving on to other news.[38]

One has to wonder whether that editorial decision casts doubt on the seriousness of the contest. In the weeks leading up to the crowning of Professor Buckey, the newspaper did milk the story as much as it could by featuring other dreams submitted by its readers. A wise guy from Jersey City wrote in, saying he had dreamt of winning the prize for best dream. He gloried in being the talk of the town: "You may imagine my disappointment when I awoke." A Civil War veteran dreamt he was in Boston at a regimental ball, and he met there a woman he had come to know on board a steamer from Europe a few years earlier. He soon after attended a ball (in New York, not Boston) and ran into the woman he had only seen twice before—on the boat and in his dream. An even eerier one among the runner-up dreams was that of a man who had been set to go on a fishing expedition. The night before, his brother, ten years in his grave, spoke to him and warned him not to go. "I awoke the next morning too late to join the party," he reported. Two of the four on board drowned that day.[39]

Coincidence? It turns out that, like the dual dream, the shipwreck dream has had a very long history. Not only did previous generations in the United States record it, but the ancient Greeks and Romans made it a part of their dream lore as well. According to Cicero, while on a journey, Simonides found the body of a stranger and had it properly buried. Soon after, the dead man came to him in a dream and warned him not to board the vessel that awaited him. Simonides did as instructed, learning afterward that all on board perished.

Just because it was something of a trope did not mean that the shipwreck dream, or its ilk, was merely imagined. "The greatest men of antiquity have held the faith," wrote the distinguished mid-nineteenth-century French physician Brierre de Boismont, that "the truth is sometimes revealed to us in our dreams." In its English translation, his study was titled *On Hallucinations: A History and Explanation of Apparitions, Visions, Dreams, Ecstasy, Magnetism, and Somnambulism.* Sensation was like a set of musical notes, he observed on the subject of presentiments: some individuals had the extraordinary gift of hearing, or sensing, an approaching storm well before anyone else in the vicinity, while other people (not to mention certain breeds of dog) were able to distinguish objects by scent at a distance. So why couldn't a person sense danger by tapping into something as little understood as a dream?[40]

In the mid-1880s, English-born Anna Kingsford, who studied "unconscious cerebration" with the top medical faculty in Paris, wrote an entire book about her dreams, drawn from ten years of painstaking diary-keeping. These included a good many nightmares, vividly told, with enchanted women, three-headed monsters, and desolate regions containing human-faced lions. While adhering to current medical vocabulary and making every effort to preserve "accurate judgment and complete self-possession and rectitude of mind," she, too, had the shipwreck vision in the form of "the doomed train."[41]

∽ᴪᴦ

I n earlier decades, the many thousands who collected books aimed for pure knowledge, utility, or moral improvement. Now there was little didacticism left, and the multiplying millions read to engage with inner life and inspect the larger world around them—a world connected by telegraph and telephone. As individuals opened up, they cultivated the humorous side of life, too, which was a great boon to the newspaper and magazine editors, who were first to see that exaggerating known uncertainties could make someone else's day more interesting. Readers of the popular press were discoverers who allowed themselves to fantasize and contemplated paranormal doings intently. Dreams made good copy.

The final two decades of the nineteenth century have been dubbed the "golden age" of memory studies, when the fast-developing discipline of psychology turned to the nature of memory and related pathologies. This was when déjà vu entered the popular vocabulary, when "I feel like I've been here before" underwent clinical study. Curiosity about dreams was fed by focused laboratory experiments into the association and retrieval of ideas—what William James called "laws of association." He speculated on how the past is received through inward images and why dreams appear as real as they do. He recognized a natural biochemistry that influenced feelings and actions without being consciously considered. In 1896, Henri Bergson published *Matter and Memory*, identifying spirit or soul as an entity rooted in the past but still engaged with the present. Memory is ineradicable, he said, even when removed from consciousness. Thus, a movement was under way in the study of the human will and the nature of introspection, even before Freud and his younger associate Carl Jung burst onto the scene.[42]

The most commonly reported species of dream remained the precognitive or prophetic. John Sobieski, a military man and religious reformer, emigrated from Poland as a teenager in the 1850s, settling in Council Bluffs, Iowa. In 1894, he was in Mark Twain's boyhood town of Hannibal, Missouri, to deliver an address. While there, he had a dreadful dream. "I am not at all superstitious," he reminisced a few years later, "yet there was something about the dream that so impressed me that I could not shake it off." He thought he was aboard a train, when a man of his acquaintance came over and said, "Where are you going?" Sobieski replied tearfully, "To the bedside of my dying boy." The next day, he went about his business and returned to his hotel to find a telegram waiting. It brought news that his son was dying and that he should return home right away. On the train, a short distance out of Hannibal, the conversation he had dreamt replayed word for word. John, Jr., died that day at midnight.[43]

Under the category of "true and amazing" comes this sensational headline: "MURDER SEEN IN A DREAM." It was a startling twist to a case of unchecked passion that had initially appeared to authorities as open and shut. In the mining town of Prosperity, Missouri, as the century was coming to a close, a "mysterious vision" led to the freeing of the woman wrongly accused and the arrest of the right man, who suddenly confessed everything.

Thirty-four-year-old John Thornton, night watchman at the Bulldog mine, was found with his throat cut from ear to ear on the morning of July 30, 1899. He was lying in a pool of his own blood, a bullet hole in his right temple and "an immense gaping wound." This was personal. His wife of eight years, known around town as the "insanely jealous" type, was picked up immediately. Once before, she had shot at her husband after an argument, though the bullet missed its mark on that occasion. This time, it appeared to all who knew the couple that she had been unable to contain her rage. No other theory of the crime was considered.

According to the *St. Louis Republic* reporter covering the story, it was some weeks later, while the unconvincing widow sat in Carthage jail awaiting trial, that she had a "strange visitation during her sleep," in which the dead husband appeared and revealed that her cousin, George Ray, had killed him. In the reporter's words: "When she awoke she could not control her emotions. She was sure that what her husband told her was true. Whether what she had seen was a spirit or only the dream of a disordered mind, she could not tell, but she was so fully convinced that George Ray was her husband's assassin that she could not rest until he was brought before her."

She told her jailer the dream. "Impressed by its vividness," he agreed to bring in Cousin George. A deputy paid a call, saying merely that Mrs. Thornton wished to see him. Outside her cell, he listened as she asked him flat out to tell what he knew about the murder. "For God's sake," she appealed. "I don't want to suffer for this crime." George could not turn away from her and broke down in tears. "I done it," he confessed and proceeded to give the details of his crime to the sheriff. John Thornton had repeatedly cursed and abused George, who was a consumptive, for lounging about the house and living off Thornton's wages. George's feet, swollen from rheumatism, caused him so much pain that he finally snapped. In coming clean, he gave the sheriff a complete timeline, returned the $75 he had stolen from his victim, dug up the razor he had used (and then buried in the Thorntons' stable), and pointed out the mine shaft where he had tossed the pistol.

The widow went free. One might say that she sensed the truth, but was unable to give voice to her suspicion until it was shaken out of her in an intense dream from her lonely jail cell. But that would have made her story sound altogether logical and less worthy of a headline.[44]

〜〄〜

Memory is mysterious, and all knowledge is conditional. Our dreams are sure reminders that we can never know how close we are to the truths we are seeking. We are attracted to a puzzle that falls somewhere short of impossible to solve. Why go into space? It's the lure of the majestic unknown. Why study dreams? Because they are the unknown us.

In the final decades of the nineteenth century, Americans were more attentively pursuing the limits of consciousness. Perhaps they did not know any better than their ancestors how the mind communicated, but they were beginning to establish the criteria by which emotions could be deciphered. Louisa May Alcott perceived her dream on the shore of Lake Geneva to be evidence of an enriched mind—she knew how to recognize when she was expressing the natural bias of her emotions in a dream. When, in 1879, a writer for Harper's opined, "As long as people dream, they will continue to talk about their dreams," he was treating dreams as autobiographical material that most individuals of his acquaintance were more than happy to divulge. This is what had changed.

EPILOGUE
WERE THEY LIKE US?

We long, amid a troubled world, for perfect being. We forget that what gives meaning to the notion of perfection is the events that create longing, and that apart from them a "perfect" world would mean just an unchanging brute existential thing.

—John Dewey, *Experience and Nature* (1925)

Dreams stand for longing; they always have. They serve to mediate our discontents. By illustrating emotions in the way that they do, they re-personify us independent of the will. They breathe desire into and out of us. And it would seem they do not stop until our desires are gone.

Dreams are dramatic dialogues taking place in the theater of the brain that accentuate the role of the creative imagination in the life of mind and body. Many use as fodder immediate past experience, generating, below the threshold of consciousness, summaries of emotional events. But something happens as dreams cross the threshold, leaving science to ponder this question: What is random and what is nonrandom in the movement of unconscious self-reflection into our conscious (language-generating) reality? Answers are very slowly emerging.[1]

In *Dreaming Souls,* neurobiologist Owen Flanagan raises his own prime question: What part of our identity do dreams constitute? Over the course of investigation, he resolves particulars while posing more and more hard-to-answer questions: Is the dream a place where socially unacceptable thoughts are free to play out? If we are designed to be in touch with our inner states, why are we endowed with a certain capacity to read emotions in faces, but ill equipped to read others' thoughts?

Allowing the professional study of dreams to reach across the barrier that usually separates science and the humanities, the neuroscientist states imposingly: "The self is fictional because it is a construction." For Dr. Flanagan, the narrative a person weaves about his or her self (or community and nation) is not just the sum of experience but also the stuff that upholds ideals. Consequently, in this book we have viewed dream lore as a marker of custom and tradition, and we consider its use an explicit component of the now familiar American Dream.[2]

--∿--

The theories of Freud did not emerge in a cultural vacuum. They were responsive to the states of mind chronicled in these pages. Physicians' consistent claims, from the Revolution to the Civil War, that dreams were either meaningless noise or the result of gastrointestinal distress were soundly rejected by literate mid-nineteenth-century Americans, who drew their contrary notions from poetry, dramatic fiction, and orally transmitted metaphysical speculation. They clamored for knowledge that science could not deliver.

It does not diminish our argument one bit to introduce the fact that the Viennese doctor was of foreign birth, because his dream work fed an existing hunger in America. Freud's ideas were initially met with cool regard back home and, among some of his peers, outright rejection. In America, however, after his 1909 visit to Clark University in Worcester, Massachusetts, and the appearance shortly thereafter of English translations of his German writings, Freud was greeted with tremendous enthusiasm. Something in his methodology tapped into an American fascination with the sleeping imagination that had incubated for decades.[3]

It was more than his methodology, though. Freud was investigating unconscious desire, and Americans were a people of yearning. It is curious, too, that, like the poet Coleridge and the opium eater De Quincey, Freud obtained creative insight from drug use. In his case, it was cocaine, with which he regularly self-medicated during the decade of the 1880s and as late as the mid-1890s. He felt that cocaine made him more open and able to release repressed feelings so that he could get in touch with parts of the mind that were otherwise inaccessible to him. Subsequently, he coined the term "psychoanalysis" and, treating patients for their neuroses, grew convinced that dream interpretation exposed wishes, urges, drives—whatever conditioned the living spirit. In *The*

Interpretation of Dreams, Freud was unequivocal: no dream is innocuous. From Dr. Rush to Dr. Freud, dreams always had something to say about disease or impairments to the mind.[4]

Critics have called Freud's psychoanalytical theories pseudoscience. They partake of the traditional dream-book formula and purport to decipher. Freud supervened upon the ancient dream-book phenomenon by introducing a new lexicon of symbols based on the supposed persistence of "infantile" pleasure-seeking. He went so far as to state in *On Dreams* (1901) that when it came to dream interpretation, popular dream books of the prior century, if rooted in superstition, were closer to the truth than medical orthodoxy was.[5]

What Freud was really doing in identifying neuroses was developing a critique of modern culture. That, too, helps explain why Americans were so receptive to his system. They were still looking for ways to liberate themselves by defining the unnamed essence inside them. The medical profession had not kept up with the advancing mind. Physicians of the early republic had exhibited too much complacency and an irritating refusal to acknowledge the limitations of their science; professionalism had since come to medicine, but its innovations arose less quickly than, say, communications technology. Transcendentalism, utopian experiments, the Society for Psychical Research, and ecstatic religion all reflected Americans' quest for sublime solutions to mundane problems, which the world of medicine was painfully slow in addressing. "Miracle drugs" were, as yet, nothing but those bogus items Dr. Pierce advertised in the newspapers.

Freud caught fire in a way the scientific psychology of William James and the "sixth sense" of Leonora Piper did not. A Chicago literary critic moved to New York in 1913 to edit a journal and discovered in Greenwich Village that Freudian vocabulary was on everyone's lips. Word-association games were as popular as recreational dream interpretation was. Meanwhile, James's students continued to keep philosophy and psychology close. One of these, Edwin B. Holt, published *The Freudian Wish and Its Place in Ethics,* in 1915, seeking to marry science and morality. The same idea furnished fodder for the long career of philosopher-educator-ethicist John Dewey. For a new generation of thinkers who felt the urge to unmask, inhibition and neurosis were excellent targets for their creative complaints. They aimed to improve the value of an American life by fashioning a unified American personality. How is nervous energy best employed? they asked. How can we educate our children to be emotionally healthy?[6]

At the risk of generalizing, Freud's success among Americans was that he appealed to the collective ego of a self-diagnosed rags-to-riches people whose individualism was no longer subordinate to the psychology of social responsibility that had prevailed formerly. American individualism suited a business-is-booming, rapidly urbanizing culture, and it found expression in two related, all-encompassing phrases: "American Dream" and "America's Century." As a marker of changing times, Freudian psychology was not just a fresh alternative to spiritualist mumbo jumbo; the Viennese doctor brought the phenomenon of the dream to a meaningful position in the life of the mind as the American ego was reaching for world cultural domination.

Since its first iteration in the Depression years, the American Dream has stood as a reminder that cultures throughout history have promoted social cohesion through faith in dreams and fantasies. National mythologies serve political ends no less than cultures invest their gods with world-transformative power. The Bible tells us that Joseph was made ruler over Egypt because of his proven ability as a dream interpreter. Individualized dreaming and socially binding dreaming both supply agency to a force that is essential to psychological well-being. Dr. Ernest Hartmann, a longtime student of this phenomenon, says that "big dreams," those that take us on heroic quests, put us in touch with the essence of culture. As memory connects us to the larger world, so our dreams keep pace with contemporary events. Dreaming would not matter only if history took place, and language and literature evolved emotionlessly.[7]

If we take the long view, Freudian psychology was instrumental in producing "the Self-Help Century" that sustained the fetish of the American Dream. What began with a theory of repressed desire and the decoded dream ended up jettisoning the nineteenth century's righteous, Protestant-directed, communitarian ideal of a regenerative, character-conscious society in favor of a more detached, openly self-indulgent, love-focused portrait of the storied psychic self. Even if we don't know the nineteenth century in a visceral way, we have a clear idea what makes our time different from it. Modernity began, in that sense, as post–Civil War literature stopped bathing in the relative innocence of its prewar picaresque and turned to realism, and the Gilded Age corporatized conflict. Social critics found corruptibility omnipresent in American society, requiring personal adjustment.[8]

Theirs was a time of determinism. The new literature, steeped in Social Darwinism, in effect courted Dr. Freud, who identified hidden neuroses that could be therapeutically treated. For his part, Freud was greatly influenced by literary metaphors in arriving at the unconscious language through which interpretation became possible for him. By appreciating the impulse connecting the health of the body to the health of the mind, and dreams to destiny, he offered hope of clarity. In other words, reason to dream.

~ω~

I t is a universal truth that we are all, sooner or later, meant to be forgotten. And so, dreams have always been a perfect symbol of inconstancy, transience, and impermanence. Ancient Greeks and Romans portrayed the dream variously: Homer's *Odyssey* contains innumerable dreams, some of no particular import, others that spell danger in the dreamer's waking reality—all of them defying easy interpretation. There was a "land" of dreams, where the gods appear in dim disguise and do not remain long. In Euripides, dreams emerge from the womb of a darkened earth, formidable and forbidding—"truth's shadows upfloating." As time passed, ancient reports grew richer. By the fourth century A.D., judging dream experiences as "vain imaginings" or delusions, the Roman Christian historian Jerome simultaneously recorded erotic dreams that challenged his ascetic intent. The point is that sleep visions summon up an emotional heritage less foreign to our sensibilities than if we were to study these same peoples sociologically.[9]

For centuries, philosophers have looked for words to join sense impressions to well-developed ideas. Theories of the imagination abound. One of William James's philosopher-metaphysician friends, the Nobel laureate Henri Bergson, wrote: "There is nothing mysterious about the birth of a dream. It resembles the birth of a perception." Both dream and perception describe something undeveloped and uncertain; both test the memory that keeps us intact and continuously self-shaping. As core elements of the functioning mind, dream, perception, and memory tell why the phrase "stream of consciousness" makes more than metaphorical sense. Consciousness proves the existence of individual identity, but does not actually delimit identity. The spontaneity in dreams says, "There is more to us."[10]

That "more" conjures up another category: our place in the universe. As dreams have been associated with conversations about death and "conversations" with the deceased, so have they been tied to religious systems. Why this is does not seem very complicated. Four decades ago, the cultural anthropologist Ernest Becker termed human beings anxious animals conscious of their animal limitations, with no choice but to negotiate natural feelings of inferiority. We constantly rewrite reality, he said, because we cannot bear otherwise. This is one way to explain the religious impulse. Others might say, as Julian Barnes has, that "religions were the first great inventions of the fiction writers." Dreams probably predate religion; both are useful fictions.

Becker's book *The Denial of Death* was completed when its author was still a young man, yet already in the throes of the disease that was shortly to take him. "To have emerged from nothing," he wrote emphatically, "to have a name, consciousness of self, deep inner feelings, an excruciating inner yearning for life and self-expression—and with all this yet to die."

Death of the body, the removal of a physical dimension, is an end to pain. But death of memory, of imagination, is the real tragedy. It is what makes our truths matter and our dreams more than haphazard neuron firings.[11]

~∿∂~

Regardless of what one believes about the existence or nonexistence of a godly intelligence, Becker's uncomfortable explanation well suits the ineffective eighteenth-century physician Benjamin Rush, who, perhaps willfully, perhaps unself-consciously, prescribed for himself dreams of self-preservation. This book, beyond its effort to capture the humanity of the past in new ways, has had the announced purpose of exploring the gradual modernization of a sense of self. We have shown that dreams were important in reflecting awareness of individual complexity, a modern quality little evoked in the texts of colonial times.

This is what separates the nineteenth century from its predecessor. After a while, a more introspective American ceased regarding human drives as surface phenomena, in the way Dr. Samuel L. Mitchill did when he relegated dreams to self-limiting typologies, or in the way the "sciences" of physiognomy and phrenology pressed human genius and emotions into immobile categories. Impressionist painting becomes a metaphor for the changing value of the dream as interiority was being redefined. A Renoir or a Monet of the 1860s–1880s is lively and evocative without conforming to literal likenesses—short, tentative brushstrokes present color and light in inventive ways. Dreams convert our personal histories into impressionistic paintings, reshaping memory in short virtual brushstrokes.

We say that the active sleeping mind confronts ordeals in a search for consonance, for psychological balance. Americans before Freud were reaching for this explanation, too, but without explicitly saying so. Because the language available to them was not ours, it has always been too easy to portray our ancestors as tight-lipped, stoical, and repressed. It is wrong to jump to such conclusions. Literary icons, a smattering of Civil War–era citizens (North and South), travelers, emigrants, and disconnected family members have all proven otherwise. We must listen to them. No single language can tell us what the past means or what dreams mean.

As a means of deepening the conversation about what constitutes "Americanness," we look to dreams because they constitute a relatively uncensored expression of selfhood. Were earlier Americans like us? Yes, it seems they were, insofar as they anchored their hopes to a quest for love and belonging. And no, they were not, in that the vocabulary to express love and belonging was (at least initially) self-limiting. No less significant, the disease environment they knew led them to confront the dying process with a resignation today's professionals try to sidestep with drugs—we have ways of masking the physical.

Theirs was a less populous, slow-moving world that looked and sounded different. And qualitatively? With surprising frequency, early Americans' dream accounts mention the direction of the wind or the placement of a field where an imaginary fire blazed out of control. Distances they traveled were felt in their bones. They had an intense knowledge of place. If their dreams exhibited a range of emotions similar to what we know today—anger, fear, wonder, and adoration—their emotional choices germinated in creative spaces with different contours. People who live close to nature dream more literally of survival.

Life span is only the most obvious factor separating them from us. Death of a loved one is disabling for any person, of course; in the vocabulary of early Americans, the event was accompanied by "enfeeblement"—that which had a feminizing effect on men. Dr. Comstock's 1841 physiology text reaffirmed the age-old assumption that "morbid sensitivity" led to dangerous melancholia. In this and many respects, emotional balance was understood to be easily sacrificed to natural passions. People had to remain on their guard.

The force of mass culture was less palpable, or at least less national, in the first decades of the republic. Crucially, though, the historic actors we have examined were artful, competitive, and confrontational in dreams, in ways that are largely indistinguishable from modern dream reports. We see something familiar in the uneven way they reacted: in some cases the same individual could be convinced that one of his or her dreams was garbled and unimportant, and that a second dream held a truth about the trajectory of a life that needed to be examined closely. Ralph Waldo Emerson comes to mind, as does Eliza Champlain and her aunt Mary Way. They made fun of dreams that made fun of them. They knew absurdity when they saw it. Through it all, they expressed the values of honesty and loyalty as they pursued an almost sacred quest for knowledge and understanding.

Perception and judgment cannot be divorced from feelings. The self-protective quality that attaches to inner life obliged our ancestors to counteract the challenges of night. We saw how Caroline Hentz took up her pen in 1836 because "visions of the past dim & awful floated around me, as I sat by the fading embers, in the loneliness of the midnight hour." Night blurred, confounded, fractured, and perverted memories; dream descriptions reflected this state of affairs. A combination of factors, one of which may have been their bid for control amid uncertainty, led nineteenth-century Americans to fashion a more dramatic language so that they would feel less alone.

The emerging middle class, this book-buying, poetry-reading community to which our dreamers belonged, was a typographical culture. Readers related to words on the page—it was how they built character and felt useful to themselves, their families, and society. Whatever got in the way of practical self-improvement led one to turn to a book or newspaper for re-engagement. But theirs was a soul-stirring, intensely oral culture, too. This new American doctrine of the unfettered word was aimed at expanding knowledge, deepening self-knowledge, eliminating superstition, and, yes, enlivening political democracy.[12]

One early newspaper article in particular led me to start thinking that they were more "like us" than "not like us." It appeared on the front page of the *New-York Mirror* in 1836, under the general subject "Original Essays" and with the simplest of headlines: "Dreams." The piece is couched in the ornate vocabulary of Romanticism, but the level of intelligence (and underlying puzzlement) resembles much later commentaries.

The article opens with a caveat: every dreamer is "incapacitated" as the dream is playing inside his or her head, so any reconstruction upon awakening must contain imperfect data. "What more hopeless task," the author bemoans, "than to revive the fleeting phenomena of a single dream! Almost as well might we hope to transfer to the canvass the colour of the chameleon, or the fanciful freaks of the Aurora Borealis." No matter how brilliant a dream is as it is occurring, its "rapid succession of images" gives the whole no time to "fix" in the mind. To this point, the article is strictly Emersonian.

But it was the writer's next observation that impressed me more, because the metaphor has not been superseded by any modern dream specialist. A dream is a cloud, "tossed into various shapes, swept through the azure expanse by the vagrant blast; we have a distinct perception of the form at every change; but the changes are so rapid we soon lose the order of succession." His cloud, moved by wind, cannot be bound to corporeal life nor attributed to meaningless sensation. The dream remains elusive because it does not abide by rules; it is "broken and confused" by dint of its refusal to sit still. It is not explicitly one thing or another. The writer sees the dream not as worthless noise, but as a part of identity that evades capture.

In an odd way, this description resembles that of the literary scholar and modern dream therapist Rodger Kamenetz, who takes the metaphor from the clouds to an underground storage site: "Dreams open a cellar door to depth." The experience is a "descent" through inner, not outer, "imaginal" space, though no less generative (Kamenetz's word) of a soulful power than the earlier cloud/heaven fixation. Both perspectives feed on the wandering and wondering element in the pursuit of some more tangible clue to individual identity.[13]

D reams conform to cultural expectations. They have often been granted supernatural attributes. Going all the way back to the Revolutionary generation, we find a celebrated needleworker, born Elizabeth Griscom and known to history by her married name, Betsy Ross, telling her grandchildren in the 1820s of a prophetic dream of her youth, in which she saw the letters G, R, A, and C against the sky. Twice widowed, she was remarried first to an Ashburn, then a Claypoole, having thereby "predicted" the initials of her various surnames in life.[14]

Of course, not every early American dream had to be stuffed with mystical content. Dolley Madison worried about her absent husband, knowing he was riding on bad country roads, and in her next letter told him her dream: "I saw you in your chamber, unable to move, from riding so far and so fast." A young prisoner of war, unfed for fourteen hours at a time, dreamt of "setting down to a table of the most delicious food." Another man scratched in pencil on a page of his 1785 almanac: "dream'd I pull'd out one of my teeth quite sound at ye root." To paraphrase Freud on the subject of his phallic cigar, sometimes a man with dental concerns dreams of having a bothersome tooth painlessly taken out.[15]

Quite often, as we have seen, a pious individual interprets dream imagery in religious terms, helping sustain belief in a particular vision of an afterlife. Yet in spite of his Christian beliefs, Dr. Rush did not recast what he dreamt to imbue it with a message any greater than a mundane sense of his professional responsibility. He presents us with a string of dreams whose raw images and dialogue reveal different elements of culture than if he had more conventionally ascended to heaven for a glimpse of what life and death meant.

"I see dead people" dreams never diminished, though the variety of elements in them expanded, and visits to a heavenly netherworld gave way to nonreligious mind pictures. Even more critically, the Romantics in England and America, beginning around 1815–1820, rejected the fixedness of inward nature. Lord Byron, who captivated that generation born in the period 1790–1810, left stiff sentimentalism behind and created an appetite for rapturous language. Mary Shelley, a fixture within Byron's circle, composed *Frankenstein* in 1819, a science fantasy involving the reanimation of dead tissue, symbolizing a newfound willingness to imagine the mind's plasticity. Next, the pairing of brilliant dream narratives and nightmarish visions in Thomas De Quincey's *Confessions of an English Opium-Eater* helped feed dreamers' curiosity—one might argue that De Quincey stirred a movement in America, prompting those who recorded their dreams to add more complex, more self-revealing dramas. Love letters of the era, filled with undisguised passion, illustrate a self-aware generation with emboldened spirits.

To put it in other terms, when Thomas Jefferson wrote of dreams as "nightly incoherencies," he did not consider them worth preserving and gave them no credence. By the 1840s, dream narratives had become indiscriminate texts without a self-policing component, truer sources of emotional history. The balance between self-repression and self-exposure had tilted in the direction of the latter. More individuals were choosing to interpret themselves, and more diarists and letter writers opened their hearts when they sat down, often in a candlelit mood, to write.

Ichabod Cook, the dream collector of the 1840s, was a kind of herald, sensitive to detail and eager to engage absurd dreamscapes. Clay Dillard's diary, a decade later, announced that private writings comprised "a kind of curiosity shop, where all phases of the heart are seen." Will Scott, at once her teacher and suitor, gave her an assignment to write on: "There is society, where none intrudes." It was a passage from Byron's *Childe Harold*, which masterpiece of verse their generation regularly quoted for inspiration: the society of the self was born. When she wrote to herself, "I'm dreaming. O! I'm dreaming," Clay was taking advantage of an outlet that the Romantics' engagement with language and emotion provided. Believing that "no one will ever read these pages but my self," she let her feelings flow freely.[16]

Of the literal dreams (101 male and 104 female) that are specifically mentioned in this book, the most interesting seem to find expression in written records of the decade of the 1850s—the turning point, if one has to be chosen, when formulaic dreams largely disappear. On the other hand, it is meaningful that the ratio between anxious and hopeful dreams (4.5 to 1 for men, 2.7 to 1 for women) does not vary greatly from one decade to the next over the course of one hundred-plus years. The same is true with regard to the presence of dialogue: 30 percent of men's and 24 percent of women's dreams included spoken words, and the percentages do not vary much over time.[17]

In the early decades of the republic, significant numbers of dreamers (most notably those who had encounters with deceased loved ones) could not be sure whether their visions came from heaven or some other place outside the self. In the democratized middle decades of the nineteenth century, the liberating effect of dreams was more manifest. Among scientists and philosophers, as well as journalists and average citizens, the study and appreciation of natural phenomena had moved inexorably from external reality to internal feeling.

With medicine still in a fairly primitive state, more people sought sublime solutions to terrestrial problems. They recognized what we today call "the unconscious mind," but they didn't have a name for it. It existed between the real and the divine—the "dream world" was of them, but not completely of them. Neither religion nor science was able to suggest meaningful ways to tame it. So they began to develop their own, albeit tentative, vocabulary to explain an intriguing inner world.

Curiosity about a "sixth sense" grew alongside the popularity of new communities of faith such as the Shakers and the Mormons and the fads of mesmerism and spiritualism. Arriving at the moment of disunion, of civil war, Americans were not only primed to discover the power of individual identity; they were re-engaging with the dream as a phenomenon they wished to understand better in order to communicate along some mystical spiritual channel and imaginatively reach the inner world of another. Two prominent examples of this mind-set were two of America's most exalted nineteenth-century names: Abraham Lincoln and Mark Twain. Both felt bound to their dream lives. Public figures exhibited ordinary emotions; they shared mundane concerns with common citizens.

To restate a premise put forth in the preface, you cannot understand the twentieth century's fascination with psychology unless you first understand earlier generations' fascination with dreams. Asleep, men, women, and children found both dire warnings and ecstatic communion with loved ones. A significant number of people found it impossible to ignore their dreams, because they were nothing short of provocations. Are we ourselves in dreams, they wondered; or are we encountering an invention, a "not us" with the power to seize control of the mind of a sleeping soul? The question was never effectively answered, and the discipline of psychology rose to attack the problem from a new perspective.

~√∂~

I did not expect to find in the dreams of early Americans an acute sensitivity to sounds. From Dr. Rush's graveyard dream through Louisa May Alcott's laughing and crying re-encounter with a younger version of her father, American dreamers heard powerfully. They clung to life's substance in auditory form, presumably encouraged by sound's defiance of death's total absence of sensation.

Today we know to be true what some sleep and dream theorists long ago reckoned, that the silence in sleep helps the brain recharge and restore functions. But we do not shut our ears in quite the same way as we shut our eyes. In sleep, when the guard is down, sound can either soothe or cause chaos and confusion. This makes perfect sense, inasmuch as the dream itself is a register of emotional life. When our brain exits the neurological slowdown of sleep, where alertness is biochemically inhibited, we re-enter the waking state to find that our brains now have a greater ability to shut out or dismiss objectionable noise. As every individual knows, music can literally guide one's moods.[18]

When it comes to reminiscence, we all have our personalized cues. Just think of how many unforgettable songs take the dream as an indicator of emotional well-being or loss. From Stephen Foster's wistful pair, "I Dream of Jeanie with the Light Brown Hair" (1854) and "Beautiful Dreamer" (1864), to such standards as "I'll See You in My Dreams" (1924), "Dream a Little Dream of Me" (1931), and "Boulevard of Broken Dreams" (1933), to the Chordettes' "Mr. Sandman, Bring Me a Dream" (1954), the Everly Brothers' "All I Have to Do Is Dream" (1958), and Aerosmith's "Dream On" (1973), dreamy numbers get recorded over and over, from one generation to the next. No matter how practical our engagement is with the present, personal markers of inspiration, such as the songs that stay with us, prove that we are in some ways bound backward by the romantic imagination—where we find sound.

The idea of thought being somehow musical goes back to the ancients. From Aristotle's *De Anima* to Cicero's likening the human body to an instrument plucked by the soul to music therapy practiced in the Middle Ages, music symbolized the harmony of body and soul. The tongue, a vocal instrument engaged by breath, enlarged the emotions.[19]

Aided by this acoustic inheritance, dreams retained rich meanings over the centuries because the spoken word could reveal as well as deceive. The Declaration of Independence indicted the British for being "deaf to the voice of justice and of consanguinity," to the power of speech. The psychic identity of a liberty-loving people could have been realized only in a cultural environment we might dub "the age of sensations." Spasms and convulsions, turmoil and torment, hypochondria and hysterical distempers, passion and fortitude—these were terms of the medical Enlightenment that infected literature and politics alike.[20]

We learn a great deal where personal narratives meet medical doctrine. From the Revolution forward, physicians routinely told their patients that their dreams were caused by indigestion, and for nearly a century, most people were loath to question this finding, at least publicly. The medical community's dismissal of dreams was a textbook approach, a fallback position—a stagnant solution to a dynamic problem.

As compilations of ancient wisdom were being published less, past dream authority declined and individual dreamers were empowered. It is not possible to pinpoint how or when this occurred, but beginning, at least in our examination, with the ruminative Emerson, and perhaps even earlier with the opium eater, dreamers gave themselves permission to experiment in resolving life's difficulties by exploring their fantasies. They accepted that novel scenarios could be freeing. Changing outlook was matched by changing inlook.

In the heyday of Mark Twain, personal rejection dreams, "I see dead people" dreams, and their ilk were not only not suppressed, they were noticeably more complicated. Sam Clemens was left "prostrate on the floor" in the vivid dream he had in which his betrothed fell back into the arms of her "old rejected lover," who had taken advantage of Sam's absence to ambush and win her back. Newspapers acknowledged subjects they had ignored before, such as the commonly experienced dream of public nakedness. We have no problem today seeing that the hyper-reality of a dream allows a person to create a powerful emotional experience that was never produced in the rationally negotiated environment of the waking state; it was only in the middle decades of the nineteenth century that people began to accept this variant of the self as a dreamdriven feeling that was normal.

Thus, we encounter candid admissions of the existence of interior dissonance or friction. In his memoir, Julian Hawthorne wrote of his nagging uncertainty that what springs from a mind can ever be original and not tainted by engagement with the narratives others tell us: "If a man's memory is not a virgin page for his own perceptions, but is written and crossed over with the thoughts of former persons, he is in constant doubt as to whether it is 'original,' or merely giving fresh wording to old stuff; whereas, if he writes from the heart, he is free from anxiety, for one's man heart can never see or feel like any other's."

If we apply his plaint to dream life, the question becomes: What memory is the vision being drawn from, and is it authentic? Is it possible that dream vignettes are snapshots of the essence of personality? Or perhaps they are something in between—corrupted essences, as it were. We may never know a "virgin page" or an uncorrupted memory.

Whereas the nineteenth century sought emotional truth, today we tend to privilege emotional health. For our forebears, satisfaction came from a knowledge of nature; for us, satisfaction is a long and active life. Their dreams engaged with a magical realm called "spirit"; ours, like the sleep aids we are routinely prescribed, are meant to function as adjuncts to a holistic sense of mental and physical stability.[21]

～⁊～

"There is very little about the emotions that is not metaphorically conceived," writes the Hungarian linguist Zoltán Kövecses. American counterparts George Lakoff and Mark Johnson clarify: "Metaphor is one of our most important tools for trying to comprehend partially what cannot be comprehended totally." We employ "imaginative rationality" everywhere. The relationship we have to our dreaming selves imitates the manner in which we engage with other people.[22]

The urge to reach out, to reach into the beyond, is extremely powerful, and it cannot be done without metaphor. In 1893, the Presbyterian clergyman Thomas DeWitt Talmage made headlines around the country from his base in Brooklyn, New York, when he declared dreams to be proof of the immortality of the soul: "If my soul can fly so far in the few hours in which my body is asleep in the night, how far can it fly when my body sleeps the long sleep of the grave? Oh, this power to dream, how startling, how overwhelming!"

A contemporary of Talmage's, psychologist James Sully, sought to wrest the question away from fanciful religion when he wrote in his book *Illusions*: "If, as we know, dreaming is a continual process of transformation of our waking impressions in new combinations, it is not surprising that our dreams should sometimes take the form of forecasts of our waking life, and that consequently objects and scenes of this life never before seen should now and again wear a familiar look." These two perspectives, Talmage's dream as flight and Sully's dream as metaphorical clothing, epitomize the two principal trajectories in existential thought at the end of the nineteenth century.[23]

The occasion of dreaming is everyone's ever-building epic, an episodic quest to establish to our sensory satisfaction our proper emotional place in life. Finding that metaphorical "place" is a reward, a remuneration. The twentieth-century philosopher Paul Ricoeur explained the reflexive geography of memory in history, identifying humans as adventure-bound animals whose nostalgic impulse points the way home. Everyone is always looking to put things in their proper "place." The emptiness or uneasiness that we encounter in emotional life is the haunting feeling that we are somehow adrift. Ricoeur says we should not overlook the role of habitation at the bottom of our anxious thoughts, just as we are unlikely ever to ignore the centrality of time in our conception of mortality. The mind, our principal residence, rests on shaky foundations.[24]

~∿∂~

The annual conference of the International Association for the Study of Dreams (IASD) was held on the grounds of a twelfth-century monastery in Kerkrade, the Netherlands, for five days in June 2011. Cultural history was barely represented, and few sessions tapped the dream content of the eighteenth or nineteenth centuries. The field has moved in a different direction. Some specialists see dreams as a "lost language" to be relearned in the process of spiritual healing. Others ponder whether postapocalyptic dreams have something to teach us. Still others question the importance of the data entering consciousness, given that consciousness is one limited function among many brain functions.

Among the IASD panels were these: an Italian team studying oneiric activity among anorexics; a Canadian researcher reporting on four decades of examining the "heads-up" dream, which consists of dreaming of someone not encountered for ages who suddenly reappears in one's life within days of the dream. An American presenter relived her sober pursuit to understand reincarnation, based on a childhood dream that convinced her she had belonged to the World War II French Resistance in her last life.

A universal curiosity about dreams makes their study naturally interdisciplinary. As such, the 2011 conference featured cognitive scientists, linguists, therapists, specialists in posttraumatic stress disorder, students of metaphysics, and more. The emotional force of culture and the cultural impact of emotion continue to intrigue. But what comes next? How will history inform the study of dreams in coming years?

Science says that vivid and forgotten dreams alike aid memory consolidation. Regulating emotion, they teach us to anticipate physical and perhaps also psychological threats. They help us sort through emotional expression so we can move on to the next day—that would be their evolutionary function. Even dreams of helplessness and compromised control, or outright nightmares (which, statistically, continue to far outnumber joyful dreams), serve to improve our waking moods and prospects. In fact, bland, emotionless dreams result in the person waking up less positive and less motivated.[25]

Instead of living indiscriminately, moment to moment, it appears that, owing to our dreams, we are able to reduce chaos in the surrounding environment and maximize our creative potential. Science is telling us to marvel at the complexity of consciousness, subjectivity, and sensation. At the same time, it wants to treat the existence of dream life, or autobiographical memory, as a neurological mechanism within the brain. In such experimental times as ours, that does not mean dream life is beyond manipulation from without. Dream specialists now teach "lucid dreaming," through which the dreamer can rearrange the sleep narrative to make it friendlier and more satisfying.

It is hard not to feel confused. For the humanist, whether or not dreams have, in the strictest sense, an evolutionary purpose, they reflect a distinctly human evolutionary desire to chart time via stories. As a nonscientist, I am easily persuaded by yet another dictum of modern science: memory is not just a reactive biological function or a cellular storehouse of sensory impressions and perceptions. It is originative. It creates. It fertilizes. It becomes us and all the changes in us. It stabilizes the present, gives firmer meaning to emotion, and enlarges the scope of criticism.

This puts us back again on the trail of the historical, where it is memory itself that instructs us, rightly or wrongly, that a given memory is real and verifiable. From the writings of earlier generations of Americans, we have learned that the relationship between dreams and the soul changed meaningfully over the course of one century—the nineteenth century. It moved from a transcendent other to a connected sentience, from something above and beyond to something within and without.[26]

Second, in the process of recomposing history out of dreams, we learn that individualism arose in a more interesting way than what we have been taught in accepting textbook definitions of equality in the early republic. That formula is typically linked to Alexis de Tocqueville's *Democracy in America* (1835). A cultural history of dreams makes it possible to challenge common shortcuts historians make—we reframe the study of individuality by removing it from traditional politics. Dreamers did not need a generous government in order to be persuaded of their individuality.

~∂~

S cience is fairly certain that memory is permeable and suggestible. This brings the study of history one small step closer to metaphysics. For, if thoughts travel beyond the physical body in a way comparable to, say, the movement of radio waves, then communication beyond the self might have an empirical basis. If something of this kind were ever to be detected by cognitive scientists, traditional conceptions of soul, dream, and thought-essence would look different.

Most dreams vanish quickly. But that does not have to mean they exist for a split second only. The unconscious picks up and stores signals from the environment as we have experienced it. When our minds are at rest and recycling the ill-defined materials of the universe, we may well be toying with more than internal concoctions, experiencing ourselves as more than the sum of active personal experience. It would be wonderful (in the earlier American connotation of "astonishing") if we ever learned that it is part of our nature to mingle with memories near and far, unable to slough off the particles of the world.

To call what has not yet been discovered "magical thinking" demeans those of our present who enjoy testing the powers of the mind. I am not quite prepared to dismiss all such yearning. Nor am I alone. Fewer and fewer scientists subscribe these days to the materialist point of view, which holds that matter is all there is, and that human knowledge, thought, feeling—even selfhood—are functions of neural impulses and, therefore, without metaphysical properties. The near-death experience is but one phenomenon suggesting the mutability or movement of thought and perception.

The mind is a source of emotional intelligence. We must pay attention to the connections it makes. To take one prominent example, there are twins who feel the sibling's traumas at a distance. Nor can every psychic be immediately dismissed, because select individuals have assisted law enforcement in solving cold cases. We commonly acknowledge the sixth sense as unconscious access.

Dreams are among the properties of human nature that people, past and present, have studied as they looked for an alternative to death-as-nothingness, unwilling to accept the fire of life being once and for all extinguished. That said, it is no less apparent in history that the concept of an immortal soul, the interpretive dream, and reincarnation were all originally generated by a world cultural impulse predicated on primitive, irrational fear. While so bleak an acknowledgment may be a true reading of the human condition, it does not render impossible the survivability of thought and emotion outside a single, physically constituted mind.

Complicating the issue, philosophers and neuroscientists largely agree that most thought is unconscious. In the political world, individuals identify with interest groups when they are so predisposed by brain chemistry, although they believe they arrive at their justifications through entirely independent reasoning. Writing recently that thought is tied to the physical material of the brain, neuroscientist David Eagleman states epigrammatically: "The first thing we learn from studying our own circuitry is a simple lesson: most of what we do and think and feel is not under our conscious control. . . . The conscious you— the I that flickers to life when you wake up in the morning—is the smallest bit of what's transpiring in your brain."[27]

The internal world probably contains as many undiscovered parts as the external. We see (or don't see) how humans have altered the atmosphere. Leaving aside contentious issues that register politically, such as the wasteful use of fossil fuels that pollute, no one denies that we have remade the nightscape. Stars visible to the naked eye are less numerous because human-engineered light shines up at the sky. We have invaded the night as it was known to nocturnal wildlife for millennia.

Has the interior dark changed, too? Our high-decibel, high-voltage, high-wattage world has quite possibly begun to alter our biochemistry. One can only speculate as to how today's humans have drifted from the sleep worlds of our ancestors. We are at a loss to say which psychically charged wonders of the past have been preserved and which have been displaced by modern invention. When we enter a dream-filled sleep, are our personalities more stable or less so than in earlier times? It's a great question. Losing touch with former contours of night, we can mourn, as the critic of light pollution does: "I am no longer so much afraid of the dark as I am afraid for the dark."²⁸

I have come to believe that at night the past feels closer. When our eyes are closed to physical structures, when sounds lessen, we become part of a "waiting time," and our minds exhibit a certain suppleness. Then, as mind and body prepare for the recalibration that takes place in natural sleep, our emotions begin to stir. We open to suggestion. Perhaps we release grief when we dream or court enchantment (as the ancients did), monitoring needs, feeding ourselves soul food, testing the capacity to savor life. Whatever it is that brains generate in the dark hours, those pulsations issue some kind of autobiographical message worth knowing about.

In its nightly rewiring activity, influenced by very recent events and perceptions we experienced in waking life, the brain shapes a fictive reality that does much to qualify individuality and move each of us along in our complex, active lives. That fictive reality is nothing if not the art of living. Asleep or awake, we engage the inward politics of memory. We are our emotions, our desires, our attitudes of mind. We are not at all sure of the difference between sense experience and fantasy.

It has become something of a refrain in these pages to say that we do not know precisely what dreams are and are not. If they embody anything, it is provisionality—an impermanence that defies embodiment at all. Dreams deform. Their most positive impact is to convey inclinations; they deny that there are certainties. They are at once imprecise and transformational, our fantasy rendezvous with measureless time and our practice encounter with unknown death.

I close the book as I opened it, with the polite suggestion that, like the dead, dreams linger inside us by the strength of imagination. In eulogistic tribute, it is customary to say of the deceased that he or she will "remain inside us forever." At least we know of dreams what Lord Byron told us two centuries ago: they leave a weight upon our waking thoughts.

ABBREVIATIONS

AAS	American Antiquarian Society
APS	American Philosophical Society
HSP	Historical Society of Pennsylvania
LCP	Library Company of Philadelphia
LSU	Hill Memorial Library, Louisiana State University
NYPL	New York Public Library
SHC	Southern Historical Collection, University of North Carolina–Chapel Hill
UVA	Special Collections, University of Virginia Library

NOTES

PREFACE

1. See Oxford English Dictionary for definitions and tracking of nineteenth-century usages of "subconscious" and "subconsciousness." The very first cited use was in the notebooks of Samuel Taylor Coleridge in 1806. "Subconscious" was not routinely used by students of psychology, however, until the 1880s and 1890s.

2. Two excellent books by historians have used dreams as a vehicle for understanding particular groups in society. Carla Gerona's study, *Night Journeys: The Power of Dreams in Transatlantic Quaker Culture* (Charlottesville, VA: University of Virginia Press, 2004), has had a significant impact on my thinking. So has Mechal Sobel's fascinating *Teach Me Dreams: The Search for Self in the Revolutionary Era* (Princeton, NJ: Princeton University Press, 2000), a cultural study of race. See also Susan Sleeper-Smith, "The Dream as a Tool for Historical Research: Reexamining Life in Eighteenth-Century Virginia through the Dreams of a Gentleman: William Byrd II, 1664–1744," *Dreaming* 3 (Mar. 1993): 49–68.

3. We face clear challenges in undertaking a cultural history of dreams. While eighteenth- and nineteenth-century Americans dreamt readily, those records of daily activities that add context to their sleep narratives are not always very detailed. The researcher must be wary about over-reaching. In framing some of the larger conceptual questions I am considering here, I have been helped by the work of philosopher Paul Ricoeur (1913–2005), who wrote extensively on the interrelationship of creative thought, personal identity, history, and memory. The fragility of memory must be considered in the context of historical community—our perception of reality being connected to, and legitimated by, the past. This would include trauma as well as positive forms of commemoration, i.e., acknowledgment of the enduring value of the dead. Human beings are haunted by history, knowingly and unknowingly, and tend to a nostalgia meant to help them restore things to their imagined proper place. What the reconstructive mind does in the dream state appears to replicate such battles with time and its power over corporeal man and woman. See Ricoeur, *Memory, History, Forgetting* (Chicago, IL: University of Chicago Press, 2004).

4. Ralph Waldo Emerson, *Lectures and Biographical Sketches* (Boston: Houghton Mifflin, 1904), 7.

5. Along the theoretical spectrum that extends from sequential snapshots to the full-blown, well-plotted dream narrative, a literal dream is most "raw" (as opposed to constructed) when its creative components are exposed. Even "raw" dreams are imperfect as evidence. All the dreams discussed in this book were written down, a fact that points to an unavoidable weakness in the historian's plan to provide complete clarity. Even dreams that feature dialogue are primal, visual expressions of emotions, corrupted when they appear as reasoned verbal productions. It is by no means certain that their revelations come as "worded" or "wordable" messages. Putting them into words must have the effect of masking, if not repressing, the uncontaminated essence of the dream. Note, too, that an unknown (high) percentage of dreams remains unremembered.

6. Calvin Kai-ching Yu, "Recurrence of Typical Dreams and the Instinctual and Delusional Predispositions of Dreams," *Dreaming* 20 (Dec. 2010): 254–79. Utz Jeggle, a German scholar of culture and memory, observes: "Dreams are an excursion into psychosis, while in madness one remains its prisoner even if one appears to escape it. In madness one suffers a waking dream that appears real." See Jeggle, "A Lost Track: On the Unconscious in Folklore," *Journal of Folklore Research* 40 (Jan.–Apr. 2003): 80.

7. Researchers estimate that the average individual spends an hour or more each day daydreaming—dreaming while awake. I cannot see any appreciable difference between "daydreaming" and "musing," other than that the former suggests more of "letting go." A hallucination is a delusive event; a vision quite similar to that, but tending to the mystical, or possessing religious overtones. This book looks most closely at the full-blown dream or nightmare that takes place during the hours of sleep.

8. Jefferson to Congressman Alexander Smyth, Jan. 17, 1825, Thomas Jefferson Papers, Library of Congress.

9. Andrea Rock, *The Mind at Night: The New Science of How and Why We Dream* (New York: Basic Books, 2004), 101, 181.

10. Patrick H. Hutton, *History as an Art of Memory* (Hanover, NH: University Press of New England, 1993). "Living memory is ultimately the ground of the historians' interest in the past," writes Hutton, "just as it was once the foundation of the identity of the historical actors that they now seek to understand" (quote at 72).

11. Probing studies are available that explain the diffusion of information, describe the ways of the postal system, and speak to the evolution of advanced networks such as canals and steamboats and railroads, and then the telegraph and telephone. See, notably, Richard D. Brown, *Knowledge Is Power: The Diffusion of Information in Early America, 1700–1865* (New York: Oxford University Press, 1989); John L. Larson, *Internal Improvement* (Chapel Hill, NC: University of North Carolina Press, 2000); Richard R. John, *Spreading the News: The American Postal System from Franklin to Morse* (Cambridge, MA: Harvard University Press, 1998); and idem, *Network Nation: Inventing American Telecommunications* (Cambridge, MA: Harvard University Press, 2010).

12. Rock, *The Mind at Night,* 134, based on an interview with LaBerge.

CHAPTER 1: GEORGE WASHINGTON
APPEARS BEFORE BRYAN FAIRFAX

1. A. Roger Ekirch, *At Day's Close: Night in Times Past* (New York: W. W. Norton & Company, 2005), 267–72; Marla R. Miller, *Betsy Ross and the Making of America* (New York: Henry Holt & Company, 2010), 64–67. Elisabeth Bronfen writes that "the setting of the sun has always been connected with the advent of a different way of thinking and behaving. . . . Our sense of distance and measure changes, the contours of the persons or objects we meet become blurred, we encounter a sense of disorientation, which can be either fascinating or threatening." See Bronfen, "Night and the Uncanny," in Jo Collins and John Jervis, eds., *Uncanny Modernity: Cultural Theories, Modern Anxieties* (Hampshire, UK: Palgrave Macmillan, 2008), 51–67, quote at 51; also Raymond J. Weisman, "Night in America: Staying Awake, Sleeping and Dreaming from Colonial to Modern Times," Ph.D. dissertation, Columbia University, 2008.

2. *Pennsylvania Gazette,* June 15, 1738.

3. "The Diary of Rev. Silas Bigelow," *Proceedings of the Worcester Society of Antiquity* 17 (Feb. 1900): 258–68.

4. *Autobiography of Benjamin Rush,* ed. George W. Corner (Westport, CT: Greenwood Press, 1970), 85–86; Carl A. L. Binger, "The Dreams of Benjamin Rush," *American Journal of Psychiatry* 125 (1969): 1655.

5. *Autobiography of Benjamin Rush,* 185; William Buchan, *Domestic Medicine* (Edinburgh: Balfour, Auld and Smellie, 1769), chap. 6, "Of Sleep and Clothing."

6. Jefferson to Rush, Sept. 12, 1799, *Papers of Thomas Jefferson,* ed. Julian P. Boyd et al. (Princeton, NJ: 1950–), 31:183.

7. Lucia Dacome, "'To What Purpose Does It Think?': Dreams, Sick Bodies and Confused Minds in the Age of Reason," *History of Psychiatry* 15 (2004): 395–416; Thomas Arnold, M.D., *Observations on the Nature, Kinds, Causes, and Prevention of Insanity, Lunacy, or Madness* (London: G. Ireland, for G. Robinson, and T. Cadell, 1782), 112.

8. William Broadum, M.D., *A Guide to Old Age, or a Cure for the Indiscretions of Youth* (London: J. W. Myers, 1795), 6–8.

9. "Lecture Notes on Sleep," Rush Family Papers, vol. 168, LCP.

10. In the Anglo-American community of this era, sexual satire of all kinds found its way into print, gender inversion was a regular theme onstage, bawdy houses were a permanent part of the landscape in major cities and towns, and crude humor among men was quite common-place—post-Revolutionary American men were not Victorians. It was largely in literature and Sunday sermons that the illusion of a sweet, high-minded domesticity was sustained. One thing that comes through his dream, at least, is that John Mifflin exhibited a pronounced need to find another person to confide in. See *John Fishbourne Mifflin Diary,* 1786–87, HSP.

    For a full treatment of the affectionate friendship of Mifflin and Gibson, see Caleb Crain, *American Sympathy: Men, Friendship, and Literature in the New Nation* (New Haven, CT: Yale University Press, 2001), chap. 1, "In the Pear Grove: The Romance of Leander, Lorenzo, and Castalio." Crain offers possible interpretations of the dream, including a suggestion that the river "represents the sentiments carrying the men along" and the missing oar "an attempt to navigate their passions without recourse to what makes their bodies sexual and male." He does not insist on a sexual relationship, though one seems at least as likely as not; and he marvels at the "thoroughness and honesty" Mifflin exhibits in the telling. Overall, Crain shows Mifflin, as fond as he was of Gibson, willing to toy with Gibson's emotions. See esp. 48–49.

    Carla Gerona also examines the Leander-Lorenzo writings and suggests that nudity might symbolize purity in this instance. See Gerona, *Night Journeys: The Power of Dreams in Transatlantic Quaker Culture* (Charlottesville, VA: University of Virginia Press, 2004), 216–18. Concerning sexual mores and the range of sexual practices in print and in public and private places, see esp. the copiously illustrated Vic Gatrell, *City of Laughter: Sex and Satire in Eighteenth-Century London* (New York: Walker & Company, 2006).

11. J. Adams to A. Smith, Aug. [?], 1763, *Adams Family Correspondence,* ed. L. H. Butterfield (Cambridge, MA: Harvard University Press, 1963–), 1:7; Edith B. Gelles, *Abigail and John: Portrait of a Marriage* (New York: William Morrow, 2009), 16–19.

12. A. Adams to J. Adams, Sept. 10, 1777; J. Adams to A. Adams, Oct. 7, 1777, in *Adams Family Correspondence,* 2:339–40, 352.

13. A. Adams to J. Adams, Oct. 21, 1775 and Aug. 1, 1781, *Adams Family Correspondence,* 1:305, 4:190.

14. A. Adams to J. Adams, Jan. 1, 1797, Adams Papers, microfilm, reel 383.

15. *The Diary of William Maclay and Other Notes on Senate Debates,* eds. Kenneth R. Bowling and Helen E. Veit (Baltimore, MD: Johns Hopkins University Press, 1988), chap. 8, entry of May 30, 1790; Joanne B. Freeman, *Affairs of Honor: National Politics in the New Republic* (New Haven, CT: Yale University Press, 2001), chap. 1; Henry Laurens to William Livingston, Oct. 1, 1778, in *Letters of Delegates to Congress,* 11:4, accessed online at Library of Congress (American Memory).

16. *Ambrose Searle Diary,* cited in *Papers of George Washington, Revolutionary War Series,* ed. Dorothy Twohig et al. (Charlottesville, VA: University Press of Virginia, 1985–), 7:43n; Fairfax to Washington, Feb. 17, 1793, *Papers of George Washington, Presidential Series,* ed. Philander D. Chase et al. (Charlottesville, VA: University Press of Virginia, 1985–), 12:157.

17. Thomas Bruff to Washington, ca. 1797, *Papers of George Washington, Retirement Series,* ed. W. W. Abbott et al., 4 vols. (Charlottesville, VA: University Press of Virginia, 1998–99), 1:537–38.

18. Roy Porter, *Flesh in the Age of Reason* (New York: W. W. Norton, 2003), 188–89; Paul Tankard, "Samuel Johnson's 'History of Memory,'" *Studies in Philology* 102 (Winter 2005): 116.

19. William Widger diary, extracted in Jesse Lemisch, "Listening to the 'Inarticulate': William Widger's Dream and the Loyalties of American Revolutionary Seamen in British Prisons," *Journal of Social History* 3 (1969–70): 1–29; see also Paul A. Gilje, *Liberty on the Waterfront:*

American Maritime Culture in the Age of Revolution (Philadelphia: University of Pennsylvania Press, 2004), 33–34.

20. *The Complete Essays of Montaigne,* trans. Donald M. Frame (Stanford, CA: Stanford University Press, 1958), 27.

21. Samuel Forman Conover, *Inaugural Dissertation on Sleep and Dreams; Their Effects on the Faculties of the Mind, and the Causes of Dreams* (Philadelphia, 1791), 1–16.

22. Charles Bonnet, *Conjectures Concerning the Nature of Future Happiness* (Charleston, SC: John Dixon Nelson, 1800), 12–13.

23. *Science against the Unbelievers: The Correspondence of Bonnet and Needham, 1760–1780,* eds. Renato G. Mazzolini and Shirley A. Roe (Oxford, U.K: The Voltaire Foundation, 1986), 3–10, 62–76. In a letter from Bonnet to John Turberville Needham (1713–1781), dated Feb. 17, 1770 (in French), the Swiss thinker laid out his argument, defending himself against the charge that he had reduced religion to the level of physics. See ibid., 280–86.

24. Conover, *Inaugural Dissertation on Sleep and Dreams,* 16–23. Whatever else the physician-in-training might have thought privately, he felt obliged to curry favor with men who were the pillars of society, a society in which one dreaded being accused of atheism. Toward the end of the dissertation, Conover took a soft swipe at orthodox Christian faith, then immediately tempered his language: "An attempt to explain all the dreams recorded in the Old and New Testament, upon the same physical causes as we do those of the present day, would, perhaps, suggest a hint favourable to deistical principles," he wrote. "Far be it from me, however, that I should entertain, or even wish to support, an idea, so unfriendly to moral science, to the happiness, and to the good order of society."

25. James Beattie, *Dissertations Moral and Critical* (Philadelphia, PA: Hopkins and Earle, 1809), 1:308–40, 2:1–29; Ekirch, *At Day's Close,* 312. Beattie had a significant following in America. He was a dynamic moral philosopher, whose work was related in scope to another, better known Scot of his generation, Adam Smith, whose humane *Theory of Moral Sentiments* (1759) influenced as many of the Revolutionary generation as his market-focused *Wealth of Nations* (1776) has since. Smith preached a gospel of positive emotional engagement, urging an investment of sympathy toward any and all. He saw a violent assault against the inner person taking place even within the civilizing process. Beattie believed that while human knowledge was notoriously imperfect, and people possessed unequal abilities by nature, ethical and intellectual progress in society was guaranteed by a progressive historical impulse. See also Nicholas Phillipson, *Adam Smith: An Enlightened Life* (New Haven, CT: Yale University Press, 2010).

26. Conover, *Inaugural Dissertation on Sleep and Dreams,* 23–24.

27. "Valley Forge 1777–1778: Diary of Surgeon Albigence Waldo, of the Connecticut Line," *Pennsylvania Magazine of History and Biography* 21 (1897): 299–323.

CHAPTER 2: FROM A LOFTY SCAFFOLD, JOHN ADAMS SPIES AN ELEPHANT

1. *The Autobiography of Benjamin Rush,* ed. George W. Corner (Westport, CT: Greenwood Press, 1970), 28–30; David Freeman Hawke, *Benjamin Rush: Revolutionary Gadfly* (Indianapolis: Bobbs-Merrill Co., 1971); for a recent treatment, see Sari Altschuler, "From Blood Vessels to Global Networks of Exchange: The Physiology of Benjamin Rush's Early Republic," *Journal of the Early Republic* 32 (Summer 2012): 207-32.

2. *Autobiography of Benjamin Rush,* 357.

3. Richard Cullen Rath, *How Early America Sounded* (Ithaca, NY: Cornell University Press, 2003). Professor Rath is comparing the eighteenth century with the seventeenth, to show how an America of still meager population evolved into something more enlightened and sophisticated; Leigh Eric Schmidt, *Hearing Things: Religion, Illusion, and the American Enlightenment* (Cambridge, MA: Harvard University Press, 2000), quote at 75.

4. A. Roger Ekirch, *At Day's Close: Night in Times Past* (New York: W. W. Norton, 2005), 292–93, 300–12.

5. Ibid., 91, 110, 132; Schmidt also highlights the symbolic meaning of trumpet sounds in early American religious life, in *Hearing Things,* 60–61.

6. *Autobiography of Benjamin Rush,* 335–36.
7. Benjamin Rush, *Medical Inquiries and Observations upon the Diseases of the Mind* (Philadelphia: Kimber and Richardson, 1812), 162, 329. To elevate a theory, in this case, he quoted the poet William Cowper passionately and at length. "How slender the tenure by which we hold our intellectual and moral existence!" Rush exclaimed, launching into "Well might the eloquent Mr. Cowper, from his view of the mind of man, consider it as 'A harp whose chords elude the sight / Each yielding harmony dispos'd aright.'" Nothing is clearer in Cowper's celebrated lines from "The Task" (1785) than its combination of soulfulness and musicality:

    > *There is in souls a sympathy with sounds:*
    > *And as the mind is pitch'd the ear is pleased*
    > *With melting airs, or martial, brisk or grave;*
    > *Some chord in unison with what we hear*
    > *Is touch'd within us, and the heart replies.*

    Other relevant lines in Cowper's "The Task" read: "The poet's or historian's page, by one / Made vocal for th'amusement of the rest; / The sprightly lyre, whose treasure of sweet sounds / The touch from many a trembling chord shakes out." As to Rush's other linguistic-musical resonances, the Scottish philosophers who influenced him simply oozed an appreciation for vibrating nerves and related sensory stimuli. Jean-Jacques Rousseau wrote extensively on the relationship between music and language, believing that a community's distinctiveness formed around the musical elements in its language and that the music of language expressed the passions that best evidenced cultural cohesiveness. See Roy Porter, *Flesh in the Age of Reason* (New York: W. W. Norton, 2003); John T. Scott, "Rousseau and the Melodious Language of Freedom," *Journal of Politics* 59 (Aug. 1997): 803–29.

    For a keen discussion of the telegraphic metaphor and how the second half of the nineteenth century pictured the neurophysiological world, see Randall Knoper, "American Literary Realism and Nervous Reflexion," *American Literature* 74 (2002): 715–45; for verification, see Eli F. Brown, M.D., *The Eclectic Physiology* (Cincinnati and New York: Van Antwerp, Bragg,and Co., 1884), chaps. 11 and 12.
8. Joseph Priestley, "Some Thoughts Concerning Dreams," *Medical Repository* 5 (Oct. 1802): 125–29.
9. *Autobiography of Benjamin Rush,* 229–31; Edwin S. Gaustad, *Sworn on the Altar of God* (Grand Rapids, MI: Wm. B. Eardmons, 1996), 112–13; Eugene R. Sheridan, Introduction to *Jefferson's Extracts from the Gospels,* ed. Dickinson W. Adams (Princeton, NJ: Princeton University Press, 1983).
10. *Autobiography of Benjamin Rush,* 357–58.
11. The literature on sensibility is vast. See esp. Porter, *Flesh in the Age of Reason;* G. J. Barker-Benfield, *The Culture of Sensibility: Sex and Society in Eighteenth-Century Britain* (Chicago: University of Chicago Press, 1992); Paul-Gabriel Boucé, ed., *Sexuality in Eighteenth-Century Britain* (Manchester, UK: Manchester University Press, 1992); D. T. de Bienville, *Nymphomania, or, a Dissertation Concerning the Furor Uterinus . . .* (London: printed for J. Bew, 1775).
12. Lucia Dacome, "'To What Purpose Does It Think?': Dreams, Sick Bodies and Confused Minds in the Age of Reason," *History of Psychiatry* 15 (2004): 401, 407.
13. Benjamin Rush and Julia Stockton Rush, *My Dearest Julia: The Love Letters of Dr. Benjamin Rush to Julia Stockton* (New York: Neale Watson Academic Publications, 1979), 12–15, 46. To a female correspondent in England, he later wrote of a "sweet song" that "opened an avenue to my heart." Rush to Lady Jane Wishart Belsches, Apr. 21, 1784, *Letters of Benjamin Rush,* 328.
14. Anticipating his late years' statements on the harmonious association of spiritual consolation and Enlightenment science, Rush acknowledged to his bride-to-be that there were "only two ways of being happy in matrimony, viz by living agreeable to the laws of religion, or reason." See Benjamin Rush, *Essays Literary, Moral, and Philosophical* (Philadelphia: Thomas and William Bradford, 1806), 19, 57–92. In his *Account of the Influence of the Military and Political Events of the American Revolution upon the Human Body,* Rush wrote that hysterical women who placed their hopes in the Revolution were actually cured of their emotional debility at war's end. See George E. Rosen, "Political Order and Human Health in Jeffersonian Thought,"

Bulletin of the History of Medicine 26 (1952): 32–44. It is also important to note that Dr. Rush held conventional views when it came time to write to a young woman embarking on matrimony: "The subordination of your sex to ours is enforced by nature, by reason, and by revelation." Rush to Rebecca Smith, May 1792, in *Letters of Benjamin Rush*, ed. L. H. Butterfield (Princeton, NJ: Princeton University Press, 1951), 617.

15. *Autobiography of Benjamin Rush*, 359–60. It is striking that, from start to finish, the dream is constantly marked by sound and dialogue. Note, too, that verbs and adjectives are not made pretty. Just as Rush's patients died of malignancies, his speaking dream characters are not above (or beyond) maligning. He appears to repress little.

16. Ibid., 243.

17. Ibid., 369–71; Richard Bell, *We Shall Be No More: Suicide and Self-Government in the Newly United States* (Cambridge, MA: Harvard University Press, 2012), 13.

18. As further examples of these qualities, amid the French Revolution, Rush bemoaned to a Londoner the beheading of King Louis XVI: "His execution was unjust, unconstitutional, illegal, impolitic, and cruel. . . . He was the best king in Europe and the honestest man in the French nation." And, more optimistically: "Chaos existed before the order and beauty of the Universe," and France would emerge from its moral darkness. Rush to John Coakley Lettsom, Apr. 26, 1793; to Julia Stockton Rush, Aug. 21, 1793; to Jefferson, Mar. 12, 1802, *Letters of Benjamin Rush*, 635, 638, 847.

19. Rush to Jeremy Belknap, Aug. 19, 1788, ibid, 482. For opposition to the death penalty, see, for example, Rush to Thomas Eddy, a Quaker, Oct. 19, 1803, *Letters of Benjamin Rush*, 875.

20. *Autobiography of Benjamin Rush*, 226, 336–37. Rush's intellectual generation took an interest in what Andrew J. Lewis denotes a "theology of nature." God's mercies arrived seasonally with bird songs, blooms, and the ever-changing landscape. Nature's "delights" led to an enlarged appreciation of God. Rush himself cited a line in Corinthians, "the Earth is the Lord's," as part of his belief in a divine intelligence manifest in physical nature. See Lewis, *A Democracy of Facts: Natural History in the Early Republic* (Philadelphia: University of Pennsylvania Press, 2011), chap. 4.

    When in his forties, around the time he says his faith began to deepen, Rush wrote to his sister-in-law that he expected biblical truths to make sense in the way nature's secrets were being slowly uncovered by science. Both contained "mysteries" that were being "brought to light" by chance and at times even by "persons of little or no education." He proclaimed: "I never read a chapter in the Bible without seeing something in it I never saw before." Rush to Mary Stockton, Sept. 7, 1788, *Letters of Benjamin Rush*, 483–84.

21. At some point in his evolution as a clinical physician, Rush concluded that all illness was brought on by "morbid excitement" and could be boiled down to capillary tension. Fever was the result of convulsive action in blood vessels and opiates lifesaving because they lessened all negative emotional stimuli. Prone to the dramatic, he had the audacity to lecture his students that there was "only one disease in the world." He was prepared to deplete the body of 80 percent of its blood in order to save the patient. Historian of medicine Richard Harrison Shryock described Rush's perspective this way: "He declared that the doctrine of one disease had done for medicine what a belief in one God had achieved in religion!" Shryock, *Medicine and Society in America, 1660–1860* (Ithaca, NY: Cornell University Press, 1980), 69–70. Most recently, on the wrongheadedness of Rush's medical practice, and the medical environment generally, see Elaine Breslaw, *Potions, Lotions, Pills, and Magic: Health Care in Early America* (New York: New York University Press, 2012).

22. Rush to Julia Stockton Rush, Aug. 25, 1793, *Letters of Benjamin Rush*, 640–41; Robert V. Wells, "A Tale of Two Cities: Epidemics and the Rituals of Death in Eighteenth-Century Boston and Philadelphia," in Nancy Isenberg and Andrew Burstein, eds., *Mortal Remains: Death in Early America* (Philadelphia: University of Pennsylvania Press, 2003), 56–67. In the last months of the crisis, Philadelphia's Charles Willson Peale, the portrait painter who captured the likenesses of the founders, received a letter from his brother-in-law in New York, giving a sense of life's fragility at the time of the scourge: "It affords me great Consolation to find your Family still in the Land of the Living—but how long this may be the case God only knows. Death's Shafts fly thick around you, and no one knows who they will light on." John DePeyster to Peale, Oct. 2, 1793, Peale-Sellers Family Papers, APS.

23. Rush Family Papers, vol. 169, LCP.

24. "Lecture Notes on Sleep," Rush Family Papers, vol. 168, LCP.

25. John Fishbourne Mifflin Diary, entry of Nov. 27, 1786, and passim.

26. *Autobiography of Charles Caldwell, M.D.,* ed. Harriot W. Warner (New York: DaCapo Press, 1968 [Philadelphia, 1855]), quotes at 200.

27. *Diary of John Quincy Adams,* ed. Robert J. Taylor et al., 2 vols. (Cambridge, MA: Harvard University Press, 1981), 1:395; see also ibid, 2:124 on the "impatient" imagination.

28. David Hall, *Worlds of Wonder, Days of Judgment: Popular Religious Belief in Early New England* (New York: Harvard University Press, 1990).

29. Royal Society (Great Britain), *Philosophical Transactions, Giving Some Account of the Present Undertakings, Studies, and Labours, of the Ingenious* (London: S. Smith and B. Wolford, 1750).

30. "Janet Livingston's Memoir," *Livingston Papers* (Transcripts and Originals), NYPL.

31. *A Dream or Vision of the Night* (New London, CT: T/ Green, 1766).

32. *The American Wonder: or, the Strange and Remarkable Cape-Ann Dream* (Salem, MA: E. Russell, 1776).

33. "Philo-Alethias on the Present State of America," in Peter Force, ed., *American Archives,* series 5, 2:967 (Documents of the American Revolution, online). The dateline is Delaware, Oct. 10, 1776.

34. Andrew Burstein, *Sentimental Democracy: The Evolution of America's Romantic Self-Image* (New York: Hill & Wang, 1999), chap. 4; *Pennsylvania Magazine,* Feb. 1775 & Mar. 1776.

35. Benjamin Rush, *Medical Inquiries and Observations upon the Diseases of the Mind* (Philadelphia: Kimber & Richardson, 1812), 301–4.

36. Joel Barlow, *The Vision of Columbus* (Hartford, CT: Hudson and Goodwin, 1787), quotes from Books 1 and 5.

37. "A Dream," broadside published in Germantown, PA, 1793, accessed at Early American Imprints, Series I (Evans); "Memorandum of a Dream," 1799, Miscellaneous Boxes M, American Antiquarian Society. I am grateful to Tracey Kry, assistant curator of manuscripts at the AAS, for sending this fascinating, newly acquired dream my way.

38. R. Po-chia Hsia, "Dreams and Conversions: A Comparative Analysis of Catholic and Buddhist Dreams in Ming and Qing China," *Journal of Religious History* 34 (June 2010): 111–41.

39. *The Complete Fortune-Teller; or, An Infallible Guide to the Hidden Decrees of Fate* (New York: n.p., 1799), 100; *The Oneirocritic* (New York, 179?); *The Universal Dream-Dictionary* (Philadelphia: H & P Rice, 1797); Harry B. Weiss, *Oneirocritica Americana: The Story of American Dream Books* (New York: NYPL, 1944), 9–10.

40. *The Dreamer's Class Book; or, a New and Original Dream-Book* (London: Dean & Munday, 1826), 12, 18, 21, 25. Typical of the mix of moods presented in the guides, *The Universal Dream-Dictionary* interspersed bawdy rhyme:

> To dream of bird's nests signifies
> In maidens ripe virginities:
> But if the birds away be flown
> It shews her maiden-head is gone.

41. *Universal Interpreter of Dreams and Visions* (Philadelphia: Stewart & Cochran, 1797), 56.

42. *The Astrologer's Magazine; and Philosophical Miscellany* (London: W. Locke, 1794); J. C. Lavater, *Essays on Physiognomy* (Boston: William Spotswood and David Weat, 1794), quote at 31; "Of the Passions, as They Display Themselves in the Look and Gesture," *Universal Asylum and Columbian Magazine* (Jan. 1791).

43. *Autobiography of Charles Caldwell, M.D.,* 365–66, 371–72.

44. S. R. F. Price, "From Freud to Artemidorus," *Past & Present* 113 (Nov. 1986): 3–37; Christine Walde, "Dream Interpretation in a Prosperous Age? Artemidorus, the Greek Interpreter of Dreams," in David Shulman and Guy G. Stroumsa, eds., *Dream Cultures: Explorations in the Comparative History of Dreaming* (New York: Oxford University Press, 1999), chap. 7; Weiss, *Oneirocritica Americana,* 5; Robert Moss, *The Secret History of Dreaming* (Novato, CA: New World Library, 2009), 33–36. The advent of typographical culture meant that Artemidorus was already appearing in English, French, Italian, and German at the time the North American colonies were first settled. Keith Thomas writes of the popularity of dream interpretation

guides in Elizabethan England, noting that the work of Artemidorus was in its twentieth printing by 1722. See Thomas, *Religion and the Decline of Magic* (New York: Scribner, 1971), 129–30.

45. Francis Hopkinson, *The Miscellaneous Essays and Occasional Writings of Francis Hopkinson, Esq.*, 3 vols. (Philadelphia: T. Dobson, 1792), 2:170.

46. *Osborne's New-Hampshire Spy,* Apr. 24, 1789, and repeated in the *United States Chronicle* (Providence, RI), July 16, 1789.

47. Carl Van Doren, *Benjamin Franklin* (New York: Viking, 1938), 651–52.

48. Ibid., 760; *The Life and Essays of the Late Dr. Franklin* (Brattleboro, VT, 1814), 208–14; *Essays and Letters by Dr. B. Franklin* (New York: R. & W. A. Bartow & Co., 1822), 120–26.

49. *The Spectator* (Philadelphia, 1851), 2:151–55.

50. Ibid., 4:30–34.

51. Paul Ricoeur, *Memory, History, Forgetting* (Chicago: University of Chicago Press, 2004), 417.

52. *Autobiography of Benjamin Rush,* 55, 95, 141, 183.

53. Rush to Gates, Dec. 26, 1795, *Letters of Benjamin Rush,* 767; on Cobbett suit, see ibid, 1213–18. Rush had felt for Gates's situation fifteen years before the cited letter, writing John Adams at the time that he was "under persecution from a faction in Congress," despite his battlefield success and popularity among the troops. Rush to Adams, Oct. 23, 1780, ibid, 256. A discussion of Rush's talking to himself during the epidemic is found in a less than glowing portrait of him by one of his students; see *Autobiography of Charles Caldwell,* 184.

54. Rush to Adams, Oct. 17, 1809, ibid, 1021–22. When word of his death reached Jefferson, the Virginian wrote the New Englander of their friend's honesty and benevolence; then, reckoning that, after themselves, only two signers of the Declaration of Independence still lived, he intoned: "We too must go; and that ere long." Jefferson to Adams, May 27, 1813, *The Adams-Jefferson Letters,* ed. Lester J. Cappon (Chapel Hill, NC: University of North Carolina Press, 1959), 323.

55. Rush to Adams, July 13, 1812, *Letters of Benjamin Rush,* 1150–52; Adams to Rush, July 19, 1812, Adams Papers (microfilm), reel 118. Adams added his thoughts about the nature of human feelings: "Feelings which make us delight and glory in existence, and ardently wish and pray for Immortality." He believed, he said, that "Nature has ordained that early impressions on our Minds should be durable," that "ideas and sensations acquired and felt in the Cradle . . . seldom leave us till we die."

56. Adams to Rush, Nov. 29, 1812, John A. Schutz and Douglass Adair, *The Spur of Fame: Dialogues of John Adams and Benjamin Rush, 1805–1813* (San Marino, CA: The Huntington Library, 1966), 254–55.

57. Rush to Adams, Mar. 23, 1805, *Letters of Benjamin Rush,* 892–93. Seven years later, Rush used the same Latin vocabulary in another letter to Adams, except this time it was "The tale is told of the American republic." Ibid., 1169.

58. Rush to Adams, Sept. 16, 1808, ibid, 976–79.

59. Rush to Adams, Feb. 20, 1809, ibid, 994–96; "Letters & Thoughts," Rush Family Papers, vol. 79, LCP, repeated almost verbatim in *Autobiography of Benjamin Rush,* 187. Rush read of the episode of the "pious merchant" in *On Beneficence,* a recently published book by a Methodist minister.

60. *Black Hawk: Life of Black Hawk, or Mà-ka-tai-me-she-kià-kiàk,* ed. J. Gerald Kennedy (New York: Penguin, 2008), 9–10. First published 1833.

61. George Henry Loskiel, *History of the Mission of the United Brethren among the Indians in North America* (London: John Stockdale, 1794), 40. Translated from the German. Loskiel lived in Pennsylvania from 1801 until his death in 1814.

62. Ibid., 13, 63, 142. These impressions are comparable to those in Jonathan Carver, *Three Years' Travel through the Interior Parts of North-America* (Philadelphia: Joseph Crukshank, 1789). Captain Carver emphasized fasting and dreaming in terms of military decision making as well as the hunt.

63. Lee Irwin, "Dreams, Theory, and Culture: The Plains Indian Vision Quest Paradigm," *American Indian Quarterly* 18 (Spring 1994): 229–45, quotes at 235, 238; Anthony F. C. Wallace, "Dreams and Wishes of the Soul: A Type of Psychoanalytic Theory among the Seventeenth-Century Iroquois," *American Anthropologist* 60 (1958): 234–48.

64. Olaudeh Equiano, *The Highly Interesting Narrative and Other Writings,* ed. Vincent Carretta (New York: Penguin, 1995), 86–87, 127, 201.

65. Rush Family Papers, vol. 79, LCP.

66. Rush, *Essays Literary, Moral, and Philosophical,* 305–10. Southern whites of this era recorded dreams in which their slaves actively figured in the narrative: in 1776, after nine of his bondmen fled to the British lines, both Virginian Landon Carter and his daughter had dreams about them—in the father's dream, the escapees were "most wretchedly meager and wan." For this and comparable examples, see *Philip D. Morgan, Slave Counterpoint* (Chapel Hill, NC: University of North Carolina Press, 1998), 378.

67. Mechal Sobel, *Teach Me Dreams: The Search for Self in the Revolutionary Era* (Princeton, NJ: Princeton University Press, 2000), 40.

68. Rush Family Papers, vol. 79, LCP.

69. Rush Family Papers, vol. 169, LCP.

CHAPTER 3: DEPLETED OF ENERGY, HEMAN HARRIS LEAVES HIS BODY

1. Nicholas Peter Isaacs, *Twenty Years before the Mast* (New York: J. P. Beckwith, 1845), 6–7.

2. "Dream of Nathaniel Newlin Related by Himself," undated, APS.

3. "The Final Departure," in the *Freeman's Oracle or New-Hampshire Advertiser,* Jan. 20, 1789. Similarly, in neighboring Vermont, a newspaper reported on a man who had dreamt of a woman plotting to kill him—he was saved by posting trusted servants by his door in the night. Elsewhere, it was reported that a man staying at a tavern dreamt he was being pursued by someone with a pistol and, half conscious, flung himself from a third-story window. Fortunately, he landed safely. "A villain wants to shoot me!" he exclaimed to no one in particular, before coming to his senses. See "Remarkable Dream," *Vermont Journal,* Mar. 10, 1790; *Connecticut Journal,* Aug. 26, 1802. For other predictive dreams, set specifically in a religious context, see Susan Juster, *Doomsayers: Anglo-American Prophecy in the Age of Revolution* (Philadelphia: University of Pennsylvania Press, 2003), chap. 2.

4. Paul A. Gilje, *Liberty on the Waterfront: American Maritime Culture in the Age of Revolution* (Philadelphia: University of Pennsylvania Press, 2004), 58; Susan Vanzanten Gallagher, "Jack Blunt and His Dream Book," *American Literature* 58 (Dec. 1986): 614–19.

5. Entry of Nov. 20, 1798, in *The Diary of Elizabeth Drinker,* ed. Elaine Forman Crane, 3 vols. (Boston: Bancroft & Holley, 1991), 2:1112–13.

6. Edward Young, *The Complaint or Night Thoughts on Life, Death & Immortality* (Glasgow: Richard Scott, 1798), quotes from "Night the Second" and "Night the Third"; Althea Hayter, *Opium and the Romantic Imagination* (London: Faber and Faber, 1968), 68; *The Universal Interpreter of Dreams and Visions* (Philadelphia: Stewart & Cochran, 1797), introd.

7. Barbara Tedlock, "Sharing and Interpreting Dreams in Amerindian Nations," in David Shulman and Guy G. Stroumsa, eds., *Dream Cultures: Explorations in the Comparative History of Dreaming* (New York: Oxford University Press, 1999), chap. 3; Matthew Dennis, *Seneca Possessed: Indians, Witchcraft, and Power in Early America* (Philadelphia: University of Pennsylvania Press, 2010), 67.

8. *American Mercury* (Hartford, CT), Apr. 6, 1789.

9. Andrew Burstein, *The Inner Jefferson: Portrait of a Grieving Optimist* (Charlottesville, VA: University of Virginia Press, 1995), 60–62; Angela Rosenthal, "Raising Hair"; Christiane Holm, "Sentimental Cuts: Eighteenth-Century Mourning Jewelry with Hair," *Eighteenth-Century Studies* 38 (Fall 2004): 1–16, 139–43.

10. *Universal Interpreter of Dreams and Visions,* 40.

11. "Extraordinary Character of a Young Lady," *Rural Magazine, or, Vermont Repository* 1 (1795-96): 323–24.

12. *The Oneirocritic* (New York: N. Ogden, 179? (exact year unknown)); *The Universal Dream-Dictionary* (Philadelphia: H & P Rice, 1797); Elizabeth Reis, "Immortal Messengers: Angels, Gender, and Power in Early America," in Nancy Isenberg and Andrew Burstein, eds., *Mortal Remains: Death in Early America* (Philadelphia: University of Pennsylvania Press, 2003), 163–75.

13. "A Remarkable Dream," dated Dec. 26, 1782, in Ann Vaux correspondence, Vaux Family Papers, HSP. Many versions of this dream exist. See Carla Gerona, *Night Journeys: The Power of Dreams in Transatlantic Quaker Culture* (Charlottesville, VA: University of Virginia Press, 2004), 160–64.

14. Mary Grew Diary, Nov. 4, 1792, in William John Potts Papers, HSP. A tale, highly doubtful to us, but that we can assume many readers supposed true in 1789, told of a woman who woke in a panic from a dream in which, after attending a ball, she was "violently whirled" by angels and sent "down, down, down! through darkness and thunderings and sulphur." Whatever anxious anticipation she might have felt about the actual ball she had lately been invited to gradually diminished in her mind, though friends urged her to heed her dream. Of course, she did attend and, on her return home, "fainted away and died" in her bed. The same source reported on a man who worried about an oft-inebriated friend and had a dream in which the friend was dead; he went to the man's lodgings and found him "quite cold, having been dead some time." See *Pennsylvania Mercury,* Feb. 19 and Sept. 4, 1789.

15. *A Dream of Mr. Heman Harris, in His Last Sickness, a Little Before His Death* (Worcester, MA, n.p., 1798).

16. Aaron Warner, *A Remarkable Dream, or Vision, Which Was Experienced on the Night of the 20th of May, 1799* (Hartford, CT: John Babcock, 1801).

17. Dream of Dec. 19, 1803, in *Two Very Singular Dreams* (Augusta, ME: A. M. M. Millan, 1804). Richardson's hell appeared a tempestuous sea, "its motion . . . lashing and foaming as in a great fury." At one point, he repeats the phrase "mixed streams," which can be read as a homonym for "mixed dreams." "When I was awaked," the dreamer concluded, "I was so weak and out-done, that I could not have stood on my feet . . . my whole flesh felt as numbed."

18. Entry of May 5, 1794, in *The Literary Diary of Ezra Stiles,* ed. Franklin Bowditch Dexter (New York: A. Finley, 1901), 3:523.

19. Entries of Nov. 20, 1772, and Jan. 18, 1774, in ibid., 1:301–2, 431.

20. Entries of May 14, 1787, Sept. 27, 1788, and Nov. 9, 1788, in *Ann Head Warder Papers,* HSP. The Mary Grew dream of her husband, while she was abroad, is both typical and unusual: this species of dream was most always recorded by a female, but it was usually the husband who traveled and she who experienced him by her side in dreams from home; Young, *The Complaint or Night Thoughts,* "Night the Seventh," 13.

21. Kelly Bulkeley and Patricia Bulkley, *Dreaming Beyond Death: A Guide to Pre-Death Dreams and Visions* (Boston: Beacon Press, 2005), 11–12, 40, and passim. Mother and son, Kelly Bulkeley holds a Ph.D. in religion and psychological studies from the University of Chicago Divinity School; Reverend Patricia Bulkley has worked as a hospice counselor.

22. It is easy to illustrate. Modern metaphors describe emotion at the ready: anger is hot, boiling energy; someone is "on fire" with passion; a person "storms" out of a room. Our needs are elemental. We are "hungry for more" and require "food" for thought. We feel we need rescuing from real and imagined ills—medical intervention is a constant factor in our lives. Love and friendship "cure" loneliness; time "heals" when we need to rebound from an emotional affliction. In this section, I draw principally on George Lakoff and Mark Johnson, *Metaphors We Live By* (Chicago: University of Chicago Press, 1980); and Zoltán Kövecses, *Metaphor and Emotion: Language, Culture, and Body in Human Feeling* (New York: Cambridge University Press, 2000).

23. Scientists of the twenty-first century have begun to speculate on the evolutionary function of belief in religion, examining whether the brain is wired for such belief, and in this way they sidestep the more sensitive question of God's existence.

24. *Fanny: or the Happy Repentance* (Litchfield, CT: Thomas Collier, 1789), 38. This was a French novel of sensibility, translated into English and first published in the United States in 1785; *The Fatal Effects of Seduction: A Tragedy* (Bennington, VT: Hasswell and Russell, 1789), in which the power-engrossing patriarch who was the heroine's unsympathetic father, was married to reason alone; for him, dreams were uniformly the products of "disturb'd imagination" and no better than the ravings of a madman.

25. For contextualization of the preceding and Scottish referents in Brown's psychological novels, see esp. Susan L. Manning, "Enlightenment's Dark Dreams: Two Fictions of Henry Mackenzie and Charles Brockden Brown," *Eighteenth-Century Life* 21 (1997): 39–56.

26. Gerona, *Night Journeys,* quotes at 144, 191–92.

27. Ibid., 227–36. See also Mechal Sobel, *Teach Me Dreams: The Search for Self in the Revolutionary Era* (Princeton, NJ: Princeton University Press, 2000), chap. 5 and 206–9.

28. Eric Gardner, "'The Complete Fortune Teller and Dream Book': An Antebellum Text 'By Chloe Russel, a Woman of Colour,'" *New England Quarterly* 78 (June 2005): 259–88; *The Complete Fortune-Teller; or, An Infallible Guide to the Hidden Decrees of Fate* (New York, n.p., 1799); Sobel, *Teach Me Dreams,* 259n.

29. Louisa Adams Park Diary, Park Family Papers, AAS.

CHAPTER 4: ELIZA CHAMPLAIN SEES ANGELS OVER CONNECTICUT

1. Miles King to Jefferson, Aug. 20, 1814, *The Papers of Thomas Jefferson, Retirement Series,* ed. J. Jefferson Looney (Princeton, NJ: Princeton University Press, 2010), 7:573–89.

2. *Jefferson's Literary Commonplace Book,* ed. Douglas L. Wilson (Princeton, NJ: Princeton University Press, 1989), 59; Andrew Burstein, *Jefferson's Secrets: Death and Desire at Monticello* (New York: Basic Books, 2005), chap. 9.

3. *A Selection of Eulogies, Pronounced in the Several States in Honor of Those Illustrious Patriots and Statesmen, John Adams and Thomas Jefferson* (Hartford, CT: D. F. Robinson and Co., 1826), 137; Andrew Burstein, *America's Jubilee* (New York: Alfred A. Knopf, 2001), chap. 11, quote at 276.

4. Hannah Spahn, *Thomas Jefferson, Time, and History* (Charlottesville, VA: University of Virginia Press, 2011), 90–91, 200–1; Jefferson to Nathaniel Macon (U.S. senator from North Carolina), Jan. 12, 1819, Thomas Jefferson Papers, Library of Congress; Karl Lehmann, *Thomas Jefferson, American Humanist* (Charlottesville, VA: University of Virginia Press, 1985), quote at 141; see also Peter S. Onuf and Nicholas P. Cole, eds., *Thomas Jefferson, the Classical World, and Early America* (Charlottesville, VA: University of Virginia Press, 2011).

5. Burstein, *America's Jubilee,* 262.

6. Ellen Randolph Coolidge to Virginia Randolph Trist, May 13, 1828, in Ellen Coolidge Correspondence, UVA.

7. Anthony Morris to Anna Coles Payne Causten, June 26, 1837; Dolley Madison to James Madison, Oct. 26, 1805; Dolley Madison to Eliza Collins Lee, July 26, 1836, in *The Papers of Dolley Madison Digital Edition,* ed. Holly C. Shulman (Charlottesville, VA: University of Virginia Press, Rotunda, 2008); Ralph Ketcham, *James Madison: A Biography* (Charlottesville, VA: University of Virginia Press, 1990), 377–80; Catherine Allgor, *A Perfect Union: Dolley Madison and the Creation of the American Nation* (New York: Henry Holt & Co., 2006).

8. Thomas Paine, *Examination of the Passages in the New Testament . . . to Which Is Prefixed an Essay on Dream* (New York: n.p., 1807), 5–7.

9. Ezra Stiles Ely, *Conversations on the Science of the Human Mind* (Philadelphia: A. Finley, 1819), 204–6.

10. Paine, *Examination of the Passages in the New Testament,* 7–8. For a good analysis of the Unitarian criticism of Paine's work, see Franklyn K. Prochaska, "Thomas Paine's The Age of Reason Revisited," *Journal of the History of Ideas* 33 (Oct.–Dec. 1972): 561–76.

11. Ann Taves, *Fits, Trances, and Visions: Experiencing Religion and Explaining Experience from Wesley to James* (Princeton, NJ: Princeton University Press, 1999); Elizabeth Reis, "Immortal Messengers: Angels, Gender, and Power in Early America," in Nancy Isenberg and Andrew Burstein, eds., *Mortal Remains: Death in Early America* (Philadelphia: University of Pennsylvania Press, 2003), 163–75; for a compelling discussion of the multiple versions of Ann Lee's life, see also Jean M. Humez, "'Ye Are My Epistles': The Construction of Ann Lee Imagery in Early Shaker Literature," *Journal of Feminist Studies in Religion* 8 (Spring 1992): 83–103.

12. The publication of Frederick's dreams reminds us that people of color were as likely as whites to be believed when it came to dream reports. See Frederic W. Swan, *Remarkable Visionary Dreams of a Mulatto Boy, in Northfield, Mass. by the Name of Frederic W. Swan, Aged Thirteen Years* (Chesterfield, NH: Joseph Merriam, 1822); *Columbian Magazine,* Oct. 1786; Mechal Sobel, *Teach Me Dreams: The Search for Self in the Revolutionary Era* (Princeton, NJ: Princeton University Press, 2000), 42–43, 47–48. Of the genre in general, see Ann Kirschner, "'Tending

to Edify, Astonish, and Instruct': Published Narratives of Spiritual Dreams and Visions in the Early Republic," *Early American Studies* (Spring 2003): 198–229.

13. It was Mitchill's encyclopedic, statistically overburdened *Picture of New-York* that in 1809 inspired the twenty-five-year-old satirist Washington Irving to pen *A History of New-York*, a high-spirited, pseudoscientific mock history of the Empire State. At Columbia, Dr. Mitchill had taught the author's older brother, Dr. Peter Irving, in the 1790s. See Andrew Burstein, *The Original Knickerbocker: The Life of Washington Irving* (New York: Basic Books, 2007), chap. 4.

14. Charles Mais, *The Surprising Case of Rachel Baker, Who Prays and Preaches in Her Sleep* (New York: n.p., 1814), 5–14, 17, 27–29. Venturing that somniloquism was something the medical profession was equipped to explain, Mitchill gave the example of an ostensibly baffling dream whose interpretation was actually easy and quite rational: "During a calamitous war," he wrote, "a farmer buried some pieces of gold in his field." He forgot where he had dug until fifteen years later, when he woke one night "in a fit of somnambulism, and went forth to the field." His wife found him with the gold in his hands and let him know he had been sleepwalking. Upon which, "he immediately related to her and the family the dream by which he was instructed where to find the precious metal, which he produced as proof of the correctness of his recollection during that dream."

15. Robley Dunglison, the personal physician of Thomas Jefferson, who taught medicine at the University of Virginia and in Philadelphia, published his *Dictionary of Medical Science* in the 1850s—a true compendium of the vocabulary of early American medical studies. In it, he defines "somnium" as "a confused assemblage . . . of ideas and images, which present themselves to the mind during sleep," attributing the coining of the term to Dr. Mitchill, who, in Dunglison's words, "used the word Somnium to signify the state between sleeping and waking, in which persons perform acts of which they are unconscious." See Dunglison, *Dictionary of Medical Science* (Philadelphia: Blanchard and Lea, 1860), 849.

16. *Devotional Somnium; or, a Collection of Prayers and Exhortations Uttered by Miss Rachel Baker* (New York: S. Marks/Van Winkle and Wiley, 1815), 29–32.

17. Daniel E. Williams, "Reckoned to Be Almost a Natural Fool: Textual Self-Construction in the Writings of Jonathan Plummer—No Hermaphrodite," *Early American Literature* 33 (1998): 149–72.

18. Undated letter of 1820, apparently to Elizabeth Way, New London, CT; Mary Way to Eliza Way Champlain, Feb. 17, 1821, in Way-Champlain Family Papers, AAS.

19. Eliza Way Champlain to Elizabeth Way Champlain, Oct. 10, 1822, in ibid.

20. Elizabeth Way Champlain to Eliza Way Champlain, undated letter, ca. Oct. 1822, and Jan. 26, 1823, in ibid.

21. Eliza Way Champlain to Elizabeth Way Champlain and Mary Way, May 18, 1825, in ibid.; Burstein, *America's Jubilee*, 105–7, 127–29.

22. Eliza Way Champlain to Edward Riley, Mar. 2, 1826, in Way-Champlain Family Papers, AAS.

23. Benjamin Rush to Julia Stockton, Dec. 2, 19, and 21, 1775, in *My Dearest Julia: The Love Letters of Dr. Benjamin Rush to Julia Stockton* (New York: Neale Watson Academic Publications, 1979), 25, 34–36. Rush belittles love, in theory, by comparing it to a friendship, rationally engaged and improved over time: "Love is founded in caprice, & is seated only in the imagination."

24. Eliza Way Champlain to Edward Riley, Apr. 19, 1826, in Way-Champlain Family Papers, AAS.

25. Eliza Way Champlain to Edward Riley, May 12, 1826, in ibid.

26. Robert Morrison, *The English Opium-Eater: A Biography of Thomas De Quincey* (New York: Pegasus Books, 2010), 9–12, 65, 81–82, 106–7; Thomas De Quincey, *Confessions of an English Opium-Eater*, ed. Barry Milligan (London: Penguin, 2003), 9, 19–26, 30–31.

27. De Quincey, *Confessions of an English Opium-Eater*, 47, 51. Compare Charles Baudelaire's 1851 "Du Vin et du Hachisch"; the poet, who translated De Quincey's *Confessions* into French, became addicted to opium after contracting syphilis. He marveled at the penetrating vividness of all drug-assisted hallucinations.

28. De Quincey, *Confessions of an English Opium-Eater*, 62–63, 68, 80–86; on the Malay, De Quincey's social snobbery and racial prejudice, and the fears of his wife, see Morrison, *The English Opium-Eater*, 187–88, 198.

29. Eliza Way Champlain to Edward Riley, May 12, 1826; to Mrs. Samuel M. Fitch, May 21, 1826, in Way-Champlain Family Papers, AAS.

30. Morrison, *The English Opium-Eater,* 110, 133.

31. Jennifer Ford, *Coleridge on Dreaming: Romanticism, Dreams and the Medical Imagination* (Cambridge, UK: Cambridge University Press, 1998), 33, 66, 133–36, 164–66, 181, 196. In her seminal study of the subject, Alethea Hayter wrote critically of Coleridge's claim: "his dreams were about his family and friends and his school, and very occasionally about historical or legendary figure. They contained practically no landscapes, and very little sense of place at all. . . . He occasionally dreamed words and sentences, and once some lines of poetry, but these were aphoristic or grotesque, not lyrical and evocative." See Hayter, *Opium and the Romantic Imagination* (London: Faber and Faber, 1968), 215. For a more recent discussion of how Coleridge exaggerated the dream-borne impetus behind "Kubla Khan," see Owen Flanagan, *Dreaming Souls: Sleep, Dreams, and the Evolution of the Conscious Mind* (New York: Oxford University Press, 2000), 186–88.

32. *The Works of Lord Byron* (Ware, UK: Wordsworth Editions, Ltd., 1994), 90–94. Evidencing the power poets had, take the case of Ralph Rylance, a failed Romantic who wished he could be another De Quincey and worm his way into the poets' circle. He wrote down dreams (professedly real) that featured his literary models: Shakespeare, Milton, Coleridge, Shelley, and Byron. "In this part of my dream," he wrote to a friend in 1818, "methought there came along the walk by the laurel hedge, a man of middle age, stout, well built, and of fair proportion, wearing doublet and hose of the fashion of Queen Elizabeth's day." All that survives of the dreamer's ambition is a crude notebook titled "Rylance's Visions." See Rylance to John Dovaston, Dec. 22, 1818, Department of Rare Books and Special Collections, Princeton University Library.

33. Lord Byron, *Childe Harold's Pilgrimage. Canto the Third* (London: J. Murray, 1816), 43, 77; *John Keats and Percy Bysshe Shelley* (New York: Modern Library, n.d.), 572; *The Journals of Mary Shelley,* ed. Paula R. Feldman and Diana Scott-Kilvert (Baltimore, MD: Johns Hopkins University Press, 1987), 118–19, 451–56; Flanagan, *Dreaming Souls,* 188–89; Ford, *Coleridge on Dreaming,* 99.

34. *Liberty Hall & Cincinnati Gazette,* Apr. 29, 1825; *New-London Gazette,* Oct. 27, 1824; "Literary Thermometer: A Dream," *City Gazette* (Charleston, SC), Sept. 22, 1825, reprinted from *New-York Mirror.*

35. Eliza Way Champlain to Edward Riley, May 12, 1826, in Way-Champlain Family Papers, AAS.

36. Lydia Richards to Charity Bryant, Apr. 14, 1811, and Mar. 15, 1815, Bryant-Drake Papers, Henry Sheldon Museum, Middlebury, VT. I am grateful to Rachel Hope Cleves for sharing her extensive research on these women.

37. Vaux to Wurts, Feb. 12, 1823, in Vaux Family Papers, HSP; "A Belief in Dreams," in *Philadelphia Album & Ladies Literary Gazette,* Dec. 4, 1830. Questions about the legal application of dream testimony were critically highlighted in a Vermont case. A decade before the Seixas episode, two individuals of the same family were convicted of murder based in part on someone's dream that the victim was buried under a particular tree. The shocking disinterment of a skeleton there made the defendants appear guilty; but years later, the alleged victim was identified as an asylum inmate in New Jersey. The justice system had leaped to conclusions about the identity of the skeleton. See "The Dead Alive!" *Providence Patriot,* Dec. 18, 1819.

38. Jane Bayard Kirkpatrick Journal, entry of Apr. 12, 1825, also Aug. 21 and Oct. 12, 1824, and Oct. 1, 1826, Special Collections and University Archives, Alexander Library, Rutgers University. I am grateful to Lucia McMahon for providing this valuable material, since published in McMahon, *Mere Equals: The Paradox of Educated Women in the Early American Republic* (Ithaca, NY: Cornell University Press, 2012).

39. Bert O. States, "Dream Bizarreness and Inner Thought," *Dreaming* 10 (Sept. 2000): 179–92.

CHAPTER 5: HENRY DAVID THOREAU GAINS EVIDENCE OF REINCARNATION

1. Entry of Mar. 9, 1846, in Caroline Lee Hentz diary, SHC; Johanna Nicol Shields, *Freedom in a Slave Society: Stories from the Antebellum South* (New York: Cambridge University Press, 2012), 39ff.; Charles Baudelaire, *On Wine and Hashish* (London: Hesperus, 2002), 41. An increased interest in dream representations and interpretation in France from the 1840s through the 1860s coincided with similar developments in the United States. See Stefanie Heraeus, "Artists

and the Dream in Nineteenth-Century Paris: Towards a Prehistory of Surrealism," *History Workshop Journal* 48 (1999): 151–68.

2. See Andrew Burstein, *The Original Knickerbocker: The Life of Washington Irving* (New York: Basic Books, 2007).

3. *The Complete Works of Washington Irving: Journals and Notebooks,* ed. Nathalia Wright et al., 5 vols. (Madison, WI, and Boston: Twayne Publishers and University of Boston Press, 1969–81), 3:254ff.

4. Ibid., 3:543–47.

5. Samuel Johnson, *Rasselas,* chaps. 26, 29, 32, and 44.

6. Lewis Gaylord Clark, ed., *The Literary Remains of the Late Willis Gaylord Clark* (New York: Burgess, Stringer, and Co., 1844), 66–67.

7. William Dunlap, *Thirty Years Ago; or, the Memoir of a Water Drinker* (New York: Bancroft & Holley, 1836), chap. 17.

8. Elizabeth G. Wirt to William Wirt, Dec. 26, 1825; William Wirt to Elizabeth G. Wirt, Dec. 27, 1825, in William Wirt Papers, Maryland Historical Society; Andrew Burstein, *America's Jubilee* (New York: Alfred A. Knopf, 2001), 49–50.

9. Salmon Chase Journal, in *The Salmon Chase Papers,* ed. John Niven, 5 vols. (Kent, OH: Kent State University Press, 1993), 1:93–94.

10. Ibid., 97–99.

11. Ibid., 102–3, 105, 109.

12. J. L. Comstock, *Outlines of Physiology, Both Comparative and Human* (New York: Robinson, Pratt, & Co., 1841), 206–7, 226–30.

13. Entry of May 2, 1835, in Jack Larkin and Caroline Sloat, eds., *"A Place in My Chronicle": A New Edition of the Diary of Christopher Columbus Baldwin, 1829–1835* (Worcester, MA: AAS, 2010). I thank Jack Larkin for directing me to this passage.

14. Comment regarding Coleridge is from a letter to his aunt, Dec. 29, 1829, in *Journals of Ralph Waldo Emerson,* ed. Edward Waldo Emerson and Waldo Emerson Forbes (Boston: Houghton Mifflin, 1909–14), 2:277; Robert Morrison, *The English Opium Eater: A Biography of Thomas De Quincey* (New York: Pegasus Books, 2010), 356.

15. *Journals of Ralph Waldo Emerson,* 2:284; "Demonology," in *Lectures and Biographical Sketches by Ralph Waldo Emerson* (Boston: Houghton Mifflin, 1904), 3–6.

16. Ibid.; *Journals of Ralph Waldo Emerson,* 2:448, 3:334, 3:532–33. Rudolph Kurz, a fur trapper who plied the western reaches of the Missouri River, in North Dakota, at mid-century, thought similarly. The rugged westerner went as deep as the New England thinker when he speculated on the "self-consciousness, intelligence, and sensibility" that made animals "kindred" to humans "in their mental faculties and feelings." They had their own form of speech and means of expressing thoughts through their eyes. Kurz wrote: "That a dog possesses the imaginative faculty is clearly shown by his actions while dreaming." All its mind lacked was an engagement with the unknown that humans felt. See *Journal of Rudolph Friedrich Kurz,* ed. J. N. B. Hewitt (Washington, D.C.: U.S. Government Printing Office, 1937), 52, 120, 163, 255, 322. Kurz lived from 1818 to 1871.

17. *Journals of Ralph Waldo Emerson,* 3:463; "Demonology," 7–9.

18. *The Journals and Miscellaneous Notebooks of Ralph Waldo Emerson,* ed. A. W. Plumstead and Harrison Hayford (Cambridge, MA: Harvard University Press, 1969), 7:327, 525; Jonathan Bishop, *Emerson on the Soul* (Cambridge, MA: Harvard University Press, 1964), 41.

19. *The Journals and Miscellaneous Notebooks of Ralph Waldo Emerson,* 7:544. In a dream he recorded many years later, on Oct. 24, 1866, Emerson noted that an obstinate youth "disliked my way of laughing."

20. Discontinuities always plagued him. For instance, "I struggled hard last night in a dream to repeat & save a thought or sentence spoken in the dream; but it eluded me at last." And again: "I wish I could recall my singular dream of last night with its physics, metaphysics, & rapid transformations,—all impressive at the moment, that on waking at midnight I tried to rehearse them, that I might keep them till morn. I fear 'tis all vanished." Or: "there is a rush from some quarter to break up the drama into a chaos of parts, then of particles, then of ether, like smoke dissolving in a wind." See various entries, Sept. 1, 1867, through 1872, in *The Journals and Miscellaneous Notebooks,* 16:70, 165, 177–78, 257.

21. Entry of Jan. 26, 1838, *Journals of Ralph Waldo Emerson,* 4:388.

22. The first chapter of Cooper's *The Pioneers* (1823) opens with genuflection before the "limpid lakes and thousand springs" of central New York State: "The mountains are generally arable to the tops, although instances are not wanting where the sides are jutted with rocks . . . neat and comfortable farms, with every indication of wealth about them, are scattered profusely through the vales, and even to the mountain tops. Roads diverge in every direction from the even and graceful bottoms of the valleys to the most rugged and intricate passes of the hills." This is inhabitable space, but it sounds like a dreamy "lost horizon." See James T. Callow, *Kindred Spirits: Knickerbocker Writers and American Artists, 1807–1855* (Chapel Hill, NC: University of North Carolina Press, 1967), chap. 5; Beth L. Lueck, *American Writers and the Picturesque Tour* (New York: Routledge, 1997); Andrew Burstein, *Sentimental Democracy* (New York: Hill & Wang, 1999), 281–82.

23. Matthew W. DeVoll, "Emerson and Dreams: Toward a Natural History of Intellect," *American Transcendental Quarterly* 18 (June 2004): 69–87; Bishop, *Emerson on the Soul.*

24. Bunyan was a staple in early Americans' private libraries, the dream allegory thus widely understood. The Philadelphia diarist Elizabeth Drinker had read *Pilgrim's Progress* three times before her 1798 dream of a dinner guest's choking on roast pork.

25. Nathaniel Hawthorne, *The Celestial Rail-Road; or, Modern Pilgrim's Progress* (Philadelphia: Merrihew and Thompson, 1844); Jerry A. Herndon, "Hawthorne's Dream Imagery," *American Literature* 46 (Jan. 1975): 538–45; *The Memoirs of Julian Hawthorne,* ed. Edith Garrigues Hawthorne (New York: Macmillan, 1938), 97–98, 205–6. For a different perspective on Emerson's thinking, stressing the worldliness, skepticism, and the "threat of illusion" in his later years' writings, see David M. Robinson, *Emerson and the Conduct of Life* (New York: Cambridge University Press, 1993).

26. Henry D. Thoreau, *A Week on the Concord and Merrimack Rivers* (Boston: James Munroe & Co., 1849). Were it not a literal dream that sparked the discussion, Thoreau surely would have embellished his prose for some purpose. Instead, he chose not to detail the argument or the vision, using the mere occasion of this particular dream to explain how it was that dreams served larger purposes in an individual's life.

27. Entry of Oct. 19, 1851, in *The Journal of Henry David Thoreau,* ed. Bradford Torrey and Francis H. Allen (Salt Lake City: Gibbs M. Smith, 1984), 3:80–81; Ednah D. Cheney, ed., *Louisa May Alcott: Her Life, Letters, and Journals* (Boston: Little, Brown, 1928), 29; Sarah Elbert, *A Hunger for Home: Louisa May Alcott and Little Women* (Philadelphia: Temple University Press, 1984), chap. 2.

28. Thoreau, *A Week on the Concord and Merrimack Rivers.*

29. Entry of Nov. 21, 1852, in *The Journal of Henry David Thoreau,* 4:415. Robert Moss tells of a tribe in eastern Bolivia that enumerates three souls, two of which can travel in dreams, even entering other times. See Moss, *The Secret History of Dreaming* (Novato, CA: New World Library, 2009), 5.

30. Entry of Oct. 29, 1857, in *Journal of Henry David Thoreau,* 10:141.

31. Entry of June 8, 1841, vol. 16, in Ichabod Cook Journals, AAS; *Macon Telegraph,* Aug. 28, 1830.

32. Entry of June 7, 1842, vol. 19, in Ichabod Cook Journals, AAS.

33. Entries of Mar. 1841, vol. 17, in ibid.

34. Andrea Rock, *The Mind at Night* (New York: Basic Books, 2004), 71–73.

35. Entry of May 4, 1841, vol. 17, in Ichabod Cook Journals, AAS.

36. *Religious Messenger* (Norwich, CT), July 16, 1831, and July 28, 1832.

37. Ichabod Cook, *A Brief Examination of Some of the Most Prevalent False Doctrines and Ceremonials of the Christian Sects* (Providence, RI: Knowles & Vose, 1847), 85, 147.

38. Ibid., 148–55.

39. "One Dream Better Than a Dozen Doctors," *Plattsburgh Republican,* Nov. 8, 1845.

40. George L. Prentiss, *The Life and Letters of Elizabeth Prentiss* (New York: Anson D. F. Randolph & Co., 1882), 44, 106 (letters of Jan. 14, 1841, and Mar. 3, 1847). Two years after the latter, Elizabeth was still seeing Abby in her dreams, now in the company of her own late mother: "They came together to see me," she wrote, "and both seemed so well and happy." Letter of Feb. 17, 1849, ibid., 114.

41. "Fanny" to Octavia Aurelia Wyche, Mar. 21, 1848, in Wyche-Otley Papers, SHC. In a letter written to another of her uncles not long after, Octavia underscores her interest in the life and poems of Lord Byron—in particular "the picture in private life"—suggesting that despite her youth, she is not averse to sexually tinged conversation, in ibid., June 10, 1848.

CHAPTER 6: CLAY DILLARD LEARNS A STRANGE LANGUAGE

1. Dell Upton, ed., *Madaline: Love and Survival in Antebellum New Orleans* (Athens, GA: University of Georgia Press, 1996), 93–95.
2. Ibid., 119.
3. Ibid., 121, 133–34.
4. Ibid., 26.
5. Ibid., 135–36, 145.
6. Ibid., 149, 157; Lord Byron, *Childe Harold's Pilgrimage. Canto the Third* (London: J. Murray, 1816), 19.
7. Upton, ed., *Madaline,* 186, 189–92.
8. Ibid., 218–26.
9. Ibid., 285, 326.
10. Ibid., 299, 301.
11. Entries of Apr. 1854 to June 1855, William George Scandlin Papers, AAS.
12. It is unclear whether Maria Edgeworth knew of the school. Its founder was North Carolina governor John Motley Morehead, a Whig politician from Greensboro who championed strong public schools. He does not seem to have known the author personally. Curiously, though, a different North Carolina teacher, with no ties to the school, struck up a correspondence with the famous author that blossomed into a rich friendship through the mails. Rachel Lazarus was the daughter of a successful businessman who lived in Warrenton, one hundred miles from Greensboro, and subsequently in Wilmington, even farther away from the Edgeworth school. In 1815, she wrote a piece of fan mail to the Irish author in praise of *Practical Education.* This led to a lively correspondence of some twenty-five years. Lazarus and Edgeworth exchanged books as well as detailed thoughts on the literature of their day, from Sir Walter Scott to Washington Irving. See Edgar E. MacDonald, ed., *The Education of the Heart: The Correspondence of Rachel Mordecai Lazarus and Maria Edgeworth* (Chapel Hill, NC: University of North Carolina Press, 1977); entry of Apr. 3, 1836, in Caroline Lee Hentz Diary, Hentz Family Papers, SHC; comparison of sales with J. F. Cooper, in Ronald J. Zboray, *A Fictive People: Antebellum Economic Development and the American Reading Public* (New York: Oxford University Press, 1993), Table 16, 165.
13. Mary Lewis Rucker Edmunds, *Letters from Edgeworth or the Southernization of Minna Alcott* (Greensboro, NC: Greensboro Preservation Society, 1988), 8–9, 13, 68–70. She is no apparent relation to Bronson or Louisa May Alcott.
14. This and subsequent diary entries are all part of a single volume, in C. Clay Dillard Papers, SHC.
15. *Annual Catalogue of the Teachers and Pupils of Edgeworth Female Seminary, Greensboro, N.C.* (Salisbury, NC: Miller & James, 1854); *Annual Catalogue of Edgeworth Female Seminary, Greensboro, N.C.* (Salisbury, NC: Bell & James, 1856).
16. *North Carolina Troops, 1861–1865: A Roster,* vol. 6, comp. Weymouth T. Jordan, Jr. (Raleigh, NC: North Carolina Office of Archives and History, 1977), 538, 639.
17. *Diary of Spencer Kellogg Brown, His Life in Kansas and His Death as a Spy, 1842–1863,* ed. George Gardner Smith (New York: D. Appleton & Co., 1903), 114ff.
18. "Faulkner Link to Plantation Diary Discovered," *New York Times,* Feb. 10, 2010.
19. Francis Leak Diary, Oct. 18, 1854, SHC.
20. B. F. Barrett, *Life of Emanuel Swedenborg* (New York: S. Colman, 1841); *A Sketch of Swedenborg, and Swedenborgians* (Boston: Otis Clapp, 1842), quotes at 7, 10; for a more profound examination of these cultural phenomena, connecting the earlier Coleridge–De Quincey mind-set to the Emerson, Hawthorne, and Poe points of view, see Bruce Mills, *Poe, Fuller, and the Mesmeric Arts: Transition States in the American Renaissance* (Columbia, MO: University of Missouri Press, 2006).

21. Diary, George N. Thurston Papers, LSU; Robert Stuart to Ellen Cairns Stuart, Oct. 31, 1856, in *Stuart Letters of Robert and Elizabeth Sullivan Stuart and Their Children, 1819–1864* (New York: privately printed, 1961), 2:763–64.

22. *Mollie: The Journal of Mollie Dorsey Sanford in Nebraska and Colorado Territories, 1857–1866* (Lincoln, NE: University of Nebraska Press, 1959), 32, 39.

23. Ibid., 48–49.

24. Ibid., 54–55.

25. Ibid., 68, 80.

26. Ibid., 84.

27. Ibid., 84–85.

28. Ibid., 109, 172–73. Mollie gave birth to a healthy boy on September 22, 1862—the day, she notes, that President Lincoln issued the Emancipation Proclamation. When Albert "Bertie" Sanford was a year old, she took him back to Nebraska to meet his grandfather. At her former log cabin home, she jotted down a simple rhyme: "Is it me? or am I dreaming? / Are these scenes to me but seeming?" Later in the war, the Sanfords bought a 160-acre ranch ten miles from Denver. Byron worked at the U.S. Mint and became a trustee of the University of Colorado; he lived eighty-eight years and died in 1914; Mollie, then seventy-six, lived just three months more. Ibid., 177, 180, 195.

29. Isaac Watts, *Divine and Moral Songs for Children* (Keene, NH: John Prentiss, 1805); *The Sunday School-Teacher's Dream* (Philadelphia: American Sunday School Union, 1837).

30. Entry of July 12, 1858, in Kimberly Harrison, ed., *A Maryland Bride in the Deep South: The Civil War Diary of Priscilla Bond* (Baton Rouge, LA: Louisiana State University Press, 2006), 75.

31. Elizabeth Emma Stuart to William Chapman Baker, Nov. 4, 1858, in *Stuart Letters*, 2:890.

32. "A Physician's Dreams," *Harper's Weekly* (Dec. 17, 1859): 810; Ann Fabian, *Card Sharps, Dream Books, and Bucket Shops: Gambling in 19th-Century America* (Ithaca, NY: Cornell University Press, 1990), 143–49.

33. Entry of May 10, 1847, in *William Clayton's Journal: A Daily Record of the Journey of the Original Company of Mormon Pioneers from Nauvoo, Illinois, to the Valley of the Great Salt Lake* (Salt Lake City: The Deseret News, 1921), 139–40.

34. Charles G. Leland, *The Poetry and Mystery of Dreams* (Philadelphia: E. H. Butler & Co., 1856), v–vi, 9.

35. Walt Whitman, "One's-Self I Sing," in *Leaves of Grass*. The poem begins: "One's-self I sing, a simple separate person."

36. See Tali Sharot, *The Optimism Bias: A Tour of the Irrationally Positive Brain* (New York: Pantheon, 2011).

CHAPTER 7: LINCOLN DREAMS HE'S DIED

1. "Singular Dream of Mr. Calhoun," first published in Lippard's weekly, the *Quaker City;* subsequently reprinted in his collection, *The White Banner* 1 (1851): 118–20. The piece is one of a dozen "Legends" in *The White Banner* and is followed by a kind of parable, "Brotherhood Versus Atheistic Sectarism," which also opens with a manufactured dream. Clearly, Lippard was not trying to convince anyone that Calhoun's dream was to be taken literally. It was his trademark to mingle historical fact with dramatic license; in *The Battle-Day of Germantown* (Philadelphia: A. H. Diller, 1843), he detoured from the fog of Revolutionary battle to tell a ghost story: "And as the battle draws to a crisis . . . , let me for a moment turn aside from the path of regular history, and notice some of the legends of the battlefield" (18).

2. *Wisconsin Democrat*, Mar. 9, 1850; Eliza Green Reid to Mrs. Andrew P. [Margaret Green] Calhoun, Mar. 25, 1850, in *The Papers of John C. Calhoun*, ed. Clyde N. Wilson and Shirley Bright Cook (Columbia, SC: University of South Carolina Press, 2003), 27:242–43.

3. George Lippard, *The Quaker City* (Philadelphia: Leary, Stuart, & Co., 1876), 312–14.

4. "Resolutions Dictated to Joseph A. Scoville by John C. Calhoun a Few Days Before His Death," in *Papers of John C. Calhoun*, 27:245; E.W. Huntington to John McLean, June 15, 1850, as cited in Charles Wiltse, *John C. Calhoun, Sectionalist, 1840–1850* (Indianapolis: Bobbs-Merrill, 1951), 479.

5. Randall Fuller, *From Battlefields Rising: How the Civil War Transformed American Literature* (New York: Oxford University Press, 2011), 34–42.

6. *A Plantation Mistress on the Eve of the Civil War: The Diary of Keziah Goodwyn Hopkins Brevard, 1800–1861,* ed. John Hammond Moore (Columbia, SC: University of South Carolina Press, 1993), 7–11, 22, 24.

7. Ibid., 65–66, 108–10, 115.

8. Edward E. Baptist, "Dreams So Real: Secession and Fantasy Fiction," unpublished paper, 2004, courtesy of the author, a professor of history at Cornell University.

9. Statement of purpose in the *American Theological Review* (May 1859): 326–33; "The Moral Aspects of the Present Struggle," in *American Theological Review* (October 1861): 710; *Henry Boynton Smith: His Life and Work,* ed. Elizabeth Lee Allen Smith (New York: A. C. Armstrong & Son, 1881), quotes at 90, 230, 251.

10. Tayler Lewis, "The Two Schools of Philosophy," *American Theological Review* (Jan. 1862): 102–35; biographical information on the author from his obituary in the *New York Times,* May 13, 1877.

11. Ward Hill Lamon, *Recollections of Abraham Lincoln, 1847–1865,* ed. Dorothy Lamon Teillard (Washington, D.C.: Dorothy Lamon Teillard, 1911), 266–67; Douglas L. Wilson, *Honor's Voice: The Transformation of Abraham Lincoln* (New York: Alfred A. Knopf, 1998), 188–89.

12. Speech before Congress, Jan. 12, 1848, in Abraham Lincoln Papers, Library of Congress (accessed online); Wilson, *Honor's Voice,* 188–93, 197–98. Here, Wilson also describes Lincoln's attachment to Byron's *Childe Harold's Pilgrimage.*

13. Lamon, *Recollections of Abraham Lincoln,* 111–13.

14. Helen M. Rauschnabel to Mary Todd Lincoln, May 7, 1861, Abraham Lincoln Papers, Library of Congress, transcribed and annotated by the Lincoln Studies Center, Knox College, Galesburg, IL.

15. "General M'Clellan's Dream," Library of Congress, Printed Ephemera (Broadside), portfolio 236; repeated almost verbatim in the *Easton* [MD] *Gazette,* Feb. 1, 1862. After the war, when he was running for president, General Ulysses Grant was said (in the same manufactured format) to have had a dream in which the late President Lincoln appeared to him. See *General Grant's Dream! A Singular and Startling Occurrence* (Philadelphia: C. W. Alexander, 1868), broadside at LCP.

16. Custer to Lydia Ann Reed and David Reed, July 13, 1862, in George Armstrong Custer Papers in the Elizabeth Bacon Custer collection, Little Bighorn National Monument. I am most grateful to T. J. Stiles for sharing his research on the Custers and sending this fascinating dream.

17. Mary Ware Allen Johnson to Harriet Hall Johnson, Aug. 5, 1861, in Allen-Johnson Family Papers, AAS.

18. Entry of Sept. 9, 1861, in *Journals and Miscellaneous Notebooks of Ralph Waldo Emerson* (Cambridge, MA: Harvard University Press, 1960–82), 15:146–47.

19. Entry of Jan. 9, 1862, in ibid., 158.

20. Charles Tenney to Adelaide Case, Jan. 1, 9, 13, and 23, 1862, in Tenney-Case Papers, UVA.

21. Adelaide Case to Charles Tenney, Feb. 18, 25, Mar. 1, 1862, in ibid.

22. Charles Tenney to Adelaide Case, Feb. 15, July 4, and Oct. 23, 1862; Adelaide Case to Charles Tenney, May 27, 1862, Jan. 7 and 15, 1863, in ibid.

23. Entry of Jan. 21, 1863, in *The Journal of Louisa May Alcott,* ed. Joel Myerson and Daniel Shealy (Athens, GA: University of Georgia Press, 1997), 116–17; Martha Saxton, *Louisa May: A Modern Biography of Louisa May Alcott* (Boston: Houghton Mifflin, 1977), chap. 14.

24. Thomas R. R. Cobb to Marion Lumpkin Cobb, Feb. 12, 1861, in *The Correspondence of Thomas Reade Rootes Cobb, 1860–1862* (Washington, D.C.: Southern History Association, 1907).

25. "A Singular Prophecy," first appearing in the *Mobile Advertiser,* as reported in the *Daily True Delta* (New Orleans), Apr. 5, 1862; see also *Staunton* [VA] *Spectator,* Apr. 15, 1862.

26. *Saturday Evening Gazette,* Apr. 25, 1863; *Richmond Examiner,* June 24, 1864.

27. George Pickett to LaSalle Corbell Pickett, Apr. 15, 1863, in *The Heart of a Soldier, as Revealed in the Intimate Letters of General George Pickett* (New York: Seth Moyle, 1913). Pickett admitted in the same letter home that General Grant's numbers were far superior, that the South's ports were closed to the world, and that the cause remained uncertain. This was two months before Gettysburg and the brutal onslaught for which history knows him best. On July 3, 1863, the

usually cautious general accepted the order to send his men across open field to be mowed down by Union rifles and artillery.

28. Edward Binns, *The Anatomy of Sleep* (London: John Churchill, 1842), 1, 31, 204–13; "A Strange Dream," in *Daily Gazette and Comet,* Oct. 16, 1860.

29. Binns, *The Anatomy of Sleep,* 295, 387; Gerald F. Linderman, *Embattled Courage: The Experience of Combat in the American Civil War* (New York: Free Press, 1987), 102–13.

30. Elliott Ashkenazi, ed., *The Civil War Diary of Clara Solomon: Growing Up in New Orleans, 1861–1862* (Baton Rouge, LA: Louisiana State University Press, 1995), 99, 122–27, 427–29.

31. Sarah Hildreth Butler to Blanche Butler Ames, Apr. 1865, in *Chronicles from the Nineteenth Century: Family Letters of Blanche Butler and Adelbert Ames* (Clinton, MA: privately published, 1957), 1:109–10.

32. Mary D. Robertson, ed., *Lucy Breckinridge of Grove Hill: The Journal of a Virginia Girl* (Kent, OH: Kent State University Press, 1979), 93–98, 115, 124, 140, 181–82. Nancy E. Moore, a pacifist and Shaker in Kentucky, recorded the dreams of members of her community: a February 1863 dream of Lucetta Buchanan featured "beautiful well formed fruit Trees full of ripe fruit which was of a clear transparent whiteness about the size of our Binford Peaches, but they were not peaches." As the dream proceeds, she imagines the taste of the mysterious fruit ("so good and extremely delightful") and wishes to share it with neighbors. Dreams of fields of corn (denoting specific locations, as "on the south side," etc.) and other products of their environment distinguish the Shaker community of dreamers, who believed that news sometimes reached them, "before it came to the newspapers," by way of "a spiritual Telegraph." Ibid., v, 125, 145. See *The Journal of Eldress Nancy,* ed. Mary Julia Neal (Nashville, TN: Parthenon Press, 1963), 105.

33. Tom Wylie Neal, Hazen, AR, "Born in Slavery: Slaves Narratives from the Federal Writers' Project," Arkansas Narratives, vol. 2, part 5; Nancy J. Fairley, "Dreaming Ancestors in Eastern Carolina," *Journal of Black Studies* 33 (May 2003): 545–61; Mechal Sobel, *Teach Me Dreams: The Search for Self in the Revolutionary Era* (Princeton, NJ: Princeton University Press, 2000), 42–43. Sobel reports on a white Moravian minister in North Carolina in the 1830s who complained that blacks based their conversions "so much on dreams, visions, and other fantasies." Ibid., 240.

34. Charles Ball, *Fifty Years in Chains* (Mineola, NY: Dover, 1970), 39. First published in 1836.

35. C. L. Innes, ed., *Slave Life in Virginia and Kentucky: A Narrative by Francis Fedric, Escaped Slave* (Baton Rouge, LA: Louisiana State University Press, 2010), 86–87. Two versions of Fedric's life were published on the eve of, and during, the Civil War.

36. John Randolph to John Brockenbrough, Feb. 24, 1820, in Kenneth Shorey, ed., *Collected Letters of John Randolph of Roanoke to Dr. John Brockenbrough* (New Brunswick, NJ: Transaction Books, 1988), 27; Robert Dawidoff, *The Education of John Randolph* (New York: Anson D. F. Randolph & Co., 1979), 63; Andrew Burstein, *America's Jubilee* (New York: Alfred A. Knopf, 2001), 172–73, 191. "Shame and manly pride went hand in hand," wrote Eugene Genovese of the planter mind-set; on the subject of paternalism, widely discussed by historians, start with Genovese, *Roll, Jordan, Roll: The World the Slaves Made* (New York: Pantheon Books, 1974), 87ff., quote at 122.

37. E. Thomas, *A Concise View of the Slavery of the People of Colour in the United States* (Philadelphia: E. Thomas, 1834), 27–28.

38. *Wooster* [OH] *Republican,* Nov. 12, 1863; Scott E. Casper, *Constructing American Lives: Biography and Culture in Nineteenth-Century America* (Chapel Hill, NC: University of North Carolina Press, 1999), 257–62; *Crete and James: Personal Letters of Lucretia and James Garfield,* ed. John Shaw (East Lansing, MI: Michigan State University Press, 1994), 48–53. Demonstrating his penchant for suggestive moods, reveries, and illusions, Garfield wrote to his future wife on November 10, 1855: "I alone here in my quiet room—the light from my open stove is dancing out and painting fantastic shapes on the further side of the room and I sitting here indulging in the reveries which their shadowy shapes suggest and yearning to share them and the scene with you." Ibid., 56.

39. Charles Tenney to Adelaide Case, Apr. 11, 1862, in Tenney-Case Papers, UVA.

40. *The Farmer's Cabinet,* Mar. 27, 1862; entry of July 6, 1863, in Charles F. Herberger, ed., *A Yankee at Arms: The Diary of Augustus D. Ayling, 29th Massachusetts Volunteers* (Knoxville, TN: University of Tennessee Press, 1999), 126; Hampton Smith, ed., *Brother of Mine: The Civil*

War Letters of Thomas and William Christie (St. Paul, MN: Minnesota Historical Society Press, 2011), 8, 206.

41. *Salem Register,* Oct. 19, 1863.

42. *North American,* July 11, 1863 (a Philadelphia paper, citing a Cleveland source); *Arrest and Trial of Frederick F. Streeter, for the Murder of the Coy Family with an Account of His Escape from Prison, His Subsequent Recapture, and Some Incidents of His Life* (Medina County, OH: Gazette Print, 1864).

43. "Private Journal of Sarah L. Wadley," entry of Aug. 6, 1863, SHC.

44. *Journal of Eldress Nancy,* 201. The understated emotion in this dream contrasts with that of a male member of the sober Shaker community, who, a short time before, told a dream of panic. He had to rescue a brother who had been dispatched on the river with one hundred bushels of potatoes to market, but who he sensed was in trouble. The boat had sprung a leak and was sinking. Ibid., 188.

45. Thomas Spight to Virginia Barnett, Feb. 6, 1865, McCain Library, University of Southern Mississippi, Hattiesburg, MS; William F. Brand to Kate Armentrout, Jan. 21 and Apr. 10, 1864, in William F. Brand Papers, UVA and *The Valley of the Shadow* (valley.lib.virginia. edu); Donald C. Maness and H. Jason Combs, *Do They Miss Me at Home? The Civil War Letters of William McKnight, Seventh Ohio Volunteer Cavalry* (Athens, OH: Ohio University Press, 2010), 128–30; similarly, see Mauriel Phillips Joslyn, *Charlotte's Boys: Civil War Letters of the Branch Family of Savannah* (Berryville, VA: Rockbridge Publishing, 1996), 175–273. Columbus Sykes, a Mississippi soldier, saw his dreams about the sweet home life left behind as a sign of weakness, believing his mind should be fixed on destroying "the hated foe." See Ted Ownby, "Patriarchy in the World Where There Is No Parting? Power Relations in the Confederate Heaven," in Catherine Clinton, ed., *Southern Families at War: Loyalty and Conflict in the Civil War South* (New York: Oxford University Press, 2000), 229-44.

46. *Plain Dealer,* Nov. 5, 1863.

47. *Chronicles from the Diary of a War Prisoner in Andersonville and Other Military Prisons of the South in 1864* (Wichita, KS: J. W. Northrup, 1904), entry of July 13, 1864; John L. Ransom, *Andersonville Diary, Escape, and List of the Dead* (Auburn, NY: John L. Ransom, 1881), 14, 58; Linderman, *Embattled Courage,* 258–60.

48. *Diary of Gideon Welles, Secretary of the Navy under Lincoln and Johnson* (Boston: Houghton Mifflin, 1911), 2:273, 278–83.

49. Lamon, *Recollections of Abraham Lincoln,* 114–19, 279–81; Kenneth Cmiel, *Democratic Eloquence: The Fight over Popular Speech in Nineteenth-Century America* (Berkeley, CA: University of California Press, 1990), 59–60, 116–18; Garry Wills, *Lincoln at Gettysburg: The Words that Remade America* (New York: Simon & Schuster, 1992). I have given Lamon's account credence in most instances, in consultation with Professor Douglas L. Wilson, who regards Lamon as essentially truthful. There are certainly Lincoln scholars who are suspect of Lamon's narrative, but Wilson is convinced that the substance of Lincoln's dreams, as recorded, are true.

50. *Crete and James,* 44–48.

51. Ibid., 80–81, 207, 210, 217–18; Theodore Clarke Smith, *The Life and Letters of James Abram Garfield* (New Haven, CT: Yale University Press, 1925); Candice Millard, *Destiny of the Republic: A Tale of Medicine, Madness, and the Murder of a President* (New York: Doubleday, 2011), 87, 90, 122.

52. *The Salmon P. Chase Papers,* ed. John Niven, 5 vols. (Kent, OH: Kent State University Press, 1993–98), 1:528–30, 665, 695, 701; on Dr. Perry, and Kate and William Sprague, see James P. McClure et al., eds., *"Spur Up Your Pegasus": Family Letters of Salmon, Kate, and Nettie Chase, 1844–1873* (Kent, OH: Kent State University Press, 2009).

53. Lucius P. Mox to Jennie, Apr. 30, 1865, Pennsylvania Historical and Museum Commission, Harrisburg, PA, via *The Valley of the Shadow* (valley.lib.virginia.edu).

CHAPTER 8: MARK TWAIN CAN'T RESIST A MUSHY APPLE PIE

1. Ednah D. Cheney, ed., *Louisa May Alcott: Her Life, Letters and Journals* (Boston: Little, Brown, 1928), 203–4; for an excellent analysis of Alcott's state of mind, see Roberta Seelinger Trites,

Twain, Alcott, and the Birth of the Adolescent Reform Novel (Iowa City, IA: University of Iowa Press, 2007), which conveniently links two prominent authors whose dreams are independently discussed in this chapter.

2. *The Journals and Miscellaneous Notebooks of Ralph Waldo Emerson,* ed. William H. Gilman et al. (Cambridge, MA: Harvard University Press, 1960–82), 16:126–27.

3. Ibid., 172–73.

4. Ibid., 177–78, 257. Recall, in "Demonology," the combatant metaphor: "We call the phantoms that rise [in dreams], the creation of our fancy, but they act like mutineers, and fire on their commander."

5. Samuel L. Clemens to Olivia Langdon, Dec. 19–20,1868, and May 13 and 24, 1869, in Mark Twain Papers (Bancroft Library, University of California, Berkeley), accessed online at www.marktwainproject.org. In the postbellum decades, courtship letters, North and South, systematically invoked the dream motif, often mixing metaphorical hopes and dreams with actual dreams. For instance, trying to impress Cora "Dixie" Bailey in southwest Virginia, Robert Talbert mock complained about his unconsummated dreams proving "phosferescent, a light without heat"; he wished Cora "sweet dreams," and she in turn bade him "dream of what you fancy." A month before they were wed, still living miles apart, he again expresses angst, this time: "the current of my life moves on undisturbed" except "while I was dreaming of you." Such expressions were meant to suggest that dream time was altered time. Letters of 1886–87, in "Love Is Our Penman," unpublished typescript, Washington County Historical Society, Abingdon, VA.

6. Clemens to Langdon, May 13 and 24, 1869, in Mark Twain Papers.

7. Clemens to Langdon, Dec. 14, 1869, in ibid.

8. On the relationship between feelings and reactions, memory and desire, see Antonio Damasio, *Looking for Spinoza: Joy, Sorrow, and the Feeling Brain* (New York: Harcourt, 2003), esp. 49–57, 91–96. Dr. Damasio explains that some sensations that are not shown outwardly are nonetheless deeply felt: "Feelings are not a passive perception or a flash in time" (quote at 92).

9. *Autobiography of Mark Twain,* vol. 1, ed. Harriet Elinor Smith (Berkeley, CA: University of California Press, 2010), 270–73; on Perkins, see *Illustrated Popular Biography of Connecticut,* comp. J. A. Spalding (Hartford, CT: Press of the Case: Lockwood and Brainard Company, 1891), 104. Gregg Camfield offers a good explanation attesting to the essential honesty of Twain's autobiography; see Camfield, *Sentimental Twain: Samuel Clemens in the Maze of Moral Philosophy* (Philadelphia: University of Pennsylvania Press, 1994), 220–27. The indigestion explanation, so often evoked since the eighteenth century, continued to be advanced at this time; see also "Dreams and Their Causes," *Anderson Intelligencer* [Anderson Courthouse, SC], Nov. 24, 1870, which added to the general understanding the results of recent experiments: "A pair of tweezers was held a little distance from [the dreamer's] ear, and struck with a pair of scissors. He dreamed that he heard the ringing of bells." And thus, "one very important class of our dreams is due to our bodily sensations."

10. *Autobiography of Mark Twain,* 274–76.

11. Clemens to William Dean Howells, Nov. 17, 1878, in Mark Twain Papers.

12. Alexander E. Jones, "Mark Twain and Sexuality," *PMLA* 71 (Sept. 1956): 595–616; Camfield, *Sentimental Twain,* chap. 4; Harold K. Bush, Jr., *Mark Twain and the Spiritual Crisis of His Age* (Tuscaloosa: University of Alabama Press, 2007), esp. chap. 7. For interview comments on nakedness, see *Mark Twain: The Complete Interviews,* ed. Gary Scharnhorst (Tuscaloosa: University of Alabama Press, 2006), 562–63.

13. *Harper's,* Dec. 1912. This story was rejected by three separate magazines during Twain's lifetime. See Everett Emerson, *Mark Twain: A Literary Life* (Philadelphia: University of Pennsylvania Press, 2000), 244, 273–74, quote at 273; idem, *The Authentic Mark Twain: A Literary Biography of Samuel L. Clemens* (Philadelphia: University of Pennsylvania Press, 1984), 221–22; Jeffrey L. Duncan, "The Empirical and the Ideal in Mark Twain," *PMLA* 95 (Mar. 1980): 201–12.

14. Lee Clark Mitchell, "Lines, Circles, Time Loops, and Mark Twain's *A Connecticut Yankee in King Arthur's Court,*" *Nineteenth-Century Literature* 54 (Sept. 1999): 230–48; Ann Taves, *Fits, Trances, and Visions: Experiencing Religion and Explaining Experience* (Princeton, NJ: Princeton University Press, 1999), 226ff.

15. *The Memoirs of Julian Hawthorne,* ed. Edith Garrigues Hawthorne (New York: Macmillan, 1938), 122.

16. Gerald E. Myers, *William James: His Life and Thought* (New Haven, CT: Yale University Press, 1986), chap. 12; Linda Simon, *Genuine Reality: A Life of William James* (New York: Harcourt Brace, 1998); Deborah Blum, *Ghost Hunters: William James and the Search for Scientific Proof of Life after Death* (New York: Penguin Press, 2006); Taves, *Fits, Trances, and Visions,* 253–58; John J. Cerullo, *The Secularization of the Soul: Psychical Research in Modern Britain* (Philadelphia: Institute for the Study of Human Issues, 1982).

17. William James to Alice Howe Gibbens James, June 26, 1885; to Catharine Walsh, June 28 and July 11, 1885, in *The Correspondence of William James,* ed. Ignas K. Skrupskelis and Elizabeth M. Berkeley (Charlottesville, VA: University of Virginia Press, 1992–), 6:40–44; Simon, *Genuine Reality,* 195–99.

18. J. E. Kimball, to Isaiah T. Williams, Oct. 24, 1885; undated letter from Cosmic Club, Isaiah T. Williams Papers, NYPL.

19. Martha U. Osgood to Williams, 1879 [no month], Oct. 13, 1879, June 22, 1880, Aug. 28, 1881, Aug. 29 and Sept. 30, 1882; poem contained in a letter from the 1880s is undated but can be traced to the international press circa 1851. All in Isaiah T. Williams Papers, NYPL.

20. *Elevator,* Nov. 1, 1867. Presumably, the *Elevator* was meant to elevate the mind. Whether it did so, or pandered more to the popular imagination, is open to debate. It confirmed, at least, what had come into Sam Clemens's mind around the same time, when he had a hellish dream, thought he had lost his darling Livy, and told her the next day that he believed it entirely possible that a life-testing dream of that ilk could turn hair white overnight.

21. *North American* (Philadelphia), Nov. 18, 1891.

22. T. J. Stiles, *The First Tycoon: The Epic Life of Cornelius Vanderbilt* (New York: Alfred A. Knopf, 2009), 277, 560.

23. Margaret Dickins to Francis Dickins, Oct. 1883, in Francis A. Dickins Papers, SHC. Similarly, see "The Land of Dreams," in *Pittsburg Dispatch,* Apr. 7, 1889, reporting on a man who dreamt that his wife was injured in a buggy accident, which then occurred, precisely as dreamt, the following day; the dreamer died in the months following.

24. "A Horrible Dream. A Railroad Man Quits the Road to Avoid Killing His Wife," *Philadelphia News,* as reprinted in the *Washington Bee,* June 23, 1888; "A Presentiment in a Dream," *Daily Globe* (St. Paul, MN), June 8, 1879.

25. *Chicago Times,* July 3, 1888; *Biographical Directory of the American Congress* (Washington, D.C.: U.S. Government Printing Office, 1950), 1681. Pierce's dream-infused poetic ads also appeared in small-town papers, such as the *Nicodemus Cyclone.* Nicodemus was a community in north-central Kansas, formed after the war by a group of ex-slaves. "Pierce's Pleasant Purgative Pellets" were manufactured at a Buffalo, New York, laboratory. They were herbal, and Dr. Pierce offered a $500 reward to anyone who could detect any injurious ingredient. See *Nicodemus Cyclone,* Feb. 3, Mar. 16, and May 1, 1888; *New York Times,* Feb. 25, 1876.

26. *Dodge City Times,* June 5, 1880; "Hints from Beyond," *National Republican,* Aug. 30, 1884.

27. *The Climax* (Richmond, KY), Nov. 20, 1889.

28. *Daily Picayune,* Sept. 24, 1880.

29. *Diary of Annie L. Van Ness, 1864–1881* (Alexandria, VA: Alexander Street Press, 2004), entry of Dec. 1864; Emily P. Beale to Dr. Horace Binney Hare, Feb. 18, 1868, and M. Coxe to unknown recipient, "Emily's Dream—Private & Confidential," undated, both in Hare-Willing Family Papers, APS; Blanche Butler Ames to Adelbert Ames, May 24, 1870, in *Chronicles from the Nineteenth Century: Family Letters of Blanche Butler and Adelbert Ames, Married July 21, 1870* (Clinton, MA: privately published, 1957), 1:140–41.

30. "The Land of Dreams," in *National Tribune,* Jan. 14, 1882.

31. *"A Secret to Be Burried": The Diary and Life of Emily Hawley Gillespie, 1858–1888,* ed. Judy Nolte Lensink (Iowa City, IA: University of Iowa Press, 1989), 309, 343.

32. *Wichita Daily Eagle,* Aug. 9, 1890.

33. James Sully, *Illusions: A Psychological Study* (New York: D. Appleton and Company, 1891), 38–40 and chap. 7. This book was first printed in London in 1881; *Sensation and Intuition,* in 1874.

34. *The Memoirs of Julian Hawthorne,* 154–59.

35. Wordsworth shared a draft of this poem with fellow Romantic Samuel Coleridge in the early years of the nineteenth century, a time when they collaborated and regularly compared notes. His ode opens with nostalgic celebration of innocent youth, "when meadow, grove, and stream" seemed to reflect "the glory and the freshness of a dream." Purer visions are lost as the child becomes a man. Later in the same poem, Wordsworth contributes that quotable couplet: "Whither is it fled, the visionary gleam? / Where is it now, the glory and the dream?"

36. Julian Hawthorne, *A Dream and a Forgetting* (Chicago, New York, and San Francisco: Belford, Clarke, & Co., 1888).

37. *Evening World,* Mar. 5, 1889; Cazenovia Junior College for Women, William Reddy, W. S. Smyth, *First 50 Years of Cazenovia Seminary, 1825–1875* (Cazenovia, NY: n.p., 1877), 238.

38. "A Dream and Vision, with Queries," reprinted from the *London Magazine,* in *Scots Magazine* 27 (June 1765): 308–9.

39. "Seen in Sleep," *Evening World,* Feb. 15, 1889. The subheading for this article reads: "The Crop of Dreams Still Packs Our Mail-Bags."

40. A. Brierre de Boismont, *On Hallucinations: A History and Explanation of Apparitions, Visions, Dreams, Ecstasy, Magnetism, and Somnambulism* (London: Henry Renshaw, 1859), 177ff. The first American edition was published in 1853. In "Dreams That Come True," the *Sacramento Daily Union* reported (Dec. 15, 1889) on the historical dream of the "ill-fated ship," by way of illustrating the real possibility that too many respectable people have experienced "remarkable revelations and warnings in visions" for all such testimony to be without merit. "Granting that ghost stories are sometimes the product of imagination or indigestion," the article opened, "there are many records of supernatural appearances and revelations which seem to defy skepticism."

41. Anna Bonus Kingsford, *Dreams and Dream-Stories* (London: George Redway, 1888). The author died at age forty-two, just before the book's publication. Unfortunately, her literary style is such that it is not always possible to separate raw dream reports from the embellished.

42. Daniel L. Schacter, *The Seven Sins of Memory: How the Mind Forgets and Remembers* (Boston: Houghton Mifflin, 2001), 88–90; Myers, *William James,* chap. 6.

43. *The Life Story and Personal Reminiscences of Col. John Sobieski* (Shelbyville, IL: Douthit & Son, 1900), 279–80. Similarly, "Francis Meeks, a negro boy, 18, died suddenly [in his sleep]. . . . During the night the boy's mother dreamed that he was dead, and awoke to find her dream true." See "Dreamed of Dreaming the Truth," *Daily Morning Astorian* [OR], Oct. 14, 1885.

44. "Murder Seen in a Dream," based on a dispatch to the *St. Louis Republic,* as reported in the *Times-Picayune* (New Orleans), Sept. 9, 1899. Once again, the concept was not new; see, for example, "Most Singular Discovery of a Murder by Dreaming," *Morning Post* (London), July 21, 1818, in which a woman stopped the drowning of a child in a privy by dreaming of it as it was happening. Countless prophetic dreams found the way into U.S. papers in the 1880s and 1890s. See also "Mental Phenomena: Remarkable Dreams That Have Come True," *Salt Lake Herald,* June 17, 1888, which collects reports from a number of places around the country.

EPILOGUE

1. These are the questions examined by Kenneth C. Bausch in "Visions, Hallucinations, and Dreams in the Context of Body Wisdom and Chaos Theory," *NeuroQuantology* 9 (Mar. 2011): 129–34. Bausch is a former priest and current systems science scholar who uses chaos theory to explain how random elements enter our thoughts and suggest solutions to life's concerns. Because we talk to ourselves in ways other than verbal, he says, we can understand where faith comes from by studying that which is drawn from the "chaotic unconscious." One way or another, we derive our perceptions of the world and our place in it from conversations that are beyond the conventionally verbal, which is another reason that dreams are useful as historical artifacts. On the implications of dream creativity, see Gordon G. Globus, *Dream Life, Wake Life: The Human Condition through Dreams* (Albany, NY: SUNY Press, 1987), esp. 56–62.

2. Owen Flanagan, *Dreaming Souls: Sleep, Dreams and the Conscious Mind* (New York: Oxford University Press, 2000), 8, 40–46, 51, 136–37, 143, 148–49, 153. The fanciful dream imagery we identify as the brain's sleepy-time concoction is not the only illusion that tampers with the "real" self. When we write down our dreams, fully awake, we do not see how we impose a

narrative form on what, in its essence, may lack the structure or connectedness that our wide-awake brain attributes to it. In the end, Dr. Flanagan describes the brain as "the seat of our soul whether we are asleep or awake," a conclusion that is not vastly different from common understandings in the early years of the nation.

3. F. H. Matthews, "The Americanization of Sigmund Freud: Adaptations of Psychoanalysis before 1917," *Journal of American Studies* 1 (Apr. 1967): 39–62; Peter Gay, *Freud: A Life for Our Time* (New York: W. W. Norton, 1988), 206–12. In Europe, only 351 copies of *The Interpretation of Dreams* sold in the first two years of the twentieth century; Freud himself was fixated on the negative reviews, underplaying the complimentary ones. See Louis Breger, *Freud: Darkness in the Midst of Vision* (New York: John Wiley & Sons, 2000), 148–49.

4. Howard Markel, *An Anatomy of Addiction: Sigmund Freud, William Halsted, and the Miracle Drug Cocaine* (New York: Pantheon, 2011).

5. Maureen Perkins, "The Meaning of Dream Books," *History Workshop Journal* 48 (Autumn 1999): 102–13; Peter D. Kramer, *Freud: Inventor of the Modern Mind* (New York: HarperCollins, 2006), chap. 6. In 1899, Freud wrote to a colleague: "A theory of sexuality may be the immediate successor to the dream book." See Breger, *Freud: Darkness in the Midst of Vision*, 147. Or as dream therapist Rodger Kamenetz puts it: "From Genesis to Freud, interpretation always writes over the dream." See Kamenetz, *The History of Last Night's Dream* (New York: HarperCollins, 2007), 11.

6. Matthews, "The Americanization of Sigmund Freud," 54–60.

7. Ernest Hartmann, *Dreams and Nightmares: The New Theory on the Origin and Meaning of Dreams* (New York: Plenum Press, 1998), 239–41. This is what relates the literal dream to the enriched metaphor of the American Dream (or the evolution of America's romantic self-image). But in terms of ethical awareness, we are only marginally better off than the nineteenth century—left to puzzle through our personal being-ness as we argue the attributes of national identity.

8. Both the nineteenth and twentieth centuries understood the pursuit of happiness through a literature steeped in medical vocabulary and states of mind. Romantic novels inherited from the medical Enlightenment the ideal of imaginative "fellow feeling" (sustained by a healthy balance within the sympathetic nervous system), while threats to the mind's composure loomed ominously over protagonists' thoughts and actions. Stock characters included the susceptible young woman in need of protection, the resilient man of feeling, and his opposite, the libidinous rake; these types were succeeded by the courageous frontiersman, the noble savage, the reformed bad boy, etc. Twain was among the last of notable American authors to indulge nostalgia for a simpler America, as the scientific skepticism of modern society took control of his later work.

9. Patricia Cox Miller, *Dreams in Late Antiquity: Studies in the Imagination of a Culture* (Princeton, NJ: Princeton University Press, 1994), 14–44, 205–9.

10. Henri Bergson, *The World of Dreams* (New York: Philosophical Library, 1958), 37.

11. Ernest Becker, *The Denial of Death* (New York: Free Press, 1973), 49–52, 87–88; Julian Barnes, *Nothing to Be Frightened of* (New York: Alfred A. Knopf, 2008), 78.

12. Carolyn Eastman, *A Nation of Speechifiers: Making the American Public after the Revolution* (Chicago: University of Chicago Press, 2009); Kenneth Cmiel, *Democratic Eloquence: The Fight over Popular Speech in Nineteenth-Century America* (Berkeley, CA: University of California Press, 1990); Thomas Gustafson, *Representative Words: Politics, Literature, and the American Language, 1776–1865* (New York: Cambridge University Press, 1992); David Simpson, *The Politics of American English, 1776–1850* (New York: Oxford University Press, 1986).

13. *New-York Mirror,* Jan. 23, 1836; Kamenetz, *The History of Last Night's Dream,* 158–159.

14. Marla R. Miller, *Betsy Ross and the Making of America* (New York: St. Martin's Press, 2010), 7.

15. *An Almanac Calculated for the Island of Grenada, for the Year of Our Lord MDCCLXXXV* (Grenada: George Burnett, 1785). I thank Carolyn Eastman for the citation. Similarly, "Last night I dreamed that I pulled out two of my front teeth with my finger & thumb." Rev. John Newton Diary, entry of Mar. 4, 1782, in Hargrett Rare Book and Manuscript Library, University of Georgia Libraries. I thank Spencer McBride for the citation.

16. The passage is from Canto 4 and reads as follows:

> *There is a pleasure in the pathless woods,*
> *There is a rapture on the lonely shore,*
> *There is society, where none intrudes,*
> *By the deep sea, and music in its roar:*
> *I love not man the less, but Nature more,*
> *From these our interviews, in which I steal*
> *From all I may be, or have been before,*
> *To mingle with the Universe, and feel*
> *What I can ne'er express, yet cannot all conceal.*

17. I have found no hard statistics to reliably compare (in gender or other terms) these tentative percentages of anxious to hopeful dreams in early America against the dream experiences of modern subjects; the general perception remains today that anxious dreams and nightmares significantly outnumber happy, upbeat dreams.

18. See Don Campbell and Alex Doman, *Healing at the Speed of Sound: How What We Hear Transforms Our Brains and Our Lives* (New York: Hudson Street Press, 2011).

19. Charles Burnett, "Perceiving Sound in the Middle Ages," in Mark M. Smith, ed., *Hearing History: A Reader* (Athens, GA: University of Georgia Press, 2004), 69–84.

20. As the new American republic claimed a morally secure position within the community of nations, it recorded its political values in terms that directly related to the potent eighteenth-century language of sensation: the tremors and vibrations of responsive nerves—sympathies—informed a charitable spirit conducive to democracy. What we hear makes us feel, and what we say about republican government accords with a generous sensibility, with a compassionate feeling toward the mass of humankind. Such constructions were integral to the popularly evolving American self-image. See Roy Porter, *Flesh in the Age of Reason* (New York: W. W. Norton, 2003); Andrew Burstein, *Sentimental Democracy* (New York: Hill & Wang, 1999); idem, "The Political Character of Sympathy," *Journal of the Early Republic* 21 (Winter 2001): 601–32.

21. Elsewhere in his memoir, Hawthorne notes of his literary coming-of-age that emotional truth was rarely ever told within, and that the only truth lay, perversely, in the external workaday journey: "Your brains, children, are the least valuable and individual parts of you," he needled. "They are poor, promiscuous servants on the road of Life." *The Memoirs of Julian Hawthorne*, ed. Edith Garrigues Hawthorne (New York: Macmillan, 1938), 185, 202.

22. Zoltán Kövecses, *Metaphor and Emotion: Language, Culture, and Body in Human Feeling* (New York: Cambridge University Press, 2000), 85; George Lakoff and Mark Johnson, *Metaphors We Live By* (Chicago: University of Chicago Press, 1980), 193.

23. Articles on Reverend Talmage's sermon were prominently featured in such widely divergent newspapers as *Peninsula Enterprise* (Accomac Courthouse, VA), Apr. 1, 1893, the *Iola Register* (KS), Apr. 7, 1893, and the *Banner Democrat* (Lake Providence, East Carroll Parish, LA), May 20, 1893, but Talmage also acknowledged the long-held view that "the vast majority of dreams are merely the result of disturbed physical conditions and are not a supernatural message"; James Sully, *Illusions: A Psychological Study* (New York: D. Appleton and Company, 1891), 275; Marina Van Zuylen, *Monomania: The Flight from Everyday Life in Literature and Art* (Ithaca, NY: Cornell University Press, 2005), chap. 3. Note that Freud expressed a general ambivalence about prophetic dreams and telepathic phenomena; see Gay, *Freud: A Life for Our Time*, 443–44.

24. Paul Ricoeur, *Memory, History, and Forgetting* (Chicago: University of Chicago Press, 2004), esp. 147–56.

25. Emotions evolved as brain states, not as conscious feelings. Because our cultural selves like to think of life as a good story, it is no doubt discomforting to learn that modern neuroscience has reduced dreams to the building blocks of life. If Dr. Flanagan insists that dreams are evolutionary side effects, and not central or unified functions of historical adaptation, Antonio Damasio explains that emotions themselves are "complicated collections of chemical and neural responses," whose purpose is to "assist the organism in maintaining life." While fully acknowledging that learning and culture give emotions new meanings, Dr. Damasio underscores that emotions are "biologically determined processes" connected to the survival instinct. See Antonio Damasio, *The Feeling of What Happens: Body and Emotion in the Making*

     of Consciousness (New York: Harcourt, 1999), chap. 2, quote at 51; Flanagan, *Dreaming Souls,* 194–95; Andrea Rock, *The Mind at Night* (New York: Basic Books, 2004), 102–3.

26.   To update the nineteenth century's dream soul and translate it into neurobiological terms of the twenty-first century is to say that our dreams are twofold, at least: (a) the byproduct of sentience, the alert cognitive state manifest through neural firings; and (b) an imprint derived from our social-emotional experience.

27.   Bert O. States, "Dreams: The Royal; Road to Metaphor," *SubStance* 30 (2001): 104–18; David Eagleman, *Incognito: The Secret Lives of the Brain* (New York: Pantheon, 2011), 4; Jonathan Haidt, *The Righteous Mind: Why Good People Are Divided by Politics and Religion* (New York: Pantheon, 2012). Animation of thought leaves open the possibility that history is more a thing of shared imagination than we even suspect; it would be to question the entire construction of individuality (or greatness) as a driving force in history. And it would mean that, with all the dissonance we know, we are actually "reaching out" in order to reshape our interior emotional selves and counter natural (physical) forces of disorder and disintegration—in other words, that we dream, at least in part, in order to connect.

28.   Paul Bogard, Introduction, and Laurie Kutchins, "Nocturnes," in Bogard, ed., *Let There Be Night: Testimony on Behalf of the Dark* (Reno, NV: University of Nevada Press, 2008), 2–5, 35–45.

INDEX